MARKET DOMINANCE AND ANTITRUST POLICY, SECOND EDITION

For Mark and Harry

Market Dominance and Antitrust Policy, Second Edition

M.A. Utton

Professor of Economics, University of Reading, UK

Edward Elgar

Cheltenham, UK • Northampton, MA, USA

Published by
Edward Elgar Publishing Limited
Glensanda House
Montpellier Parade
Cheltenham
Glos GL50 1UA
UK

Edward Elgar Publishing, Inc.
136 West Street
Suite 202
Northampton
Massachusetts 01060
USA

A catalogue record for this book
is available from the British Library

Library of Congress Cataloging in Publication Data
Utton, M. A. (Michael A.), 1939–
    Market dominance and antitrust policy / Michael A. Utton.–2nd ed.
        p. cm.
    includes index.
    1. Industrial concentration. 2. Market share. 3. Antitrust law. I. Title.
    HD2757 .U88 2003
    338.8–dc21

                                                                      2002029832

ISBN 1 84064 728 0 (cased)
Printed and bound in Great Britain by Biddles Ltd, *www.biddles.co.uk*

Contents

Figures and tables

Preface to the first edition

Even to the casual observer it might appear that problems of market dominance and antitrust policy are almost daily in the news. Amongst the more prominent examples are the following: officials of the European Commission pay unannounced visits to the headquarters of some of the most famous companies in the world and seize documents that appear to show that they have been colluding on prices; a takeover bid for a highly respected and long-established UK confectionery firm is made by a foreign company and is allowed to proceed unhampered despite widespread protest; in the aviation industry a company whose name is a household word is accused of using predatory tactics to ruin a much smaller competitor; in the UK the most prestigious and successful brewing companies are horrified to learn that the Monopolies and Mergers Commission have recommended that they should be forced to divest themselves of a large proportion of their retail outlets or pubs; in the US the most successful computer software company is accused of anticompetitive behaviour. Many other examples could be cited and in subsequent chapters we will look in detail at cases from the EU, the US and the UK involving collusion, mergers, the market conduct of dominant firms and the market power that may or may not derive both from vertical integration and from vertical restraints.

The issues and institutions involved, like industry itself, are complex. The book is therefore structured in a way which we hope will allow the reader to make sense of the complexity. There are four sections. Part I contains an analysis of market dominance and its possible extent, with a preliminary review of the institutions used to deal with it. The core of the book is then contained in Parts II and III, distinguishing horizontal from vertical issues. In Part II, particular attention is paid to the market conduct of dominant firms, which has received so much recent theoretical attention. It also contains a discussion of collusion, where the antitrust response has perhaps been the most uniform, and horizontal mergers, where despite very intensive study many issues still remain unresolved. In Part III, the emphasis switches to vertical issues: that is, those involving the relationships between firms and their input suppliers or their distributors. Both theory and policy in this area have undergone significant changes in recent years. Finally, in Part IV we raise a number of controversial questions about the effectiveness of antitrust policy, including a discussion of the appropriate sanctions both against those who infringe the law and against those who attempt to mould its application to their own purposes. We also take up sensitive questions involving conflicts between antitrust and trade policies, the international 'reach' of antitrust and foreign takeovers of domestic firms.

In courses in industrial and business economics in British universities, antitrust policy tends to be relegated to a brief final chapter or passing reference to a few well-known cases. Even though much of the preceding analysis may have led up to some apparently important policy conclusions, the next step – how these are or are not translated into actual policy – is often left unanswered or merely given a fleeting reference. On the other hand, students of competition law or competition policy may acquire a detailed knowledge of many cases without appreciating the economic analysis that may or, in some notorious instances, may not underpin them. By bringing together in each chapter of Parts II and III a discussion of the economic analysis and then the treatment of the issues in European, British and US antitrust policy, we have attempted to overcome this limitation.

The intention, therefore, is that the book should provide a useful accompaniment to courses in industrial and business economics, competition law and institutions, and in some instances microeconomics where there is an emphasis on market power issues. The level of economics assumed is no more than that usually taught to first and second year undergraduates and what little algebra is used has been largely relegated to the appendices.

Many of the topics have been discussed over several years with business economics students at Reading, and I have benefited greatly from their scepticism and readiness to challenge the conventional wisdom. I would especially like to thank Lauraine Newcombe who coped superbly with the daunting task of deciphering my handwriting and preparing the final draft for the publisher.

M.A.U.

Preface to the second edition

I have used the opportunity of a second edition to make a number of substantial changes. Some of these were necessary because the antitrust laws themselves have changed, and some were required to discuss important recent cases.

In the first category was the British Competition Act passed in 1998 and which came into effect in March 2000. The changes embodied in the Act were probably the most substantial made in the fifty years of British competition policy. In the process of aligning British policy closely with that of the European Union, much of the previous machinery was swept away and existing institutions were fundamentally altered. The detailed discussion of the previous policy, especially that involving the Restrictive Practices Act, has therefore been discarded to make way for coverage of the new policy. Similarly, fundamental changes have been made to certain aspects of European policy, especially that dealing with vertical restraints. The second edition, therefore, focuses on the changes that came into effect in 2001.

In the second category are a number of cases which not only are highly significant for antitrust policy but have been widely reported and extensively discussed. Probably the most prominent was the case brought by the US Department of Justice against Microsoft, allegedly for trying to monopolize the market for operating systems. The proposed acquisition of McDonnell Douglas by Boeing was widely reported for different reasons. The merger of two quintessentially US companies was challenged by the European Union competition authority. Until a compromise was agreed, the case threatened to rupture US–EU commercial relations. Discussion of these and other cases are included in the new edition. I have also renumbered references to Articles 85 and 86 as Articles 81 and 82 throughout, in accordance with the current Treaty of Amsterdam.

Antitrust policy continues to evolve and inevitably, at the time of writing (February 2002), the precise details of further changes in Britain (promised in the Enterprise Bill) and in the EU (concerning the future structure of car distribution) are not finalized. By the time the book is published they will be. The outcome of these and subsequent changes will have to await a further edition!

M.A.U.

PART I

ANALYTICAL AND INSTITUTIONAL BACKGROUND

1   The economic analysis of market dominance

I   Monopoly and market dominance

The immediate task of this opening chapter is to discuss some of the basic concepts that will be used throughout the book. We begin by setting out in simple terms the economic case against market dominance using the well-known tools of static theory to highlight the inefficiencies that can arise from monopolized compared with competitive markets. The discussion also allows us to compare the 'monopoly' of economic theory with the looser notion of 'market dominance' which often finds its way into antitrust cases.

Although the static analysis highlights the core of the problem, real markets do not remain frozen but are constantly undergoing change, even if the major participants try to resist. In Section II, therefore, we extend the preliminary analysis into the difficult area of dynamics and introduce a question which will recur at many subsequent points in our discussion: namely, if in many circumstances positions of dominance generate a faster rate of growth or can be eroded by pressures in the market, is 'benign neglect' a more efficient solution to the problem than direct intervention by antitrust action which may be costly, cumbersome or even wrong? In other words, we need to consider the question of how selective antitrust policy should be. In Section III we try to allay the suspicions of those who feel that antitrust action is unimportant because the losses it tries to correct and repair are trivial. There is now quite a lot of evidence that the costs, broadly interpreted, of market dominance can be considerable and, although not as important, say, as hyperinflation or the depletion of the ozone layer, are nevertheless great enough to merit detailed enquiry.

A monopolist in economic theory is the sole producer of a good or service for which there are no close substitutes. Some impediment also exists which prevents other firms from entering the market and competing with the incumbent. Under these circumstances the firm can choose that output and thence price which maximizes profit. The barrier to entry will also ensure that, whatever the size of the profit, there will be no competition to affect the firm's performance.

It will be useful for our subsequent discussion to represent these familiar results in a simple diagram. Thus, in Figure 1.1, the monopolist's demand and marginal revenue are shown as AR and MR, respectively, and long-run average cost, denoted by $LRAC$, is assumed to be roughly L-shaped and constant beyond output Q_E. This representation of the average cost curve has substantial empirical support (see Johnston, 1960; Wiles, 1961). If average costs are constant beyond Q_E, marginal costs, denoted $LRMC$, will equal average costs over this range. For profit maximization the firm will equate marginal cost with marginal revenue, resulting in an output OQ_M which can be sold for a price of P_M. The monopoly profit is represented by the rectangular area $ABCP_M$.

We can now use this simple analysis to get a preliminary answer to some basic questions of concern in antitrust. First, in what sense, if any, is the monopoly represented in Figure 1.1 inefficient? We can also introduce the related question of whether efficiency is the legitimate concern of antitrust policy. Secondly, what is the character and role of the impediment to entry in the market shown? Thirdly, what is the significance of the profits shown in the figure? And fourthly, what relation is there between the monopoly illustrated and firms in an antitrust case in a position of market dominance?

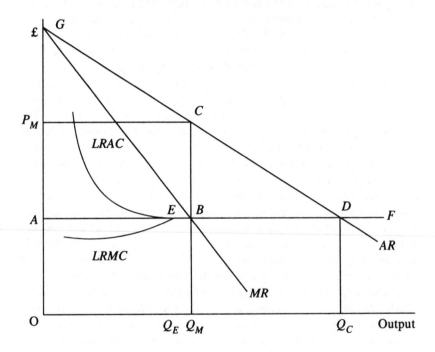

Figure 1.1   Price and output under simple monopoly

In order to address the first question we need to focus on the relationship between marginal cost and price at the equilibrium output. It is clear from the figure that at output OQ_M there is a difference CB between demand price and marginal cost. Since this difference is fundamental to the economic case against monopoly we shall spend some time examining its full implications. Any point on the demand curve represents the valuation at the margin by consumers of the unit of output specified. Thus, assuming the output is infinitely divisible, consumers' marginal valuation of the Q_M unit of output is CQ_M. The marginal resource cost of this unit, however, is only BQ_M (in the absence of production externalities). The difference, shown as CB in Figure 1.1, amounts to the mark-up of price over marginal cost. Over the entire output range Q_MQ_C consumers would be prepared to pay a price (as indicated by the demand curve) greater than the resource cost of production, indicating that such output would generate a consumer benefit. In principle consumers would be prepared to pay the monopolist a sum equal to the area $ABCP_M$ in exchange for an increase in output to Q_C, sold at a price OA. The consumers' net gain would then be the equivalent of the triangle BCD. The fact that the monopolist would restrict output below Q_C implies that resources are being misallocated: too few resources are devoted to monopoly production in order that price can be maintained above marginal cost. The monopolist's pricing behaviour therefore leads to allocative ineffi-ciency. At the heart of economists' case against monopoly is this price–cost divergence and the resource misallocation that results.

The concept of efficiency, however, is one that is often heard in discussions of the relative merits of competition and monopoly and, unless the several different meanings are kept clear, confusion is likely to occur. Thus although the monopoly may be allocatively inefficient it produces at a technically efficient scale of operations. By this we mean that the firm has built a plant of a size large enough to take advantage of all available economies of scale, where we include not only physical plant but also optimal organizational and marketing practice. By combining all factors in a way which embodies best available practice the firm is able to achieve minimum unit costs for producing and dis-tributing its output Q_M. As shown in Figure 1.1, costs can be minimized for a scale of operations Q_E or greater. For scales smaller than Q_E unit costs would be higher, as shown by the *LRAC* curve. The monopolist is thus technically efficient but allocatively inefficient.

Those familiar with the perfectly competitive model will know that in long-run equilibrium the industry will also be efficient in this sense. All firms will be producing on the minimum point of their long-run average cost curves which in this model are assumed to be U-shaped, owing to the influence of disec-onomies of scale beyond the optimum output. On the assumptions currently made, therefore, the main difference between monopoly and competition is that, in the former, prices are greater than marginal cost and this leads to allocative inefficiency. Both forms of market organization, however, are technically efficient in the long run.[1]

It is useful at this stage to introduce a further type of efficiency to which we will refer in subsequent chapters. A number of writers, stretching back as far as Adam Smith, have noted that, whereas the representation of costs in Figure 1.1 refers to the firm using the best available technology and organizational methods so as to obtain minimum costs for any level of output specified, when firms are in a protected market, incentives to achieve minimum cost may be blunted. In particular the amount of effort put into achieving the firms' objectives may be reduced at all levels of the organization so that it may operate with a considerable amount of slack. The term used for this kind of internal disorganization is 'X-inefficiency'. In terms of Figure 1.1, this would mean that, instead of operating at a point *B* on the *LRAC* and *LRMC* curve, the firm would be operating with a cost level above *B* for an output Q_M. However, if that was the case its chosen output would be to the left of Q_M, since in effect it would be attempting to obtain its objectives from a higher perceived unit and marginal cost curve than that shown. We have hesitated to use the term 'profit maximization' in this context because if the firm allows its costs to rise in the way indicated its objectives have clearly shifted and it may be pursuing 'employee and management satisfaction', rather than profit maximization.[2] For our purposes, however, it is sufficient to note that the stronger the protection for a monopoly the weaker are the incentives for X-efficiency. If competitive forces can be strengthened in a market then X-inefficiency will tend to disappear.

It is appropriate at this point to introduce the question of whether efficiency should be the major goal of antitrust policy or whether broader or indeed narrower objectives would lead to more satisfactory results. In Chapter 3 we will look in detail at what are the stated objectives of antitrust policy in the EU, the USA and the UK. For the moment we consider the issue in more general terms. One approach is to argue that ultimately the consumer interest should be paramount in antitrust questions and that this can be best achieved by the pursuit of greater efficiency through antitrust policy. Bork certainly takes this view: 'The whole task of antitrust can be summed up as the effort to improve allocative efficiency without impairing productive efficiency so greatly as to produce either no gain or a net loss in consumer welfare' (Bork, 1978, p. 91). Thus, on this view, the reduction of monopoly by removing impediments to entry is likely to have the effect of improving allocative and X-efficiency. If the incumbent firm continues to restrict output and pays insufficient attention to the level of its costs it will lose market share and its profits will be eroded. Consumers will gain through lower prices. The argument can be sustained even though the increased competition may ultimately lead to the demise of one or more of the competitors. In fact if the process of competition is effective we expect over time some firms to disappear either through bankruptcy or merger, and their place to be taken by new organizations. The speed with which the process works is one of the main concerns of Chapter 2.

Although the ultimate objective to antitrust policy may be greater efficiency and consumer welfare, by placing a greater emphasis on the competitive means to that end some writers may unwittingly allow antitrust authorities to give undue emphasis to the protection of competitors rather than to competition. Thus if the goal of antitrust is seen primarily in terms of maintaining competition this may be interpreted by lawyers, judges or antitrust administrators as requiring the continued presence of existing firms even though it might mean damaging the consumer interest because they are inefficient and are attempting to use the antitrust machinery to preserve their position. The pressures for this outcome should not be underestimated, especially where an existing market structure is dominated by one firm and where the complaint or action comes from a smaller rival. Unless the antitrust body keeps efficiency and the consumer interest firmly in mind it may serve the interests of weak competitors.

We turn now to the second question mentioned above, the character and role of impediments to entry in the monopolized market. Some impediments or barriers are quite straightforward and their effects clear-cut. The government grant of a monopoly to a single firm or individual, for example, means that no other firm can legally enter that market in the short or long run. The Stuart kings found this a useful means of raising revenue and the governments of some developing countries have granted exclusive import licences to individuals owed a favour.

Other barriers are more complex and ambiguous. The government grant of exclusive rights to a new product or process in the form of a patent has the specific purpose of encouraging and rewarding invention and innovation even though, for a time, a monopoly performance can be expected. The optimum level of innovation and change can be thought of as dynamic efficiency. There is clearly a trade-off involved between static and dynamic efficiency. Static efficiency is impaired by the use of the legal monopoly (the patent) but the grant of the patent may be the means by which new products are introduced or the costs of existing ones reduced, so that over time there are positive benefits to consumers. Furthermore, even with a patent system the impediment to new entry is likely in many instances to be less complete than in the case of a government-granted monopoly. Invention without patent infringement may frequently be possible, especially by firms already working along similar avenues of research.

Control of crucial raw materials is also often cited as an important impediment to entry. The most extreme case would be where known high-grade mineral deposits are very limited and owned by a single firm. Competitors must then either make do with inferior (more costly) materials or depend on the monopolist for their supplies. In either case their costs will be higher than those of the monopoly. A similar effect may be felt through control of prime sites for distributing a product. If the existing firm controls the best locations, other firms will have to be content with slightly inferior ones, which would again put them at a cost disadvantage. Although such extreme cases do undoubtedly exist and have been maintained sometimes for long periods, others have been much less secure simply because the very scarcity and high price of the resource provides strong incentives for finding new deposits or other methods of production and distribution.

If we move a little further down the hierarchy of entry barriers the ambiguity, not to say controversy, increases. In the markets for consumer products where incumbent firms may have very large market shares they may also have built up over a long period strong consumer loyalty and brand preference through their advertising and marketing policies. Such firms thus have a very valuable intangible asset which entrants may be unable to create for themselves in the short term, even though they may have access to the same advertising and marketing media as the incumbent. Even in the long term the degree of uncertainty surrounding the creation of a comparable intangible asset is likely to be far greater than that associated, for example, with operating a production line. In this sense, therefore, the entrant is at a cost disadvantage compared with the incumbent. Whether this kind of cost disadvantage should rank with a government-granted monopoly in the analysis of entry barriers has, however, recently been the subject of considerable dispute. A number of writers have argued that the new entrant faces similar expenditures in creating consumer brand loyalty as the incumbent firm (or firms) have incurred in the past. As long as the entrant has access to the same facilities as the incumbent, then no long-term impediment exists. To sustain their argument they can rely on a well-known definition of entry barriers by Stigler: 'a cost of production (at some or every rate of output) which must be borne by a firm which seeks to enter an industry but is not borne by firms already in the industry' (Stigler, 1968, p. 67). If the entrant can create a similar intangible asset by replicating the past expenditures of the incumbent, on this view, no entry barrier exists. The difficulty arises, however, precisely because although similar costs may be incurred by an entrant the market environment that it faces with an established dominant firm is not the same as when the latter was building its market share.

Similar considerations surround the treatment of economies of scale. If an entrant to a market where such economies are substantial can effectively reproduce the production facilities used by an incumbent firm, there is no impediment to entry, according to the Stigler view. Yet, if entry on a large and therefore technically efficient scale were to occur in such a market, the increase in output might be so great as to ensure that the market price would fall below average costs. Entry would not be viable and therefore is unlikely to take place, even though in principle a potential entrant could achieve the same cost level as the incumbent.

Clearly there are many sources of impediment to entry to particular markets and often different types will occur simultaneously. It is also evident that their precise impact on the performance of existing and entrant firms will vary considerably. In Parts II and III of the book we will be very much concerned with these effects. For the moment we simply underline the significance of entry barriers to the performance of the monopoly shown in Figure 1.1. The presence of some impediment to entry ensures that the firm retains its monopoly not only in the short term but also in the long term. If the impediment were removed the firm would still be able to charge a monopoly price in the short term but the profits that resulted would attract new resources to the market and over time the increased supplies that result would cause the price to fall to the competitive level.

We thus come to the third question posed above: what is the significance of profits shown in the simple monopoly case illustrated in Figure 1.1? As long as the firm is protected by barriers to entry its policy of output restriction and simple monopoly pricing will generate the excess profit shown as $ABCP_M$. By 'excess' we mean an amount greater than that required to retain the resources in their present use. On the usual convention that amount, the 'normal' return or opportunity costs of capital, is included in the long-run average cost curve. In a market economy the key role of returns greater than 'normal' is to attract additional resources. The presence of entry barriers frustrates this mechanism. To the extent that additional resources are kept out of a market because of some barrier (of the kind mentioned above) which allows the incumbent firm or firms to earn excess returns, the resource misallocation identified in Figure 1.1 will persist.

This conclusion would appear to have important implications for antitrust policy. Excessive profits identified amongst monopoly firms might give a good indication of a poor allocative performance, and thus be of direct policy concern. The British Monopolies and Merger Commission (MMC) often used such indicators to assist its investigations, but they have to be treated very cautiously and may be misunderstood or completely misleading.[3] In practice it may be very difficult to distinguish short- from long-term influences and those that have a benign effect (due to innovation) from those that are malign (due to entry deterrence). It may also be very difficult to obtain data that reflect even approximately the concepts used in the economic analysis of the problem. Furthermore, if monopoly firms are prone to X-inefficiency as we suggest above, recorded profits may appear modest simply because internal slack accounts for the rest. On the other hand, a monopoly which has earned only modest returns may be constrained by the threat of entry. Simply because a firm has a very large market share does not mean that it can sustain a monopoly price and earn a monopoly return. Only if its share is buttressed by barriers to entry will this be possible.

So far we have deliberately used the notion of a monopolist as the sole seller of a product for which there are no close substitutes, taken from the theory of monopoly. We have thus been able to introduce a number of concepts that will be particularly useful in the succeeding chapters. Since, however, a major task of the book is to show how economic analysis can be used to analyse antitrust problems we need now to address the question of the relationship between the monopoly of economic theory and firms in antitrust cases in positions of market dominance.

By 'market dominance' we mean the ability of a firm or group of firms persistently to hold price above long-run average costs without thereby losing so many sales that the price level is unsustainable. We have deliberately used the term 'market dominance' rather than the more frequent 'market power' in order to emphasize the central role played in many markets by one or a few large firms. The terms can, however, be used interchangeably. In the light of the foregoing discussion we can note the following points about this definition. First, a market may be dominated by more than one firm and they may either act together (through secret collusion, for example) or tacitly arrive at a price solution close to the monopoly level by acting on what they believe is their best strategy, given their anticipations of what the policy of the others will be. Thus, whereas our previous discussion proceeded on the basis of a single firm monopoly, in practice we have to recognize that a frequent case will be oligopoly and the mutual interdependence that that implies.

Secondly, the price–cost difference has to be persistent. Temporarily high prices in relation to costs may be caused by a variety of factors, including short-run fluctuations in demand or input prices. High short-term profits may result but they will not be due to market dominance. An unforeseen increase in demand will generate windfall gains even in a highly competitive market. In antitrust cases, however, 'persistence' has to be properly interpreted. Clearly whether increases in demand cause prices to rise for one, two or five years depends very much on the type of industry involved. In some cases additional supplies from new entrants may be available within weeks or months of a demand increase. They may come either from imports which were previously uneconomic because of transport costs or from new firms entering the market. In other cases technological complexities may mean that additional output from entrants will only be available after several years. Nevertheless the price increase caused by the shift in demand will not be sustainable against new entry, and the existing firms cannot be said to dominate the market in the sense defined.

Thirdly, the definition refers to prices successfully held at a level greater than average costs. Although not involving directly the concepts of perfect competition and barriers to entry, it is clear from our previous discussion that they have an important indirect bearing on the definition. In a perfectly competitive market, prices will eventually fall to the level of marginal cost. Even though there is no suggestion that the real world is populated by perfectly competitive markets, nevertheless, in those where a reasonable approximation is found, prices will in the long run be aligned with costs. The corollary is that, where serious and prolonged divergences occur between price and cost, the cause can be traced back to some impediment to entry. We may note in passing that the definition can clearly encompass different degrees of dominance implying large or small divergences between price and cost. Clearly, given the limited resources that will always be available for antitrust enforcement, it is desirable that serious cases should take precedence over minor cases, not least because these may be expected to create the largest welfare losses for consumers.

We have left until last perhaps the most difficult question of all arising from the definition of market dominance. This concerns the apparently innocuous reference to 'the market'. If a firm or firms are dominating 'the market' and if this can have important policy implications it is evident that we need to have a clear idea of what constitutes the relevant market in a particular case. In Figure 1.1 we were able to avoid the practical problems by simply drawing a downward-sloping demand curve facing the monopolist, on the assumption that the product in question had no close substitutes. The greater the gap in the chain of substitutes, the smaller will be the price elasticity of demand, *ceteris paribus*. Hence a firm or group of firms controlling all of the supply of a product for which no close substitute exists will have greater scope for raising price above cost.

When we move, however, from theory to antitrust policy some assessment of what actually constitutes the affected market has to be made. As we shall see in later chapters, large quantities of ink have been spilt and many hairs have been split in trying to catch the elusive concept. Clearly the firms themselves will argue in defence of their position that the correct market is very wide and that consequently their dominance is relatively small. Complainants and antitrust authorities are likely to think otherwise and draw the boundaries more narrowly.

One approach which has received much attention but which in practice may be very difficult to employ involves the use of cross-elasticity of demand and elasticity of supply. The cross-elasticity of demand between products X and Y may be defined as the percentage change in the quantity of X demanded resulting from a small percentage change in the price of product Y. In effect this is merely a more formal way of identifying products which are close substitutes for each other. Where the cross-elasticity is high, that is where a small change in the price of Y results in a relatively large change in the quantity of X demanded, the products can be regarded as part of the same market. Consumers will evidently switch from one product to another very readily.

Although the concept may help to clarify thinking about the scope of markets, there are practical reasons why it is of limited policy use. Estimates of cross-elasticities are not readily available or easily made. An antitrust case does not provide the ideal environment for making such estimates. Furthermore it is not clear where the cut-off points should be, even if estimates were available. In the context of an antitrust case, what constitutes a 'relatively large' cross-elasticity: 2, 5, 25 or higher? Additional adjustments would also have to be made to take account of the fact that 'close substitutability' depends not only on physical characteristics but on geographic location. Identical commodities produced several hundred miles apart and costly to transport do not constitute part of the same market.

Similar considerations apply to the elasticity of supply. The concept is defined as the percentage change in the quantity of X supplied in response to a small percentage change in the price of X. Thus, if a small increase in the price of X causes a disproportionate increase in the supply of X, supply elasticity will be high. In other words existing producers face few production difficulties in increasing their output but also other firms, using flexible production methods, can readily switch to producing X following a price increase. A further source of additional supplies may be imports. If a small price change makes the difference between profitable and unprofitable imports, clearly existing domestic firms may have little room to manoeuvre on price; that is they will have limited market dominance. In principle therefore high supply elasticity will have an important influence on the way the true 'market' is perceived.[4] The principle is of increasing importance in European Union (EU) cases where the continued removal of trade and other barriers between member states has had the effect of 'widening' the market in the way indicated. This is not to say, of course, that statistical estimation of supply elasticities is actually carried out, because the same problems arise as in the case of cross-elasticities of demand. The underlying logic, however, does have a bearing on the way a particular market is viewed and consequently how much discretion the leading firm or firms have.

The joint emphasis in the elasticity approach to both demand and supply substitutabilities is therefore correct and avoids the mistake of taking too narrow a view of the market by simply accepting at face value the alleged market share of existing firms. A seemingly different approach has been suggested by Areeda and Turner, who define a market as 'a firm or group of firms which, if unified by agreement or merger, would have market power in dealing with any group of buyers' (Areeda and Turner, 1978, p. 347). The definition appears to go directly to the heart of the problem by drawing the boundary of the market around those firms which, if acting together successfully, could raise prices. It is close to the Guidelines now used by the US antitrust authorities in merger cases which we discuss fully in Chapter 8. Some assessment has to be made both about the substitutability in demand of the outputs from the firms to be included and about the possible switches in production that may take place in firms ostensibly supplying a different market. In fact commercial history is strewn with the remains of many restrictive agreements that collapsed precisely because the participants failed to take account of the increases in supply that would occur if the price was raised. Participants clearly have a very sharp incentive to try to ensure that all suppliers are included in the agreement to make it effective. Yet they often fail. As has often been pointed out, the managements of firms have a far greater knowledge of their own industry than either lawyers or antitrust authorities. It is difficult therefore to envisage either doing any better in their attempts to define a market by drawing a ring round all actual and potential suppliers.

There is thus a considerable gulf between the concepts defined in economic analysis and their close approximation in an actual case. This does not detract from the importance of the analysis which, as we shall see, is a powerful tool for distinguishing the relevant from the misleading or false.

II   Market dominance: extensions to the preliminary analysis

The caution is reinforced when we move away from the simple, static analysis to consider more complex cases. At this stage we merely introduce three issues which will be of more detailed concern later on: significant scale economies, price discrimination and incentives for innovation.

The first and most obvious point arising out of the case illustrated in Figure 1.1 is that we implicitly assumed that costs were unchanged whether the market was supplied by one firm or by a larger group of firms. If there are significant economies of large-scale organization, as seems evident from the experience of some industries, then monopoly may be the most efficient form of organization. In particular, if the cost-reducing economies are important enough, price may be lower and output higher with monopoly than with a multi-firm competitive structure. These results can also be usefully illustrated in Figure 1.2. In the figure, market demand is shown by AR and, if production is organized by a monopoly, MR is marginal revenue. The monopolist's long-run average and marginal revenue curves are shown by $LRAC$ and $LRMC$, respectively. We have thus retained the assumption that under monopoly unit costs decline to a minimum (at output Q_N) and then remain constant over the relevant range. The profit-maximizing monopoly price is then P_M and output Q_M. All of this is the same as in Figure 1.1. However we now show the competitive supply curve as S_C. In other words, if production is organized by a large number of small-scale firms, their aggregated costs are embodied in the horizontal line S_C.[5] In this case the market-clearing price is P_C and corresponding output Q_C. Price would therefore be higher and output lower than under monopoly.

What can we say about the comparative efficiency of the two contrasting cases? As far as technical efficiency is concerned there is no question that the monopoly is much more technically efficient than the competitive industry. It uses far fewer resources to produce output Q_C or its preferred output Q_M. The resulting lower price means that consumers who, as it were, enter the market at prices between P_C and P_M have their demands satisfied by the monopolist, whereas they would have remained uncatered for by the competitive industry.[6] As far as allocative efficiency is concerned the answer to the question is more

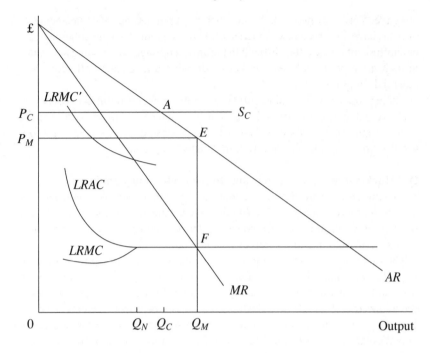

Figure 1.2   Price and output under competition and monopoly with organizational economies

complex. The fact that a greater output is sold at a lower price under monopoly implies that consumers are better off than under competition, and yet it is clear from Figure 1.2 that the monopoly output is sold at a price greatly in excess of marginal cost. At output Q_M marginal cost is FQ_M, whereas price is EQ_M, giving a mark-up over cost of EF. Thus despite the lower price the monopolist is generating considerable allocative inefficiency. Consumers are better off but they could be made even better off if a means were found of making the monopolist charge a price P_R, equal to marginal cost. Consumers would then have the full benefit of the scale economies, and the allocative inefficiency would be eliminated. We state the possibility without suggesting that there is a means readily to hand which would produce these desirable results.

Indeed, in a very real sense, the possible conflict between technical and allocative efficiency lies at the heart of many antitrust questions. In addition to the case shown in Figure 1.2, it frequently arises in slightly less extreme form in large horizontal mergers where there may be a strong probability that the merger would increase market dominance but at the same time reduce costs through economies of reorganization.[7] Similarly, a fragmented market structure may be allocatively efficient but provide an inhospitable environment for innovation. A concentrated structure may innovate more rapidly, even though in static terms it is allocatively inefficient. In each case the antitrust authority may have to decide where the balance of advantage to consumers really lies. Where a case involves two types of efficiency pulling in opposite directions, an antitrust objective which simply seeks to 'improve efficiency' is clearly ambiguous. The ambiguity is made worse if the third kind of efficiency introduced in Section I above is also considered. Suppose, for example, the market represented in Figure 1.2 is initially organized competitively but then a consortium of UK, Australian and US entrepreneurs hold out the promise of considerable resource savings by being allowed to create a monopoly in the industry and so produce the results already described. The promise may thus be of an increased output and a lower price (with also an admittedly large profit for the monopoly's shareholders). Once created, however, the monopoly faces no actual competition and, assuming it has created barriers to new entry (possibly a strong assumption), no potential competition either. The eventual performance of the firm may therefore not live up to expectations. Lethargy and inertia may mean that achievable economies remain unrealized. Actual costs stay above those shown. In other words it is possible (although difficult ex ante to predict with confidence) that X-inefficiency may cause prices to rise after the monopoly is created. In Figure 1.2, if costs are reduced to only $LRMC^1$ then the implied profit-maximizing price will be above P_C and output below Q_C. Consumers are worse off than before (they are paying a higher price) but, despite the X-inefficiency, costs for the diminished output have been reduced following the creation of the monopoly. As we shall see in Part II, the trade-offs involved in such cases can be exceedingly complex and have been the subject of much controversy.

So far we have assumed that the monopolist or monopolistic group charged a single price for the product. In such a case the contrast between competitive and monopoly pricing is thrown into sharpest relief. Simple pricing, however, is probably less common than discriminatory pricing. Anyone who has recently enquired, for example, about the price of an airline ticket between, say, London and Paris, Cologne and Madrid, or New York and Chicago is likely to have been bemused by the variety of different offers that were made, depending on such information as time of travel, date of booking, whether the trip involved a weekend, whether they were flying on to another destination, how frequently they flew with the particular airline, and so on. The information contained in the answers to these questions in effect is used to slot customers into a particular category, depending on their (approximate) demand elasticity. Instead of an airline offering a uniform price for a ticket between two destinations, different categories of customer are offered different prices where those differences bear little relationship to differences in the marginal cost of providing the service.

Even in the case of different classes of ticket ('first' and 'tourist', for example) there is no suggestion that the difference in quality of service provided is accurately reflected in different levels of cost. Many other examples of price discrimination could be quoted and the subject is dealt with at greater length in Chapter 5. For the present we shall rely on the definition offered by Stigler: price discrimination is the sale of two or more similar goods at prices which are in different ratios to marginal cost (Stigler, 1968, p. 209). The discrimination may occur between different quantities to the same group of consumers (the more purchased per time period, the lower the price) or between different groups of consumers (businessmen and tourists) or between different markets insulated from each other (the new equipment and the replacement market; the home and the foreign market). A firm with a degree of market dominance may be able to discriminate on price. In the absence of such dominance the attempt will fail because of competition.

We argued above that many antitrust problems involve a possible conflict between technical and allocative efficiency. In particular, market dominance was likely to produce divergences between price and marginal cost and hence cause allocative inefficiency. Price discrimination may make such conclusions much more ambiguous and difficult to interpret. The point can be illustrated with reference to a modified Figure 1.1, shown as Figure 1.3. The monopolist has up to now been assumed to charge a uniform, profit-maximizing price P_M. However, suppose the firm has been able to gather sufficient information about the precise demand requirements of its customers to charge different prices for different quantities purchased. Consumers only qualify for the lower prices once they have purchased the initial quantity, per period. Thus consumers are offered the initial quantity at P_1 and further quantities at P_2, P_M, P_3 and so on. The motive for such a complex price structure is clearly to increase profits. For the structure shown, profits amount to the irregular step-shaped area in the figure. They are thus considerably greater than the profits generated by simple pricing and given by $ABCP_M$. More to the point in the present context is the effect on allocative efficiency. Output is considerably increased and a large amount is sold below the simple monopoly price P_M. The discriminating monopolist will find it worthwhile to increase output up to the point where the last block of output is sold at marginal cost. In the limit, therefore, output will be at the allocatively efficient level.

For the purposes of illustration at this stage we have deliberately chosen what is probably the easiest case, price discrimination by quantity. It brings out, however, the important point that, once we move away from simple pricing, conclusions on the allocative inefficiency resulting from market dominance may be much less clear-cut. It also brings into greater prominence the question of the income distribution effects of market dominance. It is clear from Figure 1.3 that improved allocative efficiency has also created a much greater profit

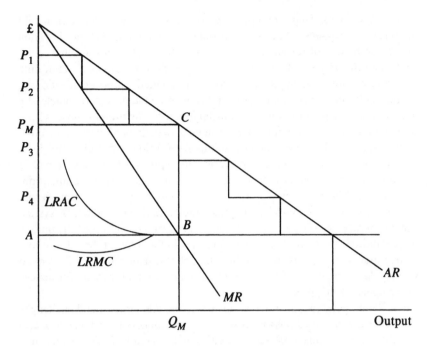

Figure 1.3 Price discrimination and allocative efficiency

for the firm and one which is only possible because of its position of market dominance. If part of such profits could be used in a number of ways to preserve dominance and stifle the emergence of competition it may be thought that the price of the improved allocative efficiency is too high and that price discrimination itself is a proper subject for antitrust scrutiny. These issues are taken up in more detail in Chapters 5 and 6.

A third qualification to the simple analysis presented in Section I above concerns the relationship between market structure and innovation. Ever since Schumpeter (1965) argued in his classic work on capitalism, socialism and democracy that the really important aspect of competition was innovation (broadly interpreted) that struck at the cost levels or demands of existing firms and, further, that adequate incentives for the inherently risky process of innovation were only available to firms with some degree of market dominance, there has been enormous controversy, both over the plausibility of his analysis and over the correct role of antitrust policy in such questions.

The efficiency concepts that we have introduced are also useful in illuminating this issue. One conclusion was that a firm or group with market dominance would create resource misallocation through operating at inefficiently low levels. Under competitive conditions this misallocation would disappear. That analysis, however, was static in that it referred to the allocation of a given bundle of resources at a particular time. The question that really concerned Schumpeter, however, was the growth of resources through time and he saw innovation, in products, processes and methods of organization, as the means to achieve economic growth. If it is true that markets dominated by one or a few firms will generate a faster rate of growth than those with a fragmented and highly competitive structure, questions of static, allocative inefficiency may become relatively unimportant. Initially the allocative inefficiency of an economy where market dominance prevails may cause it to have a lower national product than if there was universal perfect competition. However, if Schumpeter was correct, it would only be a matter of time before the concentrated economy was enjoying a higher national product. 'A system – any system, economic or other – that at every given point of time fully utilises its possibilities to the best advantage may yet in the long run be inferior to a system that does so at no given point in time, because the latter's failure to do so may be a condition for the level or speed of long-run performance' (Schumpeter, 1965, p. 83).

For Schumpeter the incentive to undertake the greater risks and challenges that innovation involved was the prospect of future monopoly profits, but he also saw the means of financing such activities as deriving from the greater than competitive returns that only firms with some prior market dominance can earn. Several writers developed his ideas in a number of ways. Galbraith (1963), for example, focused more particularly on oligopoly rather than monopoly and argued that the muted form that competition took in oligopoly allowed firms to generate sufficient profits to finance the enormous research and development costs that significant innovations now required in many industries. Furthermore, once innovations were made, the same conventions of oligopolistic competition would ensure that the innovating firm gained most of the resulting profits, rather than have them dissipated rapidly amongst a large number of rivals.[8] Compared with a fragmented industry, therefore, oligopoly was better equipped and suited for innovation. Similarly it could also be argued that the incentive to innovate was greater under oligopoly than monopoly, precisely because no single firm in an oligopoly could allow a rival to gain a significant advantage, whereas a monopolist was in sole command of the market and had no immediate competitors. Just as a monopolist may allow itself to become X-inefficient, so also it may be loath to take on the special problems associated with innovation and change.

However, this may be an unduly restrictive view of monopoly. It may apply to a few cases where barriers to entry are especially high and where technology is relatively static. In many other cases firms currently in sole command of a market and earning high profits may nevertheless feel impelled to undertake extensive research and development simply because it is impossible to predict where a path-breaking innovation may next emerge. It may come from an apparently unrelated technology and involve firms not hitherto regarded as competitors. Furthermore, if the current monopolist is successful in, for example, initiating a cost-reducing production method, it will retain all of the additional profit rather than having to share it with oligopolistic rivals. Despite patent protection, the nature of oligopolistic rivalry may be such that an innovation can often be imitated (Scherer and Ross, 1990). On this view, therefore, the incentive to innovate may be greater for a monopolist than for oligopolists. Ultimately the question of which market structure is most conducive to technical change or 'dynamic efficiency' is an empirical one which may raise a number of difficult antitrust problems. For example, will a merger between leading firms in what may already be a concentrated oligopolistic market structure intensify or weaken incentives for innovation? How far should independent firms be allowed to collaborate on expensive research and development before this affects competition between them? Are joint ventures on experimental products and processes between competing firms desirable on policy grounds or are they likely to be used as a means of collusion?

Although the factors mentioned in this section are by no means exhaustive, they should be sufficient to warn us that the simple analysis of market dominance, despite highlighting some very important features, must be treated with considerable caution when trying to apply it to policy questions. Some markets may only be able to achieve technical efficiency if they contain few firms. Very often firms having some control over their price will be able to segment the market and use price discriminations to increase their profits. Market structures which generate a faster rate of growth through innovation may have to be heavily concentrated and create static inefficiencies. All of these circumstances raise complex issues for antitrust policy because they involve a trade-off between different types of efficiency, usually, although not exclusively, between technical and dynamic efficiency on the one hand, and allocative and X-efficiency, on the other. One way of looking at antitrust policy, therefore, is as an attempt to reconcile these different types of efficiency.

III   The costs of market dominance

We have so far argued that market dominance raises important issues for public policy, but the sceptical reader may quite rightly enquire how great is their practical importance. The problems may appear significant from a theoretical point of view, but if their practical importance is negligible the scarce resources devoted to the application of economic policies could be more usefully employed elsewhere.

In this section, therefore, we discuss the probable size of the losses that may result from market dominance. It is convenient to start with a slightly modified

Figure 1.1. In Figure 1.4 we assume that costs remain constant over the entire output range. The line *AF* can be interpreted initially as the supply curve of a competitive industry (with input prices invariable with industry output). Given that market demand is *AR*, then under competitive conditions the price is *OA* and a quantity OQ_C is sold. Consumer satisfaction is then maximized in this market since marginal valuation, as reflected by the demand curve, is just equated to marginal resource cost. Another way of looking at this is to note that at this price and output configuration consumer surplus, *ADG*, is maximized. Consumers place a value on the amount of the product purchased of *ADG* greater than the resource costs involved in production with the demand and cost conditions shown. Any higher or lower price would reduce consumer surplus.

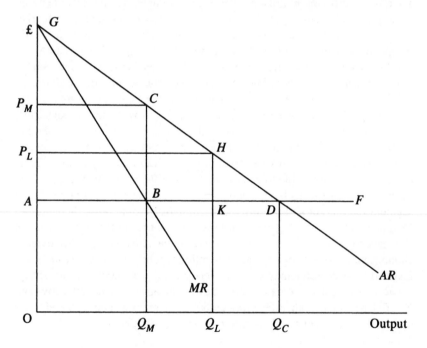

Figure 1.4   Welfare losses from market dominance

If the industry shown were to be taken over by a monopoly with no change in cost conditions occurring, price would be increased to OP_M. A close examination of the effects of this change on consumer surplus is of direct relevance to the question of how significant the effects of market dominance may be. Under the monopoly the area $P_M CBA$ becomes the monopoly profit and amounts to a direct transfer from consumers. Although this transfer may raise questions about income distribution and the relative merits of consumers as opposed to shareholders' interests and the uses to which it may be put, it is usually not treated as a matter of antitrust concern. The triangle GCP_M remains as a somewhat depleted consumer surplus. This leaves the triangle CDB. On present assumptions, when the competitive industry is taken over by the monopolist, the value represented by the triangle CDB disappears altogether. It is not transferred from one group to another; in effect the monopoly destroys that amount of value.

On the basis of this analysis, a number of researchers have therefore tried to quantify the extent of the destruction, or welfare loss. By adding up all of the welfare losses in each of the markets where dominance occurs, an estimate for the loss to a sector or a whole economy can be made. Merely to state this requirement should give some indication of the estimation difficulties involved. Consequently the figures referred to below should be taken as rough approximations rather than precise estimates. Different procedures have been used to render operational the theoretical result that output restriction leads to a welfare loss. If the full monopoly price is charged, for example, then some elementary geometry makes it clear that the triangle CDB is equal to half the area P_MCBA; that is, the welfare loss is equal to half the size of the monopoly profit. Estimates of monopoly profits can then be used to calculate the likely welfare loss. On the other hand, if a less extreme view of market dominance is taken, the welfare loss will be considerably less. For example in Figure 1.4 the expectation that the full monopoly price P_M would attract new entry and thus erode the market share of the incumbent firm (or firms) may constrain price below that level to, let us say, P_L. In this case the welfare loss, represented by HDK, would be much less. Indeed unless the incumbent firm is protected by very strong and substantial entry barriers the price is unlikely to be as high as P_M. If the existing market is in the hands of a few firms with large shares then most oligopoly theory predicts that, in this case also, price may settle below the monopoly level.

Clearly, depending on which view is taken, the empirical estimates of actual welfare losses imposed by market dominance are likely to differ. At one level this distinction lies at the heart of the different estimates made, for example, by Harberger (1954) on the one hand, and Cowling and Mueller (1978) on the other. The former favoured the more cautious approach of accepting that existing monopolists would feel some constraints on their pricing behaviour. For this assumption (as well as others which we discuss below) he was taken to task by Cowling and Mueller, who argued that the assumption inevitably meant that estimated welfare losses would be small. Harberger was, however, in very good company because, as Scherer (1987) has pointed out, Marshall in his *Principles of Economics*, first published in 1890, and characteristically in a footnote, showed that welfare losses from this source would be small, although this did not deter him from being highly critical of monopoly.

In their paper, Cowling and Mueller gave estimates using both their own and Harberger's methodology. In the present context it is convenient to contrast two sets of their estimates rather than referring to the original set presented by Harberger.[9] Using samples of the largest enterprises in the USA and UK, Cowling and Mueller estimated that the welfare losses produced if such firms were constrained to price below the monopoly level (as Harberger maintained) amounted to less than one-half of 1 per cent of the product generated in the corporate sector. These were very much in line with Harberger's original estimates and, even allowing for wide margins of error, are hardly worth bothering about. However, if it is assumed that the largest firms can charge the full monopoly price (as Cowling and Mueller suggest), the estimates rise to approximately 4 per cent of corporate sector product. This is not insignificant, but if these were the total losses, potentially removable by an active antitrust policy, many observers might feel that it should be given a rather low priority, especially since the costs of administering, monitoring and enforcing such a policy have not been included in the calculations.

Cowling and Mueller's main contribution, however, was to focus on the much wider implications of the effects of market dominance, and to give some tentative estimates of their extent. The figures just mentioned represent the welfare losses due to allocative inefficiency caused by the power to raise price above marginal cost. Their additional estimates suggest that losses from a related but distinct source may be more substantial. It was made clear in Section I above that firms' ability to maintain prices above costs rested on the presence of barriers that impeded competition. From a firm's point of view, expenditures that help to create and maintain such barriers will thus enhance their profitability. However, expenditures of this kind amount to investment in market dominance and therefore should be regarded as creating a welfare loss. For the firms concerned, the expenditure will simply be recorded as part of their costs and affect their pricing and output decisions. In practice it may be difficult for an outside observer to distinguish legitimate production and distribution costs from those designed to maintain or increase market dominance. In their study, Cowling and Mueller used the controversial assumption that all advertising expenditures had this ultimate purpose and should therefore be treated as part of the social costs of monopoly. Adding these losses to those directly due to allocative inefficiency raises the losses of gross corporate product to approximately 12 per cent in the USA and 6 per cent in the UK (the differences can be largely attributed to the much greater reliance on advertising in the USA).[10]

The activity referred to in the previous paragraph is usually termed 'rent-seeking'. A rent is the amount earned by a factor of production greater than that required to keep it in its present use. Profits due to market dominance fall clearly into this category. If the working of an economy allows the emergence of such rents, many individuals will find it profitable to expend resources for this purpose. Some advertising may have this objective but so also may expenditures on lobbying, public relations, political contributions and even bribery. To the extent that the Cowling and Mueller estimates effectively draw attention to the potential waste involved in these activities they have served their purpose. However, the argument can be taken one stage further. Firms will compete in order to obtain such rents but, as in most competitions, the majority will lose. Unlike the caucus race in *Alice in Wonderland*, everyone will not win prizes. The resources used by the losers in their unsuccessful attempt to gain rents should also be treated as one of the welfare losses indirectly resulting from the presence of market dominance in an economy. For fairly obvious reasons it is extremely difficult to measure empirically the size of such losses and there is clearly scope for a great deal of disagreement over where to draw the line between expenditures which are a normal part of the competitive process (which of course can involve the costs of bankruptcy) and those which are rent-seeking and wasteful. The tentative estimates given by Cowling and Mueller suggest that such expenditures may add a further 1–2 per cent to the social costs of market power. The estimates suggest therefore that the total effects of market power are likely to be considerable.

The estimates referred to so far have focused explicitly on the effect of market dominance on allocative efficiency and rent seeking. The potential loss due to X-inefficiency is also considerable. Referring again to Figure 1.4, suppose that the incumbent firm was confident enough of its position while charging P_M that it became complacent and internally slack so that actual costs for its output rose above AF. Precisely because the X-inefficiency extends over the entire output range rather than simply to the output contraction that occurs with market dominance, the losses it generates are likely to be much greater than those due to allocative inefficiency. The central question is then how large are X-inefficiency losses? Unfortunately here we have far less to go on than the estimates so far discussed. The 'evidence', such as it is, tends to be piecemeal, qualitative and indirect. Thus, for example, observers point to the rapid increases in internal efficiency that occurred in some UK industries in the 1960s when many cartels were abandoned in the wake of early decisions under the Restrictive Practices Act (see, for example, Swann *et al.*, 1974), which led to intensified competition. In a study of the US electricity power industry it was found that costs were significantly lower in cities where the municipality-owned plant competed with a private installation than where there was a local municipal monopoly. It has also been observed that large firms are able to reduce, sometimes drastically, their central office staff and expenditures when profitability has been reduced through competition (Scherer, 1987). A particularly interesting case involved the productivity of management consultants. After the main recommendations of the consultants were implemented in a sample of firms for which results could be quantified it was found that productivity increased by more than 50 per cent on average, and this represented an average return of more than 200 per cent over the costs of the service (Johnston, 1963). Although there was not a direct link in this case with the degree of competition, the results do suggest that firms frequently run with considerable slack. This conclusion also appears to apply to British Airways, which, in the period prior to privatization in 1987 when domestic competition was also increasing, was able to reduce its workforce and subsequently to increase its profitability (Kay and Bishop, 1988; McGowan and Trengove, 1986). Thus although the evidence is fragmentary many observers are convinced that X-inefficiency is both quantitatively significant and directly related to the intensity of competition. It is therefore likely to figure prominently in any discussion of existing market dominance or its creation through merger.[11]

Ideally we would like to be able to say how much welfare gain there can be by ensuring that the 'correct' degree of competition is maintained. We would then know the importance of antitrust policy for innovative efficiency. Unfortunately the evidence on this issue is also imprecise and far from clear-cut. For example, it is not clear from the empirical evidence which type of market structure is most conducive to rapid innovation. Industries vary considerably in the opportunities for innovation that present themselves. For long periods some industries may experience practically no alteration to their production methods and product range but then go through a period of dramatic change. Some important innovations have taken years to develop to a commercially viable stage and have involved vast expenditures, while others, equally significant, have been developed by a single person at modest cost and been quickly diffused throughout the industry.[12] After a detailed review of the empirical work, Scherer and Ross (1990) arrived at the following, balanced conclusion: 'What is needed for rapid technical progress is a subtle blend of competition and monopoly, with more emphasis in general on the former than the latter, and with the role of monopolistic elements diminishing when rich technological opportunities exist' (p. 660). We are not in a position to say by how much market dominance may retard innovation and thus affect economic welfare, although the indications are that actions which enhance dominance or facilitate collusion will tend to worsen this aspect of efficiency.

IV   Conclusion

The essence of market dominance is the ability to control the market in such a way that prices can persistently be raised above costs, leading to excessive profits. Where this occurs the market will fail to allocate resources efficiently. The task of antitrust policy can be viewed as an attempt to remove the source of that failure or to prevent its emergence. Since barriers to entry play a key role in impeding the flow of resources to their most highly valued uses we should expect antitrust authorities to be closely concerned with their analysis and control. They are likely to be especially sensitive to those actions by dominant firms which seem deliberately designed to reinforce impediments to new competition.

We saw in Section II, however, that the seemingly straightforward concept of market dominance may be very difficult to identify and interpret in practice, for a variety of reasons. Prominent amongst these was, first, the likelihood in many cases that large relative size is required for technical efficiency. Supply from a few firms rather than many could therefore be made available at lower prices, even though they were consistently above costs. Secondly, firms in a position of dominance would rarely charge a single price, preferring a more complex system of discriminatory prices which increased profitability while simultaneously making some supplies available at prices close to marginal costs. Thirdly, if the static inefficiencies caused by market dominance pale into insignificance beside the improvements that come from a faster rate of growth and if such growth is a function of a degree of market dominance, the antitrust authorities have the formidable task of deciding how much dominance to allow.

Frequently antitrust issues may boil down to a trade-off between technical and X-efficiency, on the one hand, and allocative and innovative efficiency, on the other. We could determine analytically that X-inefficiency was liable to generate considerably greater welfare losses than allocative inefficiency.

Attempting to estimate empirically the size of the losses from market dominance is hazardous and the figures should be treated with great caution. However, the general conclusion from a number of estimates is that likely welfare losses from X-inefficiency and rent seeking are considerable and certainly larger than those arising from allocative inefficiency. Direct evidence on the size of possible losses from an inferior innovative performance due to the 'wrong' level of market dominance is generally lacking. Indirect and piecemeal evidence, however, suggests that potentially the losses are considerable.

In short, the welfare losses from market dominance that antitrust policy tries to correct are likely to be substantial. Economies that are successful in removing the worst effects of market dominance or preventing its emergence are likely to register substantial gains. This does not mean, of course, that all current antitrust action is correct and effective. In some cases it may have made matters worse or been unable to eliminate the abuses of dominance.

Notes

1. We are ignoring for the moment the case where demand is relatively small in relation to available scale economies. For example, in Figure 1.1, if demand shifted sharply and permanently to the left so that it cut the *LRAC* curve to the left of *E*, the firm could still make positive profits even though it was operating at a technically inefficient scale. In this case, the firm could be classed as a natural monopoly; see Stigler (1968, ch. 6).
2. Although the concept of X-inefficiency is now widely used and seems to be backed by empirical evidence (see Section IV below) there is still considerable controversy about its analytical usefulness (c.f. Leibenstein, 1978, with Stigler, 1976).

3. For an early airing of the controversy, see Rowley (1969) and Sutherland (1971). More recent and opposing views appear in Fisher and McGowan (1983) and Kay (1987).
4. This line of reasoning has led two distinguished US authorities to argue that where appropriate all sales of 'distant' producers including foreign firms should be included in the calculation of market shares in antitrust cases. See Landes and Posner (1981). A full discussion is reserved for Chapter 4 below.
5. For simplicity we are assuming that the competitive industry can supply under conditions of constant costs. If input prices rose (fell) as the industry expanded the supply curve would have a positive (negative) slope.
6. In other words, a changeover in the organization of production from a competitive structure to monopoly creates an increase in consumer surplus of P_CAEP_M.
7. See Chapter 8 below.
8. This part of Galbraith's analysis does not really square with the more apocalyptic Schumpeterian vision of the innovator sweeping away all competition in a gale of creative destruction.
9. The interested reader can find Harberger's estimates in his 1954 paper and may also wish to consult subsequent efforts and commentary, for example in Bergson (1973), Kamerschen (1966), Schwartzman (1960) and Littlechild (1981). For a critical summary, see Scherer and Ross (1990, ch. 17).
10. The figures quoted are based on continued use of the assumption that full monopoly prices can be charged. Using the more conservative, Harberger, assumption produces much lower estimates; see Cowling and Mueller, tables 2 and 4.
11. Further examples are given in Frantz (1988).
12. For contrasting examples, see Jewkes *et al.* (1969).

2 Market dominance in practice: current perceptions and trends

I Introduction

The application of any policy to a set of economic problems is clearly not costless. Organizing and carrying out the policy uses scarce resources but also, since policy tools are by no means perfect, mistakes will be made which with hindsight show that a better economic performance would have resulted had no policy intervention occurred. Antitrust policy is no different in this respect from other forms of economic policy. Those in charge of antitrust policy therefore have to be confident that the benefits of enforcement will outweigh the costs, not only those incurred by the firms directly involved but also the costs of applying the policy itself.

The point may appear obvious, but behind it lies a very important issue which has been at the centre of antitrust discussions for at least the past decade. It concerns the speed with which unregulated markets are self-correcting, even in the face of market dominance. If those inefficiencies identified in the previous chapter are fairly quickly eroded by the forces of competition it may be better to withhold any policy intervention; the market may do the job more efficiently. Even if the record of a dominant firm appears to show that it has consistently and over a long period abused its position, it does not necessarily follow that in the absence of antitrust action it will be able to continue. An innovation from a totally unexpected source may very rapidly undermine its market share.

In the analysis of antitrust questions, therefore, great emphasis needs to be placed on the sources of market dominance. Are they likely to be short-lived and therefore require no direct policy intervention or are they so firmly entrenched that they are likely to be weakened only in the long run? In the latter case, knowledge of the foundation on which market dominance depends should act as a guide to the most effective antitrust remedy. This is what Easterbrook seems to have in mind when he says that 'the central purpose of antitrust is to speed up the arrival of the long-run' (Easterbrook, 1984, p. 2). Section II of this chapter contains a more detailed discussion of the sources of market dominance and their susceptibility to antitrust remedies.

Section III then reviews some evidence on the pattern of market dominance in the UK and the USA, but focuses particularly on an important shift of emphasis that has occurred in the last 20 years or so. Until well into the 1970s the empirical analysis of market structures as a screening device for possible antitrust action was largely based on static measures, such as the combined market share of the largest four or five sellers. Often the measurement applied only to sales of domestically produced output and took no account of international trade. More recently there has been much greater concern for the dynamics of market structure and also foreign competition. Thus for the correct analysis of market dominance the important points may not be that one firm has a current market share of, say, 60 per cent, but whether or not the rate of change of that share has been rapid and which firm or firms are providing the most immediate competition. The evidence on such issues is far less comprehensive than for the simple static measures but there is now broad agreement that it is far more important.

II   The foundations of market dominance

In their authoritative review article, Hay and Vickers (1987) distinguish between the acquisition, exercise and maintenance of market dominance. They recognize that in many ways the three are interrelated, but nevertheless find it convenient to deal with them separately. For our purposes it is useful to focus in this chapter on the acquisition of market dominance while reserving for later sections of the book a more detailed treatment of its exercise and maintenance. Although they are not intended as an exhaustive list, Hay and Vickers mention five factors that can lead to the acquisition of dominance: government grant, 'skill, foresight and industry', explicit and implicit collusion, merger and predatory behaviour. We discuss each of these in turn.

Probably the strongest foundation of market dominance comes from the government. Since sovereign power resides with the government, firms that are able to harness that power for their own ends are likely to be in an impregnable position. In important cases in the UK, firms had such power forced upon them. Thus the nationalization of industries such as gas, electricity, telecommunications, coal-mining, railways and civil aviation created unified monopolistic enterprises which were protected by statute from direct entry to their industries and from the reach of antitrust policy.[1] At the same time, however, they were constrained not only in their pricing, product and investment policies but also in their growth: they could not diversify or (for the most part) integrate vertically. In addition, of course, the power and transport industries met intense competition in some of their markets from non-nationalized enterprises (for example, the oil and road haulage industries). Assessment of their subsequent performance has produced varied results with, if anything, an emphasis on the probable X-inefficiency that resulted from their dominance rather than excessive profits.[2]

More directly relevant to the present discussion is the recent policy of privatizing or returning to the private sector most of these enterprises and, in particular, the conditions under which the policy was carried out. Thus in the case of British Telecom, which was privatized in 1984, initially a licence to provide fixed link services was granted to only one other firm (Mercury Communications) with the explicit understanding that no other entrant would be allowed for at least five years. The position of British Gas was, if anything, even stronger. Similarly the privatization of the electricity industry was in the end only able to proceed after the two generation companies had been effectively granted an exemption from any competition for 80 per cent of their sales for eight years. This last example illustrates a related point concerning the grant of positions of dominance by governments. In the USA the so-called 'utility industries' that we are discussing, although for the most part retained in private hands, have been regulated by special agencies for many years. The UK has been busily setting up rather similar agencies to regulate its newly privatized industries. What was increasingly recognized about the US system, however, was that the regulators who were supposed to ensure that positions of dominance were not abused were frequently 'captured' by the firms they were supposed to regulate. As a result they tended to operate in favour of the firms' interests rather than those of the consumer. The continued evolution of the regulatory process in the UK plus technical changes have probably meant that the tendency has been minimized. Thus, for example, deregulation in the energy sector has led not only to a complete restructuring of the once unified British Gas (it has split into two distinct companies) but to a replacement of the original and separate gas (OFGAS) and electricity (OFFER) regulators by a unified regulator OFGEM (Office of Gas and Electricity Markets). In telecommunications, persistent market growth and technical change have continued to erode BT's market share, although it remains by far the largest supplier in most markets.

Nationalization and privatization probably exemplify the difficulties associated with state-granted dominance in its most acute form. It would be wrong, however, to conclude that they were the only kinds. Wherever the state uses its authority to exclude potential competitors it is likely to enhance market dominance. It may take the form of exclusive licences, tariffs, quotas or even outright bans. For example, although the European Union (EU) is often seen (by Europeans) as a means of intensifying competition and eroding existing positions of dominance, those outside may have a different perception. Quite apart from the common external tariff which obviously inhibits imports into the EU, it has also been claimed that pressure by member firms has caused the anti-dumping procedures to be used in a highly restrictive and anti-competitive fashion.[3]

The cases of state-granted privileges mentioned so far have generally been treated with some scepticism by economists. There may be cases where they can be justified on a broader basis than simply profiting the industry concerned, but they are likely to be comparatively rare. However, a much more positive case can be made for the next category of privilege to be considered, namely patents. The recipient is granted sole right of use to the information concerned for a specified number of years and can call on the full support of the law to defend that right. The economic rationale for such exclusive or monopoly rights was indicated in the previous chapter. Innovation is both desirable but inherently risky. Adequate incentives should therefore be provided to compensate for these special risks. The prospect of future monopoly gains helps to provide such incentives. However the case is not as clear-cut as it may at first appear. The fact that a monopoly is granted to the patent holder creates the kind of allocative inefficiency and welfare losses discussed in the previous chapter. If patent lives are too long the holder will receive a greater than necessary return and consumers will suffer larger deadweight welfare losses. If they are too short the rewards to innovation will be inadequate and subsequently efforts may slacken. The issue is complicated further by the nature of competition in some oligopolistic market structures. One argument is that in concentrated oligopolies, where a handful of firms account for most of the sales, there exist strong competitive pressures to innovate and therefore there is no need for the additional incentive offered by patent protection. Individual firms know that if they do not innovate their rivals will, and they will lose their market share. They will rely on managerial secrecy and lags in the ability of rivals to imitate new products or processes to give them sufficient time to recoup the costs of research and development as well as to earn innovatory profits. On this view, therefore, patent protection is not only unnecessary but also inefficient, in that it is likely to slow down the rate at which consumers can enjoy the full benefits of innovation (that is, at competitive rather than monopolistic prices).

The point is reinforced by some recent contributions that have suggested that, if patent protection is available, oligopolistic firms will use it strategically to prolong a position of dominance, again to the detriment of consumers. One form that this can take, for example, is for a firm to protect a key patent by surrounding it with a dense stockade of minor ones, many of which may be designed to put potential rivals off the scent. The readiness of the firm using the strategy to sue any competitor suspected of an infringement will further bolster its position (Baumol and Ordover, 1985). Although few countries have as yet been persuaded by such arguments to abandon patent rights altogether, there is probably now a much greater awareness than formerly that they can be abused and that in some countries the number of years' protection allowed is overgenerous.

A second means of acquiring dominance may be 'skill, foresight and industry'. The phrase was used in a very famous US antitrust case involving the Aluminum Company of America (Alcoa)[4] which had long dominated the market. Judge Learned Hand pointed out that in the competitive process those firms which showed these characteristics in the greatest degree would very likely achieve a prominent position. It would be inconsistent for the law to acknowledge, on the one hand, the efficiency-enhancing properties of competition while, on the other, condemning firms which achieved dominance precisely because of their efficiency. Probably few would disagree with the view that firms which win a large market share by their skill and foresight should not be deprived of their position because of a misunderstanding of the notion of market dominance. If such firms can retain their position only by maintaining their efficiency, actual and potential competition are still effective and there is no market dominance in the sense defined above. Note, however, that we are using efficiency here to refer not only to technical and X-efficiency but also to allocative efficiency: that is, the alignment of price with cost.

Again the issue is not as straightforward as it appears. Judge Hand also drew attention to a point which more recently has been given greater prominence. Alcoa had built capacity ahead of demand. At any time, therefore, it was in a position to expand its own output either to meet increased demand (represented by a shift in the demand curve and an expansion of the market) or to forestall the entry of new competitors by expanding output and reducing price (the equivalent of a movement down the existing demand curve). While the former case may fall into the category of 'foresight', the latter may amount to pre-emption, a strategy deliberately designed to deter new competition. We will have much more to say about this and other strategic behaviour in Chapter 6 below. For the moment we can simply note that 'efficiency' used in such a way to maintain dominance becomes much more ambiguous from a policy point of view. In practice it may be particularly difficult to distinguish the two cases.

One further point may be mentioned while we are dealing with dominance attained by skill and foresight. Although Judge Hand did not add 'chance' to his list of virtues which may propel some firms to pre-eminence in their markets, other observers have suggested that it may play a significant role in shaping market structures. It is easy to demonstrate, for example, that, if initially all firms in a market are of equal size and all have the same chance of growth in subsequent periods but that at the end of each period it is observed that some have actually grown faster than others, then the distribution of firm sizes in the market will, over time, become more and more unequal. At first glance this result appears counter-intuitive. If all firms face the same chance of equiproportionate growth at the beginning of each period, some that grew very fast in, say, period 1 may grow very slowly in periods 2, 3 and so on, and this will tend to even things up. What this overlooks is that other firms which also grew very fast in period 1 will continue such growth in subsequent periods so that, even if in a later period, say period 6, their growth reverts to the average, by then their size will be considerably greater than that of others whose growth rate has been much smaller. The corollary is that the growth record of other firms will after a number of time periods place their size substantially below the average. Thus, if such a process is at work on the growth of firms, the effect is to widen the dispersion of firms' sizes observed at any particular time.

Very few would argue that chance factors are the only ones affecting the distribution of firm growth rates and thence their size. However, it is true that the uncertain environment in which firms have to operate subjects them to all kinds of chance occurrences: the hiring of someone who turns out to have entrepreneurial genius, the theme of an advertising campaign which affects demand out of all proportion to previous efforts involving similar expenditures, the sudden disappearance of an overseas market as the result of a change of political regime, and so on. Underlying more systematic factors, therefore, there are likely to be many other chance influences.

Furthermore, the empirical evidence indicates that, on average, larger firms tend to have a narrower dispersion of growth rates than smaller firms (Hymer and Pashigian, 1962; Singh and Whittington, 1975). Chance may project some firms into the ranks of the great but thereafter, although on average their growth rates may be smaller, the likelihood of their slipping back into a smaller size range is relatively remote. This factor will reinforce the tendency for the dispersion of firm sizes to increase over time and, although the effect may be modified to some extent by the entry of new firms, in recent decades it appears to have had little impact on the concentration of industry (Prais, 1981). In the present context the most significant aspect of the process is that once a firm has gained a dominant position it may take a very long time for it to be eroded by normal competitive influences. Considerations such as these led Williamson (1972), for example, to propose radical and dramatic remedies for removing dominant enterprises, including dismemberment.

The three remaining means of acquiring dominance mentioned by Hay and Vickers, collusion, mergers and predatory behaviour, are all discussed at length in Part II. Here we simply indicate how they may be used in this way. Collusion may be overt or tacit. The anticompetitive effects of overt collusion have been known at least since Adam Smith and in most developed countries it is strongly circumscribed by the law. In the area of antitrust economics there is now probably greater agreement on this issue than on any other. To keep the subject in perspective, however, we should note that it was not long ago that there was widespread support, including government support, for exactly the opposite position. At the height of the inter-war Depression, the UK was not alone in officially sponsoring cartels in an attempt to stave off the worst effects of the economic crisis. Even the USA modified the impact of its antitrust laws, although in the event only for a short time, before the action was declared unconstitutional. Although there is now a large measure of unanimity on the need to curb most forms of overt collusion, there is also growing support for allowing certain areas to be exempt from the full rigour of the antitrust laws. Thus, as we shall see in Chapter 11, the awesome expense of research and development in some industries and the scarcity of top-flight research teams have persuaded many observers that collaborative ventures will produce net benefits, without the adverse consequences to competition that are likely to attend other forms of collaboration.

This view poses an acute problem for antitrust authorities. One result from the analysis of oligopolistic markets is that, if firms are reasonably confident about the future actions of their main rivals, they will then be able to optimize their own behaviour in the light of that expectation. Behaviour of this kind may thus allow firms in dominant positions to earn a near-monopoly joint profit. The kind of parallel behaviour that results may be largely beyond the reach of antitrust policy. The success of tacit collusion will depend on the reliability of the individual firms' expectations and this in turn will be strongly influenced by the extent and form of the information that passes between them. For this reason antitrust policy has been directed not only against overt agreements but also against the apparently far less damaging information agreements and exchanges. Collaboration on research and development, therefore, may be more ambiguous in its ultimate effects than appears at first sight. Initially the joint efforts may be purely at the scientific and technical level and produce the benefits expected. However, at some stage the new knowledge will be converted into commercially viable product, process or service innovations and the line between collaboration and collusion may effectively disappear. In other words, collaboration in research and development may ultimately be an important means of conveying to firms which are ostensibly rivals information about future behaviour sufficient for them to maintain price at a monopoly level. This suggests that exceptions to the generally hostile stance that antitrust authorities have taken to collusion should thus be granted very sparingly, in case they become the vehicle for prolonging market dominance.

If tacit collusion fails, firms may attempt to solve the problem by merging. Historically mergers have been a significant means of attaining market dominance, as we shall see in the next section. They may also be used to re-establish dominance if it has been eroded by competition. Compared with internal growth (that is, the building of new production plant) a merger may provide the opportunity for a very rapid increase in market power. A firm with a market share of, say, 40 per cent may make three swift acquisitions of rivals with shares of 20, 10 and 5 per cent, respectively and convert what might have been a rather loose-knit oligopoly into a market dominated by one enterprise. Precisely this possibility has led to the introduction of merger control as part of antitrust policy, although not without difficulty.

If overt collusion is generally condemned and a merger is merely the most complete form of collusion it may legitimately be asked why mergers are not simply made illegal. There are a number of problems with this position. First, many mergers have nothing to do with dominance, even when they involve firms operating in the same market. Secondly, even sizeable mergers which raise the question of market dominance may simultaneously improve technical efficiency by lowering production and distribution costs. These savings would be ruled out automatically if mergers were simply prohibited. Thirdly, the threat of takeover may provide a keen deterrent against X-inefficiency. Where one firm takes over another, the top management of the acquired firm is frequently replaced by the new owners. The likelihood of this happening will be minimized if the incumbent management runs an efficient and profitable enterprise. In this case the share price will remain buoyant and therefore present a less attractive opportunity to a potential bidder. Even if the company is acquired the new owners will be far less likely to sack a successful management. Thus if the 'market for corporate control' is left open it provides an added incentive for firms to maintain a high level of internal efficiency. A blanket ban on (sizeable) mergers would remove this incentive, according to this argument. This remains, however, one of the most controversial aspects of merger policy, with many other observers claiming that the ever-present threat of takeover forces firms into an excessive, not to say obsessive, concern with the short-term at the expense of long-term strength.

The final means of acquiring dominance that we mention is predatory behaviour. Just as 'skill, foresight and industry' may be viewed as virtuous ways of attaining a dominant position, so predatory behaviour may be condemned as vicious. A firm which deliberately sets out to destroy competing firms by, say, predatory pricing, may not only succeed in creating for itself a position of market dominance but, by the precedent that this establishes in the minds of potential entrants, help to bolster its position in the long term. At this stage we can note two points about this line of argument. First, although predatory behaviour is firmly established as part of the demonology of big business in popular discussions, its actual occurrence is probably far less frequent than is commonly supposed. Secondly, when it does occur it is much more likely to be in defence of an established position than in the creation of a new position of dominance. Both questions are further discussed in Chapter 5.

Although we have discussed the factors in sequence, it should be evident that in practice a combination of several may be in operation simultaneously. Thus firms enjoying the protection afforded by government policy on inhibiting imports may also attempt to collude with close competitors or even acquire one of them if the occasion arises. Furthermore, if one path to dominance becomes closed, perhaps because of a tightening of antitrust policy in one direction, a firm may adjust its strategy accordingly or try another path: more comprehensive control of collusion may cause an increase in merger activity or greater lobbying efforts to win government protection. As we stressed in the opening chapter, however, the ability to maintain a position of market dominance which allows firms to charge prices in excess of long-run marginal cost rests ultimately on the presence of barriers to entry.

III   Some evidence on market dominance

Given the importance of market dominance in economic analysis and to antitrust policy, it is hardly surprising that considerable effort has gone into its measurement, both for single years and over time. The main purpose of this section is thus to discuss some of these estimates, largely derived from the UK.

A useful starting-point in an enquiry into possible positions of market dominance is to observe the extent to which sales are concentrated in the hands of a few sellers. If one firm makes, say, 90 per cent of the sales in a properly defined market, then, even though it is not strictly the sole seller that appears in the theoretical definition of monopoly, it is very likely to be in a position of dominance and able to control prices in its favour. However, even in these circumstances, control will only be effective if the incumbent firm is protected by some form of entry barrier. Even with high entry barriers the seller's control over price may be constrained by the buying power of customers. If the seller depends for most of its sales on the purchases of a handful of very large customers (such as other manufacturers or nationalized industries) its discretion over prices may be limited. These factors apply with greater force if, instead of a single dominant firm, the largest four or five sellers make all or most of the sales. In this case inter-firm rivalry is likely to constrain further individual firms' control over price.

Nevertheless market dominance will be found in a sub-set of those markets where sales are concentrated in few hands. Further enquiry will then be necessary to determine exactly where it is present and where, alternatively, other factors ensure it is absent. For a number of years, the Census authorities in both the UK and the USA have published information on seller concentration for a larger number of products in manufacturing industry. Thus the US Census of Manufactures regularly publishes the percentage of sales of specified products accounted for by the four, eight and 50 largest sellers. In the UK, the Census of Production includes similar information, but for the five largest sellers in more widely defined industry categories. Until 1977 this information was supplemented by data on product seller concentration. For our purposes the latter are more relevant because, for the most part, they come closer to the concept of a 'properly defined market' to which we referred in Chapter 1. However, concern with the correct market concept brings us to the first of a number of problems with the use of Census data in the preliminary analysis of antitrust questions. Although we may be able to define 'a market' satisfactorily for theoretical purposes, when we try to pin down that concept by measuring it empirically we run into difficulties, especially when using Census information. The underlying problem is that the Censuses of Manufactures or Production are designed to measure precisely that: output from manufacturing industry in a particular year. They are not designed to measure 'markets' in a way suitable for antitrust enquiry. In particular the data are largely grouped on the basis of plants using specified production methods or raw materials, rather than those making products which are close substitutes. There is a danger therefore that the output from particular plants may not be close substitutes in demand but, because they come from plants using very similar production methods, they are grouped together. More seriously, products that may be close substitutes on the demand side but which may use quite different materials or production methods may in the Census data be grouped into different categories when they are in fact part of the same 'market'.

Although this difficulty pervades all Census information and results from our wish to use it for purposes for which it was not originally intended, it is less acute, in our judgement, at the product level than at the industry level of aggregation.[5] In the discussion below, therefore, we refer largely to concentration at the product level, but we should be aware of the upward bias that is still present in most cases because of the underinclusion of close substitutes.

In the data presented below, the sales of the five largest firms are given. The number five is used in order to avoid the problem of disclosure. Census authorities are not allowed to disclose information on individual firms. In order to maximize the number of products for which concentration data could be published, the authorities decided on five as the minimum feasible number to include in the ratio. The US authorities use the four largest sellers. If fewer than five firms sell the product in the UK, the information cannot be published. In some cases which may be particularly relevant to antitrust policy, therefore, the seller concentration data are not available.

Table 2.1 shows the average level of seller concentration for a sample of 121 manufactured products in the UK over the period 1958 to 1977. In particular we should note that the last year for which product concentration data were published was 1977.[6] The first row in the table gives the simple mean value of the percentage of sales of domestic output by the five largest sellers in the sample of 121 products.[7] By 1977, on average, the five largest sellers were responsible for just under 65 per cent of the total sales, compared with 56 per cent in 1958. The whole of the average increase occurred between 1958 and 1968. After that, average concentration level appears to have stabilized. We return to the position since 1977 below. For the moment we concentrate on the difference between the two rows in Table 2.1. The first row is based entirely on sales of domestic output, rather than sales in the UK market. This betrays again the source from which such information is drawn. The Census of Production is designed to measure domestic output. The concentration data drawn from it use the same base. Imports are not included. For the UK, where import penetration has increased dramatically over the past 30 years, this is likely to be a very serious omission. In many markets the major source of competition may come from imports rather than supplies from other domestic producers. An apparently dominant UK producer may have its pricing and other decisions severely constrained by the need to compete with foreign firms in the domestic market. The second row of Table 2.1 therefore tries to take account of this factor by adjusting the published concentration data for imports. If all imports are thus included in the denominators when calculating the concentration ratios, then clearly they must be reduced. The 'adjusted' series must therefore be below the unadjusted series. If we accept, for the moment, the basis on which Table 2.1 is calculated, it is clear that, once imports are taken into account, average concentration, while increasing in the period 1958–68, was reduced in the subsequent decade practically to the level of 1958.

Table 2.1   Average five-firm concentration for a sample of 121 manufactured products, 1958–77 (unadjusted and adjusted for imports)

Concentration	1958	1963	1968	1975	1977
			Per cent		
Unadjusted	56.5	60.1	64.8	65.0	64.8
Adjusted	52.3	55.4	58.8	56.4	54.8

Source: M.A. Utton and A.D. Morgan (1983), *Concentration and Foreign Trade*, Cambridge: Cambridge University Press.

A problem with the adjusted series is that it makes no allowance for the fact that the five largest UK sellers may also control a proportion of the imports. Multinational enterprises may not only have production plants in a number of countries but also sell their finished products in all of them. To the extent that that is the case, imports are not an additional source of competition, and the adjustment made in Table 2.1 overstates their impact. Unfortunately, while everyone knows of one or two examples of large firms' responsibility for imports, there are no systematic data for a large sample on which to base firm conclusions. What the table should do, however, is to remind us that where import competition is both genuine and substantial it should modify any notion of market dominance based purely on the concentration of domestic output.

A similar point has been made by Landes and Posner (1981), who argue that a correct analysis of market dominance should focus not only on demand and products which are close substitutes, and therefore have high cross-elasticities, but also on supply and potential supply. If a small increase in price of product A is enough to make it profitable for firms hitherto producing for another market to switch to the production of A, then, argue Landes and Posner, this productive capacity should be included in the market for A. In particular, if such small price increases would cause a significant increase in imports of A then all potential imports should be viewed as part of the market. On this view actual imports may simply indicate the scope for possible increases that could occur following a price rise. Domestic firms will clearly be constrained in their price behaviour and market dominance will be reduced. The extreme version of this view has been disputed by Brennan (1982) and Schmalensee (1982a), but it again draws attention to the difficulty of defining a 'market' precisely and to the importance of imports as an actual and potential source of increased competition.

The study from which Table 2.1 is drawn also demonstrated, however, that there is an important sub-set of markets which have been heavily concentrated for a long period and where imports play a relatively insignificant role. Thus there were 35 product groups where the five largest firms throughout the period studied made more than 80 per cent of the sales, even when imports were included. In such cases the competitive impact of imports is unlikely to be very strong. It is not possible to judge from such data, however, the extent to which domestic rivalry amongst the largest sellers caused their respective market share rankings to change.

Judging by a recent analysis of the trend of concentration at the industry (rather than product) level of aggregation, the changes observed in Table 2.1 were reversed during the 1980s. Thus Clarke (1993) shows that, for a sample of 100 industries, average five-firm concentration unadjusted for imports declined from just under 44 per cent in 1980 to 40 per cent in 1989. Once allowance is made for imports, however, the decline is much more pronounced, from 30 per cent to just over 24 per cent.

It has frequently been observed that, although a measure like the share of the five largest firms in sales may be a useful first step in isolating those markets where market dominance may be present, the step is not a very large one. The concentration ratio is a static measure. We learn that the five largest firms in a certain year were responsible for, say, 85 per cent of the sales, but we learn nothing about how long that level has persisted, whether the same firms are at the top and in the same order as 10 and 20 years ago, and why sales should be so concentrated. As we stressed in the previous chapter, antitrust is only concerned with dominant positions which persist and which allow a firm or firms to raise price above the competitive level without attracting entry. If, as some economists claim, apparent positions of dominance are short-lived because abnormal profits attract new competition, then much of antitrust policy may be unnecessary: market forces will do the job more effectively. The fact that economists holding such views are still in the minority and that many countries, including developing and previously centrally planned economies, are extending or introducing systems of antitrust control, suggests that the above view of the speed of adjustment of markets is regarded as excessively optimistic. Yet the hard evidence is sparse and incomplete. For example, comparatively little is known about the rate at which large market shares are acquired and dissipated over time and how long the process may take in the absence of antitrust policy. In fact recent developments in the theory of business strategy suggest that, once attained, positions of dominance may be very difficult to dislodge.

In an interesting attempt to determine the impact of antitrust policy on market structure, Stigler presented estimates of leading market shares in six key industries for the USA and the UK over approximately the first half of the last century when US antitrust policy was in place while the UK had no specific antitrust measures. The estimates for the UK were subsequently updated to the mid-1970s and are reproduced as Table 2.2. The main reason why the sample is so small is the difficulty of gaining comparable information over such a long period. Markets and technology are evolving continuously. Many products now available were not made at all in the first decade of the last century. Any conclusions drawn from the table should therefore be treated very cautiously because the sample is unrepresentative. In four cases (cement, cars, cigarettes and soap) the leading firm experienced little loss of market share for a large part of the century (although in the seven years after 1976 this was not true in cars, where the leading firm saw its share fall from 28 per cent to 18 per cent). The most extreme case was in cement, where the market leader was formed by an amalgamation of firms in 1900 which gave it a market share of about 60 per cent. Its share was still 58 per cent 78 years later.

Table 2.2 Long-run shares of market leaders in six UK industries

Market	Stigler study*		Subsequent estimate*
Cars	31 (1924)	37 (1964)	28 (1976)
Cement	59 (1900)	60 (1959)	58 (1978)
Cigarettes	71 (1903)	65 (1959)	66 (1976)
Flat glass	29 (1904)	95 (1955)	91 (1967)
Soap	46 (1915)	59 (1961)	41 (1976)
Tyres and tubes	58 (1924)	47 (1952)	27 (1975)

* Year given in brackets.

Source: G.J. Stigler (1968), *The Organisation of Industry*, Chicago: University of Chicago Press; M.A. Utton (1986a), *The Profits and Stability of Monopoly*, Cambridge: Cambridge University Press.

In a further analysis, covering roughly the period from the Second World War until the mid-1970s, it was found that, in 19 markets where the market leader had an opening share of 50 per cent or more, substantial declines (10 percentage points or more) occurred in 11 cases and substantial increases in five. The other three remained approximately unchanged. Where the market shares declined it was nevertheless true that the firm retained its leading position but at the same time, in most instances, it was clearly having to contend with a greater degree of oligopolistic rivalry than at the beginning of the period (for example, in cigarettes, open-top cans, industrial gases, matches and wallpaper: Utton, 1986a, ch. 3).

The question of whether dominant firms can effectively 'manage' the gradual erosion of their market share over time so as to maximize their long-term profitability has been examined by Geroski (1987). After an exhaustive review of a variety of evidence on the long-term market share of dominant firms in the UK and the USA, he broadened the original hypothesis as follows. Dominant firms decline when they have become complacent and sleepy, a condition induced by the lack of any real threat to their position for a substantial period. They are then vulnerable to a sudden innovative attack from new entry where the emphasis is firmly on change (in product, process or organization). A dominant firm subject to fairly frequent challenge is likely in many instances to be able to resist successfully and maintain its position. Although, as Geroski says, this reformulation of the basic 'managed decline' hypothesis helps to explain more fully the pattern of market share actually observed, it still leaves largely unresolved the question of time. How long does it take for the sleeping giants to be aroused and reinvigorated or, alternatively, slain? If the presence and application of antitrust policy can speed up the process, so much the better.

A crucial element in the process will be barriers to entry (and exit). If entry is easy and exit costless, then market dominance in any sense relevant to antitrust policy will be absent. Any firm with a large market share in such circumstances can only retain its position by aligning prices closely to costs and keeping a firm rein on its internal efficiency. Given its crucial importance to antitrust analysis, therefore, the reader may legitimately expect the widespread availability of detailed estimates of entry conditions for a large sample of industries. As they are at least as important as the degree of concentration in the market, entry conditions should provide an equally valid starting-point for pinpointing markets that require the attention of antitrust.

Unfortunately such estimates do not exist. Thus, while it is possible to obtain official estimates of concentration, no systematic data on entry conditions are available. It is significant, for example, that two recent texts on industrial economics, Martin (1993) and Carlton and Perloff (2000), relied on the empirical estimates first published nearly 50 years ago in Bain's classic work on barriers to new competition (Bain, 1956). Rather than reproduce Bain's estimates again we rely on an analysis of entry barriers in a number of UK markets based on a large number of reports of the Monopolies and Mergers

Commission (MMC) and the Price Commission (Gribbin and Utton, 1986). The sample is therefore biased in the sense that all of the markets included had been drawn to the attention of the antitrust authorities; markets that had given no cause for concern would not have been referred to the MMC and would thus not appear in the sample. For present purposes, however, the information is sufficient to illustrate a number of important points about the nature and significance of entry barriers.

The sample of 50 markets was classified into three types of oligopoly according to the size distribution of firms within them: 'dominant firms' where the leading firm had 50 per cent or more of the market and the second largest was less than half the size of the leader; 'concentrated oligopoly' where the largest two firms had 50 per cent or more of the market; and 'loose oligopoly' where the leading two firms had less than 50 per cent of the market.

Four different sources of entry barrier were identified from a detailed examination of the reports and these were labelled as follows: technical – comprising essentially substantial economies of scale in production and possibly vertical integration; legal – involving patents or high effective tariff rates; price – depending not on structural characteristics but on behaviour, including, for example, loyalty rebates, exclusive dealing discounts and predatory pricing; and distribution – involving in some cases vertical restraints on the range of products carried by final outlets, rental only contracts and tying arrangements, and in other cases very heavy advertising which prevented access to final consumers. Once the source of the entry barriers had been identified in each market, a judgement was made about their respective significance and each case was then classified as having 'high', 'medium' or 'low' entry barriers overall. Clearly a weakness in the procedure, as indeed in the Bain study, is the degree of subjectiveness in the final evaluation. To try to minimize this effect the two authors made their initial assessments independently and then compared their results. In most cases the assessments were similar, but the point should be borne in mind when considering the comments made on Table 2.3.

As one might expect, the 'dominant firm' category had significantly different entry conditions from the other two market types. Although markets in this group amounted to only 40 per cent of the sample, they accounted for half of all entry barriers identified and 60 per cent of those classified as 'high'. In the dominant group there were, on average, 2.7 barriers, compared with 1.8 for each of the other groups. The combination of large market shares for the leaders in the 'dominant firm' group and the frequent occurrence of high entry barriers probably goes a long way to explain their significantly larger average profitability, shown in another part of the same study.

An equally important conclusion for the conduct of antitrust policy can be derived from the relative importance of the different sources of barriers, especially high barriers, shown in Table 2.3. Whereas the first two categories are essentially 'structural', the last two are 'behavioural'. More than two-thirds of the entry barriers identified were in the latter category, depending largely on the behaviour of the leading enterprises. In the past UK antitrust policy has been criticized for concentrating largely on behavioural remedies to correct positions of market dominance which have been found to be against the public interest. Firms have been required to abandon exclusive and restrictive arrangements with their customers. There has been little or no attempt to use structural remedies. If the classification given in Table 2.3 is even approximately correct, the use of behavioural remedies may be much more effective in modifying entry conditions than some critics have allowed. They can be introduced far more easily and at less cost than 'structural' remedies which might involve loss of scale economies, selective changes in trade policy or interference with intellectual property rights.

Table 2.3   Entry barriers and market structure

Barrier	Structural type								
	Dominant firm			Concentrated oligopoly			Loose oligopoly		
	H	M	L	H	M	L	H	M	L
Technical	7	2	1	1	5	1	0	3	0
Legal	5	2	2	0	2	0	2	0	1
Price	7	6	1	3	5	0	1	2	0
Distribution	11	9	1	10	9	3	3	4	1
Total	30	19	5	13	21	4	6	9	2
Number of markets	20			21			9		

Note: H = high, M = medium, L = low.

Source: Derived from J.D. Gribbin and M.A. Utton, in H. de Jong and W.G. Shepherd (eds), 1986, *Mainstreams in Industrial Organisation*, **II**, Dordrecht: Kluwer, p. 260; reprinted by permission of Kluwer Academic Publishers.

IV   Conclusion

This chapter has been concerned with two distinct issues, the means by which firms may acquire dominance (Section II) and methods of measuring and identifying markets which may require the attention of antitrust policy (Section III). Of the five methods of attaining dominance discussed in Section II, three, overt collusion, predatory behaviour and merger, are directly amenable to control through antitrust policy, which is not to say, of course, that it will be easy. A fourth, government grant (in the form for example of licences, patents, quotas and tariffs), is, by definition, the subject of policy control, although in such cases where an antitrust body recommends change in order to weaken market dominance it does not necessarily mean that its advice will be followed. Indeed, trade policy questions are usually settled in a quite different arena and changes may only rarely be used to remedy an antitrust abuse.

The remaining method, 'skill, foresight and industry', poses more difficult policy problems. It would be foolish to use antitrust to punish the efficient and innovative. The difficulty is likely to arise where an efficient firm appears to be seeking dominance rather than simply having dominance thrust upon it. Similarly, if chance factors propel some firms into a dominant position, it may subsequently be very difficult for an outside body, such as an antitrust authority, to determine whether it is maintained purely by legitimate business behaviour.

Attempts to pinpoint market dominance empirically have often used the concentration ratio in the preliminary stages. The ratio usually shows the share of the largest four or five firms in sales in the market but has a number of important shortcomings, not least its (usual) exclusion of foreign trade and static nature. It reveals neither the individual shares of the largest enterprises nor their persistence through time. There has been a much greater emphasis recently on this last point and especially on the sources of impediments to entry. However, because the concept of entry conditions or entry barriers is inherently more complex than market shares (assuming the 'market' can be properly defined), systematic data on entry barriers are generally lacking. Evidence from a sample of UK markets which has been the subject of an MMC enquiry suggested that a large proportion of entry barriers could ultimately be traced back to the market conduct of dominant enterprises. This suggests, in turn, that an emphasis in antitrust policy on behavioural rather than structural remedies may not be as ineffective as has frequently been maintained.

Notes

1. At least until the 1980s.
2. For a detailed assessment of the nationalized industries' performance, it is interesting to compare the two books by Pryke (1971, 1981), the first of which is, on the whole, favourable while the latter is, reluctantly, unfavourable.
3. The case is made in Davenport (1989) and the issue discussed in more detail in Chapter 12 below.
4. *US* v. *Aluminum Co. of America*, 44F Supp 97 (1941), 148 F2d 416 (1945).
5. For detailed discussion of this question, see Scherer and Ross (1990, chs. 3 and 11). The classic reference is National Bureau of Economic Research (1955).
6. One of the minor casualties of the cutbacks in government expenditure following the election of the Conservatives in 1979 was information on seller concentration. There is a certain irony in the fact that a government wedded firmly to the operation of free markets was responsible for reducing official information about their structure.
7. The series in Table 2.1 is used because it can be directly related to imports, as we explain in the text. However, it represents only about 44 per cent of product groups for which concentration was published in 1977. Both in size of sales and average level of concentration, the sample is close to the complete population of manufactured products (Utton and Morgan, 1983, p. 13).

3 The antitrust response: an outline of antitrust policy in Europe and the United States

I Introduction

Broadly speaking the antitrust provisions in the USA, the EU and the UK all have the same purpose. It is recognized that freely functioning markets may 'fail' because of the actions of individual firms or groups of firms acting together and that, as a result, some correcting force is necessary to try to ensure that the benefits of competition are achieved. The market failure that antitrust policy seeks to correct is the situation where competition, although in principle viable, appears to be faltering as the result of the direct actions of some firms. The remedy is essentially to maintain or restore competition. Such cases may be contrasted with a relatively small group of important industries where very strong increasing returns to scale may make competition impossible and where some other remedy has to be sought, often through regulation. In the absence of competition the regulators of such industries may nevertheless seek a competitive performance by insisting that the regulated firms pursue policies (for example, on prices) which a competitive industry would attain.[1]

Despite their similar general objective the provisions sprang from very different backgrounds. The first substantial antitrust measure of modern times was the US Sherman Act of 1890. It was passed on a wave of discontent amongst the general public and the then very large farming community at what was seen to be the overweening power of the newly created trusts, the most prominent of which were in the railway and oil industries. The first and greatest merger wave in US history was gaining momentum at the time of the Act, but, as Stigler sadly records, one of the few organized groups that did not express concern at the disappearance of many independent firms into the new amalgamations was the professional economists (Stigler, 1968).

The stimulus in the UK for the Monopolies and Restrictive Practices (Inquiry and Control) Act, 1948 was quite different. Some measures to control possible abuses of market power were envisaged in the Beveridge Report which committed post-war UK governments for the first time to policies of full employment by stimulating aggregate demand. The report recognized that, given the structure of trade union membership and of industry in the UK, successful full employment policy would generate dangerous inflationary pressures unless market power was actively controlled. In the event, the measures enacted probably fell far short of what was originally envisaged.

44

In contrast, antitrust provisions have been part of the European Union (EU) from the start. Thus the Treaty which embodies the constitution and basic rules for the development of the EU contains two articles (81 and 82) which specifically deal with antitrust issues. The founders of the Community were quite clear that the development of a unified market between member states could only proceed as long as individual firms or groups could not frustrate the growth of trade with anticompetitive actions. Thus it was seen from the start that as well as positive actions (such as the removal of internal tariff barriers and the harmonization of fiscal measures) restraining actions (in the form of curbs on collusion or on exclusionary behaviour by dominant firms) were also required.

The main purpose of this chapter is to set out briefly the main provisions of the antitrust policies applied in the three jurisdictions, especially as they relate to market dominance (Section II). Where legislative provisions have been modified over the years the current position is given. We should emphasize that a fuller discussion of the different aspects of antitrust is provided when we consider the individual issues in subsequent chapters. In Section III we consider briefly exemptions from the antitrust laws.

II   The main antitrust provisions in the USA, the EU and the UK

The original concern in all three jurisdictions was the control of collusive action by a group of firms and of problems associated with one firm attempting to monopolize a market or maintain control of a market by anticompetitive means. A notable omission in each case initially was any explicit provision against mergers.[2] Given the background of the increasing tide of mergers in the USA, the omission is surprising. What is even more intriguing in view of subsequent events is the belated correction of a similar gap in the UK provisions and the even more painful process through which the EU has had to pass in order to give birth to its own method of merger control.

The US provisions

The main provisions of the Sherman Act are deceptively simple. Section 1 deals with collusion and Section 2 with 'monopolization' or dominance. Thus, under Section 1, all contracts, combinations or conspiracies in restraint of trade are illegal. Individuals found guilty of engaging in such conspiracies are now subject to a maximum fine of $10 million, if a company, or of $350 000 if a person, or three years' imprisonment (or both), at the discretion of the court. The fines can be increased up to twice the violator's gain or twice the victim's loss. Section 2 of the Act proscribes monopolization, attempts to monopolize or combine or conspire to monopolize 'any part of the trade or commerce among the several States, or with foreign nations'. As with Section 1, violation constitutes a criminal offence, with the same level of penalties.[3]

The provisions were extended and strengthened in 1914 with the passage of the Clayton Act and the Federal Trade Commission Act. Under the Clayton

Act four specific kinds of restrictive or monopolistic practices were made illegal: price discrimination (subsequently modified by the Robinson Patman Act, 1936); exclusive dealing and tying contracts; acquisitions of competing companies (subsequently strengthened by the Celler–Kefauver Act, 1950) and interlocking directorates. In each case, however, the practice only became an offence if its 'effect may be to substantially lessen competition or tend to create a monopoly'. There is thus an important difference between a collusive act under Section 1 of the Sherman Act, which is automatically illegal, and the action of an individual firm which may be illegal according to the Clayton Act.

The main effect of the Federal Trade Commission Act was to establish the Commission (FTC) as an administrative agency with quasi-judicial powers which can conduct hearings into suspected violations of the law. Under Section 5 of the Federal Trade Commission Act all 'unfair methods of competition' were made illegal and it was up to the Commission to decide what exactly these were. Thus, whereas actions under the Sherman Act can involve criminal offences, the FTC's jurisdiction is purely civil. In practice, however, because the courts have decided that an offence under Section 5 of the FTC Act also constitutes an offence under the Sherman Act, the FTC has been able to pursue actions in the courts which in all but name amount to Sherman Act cases (Neale and Goyder, 1980, p. 5). The distinction between the two jurisdictions has thus become blurred and much may depend on the effectiveness of cooperation between the FTC and the Antitrust Division.

Cases under the Sherman Act are brought by the Antitrust Division of the Department of Justice before a Federal District Court and an appeal against a decision on a matter of law may be heard by the Supreme Court. In contrast the five-member panel of the FTC, on the recommendation of its administrative law judges, can issue a 'cease and desist' order against companies which it believes have violated the antitrust laws. An appeal against such orders largely on matters of law can be made to a Federal Appeal Court and then to the Supreme Court.

The twin and, to a degree, overlapping jurisdictions of the Antitrust Division and the FTC thus prosecute the major antitrust actions. However, both the Sherman Act and the Clayton Act allow private citizens who have suffered as a result of violations of the antitrust laws to sue for damages. If they are successful they then automatically receive triple the amount of damage incurred. Actions for triple damages have become increasingly important in recent years and we discuss the issues raised by these provisions in Chapter 11 below.

The EU provisions

The substantive antitrust provisions of the EU are embodied in Articles 81 and 82 of the Treaty of Amsterdam which are broadly similar to Sections 1 and 2 of the Sherman Act, and Regulation 4064 which deals with mergers. Section 1 of Article 81 is aimed at all agreements between enterprises, decisions by associations or undertakings and concerted practices which have as their object or effect the 'prevention, restriction or distortion of competition within the common market'. Any such agreements are automatically void under Section 2. The task of determining whether an agreement infringes Article 81 rests with the European Commission and its decisions can be appealed to the Court of First Instance.[4] To this limited extent the position is similar to that under US antitrust law, but there are important differences. First, under Section 3 of Article 81 it is possible for an agreement to be exempted from Section 1 if it is determined by the Commission that it 'contributes to improving the production or distribution of goods or to promoting technical or economic progress, while allowing consumers a fair share of the resulting benefit' and as long as it does not simultaneously give the participants the opportunity of eliminating competition in a substantial part of the market. A more detailed discussion of cases to which the Commission has given exemption is reserved for Chapter 7 below, but it has to be satisfied on all points set out in Section 3, not merely some of them. In addition to giving exemption to an individual agreement the Commission may also grant a 'block exemption' to a whole category of agreements. For example, block exemptions in the past have been granted for exclusive distribution, exclusive purchase, patent licensing, motor vehicle distribution and research and development (Merkin and Williams, 1984, p. 169).

Secondly, the EU had developed a notification procedure which has no real counterpart in the USA. Firms participating in an agreement which may infringe Section 1 of Article 81 could derive a number of benefits from notifying the Commission about the provisions. If firms were unclear, for example, whether or not their agreement constituted an infringement they could be given 'negative clearance' from the Commission. In effect this meant that there appeared to be no grounds for action under Section 1 and therefore participants could continue to operate the agreement. In addition, only those agreements which had been notified to the Commission would be considered for exemption and, finally, notified agreements which were subsequently judged to infringe Section 1 were void but participants would be exempt from fines. In contrast members of an unnotified agreement which was found to have violated Section 1 could be heavily fined. However under proposals made in 2000 the Commission planned to end the notification system in order to free resources to deal with large cross-border cartels. The proposal was part of a much larger review of EU competition policy which aimed to return to national jurisdiction control of routine cases of price fixing and abuse of market dominance. There was considerable resistance to the proposals from the legal profession and business lobbies who feared the reforms would increase uncertainties about which jurisdiction should take precedence in particular cases.

The European Commission also has the authority under Article 82 to investigate individual firms which may be abusing a dominant position within the Community. Its investigations may either be prompted by its own researches or follow complaints from aggrieved parties. Article 82 actually lists a number of practices which may constitute an abuse, namely, the imposition of unfair prices or other trading practices; the limitation of production, markets or technical developments; the application of dissimilar terms to similar conditions in order to place some trading parties at a competitive disadvantage; and the inclusion of supplementary terms which have no bearing on the main substance of a contract. In the same way that Section 2 of the Sherman Act gives wide scope for the courts to try a wide variety of possible abuses by a dominant firm, the separate paragraphs of Article 82 give potentially wide scope for investigations by the Commission. If it finds that there has been an abuse it can issue injunctions or cease and desist orders and has the power to fine the firm concerned. In pursuing its enquiries it also has wide-ranging powers of entry into firms' premises and of document seizure. Decisions by the Commission can be examined on appeal by the Court of First Instance.

Clearly the wording of Article 82 gives very wide discretion to the Commission as to how an abuse of a dominant position should be interpreted within the EU and there is a much more detailed discussion of this issue in Chapters 5 and 6. However, there is some agreement amongst observers that investigations of dominant positions have so far been much less important than those involving horizontal restrictions (Frazer, 1992; Goyder, 1998). One important reason for this may simply be a lack of information. In the case of horizontal agreements firms had a direct interest in notifying the Commission because, as we have seen, this may have led eventually to exemption and in any case gave them immunity from fines. No such benefit can flow from a dominant firm notifying the Commission about, say, its price structure or rebate schemes. Since there is no possibility of exemption, and no method of 'negative clearance', firms in a dominant position have every incentive to keep their trading practices confidential. The Commission must therefore rely entirely on its own investigations and possible complaints from customers, suppliers or competitors.

Firms which are found guilty of an offence under Articles 81 or 82 can be fined by the Commission an amount up to 10 per cent of their worldwide turnover or one million EUROS, whichever is the greater. The two articles thus establish machinery for the investigation and control of restrictive agreements and abuse of a dominant position. What of the third area of antitrust policy concerning sizeable mergers which in some circumstances may replace a previous restrictive agreement and/or create a dominant position? If dominance, once attained, is difficult to remove or restrain one might expect merger control to be at the centre of antitrust policy. In fact the Rome Treaty contained no specific provisions for dealing with mergers. Until 1990 the Commission had therefore to rely largely on action under Articles 81 and 82. In what became a landmark case, the European Court surprisingly confirmed the view of the Commission in *Continental Can* that in special circumstances mergers by an already dominant firm did fall within the scope of Article 82: a firm already holding a dominant position within the EU should be prevented from acquiring the only other substantial competitor. It was immediately apparent, however, that the decision was of rather limited application in the control of anticompetitive mergers. Thus it did not apply to mergers which might create a dominant position, only to those where dominance preceded the merger proposal. There was no pre-notification system whereby substantial mergers might be given negative clearance by the Commission. In a more recent case (*Philip Morris*), the Court made it clear that, where one company purchased shares in a major competitor, thus gaining effective control, Article 81 would apply.

Shortly after the *Continental Can* decision in 1973, the Commission produced the first of what became a whole series of proposals (in 1982, 1984, 1986 and 1988) for incorporating merger controls formally within the Community. Although it was widely recognized that some mechanism was necessary, it was not until the end of 1989 that members finally gave unanimous approval to a Directive giving exclusive power to the Commission to vet large mergers. From September 1990 the Commission has had exclusive authority to investigate proposed mergers involving enterprises with a combined worldwide turnover of at least EUROS 5 billion, as long as the total EU turnover of each of at least two of the companies is greater than EUROS 250 million, and as long as no company involved does more than two-thirds of its EU business in one member country. All other mergers will stay within the national jurisdiction of individual members (although smaller members without a well developed merger policy can ask the Commission to investigate mergers involving worldwide turnover of between EUROS 2 and 5 billion). The threshold is to be reviewed periodically and can be revised. In recognition of the increasing number of mergers involving several countries, an amendment to the Regulation was made in 1998. Mergers where the original thresholds were not met, but where three or more separate jurisdictions would be involved, could be investigated by the Commission as long as (a) global turnover was more than EUROS 2.5 billion, (b) combined EU turnover was EUROS 100 millions or more, and (c) in each member state involved, at least two merging companies would have revenue of more than EUROS 25 million. For mergers caught by the new regulation there is a fixed timetable of notification, consideration and clearance or prohibition.[5]

One of the major difficulties which held up previous acceptance of merger provisions was the desire of a number of members to incorporate broader consideration of 'industrial policy'. In the event it was finally agreed that competition should be the main ground for assessing mergers, although the

Commission has suggested that this may be more broadly interpreted than is usual. Indeed there is provision in the Directive for the Commission to take account of 'economic and technical progress' in its deliberations. Individual members may also prohibit mergers on a number of special grounds, for example to preserve national security or plurality of media ownership.

The UK provisions

Competition policy in the UK has been evolving in the half century or so since its introduction in 1948. In the following decades mechanisms were gradually developed for the investigation and control of dominant firms, restrictive agreements and large mergers. Following widespread criticism that the machinery was cumbersome and ineffective, a major reform of the policy was carried out in 1998. The Competition Act 1998, set out to correct many of these deficiencies and to bring UK policy into line with that established in the EU. The provisions became effective in 2000. [6]

The main changes are set out in Chapters 1 and 2 of the Act, dealing respectively with restrictive agreements and abuse of a dominant position. Much of the wording replicates that in Articles 81 and 82, except that the provisions apply strictly to trade within the UK. Thus in Chapter 1 all agreements or concerted practices having as their object or effect the prevention, restriction or distortion of competition are prohibited, unless specifically exempted. Compared with the previous position in the UK, agreements are to be judged on their *effect* rather than on their *form*. Members of agreements may, however, apply for exemption from the prohibition on the grounds that their agreement improves production or distribution, or promotes technical progress while passing on some of the benefits to consumers without at the same time helping members to eliminate competition. This provision exactly mirrors that in Article 81(3). As well as overt, formal agreements the provision also covers 'concerted practices' where firms in an oligopolistic market appear to pursue restrictive price and output policies without having any formal agreement. Both EU and US case law, which are referred to in Chapter 7 below, illustrate how difficult it is in practice to distinguish the intelligent but independent behaviour of an individual firm pursuing its best interests by anticipating the likely action of its rivals, from collective behaviour to rig the market against the consumer.

Chapter 2 of the Act deals with abuse of a dominant position and again follows almost exactly the wording of Article 82: any conduct on the part of one or more undertakings which amounts to the abuse of a dominant position in a market is prohibited. A list of examples of conduct which may constitute an abuse are also given, such as imposing unfair purchase or selling prices; limiting production, markets or technical development; applying dissimilar conditions to equivalent transactions; and making the conclusion of contracts subject to acceptance by other parties of supplementary obligations which have no connection with the subject of the contract. Although the list is meant to be illustrative rather than exhaustive it is clear that most forms of abusive conduct with which dominant firms have been accused in the past are covered.

Unlike Chapter 1, however, there is no provision in Chapter 2 for exemption. The explanation for this lies in the ambiguous nature of much of the behaviour cited. Thus low prices may signify technical efficiency and learning effects rather than predatory behaviour; price discrimination may allow firms to reach parts of the market not previously served; and some refusals to supply may be based on commercial judgement of a customer's financial viability rather than an attempt to exclude. Compared with the clear-cut results that generally follow from a cartel, economic analysis can give far less clear-cut assistance in the case of much market conduct by dominant firms.

The investigation of cases under both chapters lies in the hands of the Director General of Fair Trading (DGFT) who has been in overall charge of UK competition policy since 1973. The Act strengthens his position enormously by giving him and his officials authority to enter and search commercial premises, and remove documents, as necessary. Failure to comply with the requests of the DGFT for information can result in fines for the persons involved. Deliberate obstruction of the DGFT's inquiries can result in up to two years' imprisonment, plus a fine. Under the previous law, officials had no authority to enter premises and seize documents. There was no requirement on the part of companies thought, for example, to be operating an illegal agreement, to supply information to the DGFT before legal proceedings were initiated. As a result, investigations were severely hampered.

A major criticism of the previous law was the lack of appropriate remedies. Companies which were found to have operated illegal agreements for many years could merely be required to cease. Under the new law and in line with EU practice, companies found to have infringed the prohibitions in Chapters 1 and 2 can be fined up to 10 per cent of their UK turnover by the DGFT.

The role of the DGFT and his Office of Fair Trading (OFT) in the UK is thus on a par with the Competition Directorate of the EU. As we mentioned above, appeals from the European Commission are made to the European Court of First Instance. In the UK under the 1998 Act, appeals can be made to the newly constituted Competition Commission which replaces the Monopolies and Mergers Commission (MMC). Decisions under Chapters 1 and 2 may be appealed to the judicial arm of the Competition Commissoin presided over by a judge. (The first incumbent is Sir Ralph Bellamy, formerly a member of the European Court of First Instance.) The second arm of the Competition Commission fulfils a different role, to which we return below.

The prohibitive approach embodied in Chapters 1 and 2, and the substantial strengthening of the powers of the DGFT, have met many of the criticisms of the previous policy. In a number of respects, however, the 1998 Act left the previous policy unchanged. The most significant example was in respect of mergers. The established system of merger surveillance and control was retained. Under this system large mergers were initially screened by the OFT to determine whether or not the 'public interest' was involved. If the preliminary conclusion was that public interest issues were raised by the merger, the DGFT would recommend to the Secretary of State for Trade and Industry that it be referred to the Monopolies and Mergers Commission for a detailed enquiry and recommendation. The Minister did not have to follow the DGFT's advice but normally did.[7] The important point, however, was that the minister, a politician, had sole authority to refer mergers. Only those mergers which would either create or enhance a market share of 25 per cent or more, or which involved the acquisition of net assets of £70 millions or more, could be referred. If the MMC concluded that the merger would *not* operate against the public interest, it could proceed unimpeded. On the other hand, if the conclusion was that the merger *would* operate against the public interest, the Secretary of State had a discretion. The merger could either be blocked or permitted with conditions, or even permitted without conditions despite the MMC's recommendations. Although it was rare for ministers to go against the MMC, there were exceptions.[8]

Despite criticisms that political influence over the procedure should be removed, there were no provisions in the 1998 Act to deal with mergers. Shortly after the passage of the Act the government indicated that it was to undertake a review of merger policy. However, it was not until the middle of 2001 that its proposed changes were published in a White Paper.[9] Under the proposals, the power of politicians in merger policy would be removed. The DGFT would have sole authority, following the initial screening, to refer to the Competition Commission all mergers which seemed likely to lead to a substantial decline in competition. The previous 'public interest' test would thus be replaced by a competition test. Merger enquiries would be undertaken by the second arm of the Competition Commission, whose members, according to the White Paper, would be 'specialists in the field of competition and antitrust'.

This branch of the newly formed Competition Commission may also be asked by the DGFT to report on so-called 'scale' monopolies and 'complex' monopolies, under provisions set out in the 1973 Fair Trading Act. A scale monopoly refers to a situation where one firm has 25 per cent or more of a UK market and where preliminary evidence suggests that a public interest enquiry is required. A complex monopoly is where a group of independent companies, which together account for at least one-quarter of a market, engage in conduct that has the effect of restricting or preventing competition. The rationale for retaining these provisions was to cover possible gaps in the 1998 Act. Thus there are no provisions in the Act for structural remedies following an abuse under Chapter 2. If it is feared that such an abuse is likely to recur, the DGFT has indicated that a scale monopoly reference to the Competition Commission may be made, and it could, if necessary, recommend a structural remedy (such as the compulsory sale of part of the scale monopoly).[10] Similarly, the DGFT has argued that the 'complex monopoly' provision can be used to deal with situations where 'a group of companies all adopt similar practices or engage in parallel behaviour which appears to be anti-competitive but where there is no overt collusion or agreement'.[11] He does not, however, make clear why such cases cannot be dealt with as 'concerted practices' under Chapter 1 of the Competition Act.

We may finally note that all of the provisions of the Act apply to those industries (like telecommunications, gas, water, electricity and railways) formerly in public ownership but which were privatized in the 1980s and early 1990s. All of the industries are regulated by specialist agencies and they are to work in concert with the OFT to ensure that the industries comply with the Act.

III   Exemptions from antitrust policy

In all three jurisdictions there are certain areas of activity which have been given exemption from the antitrust laws.[12] Although the form of exemption differs considerably, there is a good deal of common ground over which activities should be exempt. Broadly these are agriculture, natural monopolies, labour unions and export agreements. There are obviously other cases, for example, patent rights, where exclusive use has been granted and which therefore cannot simultaneously be touched by laws affecting monopoly.

In the USA, since the Sherman Act was very widely drawn, exemptions have generally had to be specifically set out in subsequent legislation. Thus Section 6 of the Clayton Act allows for the exemption of agricultural cooperatives designed to assist members by maintaining prices. The exemption was subsequently strengthened.[13] Similarly, in the EU, where agricultural matters are dealt with by a different directorate, the Common Agricultural Policy is specifically exempted from Articles 81 and 82, and most agricultural activity in the individual member states is covered by the provision. In residual cases where it does not apply because the activity does not enter intra-European trade the separate national jurisdictions continue to apply. Such a case was the wholesale distribution of milk in the UK which for more than 60 years had been undertaken by the Milk Marketing Board. The Board was established by legislation rather than by agreement amongst producers, and was exempt from most provisions of the antitrust laws.[14] Towards the end of 1989, there were calls for the abolition of the Board (along with those for wool and potatoes) and after lengthy debate the current system was ended in 1994.

Exemption of labour unions which were never supposed to be included in the Sherman Act provisions was specifically given in Section 6 of the Clayton Act.[15] The exemption extends to arrangements designed to protect members but does not allow unions to enter into a restrictive agreement with employers either to fix final product prices or to exclude other firms from the market. Any such collusion would come within Section I of the Sherman Act.

In the EU the position is less clear-cut. Thus individual member states have their own legislation covering the usual activities of labour unions jointly negotiating the terms and conditions of employment for their members. Since these negotiations have hitherto been exclusively national in character, no specific exemption has been required. However, as the market becomes more unified, negotiations are likely to become more and more 'multinational' and it may then become necessary to make explicit what has hitherto simply been tacitly accepted, that normal trade union activities are exempt from Articles 81 and 82.

In the UK the original legislation covering restrictive agreements made no provision for those involving services rather than goods. Restrictive labour practices were therefore not included. When the law was substantially revised in 1973, however, Section 73 of the Fair Trading Act allowed the Secretary of State to refer any specific labour practice to the MMC which had to report on the public interest implications. The power remained unused until 1988, when labour practices in the television and film-making industries were referred. In the event the MMC found that the restrictions did not operate against the public interest (MMC, 1989c). The findings were thought to make it unlikely that this power under the Fair Trading Act would be used again.

The third area of exemption concerns the regulated and other 'special' industries. In the USA, natural monopolies or utilities such as water, electricity, gas and telecommunications have largely remained in the private sector but subject to regulation by a specialized agency which controlled rates of return, prices and entry. There is no blanket exemption from the antitrust laws and each industry has in effect to test the extent of its own immunity in the courts. As the break-up of Associated Telephone and Telegraph (AT and T) in 1984 following an antitrust action testifies, the immunity may not extend very far. In the EU, where such industries were frequently nationalized, special provisions were made. In particular it was recognized that, if individual members treat publicly owned enterprises differently from others, competition may be impaired and this may ultimately affect intra-Community trade. Article 86 makes clear that all publicly owned and quasi-public enterprises are subject to all of the provisions of the Treaty including Articles 81 and 82, but under certain circumstances exemption may be granted. In fact the clause under which exemption can be allowed is tightly drawn and the court has interpreted it in a very narrow way. The implication is that very few public undertakings escape the antitrust provisions (Merkin and Williams, 1984, pp. 367–9). In essence therefore the position is very similar in this respect to that of the USA. As we saw above, the UK's Competition Act applies to all of the major industries privatized and regulated in the 1980s and early 1990s. The provisions of the Act are to be applied to the industries by the OFT or the relevant regulatory agency.

In what two observers regard as a 'mercantilist remnant common to the antitrust policies of most industrialised nations' (Scherer and Ross, 1990, p. 324), the Webb–Pomerene Act of 1918 exempted from the antitrust laws all US firms participating in agreements purely concerned with exports. All such export agreements have to be registered with the FTC, which has to be sure that their operation does not impinge upon the US market. The obvious difficulty with this position is that collaboration to sell abroad may facilitate (tacit) collaboration in the domestic market. Quantitatively, however, this exemption in the USA has not been significant. In the UK, there is now provision to exempt from the Competition Act agreements designed solely to boost exports. In principle, an export agreement amongst UK producers (or groups of producers in other single member states) exclusively to increase exports to non-EU markets is beyond the reach of Article 81. For the same reason a similar agreement amongst enterprises in several member states dealing solely with exports from the Community would fall outside the scope of the existing antitrust provisions, although hitherto no test of such a case has been made. The difficulties such arrangements may cause between trading nations are discussed further in Chapter 12.

IV   Conclusion

The purpose of this chapter has been to give a brief outline of the main antitrust provisions in the three jurisdictions. Although they differ considerably in age and approach (the US system is largely judicial, the EU both administrative and judicial and the UK system largely administrative) they all have in common the objective of controlling or correcting market dominance, whether exercised by a single firm or by a group of firms coordinating their activities.

Under EU and UK law it is possible for a restrictive agreement to be exempted from the antitrust laws. However, no such exemption from Section 1 of the Sherman Act in the USA is possible. As we saw in Section III, some groups or activities were given exemption in all three jurisdictions, although in the USA this was usually effected by special legislation after the original antitrust laws were in place. Broadly speaking, these exemptions relate to the collective activities of labour unions, special industries regulated usually on grounds of natural monopoly, agricultural cooperatives or marketing boards and, more controversially, export agreements.

Very large areas of the economies thus remain subject to the various antitrust laws. In the succeeding parts of this book the way in which antitrust policy has evolved and continues to evolve is examined through a discussion of leading cases from the three jurisdictions. It should be clear from the terse clauses on market dominance and restrictive agreement quoted from the Sherman Act and the European Treaties that the substance of antitrust policy derives essentially from the case law and this depends on judicial or administrative interpretation. How far economic analysis of the issues of market dominance is also reflected in these decisions is a major concern.

Notes

1. For further discussion of these issues, see Utton (1986b) and Waterson (1988).
2. Although in extreme cases Section 2 of the Sherman Act could be interpreted in this way.
3. The level of penalties has been changed over the years. The text gives those currently in operation.
4. Until 1989, appeals went to the European Court. By the late 1980s, the Court's workload had become overwhelming and the new system was therefore introduced. Appeals on matters of law can still be made from the Court of First Instance to the European Court.
5. See Chapter 8 below for more details.
6. For a detailed discussion, see Utton (2000a).
7. A takeover bid for Sotheby's on which the OFT recommended no action was referred to the MMC by the minister.
8. The MMC recommended *against* the merger between Anderson-Strathclyde and Charter Consolidated, but the minister rejected this advice.
9. *Productivity and Enterprise: a World Class Competition Regime*, Cmd 5233, London: Stationery Office 2001.
10. Under the 1998 Act, the DGFT has to publish guidelines on how he will proceed. The text refers to *Guidelines – The Major Provisions*, London: OFT, March 1999.
11. Ibid.
12. We are deliberately excluding from specific discussion here those groups of practices to which the Commission has granted a block exemption. They are considered in Chapter 10.
13. By the Capper–Volstead Act of 1922.
14. Although its activities have had to be cleared by the European Commission.
15. Their position was strengthened by the Norris–La Guardia Act of 1932.

PART II

MARKET DOMINANCE: HORIZONTAL ISSUES

4 The measurement and interpretation of market dominance

I Introduction

We established in Chapter 1 a number of results concerning the inefficiency of monopoly. It was also apparent, however, that under certain conditions improvements in some types of efficiency may come at the expense of other types. In such cases complex trade-offs are likely to be involved, posing difficult problems for the policy maker. The main concern of this opening chapter of the part of the book which deals with horizontal dominance is to discuss how it might be possible to convert the formal results of monopoly theory into the operational requirements of antitrust policy. It is one thing to draw a downward-sloping demand curve and announce that this represents the situation in a monopoly market. It is quite another to determine whether a firm which appears to have a large market share, but where there are, say, a number of much smaller competitors as well as producers making apparently similar products, actually 'dominates' the market, with harmful results.

We approach this transition in two stages. First, in Section II below, we look at two indices of market dominance and assess their usefulness for highlighting the issues involved and for direct application to policy. The measures chosen are the Lerner index of market power and the Bain index of 'excess' profits.[1] Both have been discussed extensively in the present context, and the latter has been the subject of a great deal of empirical analysis and supporting use in antitrust cases. Secondly, in Section III, we review a number of antitrust cases in the light of our discussion of market dominance to see how far economic analysis has informed the practical questions of policy.

II Indices of market dominance

A useful starting-point for a discussion of the Lerner index is the observation that a firm has some degree of market power if it is able to maintain its own prices at a level above marginal cost. In Chapter 1 we noted that firms operating in a perfectly competitive market had no discretion over their price which at the profit-maximizing output would equal marginal cost. Thus any firm which can set its price above marginal cost has a degree of market power, but the key questions are these: how can this idea be made more precise and at what point does such market power become important enough to create significant losses in efficiency?

We proceed by taking first the simplest case of a single-firm monopoly and then the more complex case of a dominant firm in competition with a fringe of much smaller rivals. Thus in the first case a single, profit-maximizing firm serves the whole market. A well known result from standard microeconomic theory is that the marginal revenue of the firm can be expressed as follows:

$$MR = P\left(1 - \frac{1}{e}\right),\tag{4.1}$$

where MR is marginal revenue, P is product price and e is absolute value of the price elasticity of demand for the product. (The derivation of the expressions used in this section is given in the appendix to this chapter.) It is thus clear, for example, that a monopolist would normally operate on a portion of the demand curve where price elasticity is greater than one and where marginal revenue is positive. For price elasticities less than one the expression on the right-hand side of equation (4.1) is negative.[2] For profit maximization the firm will wish to ensure that marginal cost (MC) and marginal revenue are equal and therefore in equilibrium the following condition will hold:

$$MC = MR = P\left(1 - \frac{1}{e}\right).\tag{4.2}$$

With some rearrangement of terms we have, in equilibrium for the monopoly firm:

$$\frac{P - MC}{P} = \frac{1}{e}.\tag{4.3}$$

Expression (4.3) is usually termed the Lerner index of monopoly power (Lerner, 1934). The mark-up of price over marginal cost as a proportion of price is inversely related to the price elasticity of demand. The higher the elasticity, indicating that consumers can fairly readily switch to a substitute product, the smaller the monopoly power and the smaller the price–marginal cost difference. In the limit with demand elasticity equal to infinity the index is equal to zero; that is, the 'monopoly' price will equal the competitive price. At the other extreme, with demand elasticity equal to one or less, the index is not applicable or, in Landes and Posner's phrase, 'comes apart' (Landes and Posner, 1981, p. 942). The explanation for this can be seen by referring back to equation (4.1). The firm would not operate normally where demand was inelastic because this would generate negative marginal revenue and, assuming marginal cost was positive, could not be the short-run profit-maximizing position. If the firm inadvertently found itself operating where demand elasticity was less than one it would pay it to reduce output and raise price. For example, if demand elasticity was equal to 0.5, a 1 per cent increase in price would only reduce sales by one-half of 1 per cent. Revenue would therefore increase, but total costs would be reduced because less output was being produced. As a result profits would increase.[3]

The next point is best illustrated with a simple diagram. In Figure 4.1 all of the concepts have already been introduced in Chapter 1. The demand (*AR*) and marginal revenue (*MR*) for the monopoly firm are shown, together with its marginal cost (*MC*). The latter is here shown as increasing with output (rather than as horizontal, as drawn in Chapter 1), for reasons that will become clear shortly. The monopoly price and output are shown as P_M and Q_M, respectively. At the profit-maximizing output the price–marginal cost difference is $P_M - MC_M$ and is reflected in the Lerner index. It is clear from the figure that where marginal costs are rising this margin and hence the Lerner index give an upper estimate of the extent to which monopoly price exceeds the competitive price. If price were determined competitively output would increase to Q_C and price would fall to P_C. In the case shown, therefore, the difference between monopoly price and competitive price, $P_M - P_C$, is less than the monopoly mark-up over marginal cost, $P_M - MC_M$. Where marginal cost is constant over the relevant output range (the case used in Chapter 1) then the Lerner index gives a precise estimate of the extent to which monopoly price exceeds the competitive price.

Figure 4.1 can also be used to show the relationship between the Lerner index and the measure of 'deadweight' welfare loss also introduced in Chapter 1. The relationship will be used extensively in our subsequent discussion of the market power of dominant firms. For the case of linear demand and marginal cost curves it is easy to show that the deadweight loss of monopoly pricing and output restriction (*DW*) is related to the Lerner index (*L*) as follows:

$$DW = \frac{L(P_M Q_M)K}{2},\tag{4.4}$$

where P_M and Q_M are monopoly price and output, respectively, and where K is a constant which reflects the slope of the marginal cost curve and hence the extent to which a monopolist reduces output below the competitive level (Schmalensee, 1982a, p. 1791). In the limiting case where marginal costs are constant, K equals 1.

A number of important points emerge from equation (4.4). Whereas L is a dimensionless number, *DW* gives in money terms the amount of the welfare loss created by the firm's monopoly pricing. With limited resources available

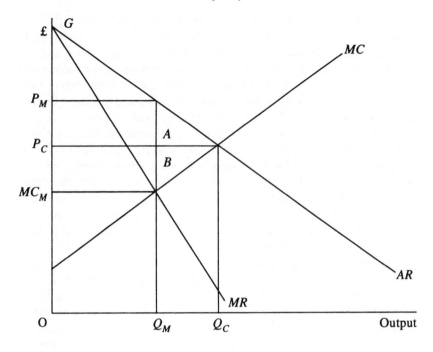

Figure 4.1   Monopoly price and welfare loss

for prosecuting antitrust cases, calculations based on equation (4.4) can determine which cases of dominance are generating the greatest losses and merit the most urgent consideration. Thus it is clear from (4.4) that two firms with equal Lerner indices but vastly different sales revenues $(P_M Q_M)$ will cause substantially different losses. Given the difficulties often encountered in attempting to define the relevant market in order to decide whether antitrust intervention should take place, it would clearly be a great advantage to be able to use a firm's sales revenue data. Together with information on the firm's costs, this would be sufficient to determine the size of the losses imposed on society.

We must recognize, however, that despite the apparent simplicity of the Lerner index its dependence on knowledge of marginal cost or the price elasticity of demand make it difficult to measure empirically. Marginal cost can rarely be known with any precision and, although estimates of demand elasticity can be made, they are not readily available and in the context of an antitrust case are likely to be seriously disputed by the firms involved. For these reasons the significance of the index is likely to remain conceptual rather than directly practical. Nevertheless its importance for clarifying antitrust analysis should not be underestimated, a point which is reinforced when we turn to the more complex case of a dominant firm in competition with a fringe of much smaller rivals. Since it is rare in practice for a firm to have a market completely to itself for any length of time,[4] the case that we are about to consider may be regarded as having broader applicability than the single-firm case. It can also be used, however, to bring out the significance of other factors that have a bearing on the dominant firm's ability to exploit its position.

A useful starting-point is the dominant firm price leadership model, which is represented in Figure 4.2. It is assumed that an established firm has a large part of the market,[5] but that there is also a great number of small suppliers selling homogeneous products. The dominant firm has lower costs than its smaller rivals. Thus, in the figure, market demand is shown as *MD*. The supply curve of the competitive fringe, that is the total supply from all fringe firms at various prices, is shown by the line S_F. At a price as high as P_2 all of the market would be served by the fringe, but at a price P_0 and below, no supplies are forthcoming from the fringe. Individual firms in the fringe act as price takers; that is, they recognize their individual supply is small enough to have no effect on price, which they take as given. The dominant firm is assumed to know how much the fringe will supply at different prices and to adjust its own behaviour accordingly. In particular this means that it treats the residual demand curve D_D as relevant for its own optimizing decision. The curve D_D is simply the market demand curve minus the supplies put on the market by the competitive fringe. It is thus only defined between prices P_0 and P_2. Marginal revenue associated with this residual demand curve is MR_D. If the dominant firm's marginal costs are MC_D then the profit-maximizing price and output for the firm are P_1 and Q_D, respectively. At a price P_1, the competitive fringe supply a total amount $Q_D Q_E$ (= OQ_F). A total amount Q_E is thus supplied at a price P_1.

A number of important points emerge from this model. First, as we would expect, the presence of a competitive fringe leads to a lower price and a greater quantity supplied than if the market is served by a single producer. In that case the monopolist would optimize by equating marginal cost to the curve marginal to the market demand curve (not shown in Figure 4.2 in order to keep it as clear as possible) and this would yield a price higher than P_1. Secondly, the slope of the fringe supply curve (and its related elasticity, to which we refer below) will govern the extent to which the smaller suppliers can capture part of the market. A more steeply sloped curve in Figure 4.2 would have meant that their combined share of the market was smaller. Thirdly, although the position shown in the figure is quite determinate, it should be recognized that it is essentially short-run. If the price set by the dominant firm allows fringe firms to earn positive profits they may be expected to expand their output capacity and supplies in the long run when they may be joined by other new entrants. In this case the fringe supply curve S_F may be expected to swivel to the right. As a result, the dominant firm's residual demand curve would shift downwards and price would be

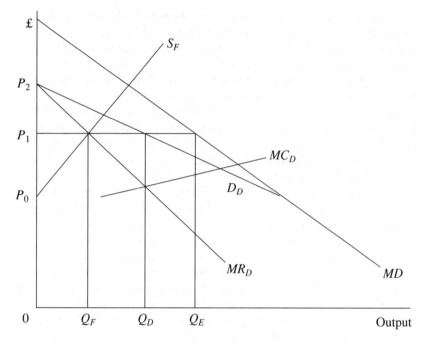

Figure 4.2   The dominant firm and the competitive fringe

reduced. Its market share and profits would also fall. In the absence of strategies designed to curb the inroads made into its market share by the fringe competition, the dominant firm would experience a continued erosion of its position. The analysis of this model underpins the declining share of the dominant firm hypothesis discussed at the end of Chapter 2 and much of the discussion in subsequent chapters in this part of the volume is concerned precisely with the type of behaviour that a dominant firm may engage in to forestall any such reductions in its market share.

For the present, however, we can focus more precisely on those aspects of market dominance which the price leadership model has highlighted: the market share of the dominant firm, the elasticity of supply of the competitive fringe and (less obviously) the price elasticity of market, as opposed to firm, demand. It is possible to show that each of these has an influence on the market power of a dominant firm. No one element alone is a satisfactory indicator. Given that in many actual antitrust cases data on market share are usually the most readily available and emphasized, this conclusion is especially important. Following Landes and Posner (1981) we can first explain the relationship between the Lerner index and these variables in the context of the dominant firm–competitive fringe model, and then discuss the implications and short-comings.

The elasticity of demand for the dominant firm is given by the following expression:

$$e_i^d = e_M^d / S_i + e_f^s(1 - S_i)/ S_i, \qquad (4.5)$$

where e_i^d is the price elasticity of demand for the dominant firm, e_M^d is the market demand elasticity, S_i is the market share of the dominant firm, and e_f^s is the elasticity of supply of the competitive fringe.[6] Also from equation (4.3) above it is evident that the Lerner index of monopoly power for the dominant firm in this case is:

$$L_i = 1/e_i^d = S_i / \left[e_M^d + e_f^s(1 - S_i) \right]. \qquad (4.6)$$

There are a number of important implications arising from these equations. First, as is clear from the first term in equation (4.5) the greater the market demand elasticity, the higher will be the dominant firm's demand elasticity, and the smaller the scope for the firm to raise price above marginal cost. This is merely a reflection of the fact that relatively close substitutes for the dominant firm's products will weaken its market power. Secondly, that power is also diminished by the ease with which existing fringe firms or new entrants can increase supplies to the market: the second term on the right-hand side of equation (4.5) shows this direct relationship between the elasticity of fringe supply and the dominant firm's elasticity of demand. Thirdly, equations (4.5) and (4.6) show that the greater the dominant firm's market share, the smaller will be its elasticity of demand and hence the greater will be its market power. The process can be seen as having two parts (Landes and Posner, 1981, pp. 946–7). Consider first a firm with a very large market share. A given reduction in output will result in a proportionately larger increase in price than if the firm had a smaller market share. To bring out this point, suppose that the elasticity of fringe supply is zero, so that from equation (4.5) it is clear in this extreme case that the dominant firm's demand elasticity is equal to the market elasticity divided by its market share. Assume also that the market elasticity of demand is one. Now compare the two cases of a firm with a market share of 90 per cent, with one with a share of 45 per cent. In the former case a 1 per cent increase in price will be sustained by a reduction in output of just over 1 per cent (because the firm's elasticity is 1.1). In the latter case, however, a 1 per cent increase in price will require a reduction of output of more than 2 per cent (the firm's elasticity is then 2.2). All else equal, therefore, a larger market share will confer more market power.

The second part of the significance of dominant firm market share for its market power relates to the supply elasticity of the competitive fringe. For a given supply elasticity, the increase in output from the fringe will be smaller, the greater the market share of the dominant firm. Thus a price increase contemplated by the dominant firm will require a smaller reduction in its output.

In general, therefore, the emphasis that antitrust authorities have frequently placed on market share is well founded. However, what the dominant firm–fringe supply model brings out, especially in its more formal representation in equations (4.5) and (4.6), is that the use of market share data alone is insufficient and under many circumstances may give a very misleading impression of both market power and the welfare loss involved. The most obvious case, and indeed one of which, we shall see, antitrust authorities have been most aware, is where a firm has an apparently very high market share but where the market demand elasticity is high, which means that the firm's demand elasticity is also high. In this case, as is evident from equation (4.6), the firm's market power may be negligible. The fact that market demand elasticity is high means that there are close substitutes in consumption for the dominant firm's product. The high share is really the result of defining the market too narrowly. If the products which are close substitutes are included in the denominator of the market share calculation a better estimate is obtained, together with a truer reflection of the firm's market power. In practice antitrust authorities often attempt such adjustments, assuming they can settle the thorny subject of precisely which products are close enough substitutes.

Equally important, but perhaps less immediately apparent, is the influence of products which are close substitutes in production, but not in consumption. The productive capacity of industry Y may be readily applied to the output of industry X. The market power of a dominant firm in industry X may then be more apparent than real if a small increase in price causes a sizeable switch in the use of industry Y's capacity to produce the same output as that of industry X. Another way of looking at this in relation to equations (4.5) and (4.6) is that one influence on the elasticity of supply from the fringe will be production from entrants to the market for X who are already established in 'neighbouring' markets. The other influence, of course, is the existing ability of fringe firms to increase their own outputs in response to an increase in price. The greater these influences are in a market the smaller will be the market power of a dominant firm, even though its apparent market share is considerable. Although estimates of fringe supply elasticity are unlikely to be available, some adjustment may be possible in an antitrust case by including in the measure of market size the output capacity that could readily be switched into producing for the market in question, as well as any surplus capacity already available to fringe operators.

In order to emphasize the point that market share information alone may be a misleading guide to the extent of market power and genuine dominance, our examples have all been in terms of overestimation. It should be apparent, however, from equations (4.5) and (4.6) that the opposite case may also occur. A relatively low market share but also a relatively low market demand elasticity (for a given level of fringe supply elasticity) can yield a high degree of market power, and so on. True market dominance with important economic effects is a complex issue which cannot easily be determined by a single indicator like market share. The dominant firm model helps to clarify more precisely the issues involved. However, we need to be aware of some important limitations of the model. Most obviously it deals with those cases where the market is overwhelmingly dominated by a very large firm with any rivals treating the price set as 'given'. There is no interdependence of decision making in the usual oligopolistic sense. If other firms in the market also have market power the effect is likely to raise prices and the Lerner index of the dominant firm. The model has very little to say either about entry deterrence (which we noted when discussing Figure 4.2) or predatory behaviour by the dominant firm, even though both subjects have been much debated (see below, Chapters 5 and 6). A particularly important limitation derives from the assumption of homogeneous products. It is assumed the products of the fringe are perfect substitutes for those of the dominant firm. In practice, of course, products may be close but not perfect substitutes. To the extent that this is the case, the model will tend to understate real market power because the constraints placed on the dominant firm's pricing behaviour will be less acute. Furthermore, the homogeneity assumption rules out non-price competition, but in many markets for final consumer goods product differentiation is the main channel of competitive behaviour. An important effect of product differentiation may be to make the precise definition of the 'market' and thence market share extremely difficult. The precise location of 'the gap in the chain of substitutes' may not be at all clear and make market share an unreliable guide to market power.

For these and other reasons, Schmalensee (1982a), for example, argues that other information can be equally important in the assessment of market dominance. The Lerner index and the market share to which it is related are essentially aspects of market structure. Schmalensee suggests that certain patterns of market conduct, especially price discrimination and predatory behaviour, which are only possible when some degree of market power exists, should also be analysed. More directly relevant in the present context is his view that under certain circumstances profitability of dominant firms, an aspect of their market performance, should also be used as an indication of market power.

This brings us to the second index, of 'excess profits', developed originally by Bain (1956). We may note first that in the simple monopoly case considered above the excess profit earned by the single-product, profit-maximizing firm is directly proportional to the deadweight loss that the firm imposes on society. In the case where demand is linear and costs are constant the loss is equal to half the excess profit. In the simplest case, therefore, 'profitability data are *exactly* as informative about [deadweight loss] as is information about price cost margins or firms' demand elasticities' (Schmalensee, 1982a, p. 1805, italics in the original).[7] Since data on profitability are usually more readily available than those on demand elasticity, there may be a greater inclination to use it to infer market power.

Bain's original line of argument was that persistent excess profit was likely to be evidence of market power and he therefore argued in favour of observing profits or profit rates over time. Using his notation (Bain, 1968), excess profits may be identified as follows:

$$\pi = PQ - C(Q) - D - iV, \qquad (4.7)$$

where π is economic profits, P is price, Q is output, $C(Q)$ are current costs attributable to output, D is depreciation of capital due to current output, V is owner's equity in the company and i is the competitive rate of interest (net of risk) so that iV represents the opportunity cost of the owner's capital. If π is zero then the company is earning no excess profits. A positive value of π indicates that the firm is earning excess profits. If competition is working normally investment from new entry will be attracted and the excess profits competed away. However, if they persist, this is likely to be due to market power, exercised in the presence of some barrier to entry.

Although on the face of it the measure appears attractive, and indeed has been widely used in a large number of empirical studies,[8] there are a number of serious difficulties in using it for the analysis of market power. Some of these are readily apparent from the definition given in (4.7). Quite apart from the well known problems with measuring depreciation accurately, the last term in expression (4.7), which distinguishes economic from accounting profits, may in practice be very difficult to determine. In particular measuring i, the firm's opportunity cost of capital or 'normal' rate of return is difficult, and yet its value may be crucial in establishing whether excess profits have been earned. The measure of i required should be net of risk because industries with similar structures but facing different risks may be expected to earn different rates of profit. Those of relatively high risk will contain an amount to compensate share-holders for this added burden. Yet there is no agreed upon method for taking account of differing risks.

Short-run fluctuations in demand (reflected in the term PQ) or current costs ($C(Q)$) may cause a firm to make exceptionally high (or low) profits yet have nothing to do with market power. If the change in demand turns out to be permanent, but if the market is working smoothly, more resources will flow in and the profits will gradually subside. Clearly the amount of time taken for this process of competition to be effective may vary considerably between markets but have more to do with technological requirements than the continued exercise of market power.

A more practical problem may arise over firms' treatment of expenditure on research and development, and advertising. Accounting conventions may mean that all such expenditures are treated as current expenses to be placed against current revenues. Yet a large proportion of the expenditures may directly create assets which continue to produce a stream of revenue into the future. In this case they should be capitalized and go to make up part of the asset base of the firm. An antitrust authority trying to screen a firm for possible abuses of market power will assess not its absolute level of profits (as in (4.7)) but the profits expressed as a rate of return on capital. Using the notation of (4.7) this would be π/V. However, if, say, advertising has been treated simply as a current cost, it will not be reflected in V and the profits to assets ratio will be overstated. Thus, unless great care is taken, a false inference may be drawn about market power.

Even if firms are using the same rules for allocating costs and an acceptable approximation for the opportunity cost of capital has been found, isolating market power by means of profit figures is still hazardous. For example, two firms apparently operating in similarly structured markets, having the same market share and with the same costs, may register quite different profit levels because of the different demand characteristics. The point is most easily illustrated by means of a diagram. Suppose there are two firms, each with the entire market in which they operate. They have the same costs (represented by *ATC* and *MC* in Figure 4.3). We also assume, for purposes of illustration, that their marginal revenue curves cut marginal cost at the same point, C. Hence, for both, the profit-maximizing output is Q_M. Prices, however, differ because of the position of the demand curves: demand D_1, giving a price of P_1, and demand D_2 a price P_2. As a result excess profits in the first market, P_1BCE are lower than in the second, P_2ACE. Thus the same level of investment yields quite different levels of excess profits. In practice, where the magnitudes would all be treated as estimates, an antitrust authority might regard case 2 as more significant than case 1, since the excess profit is greater. Given our previous discussion of the Lerner index this conclusion would be correct, *ceteris paribus*, because the greater profit margin would be a reflection of the smaller elasticity in case 2 and the greater degree of market power.[9]

A problem of a different kind may arise where a firm's apparent excess profits are small even though other indicators suggest that market power is substantial.

We referred in Chapter 1 to X-inefficiency. Firms protected from competition by some means may allow their costs to rise simply because the management takes things easy and this slackness filters through to the workshop floor. Consequently recorded profits may be very low. The term $C(Q)$ in equation (4.7) effectively absorbs what would otherwise have shown up as excess profit. In this case the absence of excess profit does not mean the absence of market power.

A different case but with a similar result is that where firms attempt to obtain or maintain a position of market power and expend resources in the process. At the extreme such a competition for market power may dissipate resources amounting to the full extent of excess profits in socially wasteful ways. Yet the recorded profits of the firms will not be high. The scramble for market power has nevertheless led to resource misallocation.

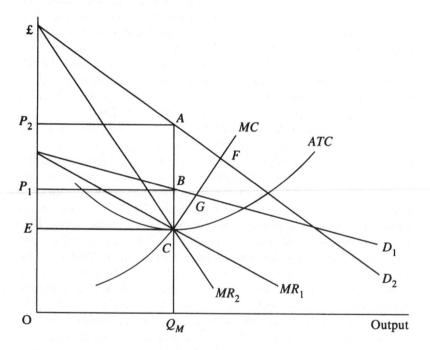

Figure 4.3   Excess profits and market power

The main point to come out of this brief discussion of profitability as an index of market power is that in any antitrust case the data have to be treated with great care if the correct inference is to be made. The use of profitability to test a number of hypotheses about market structure and market performance has recently been heavily criticized, largely on the grounds that insufficient attention has been paid to the kinds of difficulty mentioned above. However these criticisms have generally been applied to large cross-section studies involving very many industries, often several hundred. The context of an antitrust action is quite different. In that case, the antitrust authority will have some preliminary reason for investigating a particular market. There may have been complaints from customers or input suppliers. It is then quite feasible for the staff of the authority to estimate rates of return for a dominant firm, taking into account, for example, problems over the treatment of depreciation as well as advertising and R&D expenditures. While the risk-adjusted competitive return may not be known, it may be approximated. Misleading short-term fluctuations in profit can be avoided by observing returns for much longer periods. At a preliminary screening stage, therefore, carefully prepared profitability figures may be at least as helpful to an antitrust authority as market share information. Enterprises that have market shares of, say, more than 80 per cent and which have systematically made rates of return on capital several times higher than roughly comparable enterprises in similar markets may have much to explain to an antitrust authority. Such rates clearly allow for very wide margins of error or adjustment and may still be regarded as excessive. As we have seen, however, the corollary that very modest profits may signify the lack of market power does not hold.

III   Market dominance in practice

How far can the concepts used in economic analysis and discussed in the previous section be directly applied to antitrust cases involving market dominance? In this section we attempt to answer this question in two stages: first, how have antitrust authorities treated the difficult question of market definition; and secondly, having defined the market to their satisfaction, how then has the concept of market dominance itself been defined?

Market definition

In the previous section equation (4.5) indicated that a dominant firm's demand elasticity (and thence its market power) depended on the market elasticity of demand, the firm's market share and the elasticity of supply of the competitive fringe. In effect, although antitrust authorities have not generally attempted to measure the two elasticities involved, they have been very much concerned with the concepts that underlie them. Thus the correct definition of the relevant market continues to be a major preoccupation. On the demand side goods or services should be treated as being in the same market if they are close substitutes so that a small increase from the competitive price by one of them would lead to a substantial loss of sales as consumers turned to the substitutes. The reference to competitive price is significant. We have seen in Section II that a profit-maximizing monopolist will operate on an elastic portion of the demand curve. The fact that at the monopoly price demand elasticity is greater than one implies that some potential customers are switching to substitute products precisely because the price is high. In this context, therefore, evidence of substitution signifies the exercise of market power, not its absence.[10]

It is clear from equation (4.5) that the greater the range of products included as substitutes the smaller will be the market share of the dominant firm and, holding market demand elasticity and fringe supply elasticity constant, the larger will be its own demand elasticity and therefore the smaller its market power. Defendants in antitrust actions may therefore argue strongly in favour of more products being included in the correct identification of the market, rather than less. Similarly the wider the geographic area included as 'the relevant market' the lower the likely share of the dominant firm. The point has special significance in EU cases where infringements of Article 82 can only occur in a 'substantial' part of the Community, involving the whole market, that of a number of members or an important single member.

Thus on the demand side the antitrust authority has the formidable task of defining the relevant market in terms both of appropriate products and of geographic area. However, that should not be the end of this stage of the analysis. The second term on the right-hand side of equation (4.5) depends on the elasticity of supply of fringe firms. If that is high it will again tend to increase the firm's own price elasticity and reduce its market power. If we broaden our consideration of supply elasticities this may further affect the market power of the dominant firm. Where technology and entry conditions are such as to allow firms hitherto supplying other markets to switch production readily in response to small price increases to supply the market in question, then again the effective market power of the dominant firm will be curtailed.

The question of market definition arises in US antitrust actions under Section 2 of the Sherman Act and under Section 7 of the amended Clayton Act involving mergers. Similarly in the EU, cases involving Article 82 need to establish the relevant market and this has also applied to the procedure for merger control since it became operational late in 1990. In the UK the same point applies to mergers under the Fair Trading Act and abuse of dominance cases in chapter 2 enquiries.

The classic case involving the market definition issue in US antitrust law is probably the cellophane case.[11] The case was brought under Section 2 of the Sherman Act and concerned Du Pont's supply of cellophane to the US market. It was clear that Du Pont produced about three-quarters of all cellophane sold in the USA. If the relevant market consisted only of cellophane then the Supreme Court would have accepted that Du Pont had a monopoly. The defence argued, however, that cellophane was only one of a number of products making up the 'flexible packaging materials' market which included, among other things, wax paper, greaseproof paper, foil and Pliofilm. This argument was broadly accepted by a (narrow) majority of the Court. They acknowledged that every manufacturer is the sole producer of its own products but the important point is control of the relevant market and this depends on the availability of alternatives for buyers, specifically 'whether there is a cross-elasticity of demand between cellophane and other wrappings'. In assessing, albeit informally, the cross-elasticity the Court had regard to the responsiveness of demand for cellophane to changes in the price of other products and in this respect they accepted the view of the lower court which had referred to large shifts in business between Du Pont and its competitors. Thus, despite Du Pont's large share in production of a particular product, the Court accepted that its effective market share was much lower because of the high cross-elasticity of demand between cellophane and other materials. The case is interesting because of the explicit use of the concept of cross-elasticity in conjunction with market control. Nevertheless, it has been criticized for the reason already mentioned above. Customers will tend to switch to substitute products if they are confronted by monopoly or near-monopoly prices. The key issue is whether customers treat the products as close substitutes at competitive prices, a question which the Court did not address.

Another important US case where market definition was crucial involved the merger between the Brown Shoe Co and the G.R. Kinney Co.[12] The case has a number of interesting features, not least because it was the first Supreme Court decision under the amended Clayton Act; we refer to it again in Chapter 9. For present purposes, however, we will focus on the Court's treatment of market definition. Both firms involved were manufacturers and retailers of shoes. The merger therefore had both horizontal and vertical aspects. Viewed in national terms, the effect of the merger on shoe manufacturers was negligible: Brown made 4 per cent of US output and Kinney about 0.5 per cent. It was accepted, therefore, that the merger did not pose a threat to competition in the manufacturing market. The case centred on the competitive effects in retailing. Here Brown either owned or controlled through franchising arrangements about 1230 stores, while Kinney, primarily a retailer, owned over 400 stores, but at the time in the USA there were approximately 70 000 shoe outlets, of which 22 000 were specialist shoe stores. The determination of the relevant market by the Supreme Court involved both a geographic and a product element. Geographically the Court determined that the market consisted of all cities with populations of 10 000 or more and their immediate surrounding area. However, it was the product definition which caused most controversy. It again referred explicitly to the cross-elasticity of demand – 'The outer boundaries of a product market are determined by the reasonable interchangeability of use or the cross-elasticity of demand between the product itself and substitutes for it' – but then the Court confused matters by adding that 'within this broad market, well-defined sub-markets may exist which, in themselves, constitute product markets for antitrust purposes ... The boundaries of such a sub-market may be determined by examining such practical indicia as industry or public recognition of the sub-market as a separate entity, the product's peculiar characteristics and uses, unique production facilities, distinct customers, distinct prices, sensitivity to price changes and specialised vendors'. The Court then distinguished three 'sub-markets' in the case, men's, women's and children's shoes. The combined sales of the two firms exceeded 20 per cent of the local market in 32 cities for women's shoes and in 31 cities for children's shoes. According to the Court, this was sufficient to find a substantial lessening of competition.

There are a number of comments that can be made about the Court's interpretation of the market in this case. First, although it refers to the relevance of the cross-elasticity of demand (as in the cellophane case) it does not give any indication of how large the cross-elasticity should be for antitrust purposes. Since in the limit all consumer goods are more or less substitutable some cutoff point is necessary, otherwise the Court might just as well confine itself to discussing 'close substitutes', especially since no numerical estimates of cross-elasticities were given in the proceedings. Secondly, and more important, the idea of a 'sub-market' is unknown in economics and seems mainly to obscure further what is already a difficult area.[13] In the *Brown Shoe* case the Court seemed mainly concerned to use the notion in order to distinguish the three separate lines of business, since clearly women's, men's and children's shoes are not close substitutes in demand. However, had the Court been prepared to utilize the idea of elasticity of supply, the confusion could have been avoided. It is an engineering question, which the Court does not appear to have explored, as to the extent to which production capacity for making, say, men's shoes could be modified to make women's or children's shoes, following small changes in relative prices. High elasticity of supply would suggest that all shoes should be treated as being in a common market, because small increases in the price of one product line would readily lead to a significant increase in production of that line from capacity which had previously been producing the related line. In this way the focus on market power, the ability to control prices, is retained and not obscured by the use of vague concepts such as 'sub-markets'.

Similar issues concerning market definition have occurred in a number of EU cases. The two best examples are probably *United Brands* and *Hugin*.[14] In *United Brands*, brought under Article 82, the Court had to decide whether bananas constituted a separate and distinct market. Our previous discussion might suggest that the conclusion would be that bananas were only part of a much wider market for fresh fruit, in which case the likelihood of the defendant having a dominant position would be much reduced. In the event the Court took a quite different view and argued that for the banana to form a separate market it must 'be singled out by such special features distinguishing it from other fruits that it is only to a limited extent interchangeable with them and is only exposed to their competition in a way that is hardly perceptible'. Since it found that 'a very large number of consumers having constant need for bananas are not noticeably or even appreciably enticed away from the consumption of this product by the arrival of fresh fruit on the market', it was clear that bananas did constitute a distinct market. The groups recognized as having a constant demand for bananas were the very young and the very old but although their numbers may be great the Court did not quantify their importance in the market or consider the consumption behaviour of other groups.

With almost any product some individual or groups of consumers will have much stronger preferences for it than others. Consequently some will only switch to a substitute at very high prices while others will cease consumption at much lower prices. Such information is, of course, conveyed in the elementary notion of a downward-sloping demand curve and in the expression for the market elasticity of demand in equation (4.5). The central issue is not whether some groups of consumers have strong preferences for the product in question (that should go without saying) but whether, for small departures from the competitive price, significant inter-product substitution as a whole would take place. If the answer to the question is positive then those substitute products really form part of the market in question. In the present case that would have meant the inclusion of other fresh fruit. Reference to the concepts included in equation (4.5) (particularly e^d_M in the present context) helps to focus sharply on a market definition which is of use for the analysis of market power, a focus which the Court appears to have lost in the *United Brands* case.

When discussing the cellophane case we mentioned that the US Supreme Court acknowledged that every manufacturer is the sole producer of its products but that the crucial point was control of the relevant market and this depended on the availability of alternatives for consumers. Precisely this issue arose in the *Hugin* case. Hugin was the fourth largest seller of cash registers in the UK market, where its share of approximately 13 per cent was a long way behind that of the market leader, National Cash Register, which had 40 per cent. Liptons specialized in servicing and repairing Hugin machines and had also been a main selling agent. Hugin offered Liptons a new distributorship agreement which Liptons turned down on the ground that the profit margins were too low. Thereafter Hugin refused to supply Liptons with cash registers or parts at wholesale and it was impossible for Liptons to obtain them elsewhere because of Hugin's selective distribution system.

The question initially for the Commission and then for the Court was whether Hugin's refusal to supply amounted to an abuse of a dominant position. On the face of it dominance was not involved because of the modesty of Hugin's market share and the presence of other larger competitors. The Court, however, interpreted the 'market' in this case as consisting of Hugin spare parts. By its action Hugin deprived users of freedom to use the repairer of their choice and excluded competition in the form of Liptons which had been a substitute competitor in the market for servicing and repairs. The market for Hugin spare parts was distinct because parts for their machines were not interchangeable with parts for other makes. As Fox makes clear, under US law 'a company's own brand of product is almost never a market' (Fox, 1984, p. 402). Given that there was an active market in repairs to cash register machines, it was open to Liptons to switch over to repairs for competing machines. If Hugin decided to carry out most of its own repairs it must have believed that it could do the job at least as well as Liptons, otherwise its action would be putting it at a competitive disadvantage. Neither the structure of the repair market nor the market for machines was changed by Hugin's action and it gained no increase in market leverage as a result. From whatever level the judgement of the Court in the case is viewed, therefore, it appears that, although it may have believed it was protecting customers, in fact it was protecting a competitor, Liptons, when it concluded that an abuse had occurred. The Court allowed its over-narrow interpretation of the concept of substitutes in demand to blind it to the ultimate objective in Article 82 cases of determining whether an abuse of dominant position has occurred. The irony of this case is that the Court determined that since inter-community trade was not affected, it was not obliged to proceed. However, it chose to define the market and consider Hugin's place in it without determining whether an abuse had occurred. In the circumstances it might have been better had it not gone on to give such an idiosyncratic definition of the market.

The main advantage of the concepts introduced in Section II above thus lies in forcing the analyst to keep a clear focus on what is the ultimate objective of the whole exercise, namely market dominance and the exercise of market power. It is not suggested that the various quantities in, say, equation (4.5), should be estimated in an antitrust case, but rather that they should form the frame of reference.

The interpretation of market dominance

Once an antitrust agency has delineated the relevant market for the case in hand it is a reasonably simple matter to compute the market shares of the leading firm or firms. The question we address in this section is how such information has been used and supplemented to infer the presence of market power. By now we should be more than aware of the point that market share alone may be a poor guide.

A classic statement of this point was made in the US *Alcoa* case by Judge Learned Hand. Having considered three possible definitions of the market, the judge finally settled on the one which gave the leading firm the greatest market share. This interpretation was crucial to the outcome of the case because in the judge's view a share of 90 per cent 'is enough to constitute a monopoly; it is doubtful whether 60 or 64 per cent would be enough; and certainly 33 per cent is not'.[15] Although he appeared at this stage to come very close to the position that a structural monopoly in itself was an infringement of Section 2 of the Sherman Act, he went on to consider whether Alcoa's conduct showed that intent to monopolize which the Act required. We refer below to his discussion of Alcoa's investment behaviour when discussing the strategic behaviour of dominant firms (see Chapter 6). The case clearly placed market share at the centre of an antitrust action with the presumption that the larger the share the greater the likelihood of market power. Market conduct which may be acceptable from a firm with a more modest share may be regarded as the means of maintaining dominance from a firm with a large share, and therefore amount to an infringement of the law. In the subsequent decade several important US cases took essentially the same position. Thus in the second American Tobacco case the Supreme Court again came close to making a dominant position illegal per se, even though this was not the intention of the Sherman Act; in a case against a cinema chain which had not used abusive conduct the Court nevertheless concluded that 'monopoly power, whether lawfully or unlawfully acquired, may itself constitute an evil and stand condemned under Section 2 even though it remains unexercised';[16] the United Shoe Machinery Co., which had about 85 per cent of the US market, had maintained the position over a long period by using a variety of practices, none of which individually constituted an abuse but which, taken together, were found to amount to an infringement.

At this period in US antitrust law (approximately the decade following the Second World War) any firm with a very large market share therefore appeared vulnerable to a Section 2 action even though in most circumstances its conduct amounted to no more than shrewd business practice. More recently there has been renewed interest in cases brought against some of the largest US companies. Although in one case a dramatic structural remedy was agreed, in two other long-running and important cases the prosecution was dropped, essentially on the ground that there was no substantial case to answer. The most controversial and widely reported case involved Microsoft.[17] We refer to these cases again in Chapter 6.

The European Commission and Court have had similar difficulties with the notion of dominance to their American counterparts. An infringement of Article 82 requires the authorities first to establish a dominant position within the relevant market and then to determine whether an abuse of that position has occurred. In two leading cases the Court has defined dominance with an emphasis on the ability of the offending firm to act independently of others. Thus in the Hoffman–La Roche case it considered that dominance relates to a position of economic strength enjoyed by an undertaking which enables it to prevent effective competition being maintained on the relevant market by affording it the power to behave to an appreciable extent independently of its competitors, its customers and ultimately of the consumers. Such a position does not preclude some competition which it does where there is a monopoly or quasi-monopoly but enables the undertaking which profits by it, if not to determine, at least to have an appreciable influence on the conditions under which that competition will develop, and in any case to act largely in disregard of it so long as such conduct does not operate to its detriment.[18]

It added that a number of facts may contribute to the existence of a dominant position and in particular a very large market share would be regarded as highly important.

In the *Hoffman* case, which involved the supply of vitamins, the company's share within the EU ranged from 47 per cent to 95 per cent, depending on which product was considered. With the exception of the lowest, there was a strong presumption of dominance as far as the Court was concerned on the basis of the market shares alone. Even where the share was 47 per cent, since the closest rival was much smaller and not as technically advanced, dominance could be established. Similarly, in the *United Brands* case, where the leader had a share of 40–45 per cent, although this alone did not constitute dominance, the modest size of its closest rivals and their lack of success in making any inroads into the leader's market share were sufficient.

After a review of Article 82 cases one recent observer concluded that 'once [market share] can be shown to reach 45 per cent it becomes almost impossible to claim that an undertaking lacks [market] power unless there is another undertaking in the same market with a share of equivalent size. Once a market share exceeds 65 per cent, the presumption becomes almost impossible to displace, especially if the undertakings in competition are all of relatively minor significance' (Goyder, 1998, p. 324).

The definition of the market is thus again crucial, but in EU cases it appears, at least to some commentators, to have taken on a rather different significance. It has been argued, notably by Fairburn *et al.* (1986), that, rather than establishing dominance independently and as a first step prior to an examination of evidence of abuse, the EU authorities have tended to determine that an abuse has occurred and then define the relevant market in such a way that dominance is unquestionable: 'By appropriate expansion or contraction of the boundaries of geography or product, or by appropriate invocation or disregard of entry possibilities, the market grows or shrinks in such a way that the complained of firm can be identified as a dominant producer within it' (p. 41). The authors support their conclusion from a variety of cases, some involving very large firms and large markets and others quite modest firms and relatively small markets. For example, in *Hoffman–La Roche* the main practice complained of was 'fidelity rebates' based on aggregate purchases of the whole range of vitamins produced by the company. The company's advantage over competitors in this case rested on the breadth of their products. An entrant would have to produce the whole range and then offer similar terms if it was to compete successfully. However, the 'market' could not sensibly be defined to include all vitamins because they are not substitutable by either consumers or producers. The Court relied on the company's share of particular vitamins to find against a strategy which applied to the whole range. The decision thus ultimately rests on fudging the market concept.

At the other end of the scale, Hugin's refusal to deal was condemned on the highly dubious definition of the market in terms of 'repairs of Hugin machines', to which we referred above. Similarly it is difficult to avoid the conclusion in *United Brands* that the Court objected particularly to the price discrimination used by the company and then had to 'discover' a market in which it was dominant. Fortunately for the Court, it found that United Brands was dominant in a particular geographic area and was therefore saved the embarrassment of either defining the market simply in terms of the brand of the leading company or in terms of all fruit, when it clearly would not have had a dominant position.

As we said in Chapter 3, Article 82 includes examples of behaviour that can amount to abuse of a dominant position. In the cases so far considered by the Court under this provision, it has come close to interpreting certain practices, such as price discrimination or refusal to sell, as per se illegal, even though economic analysis of these issues is far from clear-cut. In some circumstances both may impair competition and bolster the position of the incumbent, but in others (as we shall see below) the incumbent may be weakened.

In the case of the UK a single firm (scale monopoly) or a group of firms acting as a 'complex monopoly' can be investigated by the OFT as long as the market share involved is 25 per cent or greater. It is not suggested that any share above 25 per cent is 'dominant' or 'monopolistic' but simply that on the basis of preliminary evidence collated by the OFT (such as complaints from customers or suppliers, and observations on price and profit trends) it might be the case that the market conduct of the firm or firms involved is against the public interest (where this is to be interpreted largely in terms of competitive effects). There is no presumption either way that any abuse has occurred. Each case is judged on its merits. Since the legislation governing this procedure refers to the supply of specified goods or services, the question of market definition has effectively been sidestepped. Thus the OFT can investigate whether the market conduct of firms supplying, say, ice cream, instant coffee, soft drinks or beer is against the public interest. In arriving at its final assessment, it can consider whether other products compete actively with those given in the reference and therefore modify the behaviour of the leading firm, but it does not have to establish the relationship in any formal way. On the whole, therefore, the products investigated will tend to be narrower than an economic market properly defined but, as we saw in Section II above, this need not hamper a correct analysis as long as proper consideration is given to the way in which close substitute products may constrain the conduct and hence affect the performance of the companies supplying the specified product. In terms of equation (4.5) above, the dominant firm's market share (S_i) will tend to be overstated but the elasticity of market demand (e^d_M) will tend to be relatively high, implying limited market power. We examine a number of these 'scale monopoly' enquiries in Chapters 5 and 6 below, where it is evident that, although market share plays an important part in the analysis, there is by no means a precise correlation between size of market share and adverse public interest findings.

Following the passage of the 1998 Competition Act, as we saw in the previous chapter, the DGFT can initiate a chapter 2 enquiry into whether or not a particular firm has abused a dominant position. The first cases of this kind will illustrate how much has been learnt from the rather uneven experience of the EU.

IV   Conclusion

The formal analysis of market power, focusing particularly on the Lerner index, established that three factors were of the upmost importance. These were the price elasticity of market demand, the market share of the dominant firm and the elasticity of supply for fringe firms. Each was important and none alone was sufficient to establish significant market power. We argued that the main influence of such an analysis in antitrust cases should be to ensure that the focus was kept steadily on relevant issues rather than on the irrelevant. It did not imply that quantified estimates of elasticities had to be made.

Although these points may appear to be obvious, when we began to examine actual cases it was clear that antitrust authorities often had difficulty in keeping their sights clearly focused on the central issue: the presence and exercise of market power. Market definition itself continues to cause problems, even in the USA, which has had more than a century of experience of its main antitrust law. The European Commission and Court, with much less experience in such matters, have also been led to some strange decisions, including, in one case, a market definition which effectively encompassed the products of a single firm. The British approach to 'scale monopolies' and 'complex monopolies' of allowing the OFT to investigate the supply of a particular product or service avoids the often time-consuming and arcane deliberations about the boundaries of a particular market. The OFT can form its own judgement, for example, about whether other products are close substitutes in demand and whether there are ready alternative sources of supply.

Notes

1. A number of other indices have been discussed in the literature. For reviews, see Miller (1955) and Scherer and Ross (1990, ch. 8).
2. For a firm operating in a perfectly competitive market, price elasticity is infinite and marginal revenue is equal to price.
3. Where demand elasticity is fractionally greater than one, equation (4.3) suggests that the price–cost margin will be very great. The explanation for this can be seen from equation (4.2). If demand elasticity is only fractionally greater than one, at the profit-maximizing output, marginal revenue and marginal cost will both be close to zero. Hence a relatively low price will generate a relatively large price–cost margin.
4. The exceptions are likely to derive from some special grant or privilege, such as a patent or government restriction on entry.
5. In practice, how large a market share has to be before it becomes 'dominant' is the subject of much debate, which we take up in Section III of this chapter.
6. The elasticity of supply is defined as the percentage change in the quantity supplied in response to a percentage change in market price. As firms normally supply more when prices increase, and vice versa, it will be positive.
7. In more complex cases of demand and cost, however, the exact relationship does not hold and the measures have to be treated with care to obtain the correct inference.
8. Usually to test for the positive association between profitability and market concentration, *ceteris paribus*. For a review, see Scherer and Ross (1990, ch. 11).
9. The size of the deadweight loss is also greater in market 2 than in market 1. In market 2 it is shown as the area *ACF*, whereas in market 1 it is *BCG*.
10. This point arose in the US case involving Du Pont, to which we refer again below.
11. *United States* v. *E.I. Du Pont de Nemours and Co*, 351 US, 377 (1956).
12. *Brown Shoe* v. *United States*, 370 US 294 (1962).
13. This point has been underlined by Schmalensee (1987): 'New legislation might be necessary to expunge the vague concept of "sub-markets" from the law. I, for one, am tired of explaining to lawyers that I don't know what a "sub-market" is because the term is not used in economics and has never been defined clearly by judges' (p. 47, fn).
14. *United Brands* v. *Commission* (1978) 1CMLR 429 and *Hugin* v. *Commission* (1979) 3CMLR 345.
15. *United States* v. *Aluminum Co. of America*, 148, F 2d 416 (1945).
16. *United States* v. *Griffith Amusement Co.*, 334 US 100 (1948).
17. The Justice Department action against AT and T ended in a consent decree and the dismemberment of the company. The cases against IBM and the leading breakfast cereal manufacturers (brought by the Federal Trade Commission) were dropped after seven and four years, respectively. The lower court judge in *Microscoft* proposed a division of the company. On appeal this proposed remedy was dropped. The case has so far lasted for eight years.
18. *Hoffman–La Roche* v. *Commission* (1979), 3 CMLR 211. The other case involved United Brands.

Appendix

The derivations of the expressions introduced in Section II of this chapter can be found in Landes and Posner (1981) and Schmalensee (1982a).

1   Marginal revenue

The firm's total revenue (*R*) is a function of output (*Q*)

$$R = R(Q) = pQ, \text{ where } p \text{ is the price of product.}$$

Marginal revenue (*MR*) is then:

$$MR = \frac{d[R(Q)]}{dQ} = p + \frac{Qdp}{dQ} = p\left(1 + \frac{Q}{p}\frac{dp}{dQ}\right).$$

But the price elasticity of demand *e* is defined as

$$e = -\frac{p}{Q}\frac{dQ}{dp}.$$

Substituting this expression in the above equation for *MR* gives:

$$MR = p\left(1 - \frac{1}{e}\right). \tag{4A.1}$$

2   The Lerner index

For profit maximization, marginal cost (*MC*) must equal marginal revenue and so

$$MC = MR = p\left(1 - \frac{1}{e}\right), \tag{4A.2}$$

or

$$\frac{p - MC}{p} = \frac{1}{e}. \tag{4A.3}$$

Expression (4A.3) may also be written as

$$\frac{p}{MC} = \frac{e}{e-1}.$$
(4A.4)

This gives a direct way of estimating the mark-up over marginal cost, given the elasticity of demand.

3   The relationship between the Lerner index and the dead-weight welfare loss (DW)

From Figure 4.1 the deadweight loss is given by the area of the triangles A and B. From elementary geometry this area is equal to

$$DW = \frac{1}{2}(P_M - MC_M)(Q_C - Q_M)$$

$$DW = \frac{1}{2}\left[\frac{P_M - MC_M}{P_M}\right]P_M Q_M\left[\frac{(Q_C - Q_M)}{Q_M}\right]$$

$$DW = \frac{1}{2}(LP_M Q_M K),$$
(4A.5)

where $K = \dfrac{Q_C - Q_M}{Q_M}$ and L is the Lerner index. If marginal cost is rising, Q_M

exceeds $\dfrac{Q_C}{2}$ and K will be less than 1.

4   The elasticity of demand for the dominant firm

The demand for the output of firm i at a given price is denoted Q_i^d and is equal to market demand, Q_M^d minus the supply of the fringe competing firms Q_f^s:

$$Q_i^d = Q_M^d - Q_f^s.$$
(4A.6)

To derive the elasticity of demand this equation is differentiated with respect to price:

$$\frac{dQ_i^d}{dp} = \frac{dQ_M^d}{dp} - \frac{dQ_f^s}{dp}.$$
(4A.7)

Multiplying through by $-p/Q_i^d$ and noting that the elasticity of demand for firm i equals

$$\left(\frac{dQ_i^d}{dp} \frac{p}{Q_i^d} \right)$$

gives

$$e_i^d = -\left(\frac{dQ_M^d}{dp} \frac{p}{Q_i^d} \right) + \left(\frac{dQ_f^s}{dp} \frac{p}{Q_i^d} \right). \tag{4A.8}$$

Multiplying the first right-hand term by $\dfrac{Q_M^d}{Q_M^d}$ and the second by $\dfrac{Q_f^s}{Q_f^s}$ gives

$$e_i^d = e_M^d \left(\frac{Q_M^d}{Q_i^d} \right) + e_f^s \left(\frac{Q_f^s}{Q_i^d} \right), \tag{4A.9}$$

where e_M^d is the elasticity of market demand and e_f^s is the elasticity of supply of the fringe firms.

Then, given that the amount demanded equals the amount supplied and the amount demanded from the fringe equals the amount they supply,

$$e_i^d = e_M^d / S_i + e_f^s (1 - S_i) / S_i, \tag{4A.10}$$

where S_i is the share of firm i and $(1 - S_i)$ is the supply of the fringe. Equation (4A.10) is the same as equation (4.5) in the text.

5 Market conduct of dominant firms: I

I Introduction

Established firms seldom produce a single product at a uniform price for one market. The more usual case is supply of a range of products (or services) to a number of markets which may be separated geographically, physically or in time. In some markets, the firm may have considerable market power, in others practically none at all. Some markets may contain heavily differentiated products, while others may consist of well defined or graded homogeneous goods. Conditions on the buyer's side of the market may also vary considerably. The same supplying firm may thus be confronted in some of its markets by two or three powerful customers, some of whom may be government agencies, while in others it may be selling to hundreds or thousands of separate retail stores.

Once we move away, therefore, from considerations of a single market and a unique price we have to address the complex question of price discrimination in all its many guises. In a now classic discussion, Machlup (1955) distinguished three broad categories of price discrimination and, within those categories, a total of about 20 variations. Thus within the first category, where the individual is the basis of the discrimination, separate orders may be priced according to each person's own negotiations or according to the intensity with which a sold or leased article is to be used. In the second category, where different groups are identified and their differences exploited by the seller, discrimination may be revealed in many ways. The most familiar examples are by age (half-fares for children, special terms for students or the retired), by employment status and by membership of certain organizations.[1] Other examples in this broad category include discrimination according to the geographic location of the customer (for example, all customers within a particular region may be charged the same price regardless of where they are situated) or according to the use to which the product is going to be put (fluid milk for direct consumption or for further processing). An extreme form of group discrimination may occur when a firm cuts its price to a very low level in a particular geographic or product market in order to kill off the competition. In the third category, the product itself is the basis of the discrimination. Thus variants of the same basic product may have different prices bearing little relation to their cost differences: hardback books compared with paperbacks, super de luxe, top of the range, car models compared with the 'standard' model. A current example may be 'green' versions of many products for the environmentally sensitive where the price premium paid may reflect more the marketing skill of the firm than the 'friendliness' of the product.

The common characteristic linking these very diverse cases, as we saw in Chapter 1 when discussing efficiency, is the sale of the same or very similar products at different prices relative to their marginal costs. If products or services are priced differently merely because their costs are different, then no discrimination occurs. Where prices in different markets or to different customers are not strictly related to cost differences, then discrimination is occurring. Similarly, discrimination is taking place if identical prices are charged for products with different costs (because, for example, they are delivered to different locations). The main questions that arise are: why should firms employ such practices, what effects do they have and how, if at all, do they concern antitrust policy?

In Sections II and III of this chapter we analyse the economic effects of price discrimination and discuss its treatment by the antitrust authorities of the USA, the EU and the UK. In Sections IV and V we look in detail at a particular form of price discrimination which has recently received a great deal of theoretical attention and policy scrutiny, namely predatory pricing. Many legends have grown up about this subject, often featuring the little man pitting himself heroically against the enormous strength of an overweening industrial giant. The facts are in most instances, regrettably, more prosaic although, as recent antitrust history shows, this has not stemmed the steady flow of cases.

II   The economic analysis of price discrimination
It is clear at the outset that, for a firm to be able to charge different prices in relation to cost in different markets or to different customers, it must have a degree of market power. In perfectly competitive markets discrimination would be impossible. A price higher than marginal cost would find no takers. It is this prime condition necessary for discrimination that makes it of possible interest to antitrust authorities. The opportunity for discrimination will, however, only arise if, secondly, different individuals or groups have different reservation prices for the product or service. In the absence of such a difference, a firm might still be able to exploit a position of market power, but this would be through a single price rather than through discriminatory pricing. Finally, a policy of discrimination can only be sustained if resale between individuals or groups is either impossible or so costly as to be unprofitable. If resale is possible, then arbitrage will undermine the price differentials. For this reason, it is often suggested that discrimination for personal services between individuals is the most successful.

These three conditions, market power, different reservation prices and the impracticality of a resale, are normally reckoned necessary for successful price discrimination. We may note, however, that where the discrimination takes the form of a common delivered price to different customers or groups (but with different costs incurred) the first condition alone is sufficient.

The formal analysis usually proceeds by identifying three different types of price discrimination and it is convenient to retain that system here. Discrimination of the first degree refers to the extreme case where the seller is able to take advantage of their assumed complete knowledge of the reservation prices of a potential customer to their own considerable advantage. The position is illustrated in Figure 5.1.[2] The demand conditions facing a dominant firm are shown by the line *AR* and the related marginal revenue by the line *MR*. The firm's marginal and average costs are denoted *MC* and *AC* (and are assumed constant for simplicity). If the firm sold at a single price, it would maximize profit at P_S, selling an output Q_S. However, if the firm had knowledge of the maximum price individuals would be prepared to pay for different units of output, it could increase its profits considerably. Thus if the 'first' unit is indicated by Q_1, this would be sold at price P_1. The next unit would be sold at the slightly lower price P_2 (not shown in the figure) and so on down the demand curve. Under these conditions, the firm would be prepared to sell output up to point where the price of the marginal unit sold was equal to the marginal cost of production: P_c in Figure 5.1. We arrive at the rather surprising result that, if the dominant firm can discriminate in this extreme or perfect sense (with

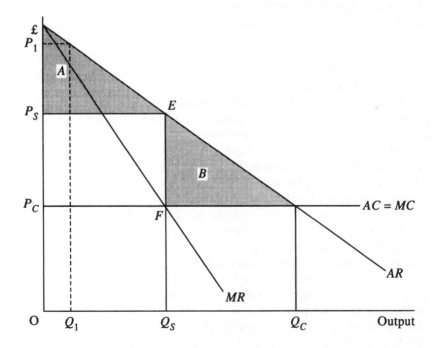

Figure 5.1   First degree price discrimination

complete knowledge of reservation prices) the output sold, Q_C, is the same as that under perfectly competitive conditions.

The implications of first degree price discrimination are important and, in modified form, have direct relevance to antitrust policy. We may note first that a dominant firm in the happy position of using first degree price discrimination has a very high profit incentive to do so. Under a single price, the firm's profits amount to $P_S EFP_C$ for the output Q_S. With discrimination, however, profits are increased by the whole of the two shaded areas A and B in Figure 5.1. Output certainly increases from Q_S to Q_C with discrimination, but so do profits. To consider the implications of this for antitrust policy, we need to look more closely at the details of the change. As far as the area A is concerned, under single pricing this was consumer surplus, but is converted into monopoly profit by the price discrimination. If antitrust policy is 'neutral' as far as income distribution is concerned, then this change will not be important. With single pricing, the area B represents the deadweight loss caused by the monopolistic restriction of output below the allocatively efficient level of Q_C (as discussed in Chapter 1). First degree price discrimination, however, eliminates the deadweight loss because output is increased to Q_C and, as we have seen, the area B accrues to the firm as part of the enhanced monopoly return. In this case, from a strict welfare point of view, there has been a net gain from the discrimination and, it may be argued, an intervention by an antitrust authority is not only uncalled for but is likely to be harmful and lead to a welfare loss. For example, if on grounds of equity single pricing was enforced, all consumers prepared to pay a price between P_C and P_S would be deprived of supplies and the deadweight loss would again be incurred.

The last observation assumes that the alternative to first degree price discrimination is single pricing by the dominant firm. In practice, the information requirements which would enable the firm to use such a refined system of price discrimination are so great as to make it infeasible or at least highly unlikely. In practice, the firm is much more likely to be able to use a modified form of discrimination based on less detailed information about reservation prices. Thus, instead of moving smoothly down the demand curve, progress may be in a series of discrete steps. The case was introduced in Chapter 1, Section III, and is illustrated in Figure 1.3. The effect is similar to that shown in Figure 5.1: both profits and output are increased. With second degree price discrimination, however, the assumption of incomplete knowledge of consumer reservation prices means that profits are rather less than with first degree discrimination. The conclusions for second degree price discrimination are thus largely the same as for the first type. In both, the alternative to discrimination is unlikely to be competitive pricing and more likely to be a single monopoly price. A fundamental change in market structure is likely to be required to induce a more competitive price structure.

In short, the conventional view is that first or (more likely) second degree price discrimination in itself should not be a target for antitrust action because, compared with the available alternatives, it actually improves economic welfare. Since price discrimination is a symptom of market power, a change in market structure (such as lowering barriers to entry) may make possible more acceptable alternatives. The welfare conclusions about first and second degree price discrimination have recently been questioned from two different perspectives. First, Williamson (1987) focuses special attention on transactions cost. In particular he argues that these types of discrimination are likely to involve the seller in considerable cost, partly for discovering the reservation prices of individuals or groups and partly for ensuring that no resale between groups takes place.[3] Purchasers have an incentive to disguise their true reservation prices and also to act opportunistically if the chance of resale at a profit arises. Assuming, therefore, that transaction costs are positive for the firm to gain full information and compliance, it still has an incentive to increase output to Q_c (Figure 5.1) as long as the gains in profits, $A + B$, exceed the transactions costs T. Indeed, the firm retains this incentive even if the following inequality holds:

$$A + B > T > B. \tag{5.1}$$

That is, it is in the firm's interest to produce output Q_c even though the transaction costs exceed the value of the deadweight loss area, B. However, a net welfare gain from discrimination only occurs for output greater than Q_s. Since, in the present case, the whole of that potential gain is exceeded by transaction costs, there will be a net welfare loss. The discrimination leads to a private gain but a social loss.

The second qualification, due to Posner (1976), involves the concept of rent seeking, which in the present context refers to the costs incurred by firms seeking to obtain or maintain positions of market power. The attraction of first or second degree price discrimination to the firm is, as we have seen, the prospect of greater profits. If it is known that discrimination will not generally be subject to antitrust control or correction, there will be a strong incentive for firms to use resources in a variety of ways (lobbying, making political contributions, heavy product promotion and so on) to create for themselves opportunities for price discrimination. The resources used in these ways impose social costs which may outweigh the potential gains indicated in Figure 5.1. In any event, it can be argued that antitrust policy which appears to condone price discrimination will send the wrong signal to firms in a dominant position.

Third degree price discrimination can occur where the seller can isolate customers either geographically (the home and exports markets) or in time (initial equipment and replacement purchases) or by end use (milk for liquid consumption or for further processing). As the antitrust cases show, variations on this form of discrimination are likely to be widespread and frequent. The formal results are, unfortunately, ambiguous.

The effects can be illustrated by the two market cases shown in Figure 5.2, although they can be generalized to any number. All of the conditions previously mentioned for successful price discrimination have to be satisfied in this case, involving a market where demand is relatively price-inelastic, market 1, and one where demand is relatively price-elastic, market 2. As in the previous cases, we proceed by comparing the price and output with a single price and no discrimination with different prices and outputs once discrimination is introduced. In the figure on the right, the line marked D_T is the combined demand for both markets 1 and 2, with the related marginal revenue, MR_T. Marginal (and therefore average) costs are again assumed constant for simplicity and shown as MC. Without discrimination, therefore, the firm would charge a single price P_S and sell output Q_S. The separate demands in the two markets are shown in the left and centre portions of Figure 5.2 as D_1 and D_2, respectively, with their related marginal revenues, MR_1 and MR_2. At the single price P_S and with those demand curves, an amount Q_S^1 would be sold in market 1 and Q_S^2 in market 2. We may also note that at these outputs in the separate markets $MC > MR_1$ and $MC < MR_2$. If discrimination was introduced, the profit-maximizing firm would want to ensure that the marginal revenues in both markets are equal, otherwise it could pay the firm to increase supplies where marginal revenue was higher and reduce it where marginal revenue was lower. At the profit-maximizing marginal revenue, therefore, the firm would reduce output and raise price in market 1 and increase output and lower price in market 2. The result would be that price would rise to P_D^1 in market 1 for an output Q_D^1 and fall to P_D^2 in market 2 for an output Q_D^2 The total profits for the firm rise to the area $[P_c P_D^1 \, ad + P_c P_D^2 \, hm]$. It can be shown that, as long as the demand curves are linear, the total output remains unchanged when price discrimination is introduced.[4] If demand curves are non-linear, which is more likely to be the general case, then total output may either rise or fall with price discrimination. We return to this point below.

For the moment we will explore more fully the welfare and possible policy implications of the effects shown in Figure 5.2, the linear demand case. The net welfare effect can be seen by focusing on the impact in both markets of the change in output, that is $Q_D^1 - Q_S^1$ and $Q_S^2 - Q_D^2$. In market 1, the welfare loss resulting from the reduction in output from Q_S^1 to Q_D^1 amounts to the loss of profit, *bced*, and the loss of consumer's surplus, *abc*. On the other hand, in market 2 the increase in output Q_S^2 to Q_D^2 involves a welfare gain represented by a gain in profit, *ghmk*, and a gain in consumer surplus of *gfh*. Clearly, since the decreased output in market 1 is exactly matched by an increased output in

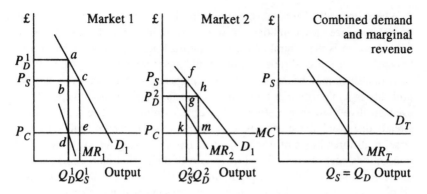

Figure 5.2   Third degree price discrimination

market 2 in this case, while P_D^1 is above P_D^2, the losses must outweigh the gains. As long as the whole of the market is served both prior to and after the introduction of price discrimination, we can conclude, therefore, that discrimination leads to a net reduction in welfare where demands are linear. Indeed, if demands are non-linear and discrimination leads to a fall in total output, there is also a net reduction in welfare.

The ambiguous cases arise where demand curves are non-linear and price discrimination leads to an increase in total output and/or allows markets to be served which would otherwise remain untapped. Unfortunately, an increase in total output alone is not sufficient to increase welfare. We can describe approximately the process at work by referring to Figure 5.2. The welfare change that occurs when price discrimination is introduced consists of two components: the net change in profits (*ghmk–bced*) and the net change in consumer surplus (*gfh–bca*) which is necessarily negative. Hence, where demand curves are non-linear and output increases, the first effect will be positive but this may be more than outweighed by the negative, second effect. Only if output increases by a sufficient amount will welfare be increased as a result of discrimination.

For cases like that represented in Figure 5.2, it is worth spending a little time explaining why the welfare effects are adverse. The different prices for the different groups of consumers introduced by the discrimination means that some consumers in market 1, where prices are raised, are denied access to the good even though they would have been prepared to pay a price at least equal to P_D^2. Similarly in the second market, where prices are reduced, there are some consumers who would not be prepared to pay the price $P^1{}_D$ in the first market. More precisely, price discrimination ensures that marginal valuations differ amongst consumers, whereas an efficient resource allocation requires that consumers' valuations at the margin should be equal.

Where does all of this leave antitrust policy? We have seen that market power is a necessary condition for price discrimination to be introduced. If market power is the central concern of antitrust policy, is it sufficient for us to conclude that price discrimination should therefore always be condemned? Although there may be some economists prepared to take this view, they are probably in a minority. For two main reasons the majority take an agnostic or even positive view of the effects of price discrimination. The first we have already discussed above and concerns the possible net welfare gains that can arise in all three kinds of discrimination. Even allowing for the presence of transactions costs or the misuse of resources under first and second degree discrimination, as well as the possibility of a net loss with third degree discrimination, sufficient cases of gains remain to suggest that each case requires a separate analysis rather than a blanket prohibition. The point is strengthened if it is believed, on the whole, that price discrimination allows the development of new areas of the market which would otherwise not be served. This was the judgement of Robinson, whose treatment of 70 years ago remains largely unchallenged. It is also the view of Phlips (1983) who made a strong case for including different varieties of the same good within the definition of price discrimination. The taxonomy of cases given by Machlup, referred to above, was certainly in this spirit. If the scope for discrimination is interpreted in this way, then not only is it almost universal, as Phlips suggests, but there is a much stronger probability that the net welfare effect is positive. The firm has a profit incentive to introduce new variations in its product to exploit hitherto dormant sections of the market. The total market served is thereby increased.[5]

The second reason concerns the distinction between persistent and systematic price discrimination, on the one hand, and spasmodic or temporary price discrimination, on the other. A dominant firm employing a consistent and uninterrupted policy of price discrimination is likely to be exercising market power to enhance its profitability. Where such cases are found, antitrust action is justified. However, where discriminatory pricing is haphazard and intermittent, it is likely to signify the breakdown of a previous pricing arrangement amongst the largest firms in the market. If a firm starts to grant secret discounts or rebates to selected customers in an effort to increase the use of spare capacity, it is unlikely that this discriminatory policy will for long go unnoticed by its competitors who will respond in a similar fashion. The previous coordinated price structure may thus be undermined, to the advantage of customers.

In short, economic analysis gives a rather unclear picture of the possible effects of price discrimination. The results are sufficiently ambiguous to suggest that a policy maker should be wary of embracing any general rule either in favour or against.

III Price discrimination in antitrust policy

The ambiguity is carried over into the three antitrust jurisdictions that we are discussing. In the USA, although price discrimination has featured in cases brought under Section 2 of the Sherman Act involving dominant firms, the Robinson–Patman Act of 1936 was specifically aimed at price discrimination. Under the Act, which was a Depression-induced amendment to the Clayton Act, it became illegal to use price discrimination where it has the effect of substantially lessening competition or tends to create a monopoly. Price differentials which reflected genuine cost differences, or introduced to meet the competition, were allowed. The language is thus very similar to that of the Sherman Act which also refers to 'lessening competition' and 'tending to create a monopoly' and, given that Robinson–Patman recognizes that price differences amongst customers may simply reflect differences in cost, there appears on the face of it to be little which conflicts with economic analysis. However, as we shall see below, the interpretation placed by the courts and the Federal Trade Commission on the main provisions of the Act has led to a general condemnation by economists, and some lawyers. Thus Posner explains that 'the economic meaning of price discrimination must not be confused with the legal meaning of price discrimination under the Robinson–Patman Act whose intricate and often perverse requirements will not be discussed' (Posner, 1976, p. 62).

In the European Union, Article 82 condemns any abuse of a dominant position and such an abuse may consist (amongst other things) of 'applying dissimilar conditions to equivalent transactions with trading parties, thereby placing them at a competitive disadvantage'. The wording thus includes discrimination where prices are dissimilar but also cases where prices are identical but costs differ. Although it conforms with the economic definition of price discrimination in that it recognizes that prices may differ because of cost differences (that is, the conditions in such a case would be dissimilar) the singling out of price discrimination in Article 82 suggests that the antitrust authorities are more likely to be hostile than in favour.

In the UK, Chapter 2 of the Competition Act includes the same wording on discrimination as is contained in Article 82. Prior to the Act the former MMC in its enquiries into the behaviour of dominant firms frequently examined various types of price discrimination but without any presumption either way about the likely consequences. It was thus able to judge each case on its merits, as economic analysis would suggest. Whether on the whole its judgements have been correct we discuss in more detail below. A number of enquiries have also involved what we have termed the most extreme form of price discrimination, predatory pricing, and they are therefore discussed in Section IV of this chapter.

Each jurisdiction thus has considerable scope for the examination and possible control of price discrimination. How have the varying degrees of hostility to it displayed in the legislation actually worked out in practice? The divergence between economic analysis and legal interpretation has probably been greatest in the USA and decisions under the Robinson–Patman Act. The problems seem to start with the wording of Section 2 of the Act which says that it is unlawful 'to discriminate in price between different purchases of commodities of like grade and quality'. Actions under Section 2 have therefore tended to be triggered by price differences which, as we have emphasized, need not involve discrimination. In fact, in one quite recent case, the Supreme Court actually identified price differences as synonymous with price discrimination. Responding to the defendant's argument that price discrimination under the Act required a price low enough to be unreasonably low or even below cost with the purpose of eliminating competition, the Court found that 'there are no overtones of business buccaneering in the Section 2 phrase "discriminate in price". Rather a price discrimination within the meaning of that provision is merely a price difference.'[6] Literally applied, this interpretation divorces the legal interpretation completely from the economic meaning. The position appeared to be made worse in a Supreme Court interpretation of the phrase 'commodities of like grade and quality'. In a case involving the sale of evaporated milk, the Court interpreted it to mean commodities having the same physical characteristics. Thus the company, Borden, which sold its own branded and advertised milk at a higher price than milk it supplied to retail chains for sale under their own label, was challenged by the Federal Trade Commission under Section 2. The company argued that the products were not of 'like grade and quality' because they were not perceived in this way by consumers. The Federal Trade Commission countered that, since the product had the same physical characteristics, to sell it at different prices was discriminatory. On appeal, the Supreme Court agreed with the Federal Trade Commission, arguing that, if price differences could be justified by minor brand differences, then all price differences could be explained in this way and the Act would be robbed of all content. If the principle stood, therefore, it meant that all competition from high-quality, low-priced, own-brand goods with national advertised brands was vulnerable.

Fortunately for both consumers and companies concerned, the eventual outcome was more in line with the logic of economic analysis. Thus the case was returned to the appellate court for a ruling on the competitive effects and it was determined that competition was not adversely affected. The court decided (somewhat perversely in view of the Supreme Court's interpretation) that, where the price difference between a premium and a standard product merely reflected the different consumer preference for the premium grade, no injury to competition resulted because it amounted to 'a rough equivalent of the benefit by way of the seller's national advertising and promotion which the purchaser of the more expensive branded product enjoys'.[7] Nevertheless, the Supreme Court's interpretation of price discrimination as 'price differences' and its identification of 'like grade and quality' with purely physical charac-teristics cannot inspire confidence in firms embarking on a new price strategy.

The positions might be retrieved by the provision in the Act that companies can defend their price differentials by showing that these were reflections of differences in cost of supply. It would not meet the point that discrimination can occur with similar prices but with different costs, but at least it should allow firms to offer an economic justification for their conduct. The onus of proof, however, lies with the defendant and there is substantial agreement that the burden is considerable (Neale and Goyder, 1980). The Federal Trade Commission has insisted on evidence of a very sharply defined relationship between cost savings and price differences for the defence to be accepted. The question has frequently arisen in cases involving a firm supplying a number of customers of different sizes and therefore with different demands. Although a supplier may judge it worthwhile to give discounts for very large orders because this assists them with production planning and helps to stabilize earnings, it may be very difficult to show very precisely what savings arise from particular orders.

For a time it looked as though the cost defence was going to require pricing schedules to be aligned with orders to individual customers if it was to be successful. In a private suit brought against American Can, for example, a carrier located in Florida argued that he was discriminated against. While he received no quantity discount because his annual order fell below the purchase threshold required, his larger competitors were able to qualify for rebates of up to 5 per cent by aggregating the purchases of their several plants. It was suc-cessfully argued that it could not cost less to supply, say, three plants located in different parts of the country if they were all owned by the same company, compared with the cost if they were all separately owned. Since canning costs were an important element in the total cost, the price discrimination against the company seriously affected their competitive position. The Fifth Circuit Court of Appeal agreed, finding that the discount structure was 'tainted with the inherent vice of too broad averaging, as a result of which it favoured a few large customers at the expense of a multitude of small buyers'.

The problem was to ensure that the 'averaging' system on which discounts were offered to different groups of customers reasonably represented the varying costs of serving them. Although the difficulty was recognized in *Borden* (referred to above) where it was pointed out that the government had never intended that price differences between any two purchasers had always to be individually justified, the averaging system used by the company was still found to be too gross. The discount structure used was insufficiently sensitive to the different cost savings made by the company in supplying different customers. In general it remains the case that defendants will find it very difficult to sustain a cost-based defence.

If a prima facie case of price discrimination is established, the Court then has to be convinced that some injury to competition has occurred. Three 'lines of injury'[8] have been distinguished by the Courts, but we will refer mainly to the first two. A 'primary' line injury involves the competitors of the company using price discrimination. The leading case, involving price reductions which were found to be predatory, can more conveniently be discussed in Section IV below, where the topic is considered at length. Secondary line injury is concerned with the effect on competitors of the firm which has been granted the discriminatory price.[9] The company, a leading seller of salt, had a discount system depending on quantities purchased both for individual deliveries and total annual orders. Delivered prices for the largest orders were nearly 19 per cent below those offered to the smallest purchasers, although only five large retail chains were big enough to qualify for the maximum discount. However, the discounts were large enough to have a discernible effect on the retail prices charged by different retailers. Hence larger purchasers were put at a competitive advantage compared with their smaller rivals. The Supreme Court had little difficulty in finding an injury to competition in this case. It was sufficient to show that the discount structure was such as to raise 'a reasonable possibility' that competition would be adversely affected rather than that the effect had already occurred.[10]

Systematic price discrimination which gives an advantage to larger firms because of their ability to place larger aggregate orders over, say, a year will enable them to undercut smaller rivals of equivalent efficiency. In this form, the discrimination will serve to maintain market power and this is a proper subject of antitrust policy. As we shall see below, this has essentially been the position also taken in a number of cases by the MMC. In general, however, the US attempt to control price discrimination through the antitrust laws has been less than a success. Criticisms have ranged from the scathingly dismissive (Bork, 1978) to the more measured assessment that the fact that it has not been more damaging to the economy says much for the resilience of competition (Scherer and Ross, 1990). The few voices that are raised in its defence tend to rest their case on grounds of equity rather than efficiency (Silcox and MacIntyre, 1986). Not surprisingly the major criticisms that have been levelled against the effects of the Robinson–Patman Act are largely a mirror image of those advantages of taking a flexible approach to price discrimination identified in the previous section. Thus it is argued that the case law of the Act has tended to inhibit price competition and to rigidify that very price discipline in oligopoly that sporadic price discrimination tends to loosen and undermine. To the extent that potential entrants to a market feel their room for manoeuvre is circumscribed by the law, entry is likely to be inhibited. Entrants in particular may deliberately wish to price low and expect to make negative returns initially while they are creating a viable market share. The threat of legal action increases the risks of what is

already a risky decision and will therefore reduce entry. To these anticompetitive effects and the inefficiency that they imply should be added the administrative burden imposed by preparing and hearing cases brought under the Act.

The Robinson–Patman Act is still on the statute book but there are signs that
the weight of opposition is bearing fruit. Traditionally the Federal Trade
Commission (rather than the Justice Department) has initiated cases under the Act.
The number of cases brought by the Commission has dwindled dramatically.

> In the last 40 years, the Antitrust Division of the Department of Justice has never
> brought a prosecution for price discrimination. In the last twenty years, the Federal
> Trade Commission (FTC) has averaged less than one prosecution under the
> Robinson–Patman Act every two years. Even private actions under the Act have
> dwindled to a very few in the face of unfavorable rulings from judges who have
> become convinced by academic writings that the price discrimination law is senseless
> and anticompetitive. (Davidow, 1992, p. 43)

A number of important cases in the EU have had to deal with price discrimination in a variety of forms. The most significant case concerned United Brands.
The company shipped bananas to the EU from Central America and had an
overall market share of about 45 per cent, varying from 20 per cent in France
to 50 per cent in Belgium and Luxembourg. It marketed its main brand under
the name of 'Chiquita' which was widely advertised in the Union. The company
sold the bananas to ripeners who sold to wholesalers who in turn sold on to
retailers. The Commission, having decided that the company had a dominant
position, then determined that it had abused this position in four ways: (i) by
requiring its ripener-distributors not to resell bananas while still green; (ii) by
charging different prices in different member states even though market
conditions were, to all intents and purposes, the same; (iii) by charging unduly
high prices to some ripener-distributors; and (iv) by refusing to supply a Danish
firm for a time, because it had taken part in an advertising campaign for the
bananas of a competing brand. In the present context, our main items of concern
are (i) and (ii). According to our analysis, the first may assist a dominant firm
in maintaining price discrimination, while the second amounts to third-degree
price discrimination itself. It also emerged that the company regularly supplied
their customers with less than the quantities they had ordered. The Commission
demonstrated that there had been considerable price differences between
member states for a number of years. For example, Belgian customers paid on
average about 80 per cent more than customers in Ireland, while the Danes paid
2.38 times more. The Court upheld the decision of the Commission on both
issues.[11] In particular 'the policy of differing prices enabled UBC [United
Brands] to apply dissimilar conditions to equivalent transactions with other
trading parties, thereby placing them at a competitive disadvantage [and] was
an abuse of a dominant position' (para. 500). It seems clear from this case that

the form of price discrimination practised by United Brands was regarded by the court as per se illegal under Article 82. Given the ambiguity of the welfare effects of third degree price discrimination and the view that in many contexts it may lead to desirable rather than undesirable results, the decision has aroused considerably controversy (Bishop, 1981; Fox, 1984). In US terms the case appeared to involve 'secondary line' injury; that is, some customers of the discriminating firm were put at a disadvantage compared with others which were receiving more favourable terms. In this case, however, the disadvantage was illusory. As Bishop scathingly puts it: 'Grocers in London do not compete with those in Frankfurt. So no one is put at a competitive disadvantage by different purchase prices for (say) bananas. Only where the good is an input for firms which compete with one another will this argument make any sense. For bananas it makes no sense at all' (Bishop, 1981, p. 289).

The Court objected strongly to the ability of the company to fix the prices at which it sold to the intermediate purchasers. In making its point, it unfortunately uses some very vague and mysterious language: for example, 'The interplay of supply and demand should, owing to its nature, only be applied to each stage where it is really manifest ... The mechanisms of the market are adversely affected if the price is calculated by leaving out one stage of the market and taking into account the law of supply and demand as between the vendor and the purchaser (the ripener/distributors)' (paras 230 and 231). It appears to object to the firm making an assessment of the retail demand conditions in the different markets and then fixing its intermediate prices accordingly. If the company had been vertically integrated into ripening and distribution it seems likely that the Court would not have objected, or at least not in the same terms. As it is, the Court's analysis and conclusions might provoke non-integrated firms into making inefficient, integrating decisions in order to continue without incurring an antitrust penalty. More generally, as Fox has pointed out, it is difficult to see how the public interest is served by transferring the ability to earn monopoly profits by discrimination from the shipper to the ripener/distributors. For if the company was forced to supply all its distributors at the same price and yet the different demand conditions in the several countries remained unchanged, it would then be the distributors who discriminated rather than the shipper.

The Court accepted that the responsibility for establishing the single banana market does not lie with the applicant. Nevertheless in its judgement it seems to have allowed an overriding concern for a unified market without artificial constraints on trading to prevail, possibly over efficiency and almost certainly over equity considerations. We have mentioned one possible inefficient effect of the judgement in the previous paragraph. It is possible, although not certain because of the ambiguity surrounding third degree price discrimination, that output may have been higher or prices more flexible with the discrimination than without it. Perhaps more important is the indirect or demonstration effect of the judgement. Traders in similar markets may be advised against discrimination, and thus price discipline in some oligopolistic markets may be tighter than it might otherwise have been.

Equity was almost certainly affected adversely by the judgement because an averaging of prices across countries (reversion to the single monopoly price in terms of Section II above) would mean that prices would rise in the poorer countries (like Ireland) and fall in the richer countries (such as Germany). Hence some relatively poor consumers who could afford to buy at the lower price under discrimination would not buy at the higher, single price. Relatively wealthy consumers have a reduction in price and some who did not purchase before would do so at the lower price. We emphasized in Chapter 3 that antitrust policy is generally concerned with the efficiency, not the income distribution effects, of market power. In many contexts, that position is sound (although we noted a number of qualifications). In the present case, however, it needs more careful consideration. In the economic analysis of antitrust policy the distribution effects are between two groups of consumers in the same country or economy and the 'neutral' treatment seems relatively uncontroversial. In contrast, the present case involves redistribution between groups in different countries within the EU. If we are correct in our conclusion that the Court was primarily concerned with market unity, it appears to have been purchased in this instance at the expense of greater efficiency and more equitable income distribution.

According to Fox, there were three factors in this case which enabled the company to sustain price discrimination and possibly earn monopoly profits. These were the restriction on resale of green bananas, which prevented arbitrage[12] and which the court prohibited; the restriction of supplies to below the distributor/ripeners' needs, which reinforced the ban on arbitrage but which neither the Commission nor the Court regarded as an abuse; and the inter-state differences in regulations, customs and consumer preferences which helped to underpin a discriminatory system (Fox, 1984, p. 411). The price discrimination itself was not the means of acquiring or maintaining market power, but simply an attempt to charge what the market would bear. Hence the remedies should have been mainly concerned with getting rid of those conditions which made price discrimination possible, especially the first two (since the last is beyond the reach of antitrust) rather than the price discrimination itself which would be likely to re-emerge in a slightly different form (practised by the distributors instead of by the shippers, for example).

The enormous range and variety of discrimination also emerges from the scale monopoly enquiries of the MMC, which spanned more than four decades. Furthermore, in a detailed examination of reports between 1959 and 1978, it was found that price discrimination, broadly interpreted, was the most frequent practice likely to be found against the public interest (Pass and Sparkes, 1980). The MMC examined each case on its merits and was not bound by any previous judgement. On the whole it has condemned discriminatory behaviour deliberately aimed at undermining or destroying competitors and discount structures which are not closely related to costs.

Largely because of the wide discretion it had in determining whether or not the market conduct of a dominant firm is against the public interest, it avoided making general pronouncements on particular issues. Even if it did, it usually left itself an escape route via a qualifying clause. Thus in its report on chemical fertilisers, it appeared to support the desirability of eliminating price discrimination: 'It seems to us that in the absence of effective price competition a monopoly supplier can generally speaking best serve the public interest by ensuring that, so far as may be practicable, his price for any one product to any particular consumer or class of consumer reasonably reflects the true cost of supplying the product to that consumer. But we cannot regard this as a rule to be applied indiscriminately' (Monopolies Commission, 1959, para. 669). Without the qualifying final sentence, the MMC appears to expect dominant firms with market power to ignore the profitable opportunities that it confers and align their prices with costs in the way that competitive firms are forced to do. If they do not, then the public interest requires that the antitrust agency should ensure a competitive result.

In the event, however, the MMC used the individual circumstances of the different cases to determine whether or not prices should be related to cost. Thus blatant forms of third degree price discrimination, which were leading to very high profits, have generally been condemned. For example, in the report on electrical equipment for mechanically propelled land vehicles, the dominant firm charged much higher prices in the replacement market, where there were many purchasers, than in the initial equipment market where the purchasers were other large firms. 'We believe that the practice is pursued for the purpose of maintaining market dominance and that the position of dominance so achieved can be used to secure an excessive rate of profit overall. We regard the practice therefore as objectionable in principle and against the public interest, in as much as it tends to perpetuate the dominance of individual component manufacturers in their particular fields, eliminating competition and providing opportunities for excessive profits' (Monopolies Commission, 1964, para. 996).

The case seems to be a textbook example of the kind of discrimination illustrated in Figure 5.2 above. There were different elasticities between the two markets and the firm exploited this information to its own advantage. However, if the situation is to be improved by the action of an antitrust agency, an important question is why demand elasticity was comparatively low in the replacement market. If the dominant firm's power in this market rested on preventing other firms from supplying replacement parts, how was this achieved? At the time the situation in the motor trade was approximately as follows. New cars were supplied with a warranty covering their overall reliability and the individual components. The warranty only remained valid so long as cars were repaired using 'genuine' replacement parts, that is those supplied by initial equipment manufacturers. If parts made by other firms were used, the warranty was void. A car manufacturer clearly has an interest in ensuring that replacement parts used in their cars are of a suitable quality. This could have been arranged by the supplier 'authorizing' the replacement parts of other firms as satisfactory for use in their vehicles. In other words the heart of the problem, as in *United Brands*, was not the price discrimination per se but the arrangements which underpinned it. The reintroduction of competition in the replacement market would have removed the basis of the dominant firm's market power. There was little discussion by the MMC of possible output effects but, as the quotation above illustrates, considerable emphasis on distribution effects in that the price discrimination provided opportunities for 'excessive' profits.

In cases concerning second degree price discrimination, the MMC generally (although not exclusively) took the view that dominant firms' price structures should be closely related to costs. In practice this meant that discounts based on consignment size were acceptable and even in some circumstances additional discounts given for total purchases within a specific period. Thus in its second report on electric lamps, after making the point that prices to individual purchasers should be related to cost of supply, it went on:

> Since distribution costs vary with the quantities delivered, the most appropriate method, and the one most conducive to efficient distribution, is a suitable scale of discounts related to the size or value of individual consignments. We would, however, see no objection in the circumstances of their industry to terms which also, if a manufacturer so wished, give some recognition to the size of the whole order (covering more than one consignment) or to the value of the total business which a buyer places with him ... We can see no reason, however, for any differentiation in treatment between one class of user buyer and another which is not related to the cost or value of the buyer. (Monopolies Commission, 1968a, para. 81)

The passage goes considerably beyond what would be allowed, for example, under the Robinson–Patman Act. The *Morton Salt* case cited above specifically excluded discounts based on total annual purchases, rather than those based on consignments and hence costs. In fact in the electric lamp report, the MMC eventually allowed only discounts based on quantities purchased. Similarly, in a report on the metal container industry, that part of the complex discount structure geared closely to purchases was accepted, while additional discounts based on exclusive buying was not (Monopolies Commission, 1970a, paras 311–12). In the report on cellulosic fibre, Courtaulds was criticized for giving additional discounts to very large purchasers even though they were not in any way related to additional cost savings (Monopolies Commission, 1968c).

It would help the cause of consistency if it were the case that second degree price discrimination was acceptable as long as the firm could demonstrate that its discount structure was based closely on consignment size and hence cost savings, while anything over and above this was unacceptable. Unfortunately such is not the case, as the reports on flat glass and wire ropes demonstrate. In both, some discounts were based on aggregate annual purchases rather than on consignment size, even though, as Pilkington's admitted, 'size of delivery has ... little bearing on cost, provided (as is the usual practice) deliveries are taken in full long loads; larger annual purchases are not therefore productive of any significant saving in delivery costs' (Monopolies Commission, 1968b, para. 73). Significantly, however, the reason given by the company for offering additional discounts was to encourage distributors to invest in modern equipment.

The pervasiveness of price discrimination throughout industry means that it is likely to feature prominently in antitrust cases. On the whole decisions by the various antitrust agencies in the three jurisdictions have not reflected in any direct way the results of economic analysis, although, as we saw, these are highly ambiguous. The idiosyncratic interpretation of price discrimination by the Supreme Court in the USA has contributed to an almost universal criticism of the workings of the Robinson–Patman Act amongst economists. Recent inaction by the authorities suggests that it may no longer be a serious policy instrument. The European Commission's judgement suggests that third degree price discrimination will be regarded as an abuse under Article 82, in order to prevent restraints on intra-Community trade rather than to improve efficiency or equity. Despite some ambiguous views expressed by the MMC in the UK, price discrimination not aimed at eliminating entrants was generally accepted as an important source of price competition in oligopolistic markets as long as the discounts offered are broadly in line with costs. In some cases, however, it was prepared to interpret this idea a good deal more generously than would be allowed in the USA.

IV   Predatory pricing

So far we have interpreted price discrimination as selling the same or very similar products at different price to marginal cost ratios. The motive for the firms concerned was to raise their profits above the level obtained from a single price. The lowest price could fall on this interpretation was to marginal cost (under first or second degree discrimination). There was no suggestion that the firm's pricing policies were designed to undermine competitors or prevent entry.

However, for a firm operating in a number of markets or selling to several distinct groups, it is a short step from this kind of price discrimination to one which is specifically tailored with the predatory intent of destroying actual or potential opposition. The argument is superficially simple but, as with many simple propositions, turns out to be exceedingly complex. Predatory pricing has therefore spawned an enormous and controversial literature.

The 'classical' story of predatory pricing is usually told in approximately these terms: a dominant firm operating in a number of regional markets or selling a range of differentiated products will cut prices to a very low level in the short run and sacrifice profits, in order to destroy a rival or deter a potential rival. Once success has been achieved, price is raised again to a monopoly level. According to legend, the old Standard Oil company used such tactics to weaken smaller rivals who were then more than willing to sell out on terms favourable to Standard.[13] A well-documented British case of approximately the same vintage involved a group of shipping companies which employed separate 'fighting fleets' to undercut and undermine a new entrant (Yamey, 1972).

One problem with this account is that it is not clear how low prices have to fall before they are predatory. After all, competition is supposed to stimulate price cuts and these generally benefit consumers. Unlike the more formal treatment of price discrimination discussed above, predatory pricing has always had a strong policy emphasis and much of the literature has been concerned with policy rules which are both workable and efficient. The dilemma is that a rule which is too harsh may condemn legitimate price competition and therefore unduly inhibit the behaviour of dominant firms. A rule which is too lax may allow predatory competition and therefore deny consumers the long-term benefits of lower prices that would otherwise have prevailed.

In order to keep our discussion relatively brief, we will proceed in the following way. First, we will consider a cost-based approach to the problem, as suggested by Areeda–Turner (Areeda and Turner, 1975), focusing particularly on which costs are relevant. Secondly, we discuss a number of criticisms that were made of the Areeda and Turner analysis and proposals, especially the point that their policy rule may lead to an over-narrow view of predatory pricing. Thirdly, this is extended to a consideration of contributions which have viewed predatory pricing as part of the wider issue of strategic behaviour. Fourthly, we consider a number of more general criticisms of the whole issue made by members of what we will characterize as the Chicago School.

Areeda and Turner's aim was to provide judges trying antitrust actions in the USA with a straightforward rule that was soundly based on economic principles and relatively easy to apply. They therefore proposed that prices should be regarded as predatory if a dominant firm reduced its price below short-run marginal cost (subject to some qualifications which are mentioned below). The core of their argument can be illustrated using Figure 5.3.

Demand and marginal revenue of the dominant firm in the market threatened by entry are denoted by *AR* and *MR* respectively. Its short-run marginal cost (*SMC*), short-run average cost (*SAC*) and average variable cost (*AVC*) are also

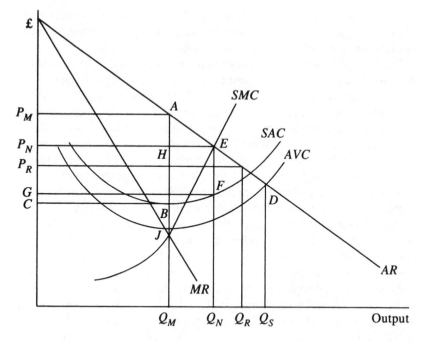

Figure 5.3   Price and cost of the dominant firm

shown. The profit-maximizing price for the firm is P_M at which an output Q_M is sold. The firm's profit is represented by the rectangle $P_M ABC$. In the face of entry, the firm may cut its price below the profit-maximizing level. Suppose, for example, it cuts price to P_N and sells an increased output Q_N. Its profits are reduced (to the area $P_N EFG$) and price is now equal to marginal cost, the level that would prevail under perfect competition. Areeda and Turner would regard any price level between P_M and P_N as acceptable. There is a net gain in consumer surplus of AEH.[14] Since price remains above average total cost, any entrant that cannot survive is not worth saving because it is inefficient compared with the incumbent. They take their argument further: a price below P_N but above average cost, say P_R, implies an inefficient use of resources: the resource costs of output $Q_N Q_R$ are greater than the valuation placed by consumers on that output. Society would be better off if it were not produced. Despite this welfare argument, however, Areeda and Turner are prepared to accept that a price below marginal costs is non-predatory, as long as it remains above average total cost. A firm that cannot compete with the incumbent when the latter is still earning positive profits must be less efficient and cannot 'compete on the merits'. Thus only price below marginal cost but where marginal cost is below average cost would be regarded as predatory, according to Areeda and Turner.

They recognized, however, that, since precise data on marginal cost are frequently difficult to acquire, in practice average variable cost could be substituted for marginal cost in the actual application of the rule. If the relationship between short-run marginal cost and average variable cost is approximately that shown in Figure 5.3, then the scope for inefficiently large production is considerably increased. Output could increase to Q_s (with its corresponding price), the whole of the output $Q_N Q_s$ would be socially inefficient and yet this would not be classed as 'predatory' under the Areeda–Turner proposal. Fortunately there is considerable evidence that at least in manufacturing industry short-run marginal cost may remain constant over a significant output range, even in the short run (Johnston, 1960). In this case, average variable cost will coincide with marginal cost and hence the practical effect of the substitution in antitrust cases may not be great. On the other hand, it may cause confusion and undue complexity in cases where the defence argues that, for the case in hand, variable costs are not a good substitute for marginal costs. The simplicity for which the rule was designed would therefore evaporate.

Apart from the points already mentioned, the Areeda–Turner cost-based rule has also been criticized on the following grounds. First, any test which depends simply on the costs of the dominant firm may create a serious information problem for any potential entrant. Such firms will know their own prospective costs and the current market price. In the absence of the threat of predatory reaction they may then be able to make a reasonable judgement about the likely success of their own entry. However, they may have little information about the incumbent firm's cost level and therefore find it very difficult to predict how large a price cut would occur if they entered. Some potentially efficient firms may be deterred by the uncertainty surrounding the extent of possible price cuts.

Secondly, the rule may allow the elimination of equally efficient smaller entrants which have fewer financial resources than the incumbent. This point is part of a more general criticism that their analysis was essentially short-run, when the essence of the predatory pricing problem is long-run. Any firm embarking on a predatory strategy would expect reduced profits or losses in the short run but expect to return to monopoly profits in the long run. For a correct analysis, therefore, the prospects in both periods need to be considered.

This leads directly to a third and more fundamental criticism of the Areeda–Turner analysis and policy rule. A number of economists, notably Scherer (1976) and Williamson (1977b) argued that the analysis was based on a very simple static model of the behaviour of dominant firms. It did not take account of more complex strategies that they could adopt to protect and strengthen their position in the market and therefore the proposed policy rule was likely to be far too lax. Much behaviour by dominant firms which had the effect of deterring entry or undermining smaller competitors would thus be beyond the reach of the rule and effectively immune from antitrust prosecution. In other words, these and other contributors to the debate viewed predatory pricing as one part of the much broader issue of the strategic behaviour of dominant firms. Strictly speaking, this is the subject of the next chapter. It is treated here merely as a matter of convenience.

The starting point for this criticism of the Areeda–Turner approach is their suggestion that where price is cut to marginal cost (or even below it) this should not be regarded as predatory because only firms technically inefficient in comparison with the incumbent will therefore be excluded from the market. Both Scherer and Williamson show that this need not be the case. By careful strategic pricing, the incumbent can exclude equally efficient firms indefinitely and still earn positive economic profits, even though these may not be the short-run maximum.

The argument can be illustrated by Figure 5.4. The demand and marginal revenue curves of the dominant firm are again shown as *AR* and *MR*, respectively. The firm's long-run average and long-run marginal costs are denoted *LRAC* and *LRMC*. It is assumed that, beyond a scale of output Q_E, all economies are exhausted and thereafter average and marginal costs are constant and therefore equal. The assumption is also made that, to achieve minimum unit cost, the scale of operations is substantial relative to the market; that is, output Q_E is a sizeable proportion of the total. The dominant firm's short-run average and marginal cost curves are shown as *SAC* and *SMC*, respectively.

The strategy of the dominant firm is to build an output capacity sufficiently large so that if entry threatens it can not only increase output considerably but do so in a way that actually reduces its own short-run costs. The increase in output and the consequent fall in price that would result would make it unprofitable for any firm to enter. The argument can be demonstrated from Figure 5.4 as follows. The dominant firm maximizes short-run profits by producing an output Q_M which sells for a price P_M: short-run marginal cost is equal to marginal revenue at this output. Note that this price is below the unconstrained monopoly price. If there was no entry threat the incumbent would have built a smaller plant to operate at minimum short-run average cost. It is assumed that a potential entrant could build output capacity with the same costs as the dominant firm. The problem for the entrant, however, is that, if it builds a plant with an output capacity of Q_E (the smallest output at which unit costs can be minimized), the effect on price of this addition to total output and the reaction of the incumbent will mean that the entrant makes losses. If the entrant produced Q_E and the incumbent continued to produce Q_M, the total output would mean that price remained above average cost. However, the incumbent firm has deliberately provided for this possibility and could increase output to Q_N. Its short-run unit costs are thereby reduced but, more important, the total output $Q_N + Q_E$ means that price will fall to P_F, below *LRAC*. The incumbent firm would have announced in advance that it has capacity to increase output, although the strategic value would not be emphasized. Its availability could be explained in terms of careful planning to meet possible increases in demand. For the potential entrant, however, the analysis suggests that the threat of increased output will be sufficient to deter and the incumbent can continue to earn abnormal profits.[15] Furthermore, if a potential entrant considers building a sub-optional plant (that is, one with an output capacity less than Q_E), the previous argument is reinforced. The entrant would have higher unit costs than the incumbent and price would have to fall by a smaller amount to make it unprofitable for the entrant. The incumbent would continue to make surplus profits.

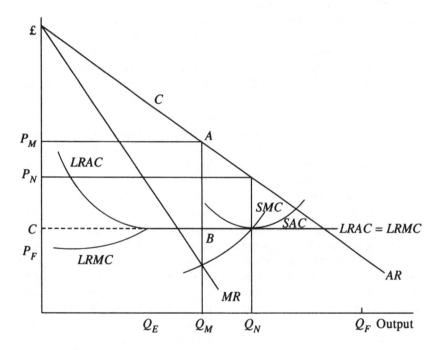

Figure 5.4   Price strategy of the dominant firm

The availability of the additional output capacity owned by the incumbent thus makes the threat of losses for the potential entrant credible and therefore entry is unlikely to take place. As far as the Areeda–Turner rule is concerned, we can now see why contributors using a strategic analysis have argued that the rule would be far too restricted and miss many cases of entry deterrence and elimination of small rivals. The strategy of the dominant firm can be introduced without violating the cost rule and without cutting prices. For this reason a number of writers have argued that a simple cost-based rule is inadequate and a more complex analysis should be undertaken in any case involving allegations of predatory pricing. The response of antitrust agencies to this conclusion is considered in Section V.

A vigorous response to both the cost-based and strategic analysis of the predatory pricing issue has been given by members of what we may characterize as the Chicago School of antitrust analysis.[16] They are generally sceptical about the suggestion that it would ever be sensible for a dominant firm to adopt a predatory price. They emphasize, for example, that any losses or forgone profits would, by definition, fall very heavily on the dominant firm precisely because it is dominant and has a large market share. A price cut as part of a predatory strategy would mean losses over the entire share. To the normal uncertainties that surround future performance, the firm would be deliberately adding another, namely that it would be able successfully to raise price once the threat of entry had been removed. Yet it will only be able to do this if there is no recurrence of the threat. Only if it has simultaneously been able to erect additional entry barriers will this be true. Otherwise, when it tries to raise price to recoup profits, entry will again threaten and the cycle will be repeated. Knowing this, the dominant firm will discount future profits more heavily and, when weighing up its available options, will reject the predatory strategy.

The argument is strengthened, according to the Chicago School, when the position of the potential entrant is examined more closely. If they anticipate predatory pricing from the dominant firm they have at least two defensive strategies of their own which will further weaken the position of the incumbent. First, they should be able to detach customers from the dominant firm by explaining to them that they would be better off in the long run by signing a contract at a competitive (non-predatory) price with the entrant, rather than continuing to buy at an uneconomically low short-run price from the incumbent. The customer's long-term interest would be served because, if the entrant was eliminated, price would rise to the pre-entry monopoly level. Secondly, if the entrant is making losses because of the predatory pricing by the dominant firm, it will be plain that this is merely a short-term phenomenon. The entrant should, therefore, be able to negotiate a loan from a financial institution on normal commercial terms because it has the prospect of making large profits once price rises again to the pre-entry level. Indeed, the mere knowledge of such a loan conveyed to the dominant firm should be sufficient to convince it that its predatory strategy has failed, and prices will therefore rise to a level that allows both entrant and incumbent to make profits.

Although superficially plausible, both arguments depend on near perfect information of the market on the part of the entrant, potential customers and potential lenders. In the first case, the entrant is likely to have to persuade customers who have been dealing with the dominant firm for a considerable time. They will know its reliability and methods of operation. In addition, they are gaining the current bonus of very low prices caused by the entrant. To change suppliers can be quite costly. To change to a supplier which is offering a higher price and the uncertain prospect of 'not so high' prices in the future strains credibility. Very much the same argument can be applied to the second point. In short, although we cannot rule out entirely these counter-strategies, the occasions on which an entrant or small rival could actually use them with any success are likely to be relatively rare.

However, the matter does not rest there. The Chicago response to the strategic analysis has two additional arguments. First, suppose that, despite the strategic manoeuvrings of the dominant firm (illustrated in Figure 5.4), entry actually takes place. The entrant incurs some sunk costs and is confronted by an increase in output by the incumbent firm. If the entrant had decided to build a plant of minimum efficient size (Q_E in the figure) the combined output of the incumbent, Q_N and the entrant Q_E gives a total of Q_F and, to clear the market, price would fall to P_F. Neither firm would make any money. In fact the incumbent firm's losses would be greater than those of the entrant because it would have to sell more. The key question then is how does the market return to equilibrium, given that the entrant has taken the plunge, incurred sunk costs and finds itself making losses? The entrant will continue to produce in the short run as long as price covers its direct or variable costs. As an alternative, it may temporarily cease production and let the dominant firm supply the entire market at a loss. When price rises, the entrant again commences production. In these circumstances, it has been argued, notably by McGee (1980), that the incumbent firm would reach an accommodation with the entrant firm and price would rise to a level which allowed them both to make positive profits. To support this conclusion, he points, secondly, to the fact that historically much entry has taken place and many dominant firm shares have been eroded, even though the process may often be lengthy and still leave them as the largest supplier in the market. In general, these contributors have argued that, in markets with imperfect information, creating overoptimistic expectations about future profitability, the type of strategy shown in Figure 5.4 will frequently fail to deter entry and that, once it has occurred, it may be very difficult to dislodge, if sunk costs are significant.

The debate over the plausibility of predatory pricing continues, although more recently the issue has also been broadened to cover strategic behaviour involving many other variables apart from price (and these developments are discussed in the next chapter). It has served to highlight a number of points that previously were not fully appreciated. First, a dominant firm may have to incur heavy costs to sustain a predatory strategy and may therefore seek an alternative. Secondly, there may be occasions, however, when predatory pricing is chosen by an incumbent firm, although these may be less frequent than is usually supposed. In particular the firm may adopt the strategy to reinforce its image as a tough competitor in the eyes of potential entrants. Thirdly, although marginal (or average variable) costs may be a useful starting-point for an antitrust enquiry, the issue is too complex to base a judgement on this criterion alone. If the policy is not to be too permissive, other features of the market have to be analysed, such as barriers to entry, the resources of the incumbent firm and (more controversially) motivation or intent. Fourthly, the detailed discussion of predatory pricing has led to some detailed analysis of feasible remedies. Since the strategy is thought most likely to be used by a dominant firm, an adverse finding in one case (and possibly a fine) will not remove the source of the problem, which derives from the structure of the market. Some contributors have therefore proposed remedies intended to deter. Baumol (1979), for example, suggested that dominant firms undercutting new entrants and increasing their output should not be allowed to rescind the price cut for a specific period, should the entrant leave the market. The firm would therefore be likely to incur heavy losses. If the policy were known in advance, they might think twice before running the risk of having to supply a substantial portion of the market at a loss. The alternative but clearly related proposal by Williamson (1977b) focused on output. Again, for a specified period after entry occurred, an incumbent firm that had increased its output (in line with the analysis illustrated in Figure 5.4) would not be allowed to reduce it to the pre-entry level, with the same loss-making implications.

V   Predatory pricing and antitrust policy

For a strategy that dominant firms may only rarely find acceptable, predatory pricing has recently taken up a great deal of time in all three jurisdictions. In the USA the practice may be dealt with under three major pieces of antitrust legislation: under Section 2 of the Robinson–Patman Act involving 'primary line' injury through price discrimination (see Section III above); under Section 2 of the Sherman Act as part of an attempt to monopolize a market; and under Section 5 of the Federal Trade Commission Act as an unfair method of competition. The first two can involve public or private actions, while the third entails public enforcement only.

US cases

In view of our discussion of price discrimination in Sections II and III, we will deal first with a notorious case brought under the Robinson–Patman Act, although most important recent actions on the issue have involved the Sherman Act. The *Utah Pie* decision has been almost universally condemned by economists but it does illustrate a number of points common to predatory pricing cases. The facts, briefly, were these. A small privately owned and family-run pie-making firm in Utah decided to enter the frozen pie market, where it met competition from three much larger companies operating on a national basis. The latter transported their products from California, whereas Utah Pie produced locally. To take advantage of its lower production plus distribution costs and to establish a position in the market, the local company undercut the established firms and rapidly gained a large market share (67 per cent in 1958). The established firms responded by cutting their prices to below their average total costs and in some instances to levels below those charged in markets close to their production plants. Utah Pie's market share fell back to 34 per cent in 1959 but had risen again to 46 per cent in 1960, when it was still the largest seller by a substantial margin. Throughout the period considered, it remained profitable. On these facts, the respondent companies were using price discrimination and the question to be determined was whether it amounted to a 'primary line' injury to competition.

A superficial reading might suggest that the case meets the 'classic' form of predatory pricing: large rivals operating in a number of geographically dispersed markets, in some of which they earned abnormal returns, could afford to support a predatory campaign in one local market where they encountered a smaller, aggressive competitor. The Supreme Court largely agreed with this interpretation, placing particular emphasis on evidence of intent by the defendants and the sales below costs. The majority decision explicitly ruled out the possibility that the defendant companies were merely responding to price cuts by the market leader. However, far from injuring competition, the general view of this market was that competition was stimulated by the price responses of the incumbent firms. During the period of price discrimination, although Utah Pie lost market share, it never lost money and fully participated in a rapidly expanding market.[17] The Supreme Court thus erroneously appears to have identified falling prices with an injury to competition and handed down 'probably the most severely criticised antitrust decision of all time' (Martin, 1993, p. 433).

A successful action under Section 2 of the Sherman Act has to show three things to establish an attempt to monopolize a market: (i) exclusionary or anti-competitive conduct, (ii) a specific intent to monopolize, and (iii) a serious probability that the attempt would be successful. Within this framework many private actions for triple damages have been brought claiming predatory pricing on the part of the defendant. In one survey of 23 such cases which had been determined, the plaintiffs had won two and lost 21 (Hurwitz *et al.*, 1981). Frequently the lower courts used some variation on the Areeda–Turner rule to reach their decision, often with some additional evidence on intent. As yet there has been no definitive Supreme Court ruling on what standards should be applied to determine whether predatory pricing has taken place. However there have been several cases where the issue has been raised and a number of legal points have been established. For example in *Matsushita*, involving the pricing strategy of Japanese television set companies operating in the USA, a long-term policy of pricing low in the USA while maintaining relatively high prices in Japan resulted in a number of private suits for triple damages, as well as action by the US Treasury under anti-dumping regulations. The majority in the Supreme Court was impressed by the fact that the low prices of the Japanese producers had been maintained over a long period. They reasoned that in this case a successful predatory strategy required not only geographic price discrimination but also intertemporal discrimination: an initial period of low prices and possibly losses followed by a subsequent period of high prices and high returns. Observing the first but not the second, the majority in the Court concluded that the actions failed. The Japanese companies, after more than two decades in the US market, trailed behind RCA and Zenith in the retail market for television sets. The majority of the Court therefore interpreted their low prices as an attempt to compete for business rather than 'an economically senseless conspiracy'. The dissenting minority in this case argued that the long-term pricing behaviour of the Japanese companies was much better understood in terms of price discrimination which involved collusion (and hence non-competitive prices) at home and dumped prices abroad. If there are important learning effects in television production (as seems possible) then the discriminating policy would be profitable without any eventual increase in the foreign price. If this is the correct interpretation of the facts of the case, then it would probably have been better suited to action under the Robinson–Patman Act.[18]

A case which ultimately followed the Areeda–Turner rule very closely involved allegations by the Federal Trade Commission (FTC) that the Borden Company had attempted to monopolize the processed lemon juice market. The company had sharply cut the price of its widely advertised brand in areas where it was meeting stiff competition from a relatively new competitor, Golden Crown. Prices were not cut in other parts of the country where competition was less intense. In other words, the allegations of predatory pricing in this case involved geographic price discrimination. Although the evidence on whether Borden had cut price below average variable cost was unclear, the administrative law judge found against the company and ordered the highly unusual remedy of compulsory licensing for the leading brand. On appeal this part of the judgement was eliminated, but the company was ordered not to sell its brand below cost or at 'unreasonably low' prices and not to discriminate between retailers within the same area. The final act of this particular drama occurred while the company was appealing against this decision and when the composition of the FTC was changing. The new majority took a more favourable view of Borden's position and got the Supreme Court to agree to a milder order regulating the company's future conduct. In particular, the company was banned for seven years from selling its leading brand in any market for less than its average variable cost (Scherer and Ross, 1990, p. 468).

The notion that predatory pricing must involve a realistic likelihood of 'recoupment' of lost profits was addressed specifically in the *Brooke Group* case. In its assessment of the claim that the defendant had sold its low-priced, generic cigarettes at a predatory level, the Supreme Court determined that, for predatory pricing to be established, it had to be proved that the firm had a reasonable chance of recouping the losses. Since in this case the market structure would not allow such a recoupment, the claim of predatory behaviour was dismissed. However, the Court declined to rule on what was the appropriate measure of costs in such cases, and so there is still no precedent on this central issue.[19]

Predatory pricing was exhaustively discussed in what became the most widely reported case in recent years. The case brought by the US government in 1998 against Microsoft has still to be finally resolved. It raised many traditional antitrust issues, including allegations of monopoly, exclusion and abusive conduct against the most stunningly successful company of the last quarter of the 20th century, but in a technological context where many claimed that the familiar legal and economic standards did not apply.

Prior to the most recent case, the US authorities had already moved against Microsoft. Following an inconclusive investigation by the Federal Trade Commission into Microsoft's licensing practices towards personal computer manufacturers, the Department of Justice took up the baton and in 1994 filed a complaint against the company alleging that it used exclusionary and anti-competitive contracts with the manufacturers to maintain an unlawful monopoly essentially concerned with 'bundling' together different products. A consent decree between the parties placed restrictions on the terms Microsoft could use in its licensing practices. However, Microsoft's interpretation of the terms of the decree was soon causing problems. Shortly after the decree was signed, Microsoft began requiring computer manufacturers to license and install its *Internet Explorer* (IE) browser as a condition for obtaining a licence for the Windows 95 operating system. Microsoft argued that, since the browser was an integral part of the operating system and not a separate product, the terms of the decree were not violated. The Department of Justice disagreed and sought an injunction. The Department was successful in the lower court but the appeal court ruled in favour of Microsoft, accepting the view that the products were 'integrated' and therefore did not infringe the consent decree. Thus the government's initial attempt to restrain Microsoft's market conduct by means of the restrictions on their licensing agreements had failed.

In retrospect these cases can be viewed merely as the prologue to the main drama. This commenced in May 1998 when the Justice Department brought an antitrust case alleging that Microsoft had monopolized the market for personal computer operating systems and browsers.[20] The case was heard between October 1998 and June 1999 with the judge giving his rulings as to the facts in November 1999 and as to the law in April 2000. According to Fisher and Rubinfeld (2001) the case raised four basic economic questions:[21] 1. Did Microsoft possess monopoly power in the market for personal computer operating systems? 2. Did Microsoft maintain its monopoly power by anticompetitive conduct? 3. Did Microsoft use its monopoly power in an anticompetitive way to distort competition in markets other than the market or markets for personal computer operating systems? 4. Did Microsoft engage in unreasonable restraints of trade? (ibid., p. 2). The first three questions involve Section 1 of the Sherman Act, while question 4 involves both Sections 1 and 2.

As we have seen, in an antitrust action involving allegations of abuse of a dominant position, it is necessary first to determine the relevant market, then establish whether the leading firm has market power within that market and finally decide whether it has used exclusionary or anticompetitive conduct to maintain or extend its market power. It is not unusual for plaintiff and defendant in such cases to disagree fundamentally on the correct definition of the market. This was certainly true in *Microsoft*. The different interpretations adopted by the two sides in the case account for much of their succeeding disagreement.

For the Justice Department the relevant market was for Intel-compatible personal computer operating systems. Buyers of Intel-compatible personal computers have no substitutes for operating systems designed to work on those systems. For a number of years Microsoft's share of this market had been 90 per cent or more. The economics of such markets made it highly unlikely that a competitive operating system would be able to displace Windows directly because of 'network effects'. In markets involving networks, demand for a product increases with the number of the users of that product or with the number of complementary goods and services for that product. 'Specifically, because of switching costs and consumers' desires for a variety of applications programs, an operating system cannot gain widespread acceptance until it has a large set of available applications. But because of economies of scale and sunk costs in software development, applications programmers do not want to write to an operating system unless there is a large base of users' (Gilbert and Katz, 2001, p. 28). According to the Justice Department this characteristic of the market amounted to a formidable 'applications barrier to entry' and much of Microsoft's objectionable market conduct was an attempt to preserve that entry barrier and thus their operating systems monopoly. In contrast, Microsoft argued that the relevant market was 'software platforms'. 'A software platform contains modules of code that are accessed through application programming interfaces (APIs). APIs provide a wide variety of features and services to software developers' (Evans *et al.*, 2000, p. 165). In this market, it was argued, Microsoft not only faced powerful competitors such as Sun and Netscape, but technology was developing so fast that any market power was always under threat.

However, the Justice Department perceived the threat to Microsoft quite differently. The Department and Microsoft agreed that Internet browsers combined with Java computer language (developed by Microsoft's rival Sun Microsystems) and server-based applications could become competitive with Windows. Java provided a so-called 'middleware' layer of software between applications programmes (such as word processing and spreadsheets) and the operating system. In principle Java offered the possibility for creators of applications to write programmes regardless of the underlying operating system. Netscape offered a threat to Microsoft because its browser, named Navigator, could provide the means by which Java gained wider acceptance as a language for applications programmes, irrespective of operating system. Furthermore, it was possible that Netscape's Navigator might develop into a direct substitute for Windows. 'These are the outcomes the government sought to preserve and Bill Gates (1995) feared when he wrote that Netscape threatened to "commoditize the underlying operating system"' (Gilbert and Katz, 2001, p. 27).

The Justice Department argued that Microsoft sought to maintain its monopoly in the market by two central strategies, predatory conduct and exclusionary behaviour in the form of highly restrictive contracts with computer manufacturers, Internet service providers and Internet content providers. We deal with these in turn while recognizing that the distinction between the two strategies can become blurred.

The Department argued that Microsoft had pursued several interrelated forms of predatory conduct. The first occurred when the company gave away *free* its Internet Explorer browser and paid Apple Computer to use its browser. According to the Department the profitability of such a policy depended on the elimination of the competition. It was therefore predatory. An interesting feature of this argument is that action relating to a complementary product (the browser) was being used to protect the main product (the operating system). It is thus consistent with the Department's central claim, that Microsoft's alleged anti-competitive conduct was all designed to protect its operating systems monopoly. However, it contrasts with the typical predatory conduct case where a firm reduces the price of a product in the short term to eliminate or weaken the competition, prior to raising the price in the long term in order to recoup its previous losses.

Microsoft's response to this claim was that the strategy did not rely for its profitability on the removal of competition. It made good business sense because it made personal computers more attractive and widened the market for operating systems and related software, thus paving the way for future revenues.

The Department, and in due course the Court, was unimpressed by this defence. If true, Microsoft should have supported any quality browser whether or not it was supplied by the company. Copious evidence produced in the trial clearly pointed to the fact that Microsoft's objective was to stifle Netscape Navigator sales. Probably the most widely quoted was that of one Department witness who testified that a high ranking Microsoft executive had said to him that the objective of the company's Internet strategy was 'to cut off Netscape's air supply ... by giving away free browsers, Microsoft was going to keep Netscape from getting off the ground' (quoted in Gilbert and Katz, 2001, p. 35). It was also difficult to square Microsoft's defence with its policy of paying Apple to take IE. If a major concern of Microsoft was the promotion of its software products, this would have been achieved by persuading Apple to use the best available browser.

The Justice Department also viewed as predatory the 'bundling' by Microsoft of IE with Windows 95 and subsequent versions of the operating system. According to the Department the tactic helped to prevent Netscape from becoming an effective platform competitor. Its objection was not simply that the browser and operating system were provided together but that Microsoft refused to offer customers the option of taking the operating system separately. Sophisticated customers could still install Netscape Navigator but the fact that Microsoft was bundling its products amounted to predation, according to the Department, because IE was installed at zero price.

In its defence, Microsoft rejected completely the notion that the browser and operating system were distinct 'products'. They claimed that integrating the two amounted to nothing more than an operating system upgrade. They noted that other operating systems, such as Sun and Linux, made similar 'bundlings', and argued further that there were efficiency gains in joint provision.

The final element of the Department's claim that Microsoft had used predatory behaviour to protect its monopoly was in its attempt to prevent Java from becoming the vehicle through which Netscape might develop into a competitor to its operating system. According to the Department it did this by developing what Microsoft itself apparently termed 'polluted Java' (Fisher and Rubinfeld, 2001, p. 50). This version of Java (J/Direct) would only run on Windows and programmers were encouraged to write applications using this version. The purpose of Microsoft incurring these additional costs, according to the Department, was predatory and designed to thwart the growth of an effective rival. It rejected, as did the Court, Microsoft's defence that it was simply applying Java to its advanced operating system for the benefit of consumers.

The Department's second series of objections all concerned exclusionary behaviour towards Internet service providers (ISPs), computer manufacturers and Internet content providers (ICPs). The restrictive conditions imposed by Microsoft on each group were seen by the Justice Department as designed to reinforce the company's overall strategy of maintaining the applications barrier to entry, and thus protecting its systems monopoly. In the case of the ISPs,

Microsoft made it easy for users to establish an account but this facility was only available if the ISP agreed to deny most or all of its subscribers a choice of browser. Computer manufacturers could neither remove IE nor feature a rival browser more prominently than IE.

In its response, Microsoft argued that the restrictive conditions occurred at a time when IE accounted for a modest share of Internet usage and they allowed the company to develop its share and thus become a more effective competitor to Netscape. In a company with little or no market power such a defence might have been accepted, especially if it could also be shown that the restrictions actually produced efficiency benefits. For a company like Microsoft, however, with enormous market power in computer operating systems and using restrictive contracts which apparently led to no specific efficiencies, their exclusionary effect seemed paramount, both to the Department and to the Court. The question of efficiency gains was crucial when the Court came to consider Microsoft's relationship with ICPs. In this case, the restriction which involved the company offering special prominence on IE at no cost to ICPs which agreed to promote IE in a number of ways was viewed as positive by the Court, rather than anticompetitive. The Court accepted that it could stimulate complementary investments between Microsoft and the ICPs, thereby leading to gains for consumers.

In April 2000, Microsoft was found guilty of violating the Sherman Act. Negotiations followed on appropriate remedies. Both sides made proposals on future market conduct, essentially the removal of restrictive contract conditions. In addition the Department proposed the much more dramatic structural remedy, of splitting Microsoft up into two separate companies. One would have the Windows operating system, while the other would have the applications programmes and all other parts of Microsoft's business.

Since Microsoft had essentially been found guilty of illegally maintaining the applications barrier to entry, a remedy which 'unbundled' Windows from IE would in principle resolve the problem. However, the Justice Department's earlier lack of success (discussed on p. 113 above) in enforcing effectively such a conduct remedy inclined the Court towards a more enduring structural solution. Breaking up very large and very successful companies carries enormous dangers. Apart from the impact costs imposed at the time of the split it is not at all clear that the form of the break-up proposed by the Court would generate efficient and competitive market structures in the future.

The Court of Appeals which gave its judgement in 2001 was much less sympathetic to the Justice Department's and lower court's stance, reserving especially harsh criticism for the way the lower court judge handled the case (and subsequent interviews with the media).[22] At the time of writing (October 2001) a new lower court hearing under a new judge to determine the ultimate penalties against Microsoft has been scheduled for the Spring of 2002. However, the prospects of a structural remedy appear to have receded.

EU and UK cases

Direct application of the Areeda–Turner rule has so far found little favour either in the EU or the UK. In *AKZO*, the leading case, the company was accused of attempting to undermine or destroy a smaller rival by its action in the UK market. The facts briefly were as follows. AKZO, a Dutch-based multinational chemical company, had approximately 50 per cent of the EU market for additives used largely in plastics production but also (mainly in the UK and Ireland) as a bleach in breadmaking. In the UK, where the predatory action was supposed to have taken place, AKZO had a market share of about 52 per cent, a small independent UK firm, ECS, had about 35 per cent and an even smaller firm the remainder. For several years prior to the case market shares had remained largely unchanged, prices had increased regularly by about 10 per cent per year (initiated by AKZO) but ECS's prices remained about 10 per cent below those of AKZO. In fact, ECS claimed that it was the lower cost producer. What triggered the events leading to the case was ECS's entry into the German market for plastic additives, quoting prices 15 to 20 per cent below those offered by AKZO to one of its leading customers. AKZO's response to this move was swift. At two meetings with ECS it was alleged that it threatened that, unless ECS withdrew from the German market, it would cut its prices substantially in the UK, 'going below cost if necessary' (Decision, 374/7). Largely on the basis of this, ECS applied for and was granted an injunction against AKZO under Article 82 and, in an out-of-court settlement, AKZO agreed not to reduce its prices in the UK with the intention of eliminating ECS as a competitor.

Despite this, AKZO's campaign appears to have been continued, a view confirmed by documents seized by Commission officials some two and a half years later. In particular, the documents set out the details of the way AKZO should respond if ECS did not withdraw from the German market. Plans were set out for detaching ECS's main customers by means of lower prices and special provision was made for the losses that the policy would involve. Evidence of the way in which the plan was put into action is detailed by the Commission. In effect, AKZO was offering far better terms to ECS's customers than to some of its own, with the result that its prices were now below (in some cases substantially below) those of ECS, who consequently lost market share.

The Commission had to decide whether AKZO's policy constituted an abuse of a dominant position under Article 82. It determined that the relevant market for the case involved the whole of the Union and, more dubiously, that AKZO held a dominant position within it. As we saw in the previous chapter, a market share of about 50 per cent would not necessarily be regarded as dominant under US law and the facts of the present case did not indicate that AKZO could set its prices independently of 'its competitors, its customers and ultimately of its consumers'. In arriving at its decision on dominance, the Commission gave no attention to the fact that in the UK a handful of very large customers (multi-plant baking concerns with many other interests) accounted for the greater part of total purchases. Although the additives in question made up only a small part of their total costs, they were unlikely to allow their suppliers to charge them a monopoly price.[23]

In arriving at its decision on AKZO's pricing strategy, the Commission explicitly considered the appropriateness of the Areeda–Turner rule. Part of AKZO's defence was that, since their prices had never fallen below their average variable cost, they could not have been predatory. The Commission considered that AKZO's prices had fallen below properly defined overall variable cost. In contrast the Court determined that most prices had fallen between average total and average variable cost but in the context they were 'unreasonably low ... with the aim of damaging ECS's viability' (*AKZO* v. *Commission* [1993] 3 CMLR 287).

Of more lasting significance, however, was its view that a cost-based test of predatory pricing should in no sense form the basis of a per se rule. The Commission argued that a cost-based rule was far too narrowly grounded on static efficiency considerations and took no account of the need to protect an effective competitive market structure (as laid down under Article 3(*f*)).[24] To establish an abuse, the whole of a dominant firm's conduct had to be taken into account and in the present case this included, inter alia, making threats, offering prices below costs to a competitor's customers and keeping prices below costs to its own customers for prolonged periods. Despite the misgivings that many observers have over the significance in such cases of the overblown rhetoric of internal memoranda, the Commission appears to have placed great weight on AKZO's plan of action seized by its officials. Together with the stance they had taken towards ECS and its customers, this was sufficient to prove an abuse. The company was therefore fined ten million ECU, the largest sum ever imposed on a company. In July 1991, AKZO's appeal was rejected by the Court which agreed with most of the Commission's findings, even though the Advocate General recommended acceptance of the appeal on the grounds that the Commission had not proved that the company had a dominant position nor given sufficient proof of the alleged abuses. The fine was, however, reduced to 7.5 million ECU, largely on the ground that this was the first case of its kind to come before the Court.

There are a number of worrying features of the case, some of which were highlighted in the opinion of the Advocate General. If the Commission and Court had depended on the analysis of price and cost, plus the evidence of intent expressed in the action memorandum, then at least it would have sent a clear signal to other firms about where the line was to be drawn between competitive and predatory behaviour. However, because of the ambiguities surrounding a cost analysis, it tries to take a wider view and in this respect it is far less convincing. In particular, it does not address the central question of whether AKZO's conduct was credible as a strategy for forcing ECS out of the German market. Its action in the UK was after all against a company which claimed to be the lower cost producer and which after several years of AKZO's strategy had about 30 per cent of the UK market. Although the Commission seemed to believe that entry barriers were high, some years previously ECS apparently had had little difficulty entering the UK market. If AKZO's policy towards ECS was an attempt to build a 'tough guy' image and thus frighten off subsequent entrants, the strategy did not appear to work in this market where previous small entrants had received similar treatment. In any case, if AKZO had succeeded in eliminating ECS and then attempted to recoup previous lost profits by raising prices to a monopoly level, there was a danger that other large chemical companies would enter the market.

The question of recoupment of previous losses was specifically raised in the *Tetra Pak* case (usually referred to as *Tetra Pak II*). The case went on appeal all the way to the European Court of Justice and involved a number of complex issues concerning the abuse of a dominant position. The one relevant here which was not dealt with explicitly in the *AKZO* case was whether the Commission had to show that a dominant firm allegedly engaged in predatory pricing had a realistic chance of recouping its previous losses. The company claimed that, since this had not been shown, the charge of predatory pricing should be dismissed. The European Court took exactly the opposite view to that of the US Supreme Court in the *Brooke Group* case (p. 113 above). Having established that some prices had been below average variable cost and some between average variable and average total cost but with the intention of eliminating a competitor, 'it would not be appropriate ... to require in addition proof that Tetra Pak had a realistic chance of recouping its losses. It must be possible to penalise predatory pricing wherever there is a risk that competitors will be eliminated' (*Tetra Pak* (No. 2) [1997] 4CMLR 724). The appeal by the company was dismissed in its entirety and the fine of ECU 75 million stood.

In both cases there is some force in the view that EU policy may tend to protect competitors, rather than competition (see Phlips and Moras, 1993).

Some early investigations by the MMC in Britain uncovered examples of what might be termed 'classical predatory pricing' where a long-established firm with a very large share of the market attacks smaller entrants and rivals through 'fighting' companies. Two examples from the 1950s involved British Oxygen, which used selective price cutting by an undisclosed subsidiary to thwart competition in particular parts of the country, and British Match, which produced special low-price brands to achieve the same purpose. In both cases, the MMC had little difficulty in concluding that such behaviour was against the public interest. Other cases have occurred occasionally since then, notably that of Hoffman–La Roche, whose practice of supplying its tranquillizers free to the hospital service in order to secure the larger and more enduring general practice part of the market was condemned by the MMC.[25] Until recently, however, they have been infrequent and part of a more complex strategy.

More recently the OFT has investigated the issue on a number of occasions. In five cases in the late 1980s, predatory pricing was the main concern, and four involved the newly deregulated local bus industry. In the first of these cases, the OFT established a framework for analysing complaints alleging predatory pricing and it was followed in all subsequent cases. The framework attempted to take account of both the Areeda–Turner cost-based approach and the wider issues which affect the credibility of a predatory strategy. It had three elements: (i) were the market conditions such as to make predatory pricing feasible; (ii) had prices below average variable costs or average total costs been charged, and if they had what were the other circumstances of the market; (iii) was there any evidence about the intent of the firm in reducing its prices? The first point recognized that predatory pricing can be costly to the incumbent. It would need funds to finance the strategy and confidence that it could make up for lost profits by subsequently raising prices again. The second point was obviously related to the Areeda–Turner proposal, although the OFT adopted a wider interpretation. While recognizing that 'there is no rational, non-predatory reason why a firm should choose to make out-of-product losses' (that is, by selling below short-run marginal cost, srmc), nevertheless:

> the Office's view is that prices can be predatory even when above srmc. If a firm is able to maintain prices which are above that level but do not contribute fully to its fixed (overhead) costs and to the minimum necessary to remunerate investment in plant and other fixed facilities by drawing on financial resources generated elsewhere in the business, other firms which are just as efficient in supplying the product(s) on which losses (in such an accounting sense) are incurred may be forced out of business. (Office of Fair Trading, 1988, p. 74)

However, because prices between short-run marginal cost and average total cost cannot unambiguously be ascribed to predatory behaviour, the third point, relating to intent, was required before a complete assessment could be made.

We will use one case to illustrate how the framework was applied. In *Highland Scottish Omnibuses*, the company was the sole supplier of bus services until the entry of a new competitor. At the time of the case, Highland Scottish was part of a public corporation which, according to both the OFT and the MMC, allowed it costless access to a fund of £300 000 in addition to its own accumulated reserves. The OFT was thus satisfied that it could finance a predatory campaign and that this course of action was not open to a new entrant solely dependent on the market concerned. Feasibility, however, also depends on the reaction of actual and potential rivals. Entry conditions are crucial. If entry is easy, the strategy will fail because the incumbent will be unable to raise prices to a supracompetitive level to recoup previous losses without attracting renewed entry. Despite the fact that local bus markets in the UK had been deregulated following the 1985 Transport Act and that all legal restrictions on entry had effectively been swept away, the OFT (and subsequently the MMC) decided that sufficient barriers remained in bus markets to make a predatory strategy viable.

To sustain this argument, the OFT mainly relied in this and in the other three cases in the bus industry on information asymmetries. In particular, potential entrants would be unsure about the precise cost levels of incumbent firms and uncertain about the reaction of incumbents to new entry. In these circumstances, incumbents would have a strong incentive to establish a reputation for toughness to deter future entrants. In effect, the OFT's position was that physical and legal barriers under regulation had been replaced by no less potent but intangible barriers. It is not clear, however, that these information problems were any greater in local bus markets than in other markets. Entrants are always taking decisions under conditions of considerable uncertainty. In fact the previous experience of the entrants in *Highland Scottish* as well as in the other cases suggested that their knowledge of the market was at least as great as potential entrants to other markets.

Since, however, the OFT was satisfied that a predatory campaign could be financed and was feasible, it proceeded to the second part of its framework, the price–cost relationship. We should note first that in *Highland Scottish* the company matched the price levels of the entrant.[26] When it compared costs with revenues in the case, the OFT concluded that revenues more than covered 'strictly variable costs' (wages, fuel, lubricants and tyres), but when 'semi-variable costs' (cleaning, maintenance and vehicle depreciation) were included costs exceeded revenues during the period when competition occurred. The case illustrates well the inevitable problems that surround a cost-based rule: precisely what costs should be included when measuring 'variable' costs? We have already seen that this caused disagreement in *AKZO*. Equally, it is not clear why vehicle depreciation should be included in variable costs in *Highland Scottish*. The definition of 'semi-variable' costs in this case was probably more broadly interpreted than a strict application of the Areeda–Turner rule would allow. There was sufficient ground, however, for the OFT to proceed to the third stage of its procedure and consider evidence of intent. Here the pitfalls graphically highlighted by Posner of relying on 'the inveterate tendency of sales executives to brag to their supervisors about their competitive prowess' (Posner, 1976, p. 190) were avoided. Instead of relying on internal memoranda (as in *AKZO*) the OFT placed great emphasis on the disproportionate increase in services by Highland Scottish during the period of competition with the entrant.

With prices reduced, some expansion of demand is to be expected. However, the incumbent's increase in (mainly unregistered) services on routes served by the entrant amounting to a 60 per cent expansion in its weekly mileage was interpreted by both the OFT and the MMC as evidence of predatory intent. Such behaviour was ruled to be against the public interest.

Thus the case illustrates clearly how the three stages of the procedure work: first, the incumbent was not only well established and with substantial funds but could also rely on intangible entry barriers; secondly, it cut its prices to a level between average variable and average total costs which was unsustainable in the long run; and thirdly, it revealed its intent by greatly increasing its services on routes covered by the entrant. Each element was necessary and, taken together, they constituted predatory behaviour in the judgement of both the OFT and the MMC.

Chapter II of the 1998 Competition Act provides for the OFT to investigate possible cases of predatory pricing which would amount to an abuse of a dominant position. In the *Guidelines* published by the OFT on Chapter II, the DGFT sets out the procedure that will be followed.[27] The form of the *Guidelines* relies mainly on the key cases determined by the European Court. The emphasis on costs and intent is retained. Thus where price is above average total cost, predatory pricing has not occurred. At the other extreme, where price is below average variable cost, predation will be assumed, although the *Guidelines* indicate that even here the DGFT would consider evidence that the behaviour was objectively justified. 'For example, a policy of loss leading might be objectively justified and would not therefore normally be predatory' (*Guidelines*, 1999, p. 12). The difficult cases would be where price was above average variable cost but below average total costs. In these cases, cost information would be looked at in great detail but in addition evidence of *intent* would be considered. Thus, for example, evidence that the pricing strategy had led to incremental losses or reduced profits would be interpreted as predatory, especially if backed up by apparent 'dirty tricks' (ibid., p. 13).[28]

VI   Conclusion

Some degree of market power is a necessary condition for price discrimination and, for this reason, it is likely to continue to feature prominently in antitrust cases even if it is merely part of a more complex strategy. The theoretical conclusions, especially in the case of third degree discrimination, are ambiguous but most observers are prepared to accept that, where prices charged are closely aligned with costs or reflect particular cost savings, the effect is likely to be pro-competitive, especially if they also contribute to a loosening of oligopolistic price coordination.

On the whole, the US antitrust treatment of price discrimination seems to score badly, especially those actions brought under the Robinson–Patman Act.

Recognition of these shortcomings may recently have led to the substantial reduction in public cases. The leading EU case has also been severely criticized as likely to lead to both inefficiency and inequity, although the court may have felt constrained by the obligation to promote the unity of the whole market. The flexibility of the UK approach allowed the MMC to assess the impact of price discrimination in different market conditions. Where price differences were related to cost differences and where there was no suggestion of predatory pricing, they were unlikely to be found to operate against the public interest.

In the public mind, the most objectionable form of discrimination is probably predatory pricing. The idea that a small independent firm may be weakened or destroyed by a powerful and arrogant competitor is widely held. In this modern version of David and Goliath, the roles of victor and vanquished are inevitably reversed. Unfortunately, the analysis of predatory pricing is far more complex than the popular version implies. A full treatment has to consider the costs and financial resources of the incumbent, the tangible and intangible entry barriers, the viability of the entrant or prey and the actual conduct of the incumbent. The antitrust agency must also be alert to the dangers to genuine competition of a policy that is either too harsh or too lax. Recent antitrust experience tends to support the view that actual cases are likely to be comparatively rare, partly because they will be expensive to the predator and partly because equally effective but less obvious strategies can be used. All three jurisdictions have paid more than passing attention to the cost-based rule suggested by Areeda and Turner. However, its oversimplification of a highly complex issue has been emphasized, particularly in the EU and the UK. A major problem in the cases (as in much economic research) has been the proper analysis of entry conditions. Unless these are difficult or are made difficult by the very fact of predatory behaviour, the strategy is not credible. At present there is a suspicion that the result of antitrust decisions on this subject may do more to preserve competitors than competition.

Notes

1. Recent developments have presumably eliminated one of Machlup's examples, namely price discrimination by sex in which there was 'reduced admission for ladies at ball games' (Machlup, 1955, p. 403).
2. This representation is derived from Williamson (1987, p. 79).
3. Advances in information technology may in many instances have lowered these costs considerably. For analysis with many examples, see Shapiro and Varian (1999).
4. The proof is, however, somewhat involved. See Robinson (1969, ch. 15) and Schmalensee (1981).
5. In practice it may be very difficult to distinguish this case from the one discussed in the next chapter, where a firm deliberately fills a finite 'product space' in order to deter new entry.
6. *FTC* v. *Anheuser-Busch, Inc.* (363 US 536 (1960)).
7. *FTC* v. *Borden Company* (383 US 637 (1966)).
8. According to some observers four, and, in principle, an indefinite number; see Martin (1993).

9. Tertiary line injury involves the firms competing with the customers of the firm granted discriminatory prices, and so on.
10. *Federal Trade Commission* v. *Morton Salt Company*, 334 US 37 (1948).
11. *United Brands* v. *EC Commission* (1978) ICMLR 429. The Court reversed the Commission's judgement on the third issue on the grounds that it had not been properly demonstrated empirically and upheld the judgement on the fourth issue.
12. There is some disagreement on this point. Bishop maintains that the nature of the product meant that there was little opportunity for resale and consequently the restriction was of 'small practical importance' (Bishop, 1981, p. 283).
13. Whether the legend is true is still the subject of some controversy; see, for example, McGee (1980), Scherer and Ross (1990). An earlier writer was convinced that some companies used even more outrageous competitive methods, including dynamiting their rivals' plants. For obvious reasons the record on this point is even more obscure than for dubious pricing strategies. See Marshall (1919).
14. There is also a transfer from the producer to consumers represented by the area $P_M A H P_N$ and an increase of HEJ in producers' surplus.
15. If the strategy failed and entry occurred, price would fall below marginal and probably average variable costs. We take up this point again below.
16. See in particular Bork (1978), Easterbrook (1981) and McGee (1980).
17. Significantly, despite winning its actions for triple damages, the success was comparatively short-lived, not because of damage from predatory pricing but from managerial inefficiency (Elzinga and Hogarty, 1978).
18. *Matsushita Electrical Industrial Co.* v. *Zenith Radio Corporation*, 106 S.Ct, 1348 (1986).
19. *Brooke Group* v. *Brown and Williamson Tobacco*, 113 S. Ct 2578 (1993).
20. *US* v. *Microsoft*, 1998, Civil Action No 98–1232 (Antitrust), Complaint, US District Court for the District of Columbia, May 18, 1998. The case is exhaustively discussed in Gilbert and Katz (2001), Whinston (2001), Fisher and Rubinfeld (2001), Klein (2001a), Comanor (2001), Levinson *et al.*, (2001), Evans *et al.*, (2000), McKenzie and Lee (2001).
21. Fisher was the Justice Department's chief economic witness in the case and Rubinfeld the Justice Department's chief economist for most of the trial.
22. See, for example, the *Financial Times*, 3–4 March 2001.
23. Indeed, following the High Court injunction against AKZO, when the price differential between AKZO and ECS widened, two of AKZO's most important UK customers approached ECS for quotations. On the strength of these lower quoted prices the customers were able to get comparable terms from AKZO (Decision, 374/9–10). This is hardly the behaviour of a company able to price without regard to its rivals or customers.
24. As in *United Brands*, therefore, there is more than a hint that the Commission may be prepared to sacrifice some efficiency for what it regards as a competitive market structure.
25. The practice was interpreted by the MMC as a means of denying entry to the whole market to a small competitor. Doctors would not want to change the brand of tranquillizers after patients left hospital. A supplier to the hospital service would therefore capture a large part of the general practice market.
26. In one case it actually undercut the entrant, but the MMC (contrary to the OFT) decided that this was done in the reasonable expectation that the entrant would be charging a similar price (MMC, 1990a).
27. Office of Fair Trading (1999), The Chapter II Prohibition.
28. In *Compagnie Maritime Belge Transports SA and others* the admission by the parties that their earnings had been reduced was treated by the European Court of First Instance as evidence of an abuse.

6 Market conduct of dominant firms: II

I Introduction

A large part of Chapter 5 was concerned with the exercise of market power. In particular, the sections on price discrimination showed how an incumbent firm could increase its profitability by varying the price to cost margin for different amounts of output or to different groups of purchasers. The exception was where our discussion extended to the use of predatory pricing by a dominant firm in an attempt to maintain its position. We also mentioned there the possibility that the firm may deliberately expand its output capacity beyond the level dictated by current and foreseeable demand as a strategy to deter entry to the market. Such capacity expansion is only one of many strategies that incumbent firms may employ to maintain their dominance. An analysis of those strategies and their implications for antitrust policy is the main focus of this chapter.

As we shall see, many of the strategies are aimed at potential rather than actual competitors. For those used to thinking of competition in terms of inter-actions between existing firms, the current focus on potential competitors may seem misplaced. After all, the familiar view of the competitive process is one where existing positions of market power are eroded over time by the growth of rivals attracted by the lure of abnormally high profits. One model describing this process was discussed in Chapter 4, where it became clear that the influence of fringe suppliers not only reduced price but would continue to erode the market share of the dominant firm unless it took defensive action.

Crucial to the successful protection of a dominant position are the conditions of entry to the market. In the extreme case of a firm protected by law from new entrants, there would clearly be no incentive for the firm to incur costs by acting strategically because it would thereby reduce its profits for no reason. The former nationalized enterprises in the UK in such industries as telecommunications, gas and electricity were protected from entry in this way, although they were not free to charge monopoly prices. Most enterprises are not in the happy position of having entry blockaded by the law. Nevertheless other factors, some of which we explore in later sections of this chapter, may give incumbent firms a degree of protection from new competition, but they may decide that they are inadequate to protect their long-term interest and therefore seek to reinforce any existing barriers by acting strategically.

It is not too much of an exaggeration to say that the role of potential competition in modifying or controlling the behaviour of existing firms has led to some of the most significant developments in the theoretical and policy analysis of industrial economics. One of these, the notion of contestability and contestable markets, emphasizes the controlling influence that the threat of entry can have under certain conditions on the behaviour and performance of firms which may appear to dominate a market. The theory is outlined in Section II, while Section III gives a brief discussion of antitrust cases where the theory has had some role. The second development, strategic behaviour to deter entry, in which incumbent firms may make a variety of expenditures to demonstrate to any potential entrants their determination to maintain their position, is then discussed at some length in Section IV. The impact of strategic behaviour on antitrust policy is considered in Section V. However, the subject can pose difficult problems for the policy maker precisely because the behaviour in question is often that expected in a competitive market.

II   Contestability and potential competition

In the opening chapter we referred to market power as the ability of an incumbent firm persistently to maintain prices above long-run marginal and average cost. A central purpose of antitrust policy is to reduce or eliminate the exercise of market power. What the theory of contestable markets does is to erect a framework of analysis where market power is completely absent. In the extreme case of a perfectly contestable market, the performance of the incumbent firms, even if they number only two, is the same as those operating in perfect competition, and there is no need for antitrust, or indeed regulatory, policy at all.

The theory casts potential competition in the leading role and relegates active competition amongst existing firms to a subsidiary walk-on part. This remarkable result is derived as follows. A perfectly contestable market is one where entry is completely free and, equally important, exit is costless. By 'free' entry is meant the ability of new participants in the market to replicate exactly the cost conditions of established firms. They must incur the same expenditures, no more, no less, in setting up their productive capacity as the incumbent has had to lay out, but can then achieve the same level of efficiency. Costless exit implies that any firm can leave the market without loss of capital. In other words, sunk costs are zero. Note the important distinctions between fixed and sunk costs: fixed costs are invariable with output but are recoverable if the firm leaves the market, whereas sunk costs are irrecoverable if the firm leaves. An aircraft leased for a given term is a fixed cost of operating in a particular market, but may be transferred readily to another market or the remaining part of the lease sold on to another operator. In contrast, the advertising expenditures incurred to promote an airline service on a particular route are specific to that market and irrecoverable if the firm ceases to serve the route.

Using these stringent assumptions, Baumol and his colleagues argue that incumbent firms will be vulnerable to what they term 'hit and run' entry (Baumol, 1982; Baumol *et al.* 1982). Any price exceeding marginal cost, implying positive profits, will provide an incentive for others to invade. They can enter, fractionally undercut the prevailing price, take all the market and then leave costlessly before the incumbent firms can respond. The discipline that such a threat imposes on incumbent firms is severe and means that, if they are to survive, they will be forced to ensure that their performance matches that of firms operating under perfectly competitive conditions. First, if two or more firms operate in the market, price will be equal to marginal cost because any deviation from marginal cost would allow at least one of the firms to make a profitable marginal adjustment in its output. Even if the market is a natural monopoly, that is economies of scale are so great in relation to demand that there is scope for only one firm to operate efficiently, the authors show that in this case price will only be sufficient to cover average cost.[1] Secondly, in equilibrium, price will be equal to average cost because, if price was below this level, firms would leave the market and, if above this level, some firms would enter. Thirdly, there will be no scope for X-inefficiency, otherwise firms would be attracted to the market by the profitable opportunities available to efficient producers. Taken together, these results imply that the number and size distribution of firms in equilibrium will be such as to ensure that output is produced at minimum total cost. In addition they also mean that there is no scope for one product to be cross-subsidized by another because there are no surplus profits available to finance such a policy.

The perfectly competitive model also generates these outcomes, but what is novel about the theory of perfect contestability is that the results hold in markets with as few as two firms.[2] Thus a perfectly contestable duopoly will meet all the desirable performance criteria: it will be technically, allocatively and X-efficient, but without any need for antitrust intervention. Similarly, a perfectly contestable natural monopoly will be forced to produce efficiently without exploiting consumers and without the cumbersome regulatory apparatus which is commonly employed. The engine driving this analysis is the 'ultra-free' entry and exit conditions and the threat of potential competition.

Before alarmed antitrust lawyers pack their bags and consider retraining for a more useful occupation, we need to look closely at the implications of the theory. Baumol recognized that the world is no more populated with perfectly contestable markets than it is with perfectly competitive markets, but this has not prevented the latter from being a powerful tool of analysis. All theories have to abstract from reality and simplify, otherwise they would merely reproduce the complexities of the world they were trying to explain. Critics of the theory have pointed out, however, that to be really useful a theory has to be robust, in the sense that small departures from its assumptions should cause only minor alterations to the predictions. They have argued that contestability theory does not stand up very well to tests of robustness. In particular, Vickers and Yarrow (1988) suggest that even a modest change in the extreme assumption of zero sunk costs can fundamentally alter the results. Their argument can be illustrated by the use of Figure 6.1. They assume a homogeneous product and constant unit (and hence marginal) costs, denoted *MC*. The demand curve is given by *D*. Social welfare will be maximized where price equals marginal cost, that is where output is Q_C. The monopoly price is P_M but the incumbent is currently charging a price P_I. An entrant which priced fractionally below P_I could earn a profit slightly less than the area of MCP_IRS for as long as it can produce optimally before the incumbent responds. As soon as the response does take place, it is assumed that price falls to *MC*, but no lower. A firm will enter the market as long as the flow of profits exceeds any sunk costs.

Three situations can be distinguished. First is the extreme case we have just been discussing: the perfectly contestable market. Sunk costs are zero and the entrant can set up fully before the incumbent responds. Any price greater than *MC* makes the market vulnerable to entry. With price at P_I therefore, hit-and-run entry could occur and, as indicated above, the entrant could earn profits fractionally less than MCP_IRS until the incumbent responded, when price would fall to *MC* and the entrant could costlessly leave the market.

The second and more realistic situation is where the incumbent can respond before the entrant is sufficiently established to start production. There is no scope for the entrant to make profits because price would fall to *MC* as soon as an entrant started production. More to the point, the presence of some sunk costs, however small, would deter all entry. Even a monopoly price, P_M, would have no impact.

The third case is where sunk costs are positive but also the incumbent takes some time to respond. As long as the scope for profit making by an entrant is less than the size of sunk costs, entry will not occur. In particular, if the response time of the incumbent is short, then sunk costs, however small, will effectively bar entry. It may even be the case that a monopoly price does not attract entry because of the flexibility of the incumbent and the need to sink some expenditures.

There is thus a strong probability that even slight departures from perfect contestability will produce dramatically different results. In these circumstances it is not tenable to argue that an imperfectly contestable market gives a satisfactory approximation to the results of perfect contestability. It may not make sense to analyse markets according to the 'degree' to which they are contestable. Baumol himself was doubtful on this, writing in 1984: 'Since perfect contestability is highly improbable in reality, it is necessary to consider the state of affairs that is likely when the requirements of contestability are fulfilled only approximately. Unfortunately, since the entire analysis is so new, the case of imperfect contestability and the attributes of a "workably contestable" market are only now being explored' (Bailey and Baumol, 1984). Critical analysis

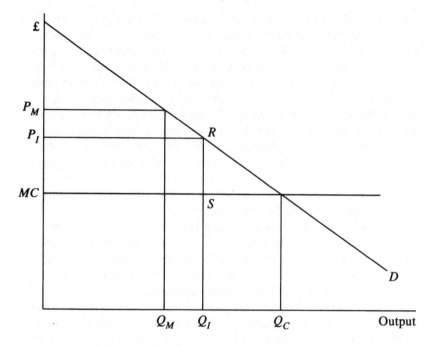

Figure 6.1   Contestability and entry

since this was written has, if anything, increased scepticism on this point, as the reference to Vickers and Yarrow indicates.

Other observers have pointed to the wealth of empirical research and antitrust cases which indicate that actual rather than potential competition has a much more potent effect on market performance. Firms with large market shares frequently have market power and exercise it. They will also take steps to create entry barriers and retaliate swiftly should entry occur. The evidence also suggests that high market shares and high entry barriers are correlated. Where actual competitors are numerous, the number of potential entrants is also high and vice versa. Hence there are relatively few cases which combine a high degree of monopoly with low entry barriers. Shepherd (1984) has been particularly trenchant in his criticism of the claims made by the authors of the theory, but a number of other writers also remain highly sceptical of its results and especially its use as a benchmark for policy (see, for example, Martin, 1993; Scherer and Ross, 1990). For a more receptive view, see Spence (1983).

An important outcome of the wide debate that has followed the original publication of the theory has been the emphasis placed on sunk costs and their role as a barrier to exit. Significant sunk costs raise considerably the risks associated with entry. Even if entrants can replicate the productive capacity of incumbents to achieve similar unit costs, they may well be deterred by the prospect of irrecoverable costs should the market turn sour.

The analysis was given greater impetus by the moves towards deregulation of certain industries that were already under way in the USA and rapidly adopted in other countries (especially the UK) in the early 1980s. One economist whose influence at a policy level was highly significant, as we shall see in the next section, was Bailey, who argued that 'the single most important element in the design of public policy for monopoly should be the design of arrangements which render benign the exercise of power associated with operating sunk facilities' (Bailey, 1981, p. 179). Although the detailed arrangements will vary from industry to industry, the two general principles should be to ensure either that access to the sunk facility (whether or not it is publicly owned) is available equally to all operators, or that the sunk investments are isolated and their use regulated in a way so as not to discriminate against new entrants.

Since, however, contestability depends on free entry as well as free exit, the two aspects have to be coordinated to prevent abuse. In practice this is where the greatest difficulties may arise. One example occurs in civil aviation and another in local telecommunications. The main sunk facility in aviation is the airport. In principle, the problem can be solved by ensuring that a separate organization (firm or public authority) owns the airport where equal access is maintained. However, the restricted availability of runways at primary airports in many major cities, plus the additional limited number of time slots which may be further curtailed by environmental concerns, mean that a strict rationing system has to be used to allocate these scarce resources. Allocation methods, however, have tended to reinforce existing market shares at the expense of new entry. Thus, for example, Bailey (1981) cites the case of slot allocation at four major US airports, under the former regulatory system. The incumbent airlines were allowed to allocate slots amongst themselves using a unanimity principle, safe in the knowledge that they had been granted antitrust immunity. In the UK, until recently, no 'additional' airline was granted slots at London's premier airport, Heathrow, partly on the grounds of congestion but also for political reasons: Heathrow was preserved as the major hub for British Airways. In 1991, what was seen as a major modification in policy took place when both American Airlines and United Airlines were allowed to purchase the slots long allocated to Pan American and Trans World Airlines, which were in financial difficulties.[3] Although a number of experiments have taken place in recent years to allocate scarce slots on a basis that does not discriminate against entry, the majority are still distributed according to so-called 'grandfather rights' which automatically favour those who have been allocated prime slots in the past.

In fixed-link telecommunications a major sunk cost is the local network of lines. Obviously a subscriber will wish to be linked to as dense a network of lines as possible. It would be very costly, not to say inefficient, to establish more than one local telecommunication network.[4] This factor has much less force in long-distance calls, where network requirements are much 'thinner'. Thus it is less costly for newcomers to enter the long-distance market than to enter the local market. According to the Bailey principle stated above, the sunk facility (in this case local telecommunications networks) should be identified and then provision made for equal access to all new entrants. As in civil aviation, the problems arise with the practicalities of ensuring genuine and equal access. If the local telephone company does not also supply the long-distance market, the central question concerns the terms on which long-distance suppliers can link into the local network. The local company will have no reason to discriminate between competing long-distance suppliers.[5] This factor was important in the restructuring of the former AT and T company in the USA in 1984. The former vertically integrated company was split essentially into eight new groupings with long-distance services kept separate from 'local' (or more appropriately 'regional') suppliers.

The problems in the industry are more complex if the aim is to stimulate competition in the long-distance market by allowing entry while maintaining an incumbent, integrated company which supplies both local and long-distance services. In this case the incumbent is in competition with the entrant in the long-distance market, but has monopoly control of local (fixed-link) services. The viability of the entrants will depend crucially on the terms negotiated for linking in to the local networks. Unfortunately, in the UK, the incumbent telecommunications company, British Telecom (BT), was privatized intact (that is, supplying both local and long distance). As a result, the terms on which the new entrant (Mercury) could use BT's local networks were a persistent cause of friction and dispute. Matters were, if anything, made worse by the initial decision of the government to license only one new entrant rather than allow open access to all financially and technically sound companies (Vickers and Yarrow, 1988, ch. 8).

Thus, in industries which are being deregulated, contestability analysis has helped to sharpen the focus on those characteristics of market structure which may require particular care, especially the need for open access to facilities embodying sunk costs. Its contribution as far as entry conditions are concerned merely reinforces the conclusions of previous analysis going back, as Baumol himself has said, at least to the work of Bain (Baumol, 1982, referring particularly to Bain, 1956).

III   Contestability and antitrust policy

The theory of contestable markets has probably had a more direct and speedy impact on policy in the USA than any other piece of economic analysis. Whether in retrospect its influence will be seen as benign or perverse is still hotly disputed. The industry mainly affected is civil aviation and the leading role was played by Elizabeth Bailey. In her 1981 paper she explained that, while a member of the Civil Aeronautics Board (CAB), the agency which had regulated the industry for 40 years and which was abolished in 1985, she had argued that the sizeable merger between Texas International and National Air should be allowed to proceed and not be blocked by the antitrust proceedings desired by the Justice Department.[6] The share of traffic on the key Houston–New Orleans route accounted for by the two largest carriers would rise from around 50 per cent to practically 75 per cent if the merger was completed. In accordance with previous Supreme Court decisions, it seemed clear-cut at the time that the Justice Department should seek to challenge a merger which apparently had such a significant impact on market structure.

Under the banner of contestability, this conventional view was successfully overruled by the CAB.[7] As Bailey explained,

> since the passage of the Airline Deregulation Act of 1978 ... there was now relative ease of entry, even for small carriers into such markets. In the Houston–New Orleans market in particular, there were eleven carriers with stations and functioning facilities already in place at both ends of this market. Therefore, the CAB reasoned that the markets were readily contested and did not find that a merger would be anticompetitive. (Bailey, 1981, p. 181)

This philosophy was carried over to a crucial phase in the post-deregulation development of the industry structure in the USA. Following the abolition of the CAB, responsibility for overseeing policy towards the industry passed to the Department of Transportation, rather than the Department of Justice. In 1986, a number of very large mergers were announced, following a period of intense price competition and entry. Applying its usual criteria, the Justice Department wanted to challenge each of the proposals, but was overruled by the Department of Transportation on grounds similar to those outlined above by Bailey. Airline markets were contestable and therefore mergers creating very large market shares did not create an antitrust problem because market power was not enhanced.

Contestability analysis was in effect applied to the industry even though it was already apparent that, despite earlier optimism, entry conditions were far from easy, partly because of the limited availability of key 'slots' and partly because of the dominance by incumbent airlines of computer-based reservation systems.[8] The empirical evidence also suggested that average fares were higher in more concentrated markets and that within such markets the leading firms had higher fares than smaller firms (Bailey *et al.* 1985). In other words, the 'traditional' view that actual competition was more important than potential competition was borne out, despite the predictions for the industry of the contestability theorists. The case illustrates clearly the danger of slipping from the theoretical limiting case of perfect contestability to the much messier real-world example where neither entry nor exit is perfectly free. Given the non-robust nature of the theory, mentioned above, there is really no reason to expect a close approximation to the theoretical results to emerge in practice.

As Shepherd (1988) has pointed out, Baumol also argued strongly in favour of a major railway merger that had occurred in 1983, on exactly the same grounds as were offered in the airlines cases: 'in a market where trucks or water carriers can enter, excessive pricing or poor service by two railroads (or even one) become a lure and must attract incursions by the more mobile carriers, which will soon enough bring the hypothetical railroads' attempt at monopolistic behavior to an end' (Baumol, quoted in Shepherd, 1988, p. 123). As a result of the threat of competition from these alternative modes, he thus argued that 'it is simply not possible for a merger to serve as a source of market power' (ibid.). As Shepherd indicates, however, while different transport modes are certainly alternatives for some cargoes and over certain distances, it is clearly by no means the universal rule, as Baumol implies. Particularly where substantial cost differences arise (as with high-bulk, low-value items which do not need to be broken down into small delivery size amounts) road transport is not a competitive substitute for rail and hence the elimination of competition between railroads, which the merger between the Santa Fe and the Southern Pacific Railroads implied, would create opportunities for the exercise of market power. In the event, in this case the regulatory agency, the Interstate Commerce Commission, was unpersuaded by the contestability arguments and rejected the merger in 1986, a decision which created havoc for the combined company (ibid., p. 115).

The publication and widespread discussion of the contestability theory in the early and mid-1980s coincided with the privatization and deregulation policies of the successive Conservative governments in the UK. It is hardly surprising, therefore, that the analysis featured quite prominently in the debates which preceded the privatization of most of the major utilities.[9] In the present context an interesting example was the experience of the local bus industry.[10] The White Paper introducing the proposals referred to local bus markets (those where the maximum journey is under 15 miles) as 'highly contestable' (Department of Transport, 1984, p. 52) and anticipated, therefore, that, once the industry was largely privatized and entry restrictions were abolished, competition both actual and potential would bring significant reduction in cost (after more than 50 years of regulation) and ensure an efficient performance.

The National Bus Company (NBC) was duly privatized as more than 70 separate units, although in most large towns and cities the municipally owned operators continued to provide major services on a profit-making basis. In view of the optimism expressed in the White Paper, subsequent events in the industry are instructive. In the decade following deregulation in 1986, the industry received more attention from the UK antitrust authorities than any other since the formation of the Monopolies and Restrictive Practices Commission (as it was then called) in 1948. More than a hundred of the restrictive agreements registered with the DGFT were found to have restrictions on prices or other terms of trading which he found objectionable (Beesley, 1990); the Office of Fair Trading reported on seven allegations of anticompetitive practices and six mergers were referred to the MMC.

A perfectly contestable market, as we have seen, would require no such pervasive scrutiny because the threat of entry prevents the emergence of market power. The White Paper implied that local bus markets would be (in Bailey and Baumol's phrase, 1984) 'workably contestable'. In four of the merger cases, however, the MMC explicitly rejected this view, without actually using the term 'contestability'. Despite evidence that economies of scale in the industry are modest and despite the abolition of the regulatory restrictions which had governed entry for more than 50 years, the MMC was convinced that the reduction in actual competition that resulted from the mergers was far more important than the impact of potential competition. It believed that the enhancement in the size of the incumbent operator as a result of merger would increase the threat of retaliation against any potential entrants, which would therefore be deterred. As a result, market power would increase. Although the MMC's interpretation in these cases is open to question, not least because the industry had been highly unprofitable since deregulation and physical entry barriers are slight, it illustrates its great scepticism of the applicability of contestability analysis once the 'perfect' conditions do not prevail. In view of the non-robustness of the theory, this scepticism seems justified.

IV   Strategic behaviour by dominant firms

The reasons given by the MMC for concluding that four of the merger cases involving local bus markets were likely to operate against the public interest provide a convenient link to the subject matter of the present section. The MMC was convinced that the merged companies would be able to intimidate potential entrants by reason of their size and established position. It considered that a 'main deterrent to entry would ... seem to be the ability of the existing operator to retaliate against a new entrant, by lowering fares, or increasing frequency, or retiming or rerouting services' (MMC, 1990a, para. 7.47). Elsewhere, in its reports on alleged anticompetitive behaviour in the same industry, the OFT has reinforced this argument by emphasizing the importance of asymmetric information as between the incumbent and the entrant:

> Asymmetries in information are likely to be very important in the bus industry where 50 years of regulation have conditioned operators to accept a lack of direct competition as the status quo so that new entrants are likely to be unsure about how existing

operators will respond to competition. In this situation, existing operators have an incentive to build up a reputation for toughness in the face of competition in order to deter new entrants. (OFT, 1989, para. 5.9)

These views expressed by the antitrust authorities reflect part of a rapidly growing literature on the strategic behaviour of dominant firms. The use of resources by the incumbent may be designed to worsen the profit expectations of a potential entrant. The fact that resources are committed makes the threat credible and entry is forestalled. What distinguishes most forms of strategic behaviour discussed in this section is thus their focus on commitment to possible future behaviour by the dominant firm designed to deter entry rather than actions aimed at removing or coercing existing rivals.

The case which the OFT had in mind, however, is the one already mentioned in the previous chapter when we were discussing predatory pricing: the incumbent commits resources to the destruction of an entrant not merely to remove the current competitor but to establish the belief amongst future possible entrants that they will meet the same fate. To the extent that the incumbent reinforces its commitment by actually using predatory pricing against an entrant to establish its reputation for toughness, the case is exceptional when compared with most other strategies discussed below. Most of the strategies involve what Spence (1981) terms 'positioning' as opposed to 'reaction' moves. The former are undertaken before entry, the latter after entry has occurred. As we observed when discussing investment in surplus capacity in the previous chapter, 'positioning' moves may appear innocent and part of the normal competitive process to an outside observer. It may thus be extremely difficult for an antitrust authority to determine whether they amount to an attempt to monopolize an industry (according to the Sherman Act) or to an abuse of a dominant position (under Article 82).

In what follows, we discuss a number of such strategies including the aggressive use of the learning curve, research and development (R & D) allied to pre-emptive patenting, and brand proliferation and excessive advertising. For convenience, the strategies are discussed separately but, of course, in practice firms may use a number of them simultaneously.

Where an industry experiences significant learning effects, an incumbent firm may legitimately claim that its allegedly uncompetitive prices can be justified and, although they may have a deterrent effect, they are not predatory. The argument proceeds as follows: where production of a complex product involves the replication of the same series of operations, it has frequently been observed that unit costs fall as the cumulative output rises, even though technology remains unchanged. Increasing experience of production, for example, may improve work lay-out and sequence as well as reducing material wastage. Although difficult to measure empirically with any precision, in some cases the reductions are thought to be considerable, possibly of the order of a 15 per cent fall for a doubling of output (Spence, 1981). In commercial aircraft production the figure is reckoned to be as much as 20 per cent (Tyson, 1992).

To the extent that such savings are unique to a firm and not transferable to others, there is a clear incentive for an incumbent to move rapidly down the learning curve by producing large outputs in the initial stages of a product's development. If learning effects are substantial, it is possible that the cost advantage they confer over rivals may persist well into the mature phase of the product life cycle. The extent of the initial advantage will clearly depend not only on the size of the savings that can be made but also on the rapidity with which the firm can realize them. Where costs are a function of cumulative output, the marginal cost is not measured by the marginal cost of current output but by the difference between marginal cost and the present value of all future cost reductions created by the production of that output. Consequently, where learning effects are present, the firm may set its prices at what appear to be an especially low level. It is thus likely to make it particularly difficult to distinguish low prices influenced by prospective learning effects from predatory pricing. Consumers gain from paying lower prices sooner rather than later, but the antitrust concern is that knowledge of the initial cost advantage achieved by the incumbent will keep entrants out so that price never falls to the competitive level.

In a somewhat similar vein, Gilbert (1981) and Gilbert and Newbery (1982) have argued that a dominant firm may have a direct profit incentive for accelerating R & D expenditures in order to acquire what Judge Learned Hand termed 'pre-emptive patents' in the celebrated Alcoa antitrust case in the USA.[11] In markets where the incumbent firm has enjoyed monopoly profits and where there is the expectation that R & D effort will produce patentable cost-reducing inventions, there is a profit incentive for the existing firm to use such expenditures strategically. The essence of the argument depends on the result that monopoly profit is higher than the joint profit shared by non-colluding oligopolists. The incumbent firm then has more to gain by protecting its position against entry (by increasing R & D and patenting the results) than has a potential entrant which, if successful, would have to share the total profit with the previous incumbent. The incumbent's expenditures are therefore greater than they would be in the absence of the entry threat, in order to secure a long-term gain in the form of monopoly profits.

Two observations can be made about this analysis. First, it only applies where patent protection is effective against entrants. However, as Gilbert (1981) admits, 'In view of the very limited monopoly power afforded by patents in most industries, pre-emptive patenting could occur in only exceptional circumstances'; and again, 'In the vast majority of industries, a wide range of technological alternatives in a given product area rules out pre-emption as a credible strategy to maintain monopoly (pp. 211, 228). We are left, therefore, with perhaps a comparatively small group of industries where patent protection is significant enough to allow incumbent firms to use such strategies. In some other cases, multiple patenting by the incumbent may raise potential entrants' costs by forcing them to undertake higher R & D expenditures than would otherwise be necessary in order to find ways round the legal stockade. Secondly, the implicit assumption is that any cost-reducing innovations are comparatively modest and would not threaten the complete elimination of the incumbent firm if introduced by an entrant. In the more dramatic case of a significant shift in cost functions, it has been shown by Arrow (1962) that a competitive market structure generates greater profit incentives to innovate than a monopoly. In this more fundamental (but comparatively rare) case an incumbent monopolist has a prospective future profit equal to the difference between its former monopoly profit and the 'new' monopoly profit produced if the profound innovation is made. In contrast, for existing and potential entrants in a competitive environment, the prize for the successful innovator will be the entire monopoly profit.

Advertising and product differentiation may provide rich opportunities for incumbent firms to attempt to protect their position against the threat of new entry. Hilke and Nelson (1984), for example, have pointed out that, in consumer goods markets, the use of various advertising strategies by the incumbent firms are likely to be used immediately prior to the attempted entry, particularly when the entrant is trying to establish the reputation of its brands amongst consumers. They have two lines of argument. First, there is a good deal of psychological evidence that the absorption of new information may be seriously impaired if individuals are suddenly confronted by large increases in data. They are likely to suffer from what the authors term 'information overload' (p. 367). Thus, if advertising in a market is normally reckoned to be the most efficient means of communicating product information, the efforts of an entrant firm may be frustrated and it may be forced to use more costly methods if the incumbent firm significantly increases its own advertising expenditure immediately prior to and during the launch of the entrant's products. The effect may be reinforced if, as seems plausible, consumers are most likely to experiment with a different product when it is new. Heavy promotional expenditure by the incumbent firm immediately following new entry may therefore adversely affect the entrant's long-run costs of supplying information to consumers. In subsequent periods, their advertising expenditures are higher than they would otherwise have been, because it is then more difficult to persuade consumers to switch brands. To the extent that such policies by the incumbent are successful, there are again the adverse consequences for allocative efficiency but there are also the social costs that result from the additional advertising both by the incumbent firm in the entry period and by surviving entrants in subsequent periods.

An analysis by Schmalensee (1978) emphasizing brand proliferation sustained by advertising reaches rather similar conclusions. In his analysis, Schmalensee assumes that there are increasing returns in production at the brand level, that there is inter-brand rivalry and relative brand immobility in product space.[12] He argues that established firms will be able to increase the number of brands sold in concentrated markets for differentiated products to the point where insufficient 'product space' remains for entrant firms to gain a viable market share. In such markets, where existing firms are reasonably confident that their established rivals' competitive responses will take non-price forms, he concludes that 'brand proliferation' will be a credible entry-deterring strategy. If the brands of existing firms are all in place prior to entry there is little likelihood that, should entry actually occur, any of the brands will move within product space, given their relative immobility. The entrant cannot therefore reckon on any reduction in the number of brands to increase profitability, if it should enter. Even if it is successful in getting an existing brand removed from the market, 'the favoured demand positions of established brands ensure that any entrant that imposed losses on an established brand would incur greater losses itself' (ibid.).

The strategies discussed above were meant to be illustrative rather than exhaustive. For much more detailed treatments, the reader is referred to Porter (1980, 1985) and Salop (1981). A number of general points emerge from the discussion when considering the implications for antitrust policy. First, all aspects of 'positioning' behaviour are concerned with entry deterrence as compared with 'reactive' behaviour which analyses competitive responses once entry has occurred. If such strategic behaviour is successful, entry is deterred but there are no 'victims' in the sense of firms which have directly suffered as a result of the incumbent's actions. There are therefore unlikely to be any 'smoking guns' which antitrust authorities could produce as evidence of exclusionary behaviour. Furthermore, as Baumol has argued when discussing the implications of the theory of contestable markets, the lack of entry to a market, even over a considerable length of time, may not signify high entry barriers and successful entry-deterring strategies used by incumbent firms (Baumol, 1982). On the contrary, if the market is 'contestable', lack of entry may signify the influence that potential competition is having upon existing firms which are constrained to maintain prices at 'competitive' levels. A dominant firm may thus be able to mount a persuasive case against the argument that it has abused its position, especially given the ambiguity that may surround recorded profit levels (to which we referred in Chapter 4) and the precise importance of sunk costs in particular markets.

Secondly, if competition policy appears to be effective against 'reactive' behaviour (overt actions taken by dominant firms once entry has occurred), incumbent firms may increasingly seek to achieve the same objective by 'positioning' since this, for the most part, has the appearance of desirable and normal business practice and is also likely to be much more difficult to pin down within the confines of existing antitrust laws. As Spence puts it: 'To the extent that probabilities against predatory behavior constrain firms' reactions to entrants, the prohibitions will increase the incentive for firms to make prior investments that reduce the need for aggressive reactions to deter entry' (Spence, 1981, p. 56).

Thirdly, while increasing attention to 'positioning' behaviour may in future have to be paid by competition policy authorities, it is not at all clear what this will involve and what effective remedies can be invoked. Spence is sceptical that 'prohibitions against predatory responses to potential entrants would have any material effect on the performance of this type of industry' (ibid. p. 59) while Schmalensee (1982b) concludes that 'recent theoretical work suggests that in many policy areas (such as tying contracts and entry deterrence) there may exist no workable rules that are generally efficiency enhancing'. As far as US antitrust policy is concerned, he recommends that the authorities should 'at least hesitate to bring cases in which there does not exist a specific relief proposal likely to enhance efficiency' (ibid., p. 27).

More generally, Williamson (1987) has argued that, where dominant firms have a well established position gained through good judgement or good fortune, they may be especially difficult to dislodge, whether or not they have resorted to strategic behaviour or infringed the antitrust laws. In such circumstances he was prepared to recommend a policy of selective dissolution in order to restore competition and improve allocative efficiency. At the time he was originally writing, the policy did have considerable support (at least in the USA, where the proposal got as far as a Deconcentration Act). Subsequently, however, and particularly during the Reagan presidencies, there was a sharp change of approach, with a major emphasis on non-intervention and curtailment of antitrust activity (Mueller, 1986; Williamson, 1987).

Dominant firms found to have abused their position have always created problems for antitrust authorities. What the recent theoretical analyses of strategic behaviour have underlined, however, is that these difficulties may be more intractable than previously thought, from the point of view of both diagnosis and ultimate remedy. In the next section we attempt to illustrate this point with some antitrust cases which have involved strategic behaviour.

V   Strategic behaviour in antitrust cases

Long before the recent upsurge of theoretical interest in strategic behaviour, commentators on antitrust policy were aware of the complexity of the issues involved. Neale and Goyder (1980) summarize succinctly the position taken by the US antitrust authorities as follows:

It is legitimate to 'make a better mousetrap', using all the skill, foresight and energy at your command, even though monopoly power accrues; but if skill and energy are reinforced with business stratagems that are directed to competitive advantage and power rather than productive efficiency as such, there comes a point where unlawful purpose is revealed. The root of the matter is just how much stratagem is within reason and at what point it becomes an intent to monopolise. (p. 106)

It is significant that this quotation is taken from their discussion of the Alcoa case,[13] one of the most frequently cited, but perhaps least followed, of all US antitrust actions involving a dominant firm. At the time, much discussion focused on the definition of the relevant market and Alcoa's share (cf. Chapter 4, Section III). In the event, Judge Hand settled on a somewhat narrow interpretation which gave Alcoa a share of about 90 per cent of production which, according to the judgement, brought it considerable market power. More germane to the present context, however, was the discussion of Alcoa's market conduct which appeared to change the possession of market power into the offence of monopolizing the market. It was accepted that under certain circumstances a firm may unwittingly find itself in sole possession of a market without having committed any antitrust offence. One example would be where limited demand interacting with economies of scale produced natural monopoly. Another case might be where a change in taste away from the product leads to the elimination of all competitors except one which remained in the market through 'superior skill, foresight and industry'.

However, Judge Hand saw Alcoa's position, which had remained largely unchanged since 1912, in quite a different light. The retention of its dominance was, in his view, not fortuitous but resulted 'from a persistent determination to maintain control'. There then followed the highly controversial and often quoted passage which seems to fit very closely the entry-deterring strategy referred to in Chapter 5 (Section IV and Figure 5.4):

The only question [about Alcoa's market conduct] is whether it falls within the exception established in favor of those who do not seek, but cannot avoid, the control of the market. It seems to us that the question scarcely survives its statement. It was not inevitable that it should always anticipate increases in the demand for ingot and be prepared to supply them. Nothing compelled it to keep doubling and redoubling its capacity before others entered the field. It insists that it never excluded competitors; *but we can think of no more effective exclusion than progressively to embrace each new opportunity as it opened, and to face every newcomer with new capacity already geared into a great organisation, having the advantage of experience, trade connections and the elite of personnel.* Only in case we interpret 'exclusion' as limited to maneuvers not honestly industrial, but actuated solely by a desire to prevent completion, can such a course, indefatigably pursued, be deemed not 'exclusionary'. So to limit it would in our judgment emasculate the Act; would permit such consolidations as it was designed to prevent. (*United States* v. *Aluminum Co. of America,* 148 F2d 416 (1945), emphasis added)

It is not difficult to see in this part of the judgement elements of both the investment in surplus capacity analysis and the aggressive use of the learning curve. What might be regarded as prudent business practice in a firm with a more modest market share was, according to Judge Hand, monopolizing behaviour when used by a firm already in possession of market power. In other words, the 'stratagems' used consistently by Alcoa went beyond the normal 'skill, foresight and industry' that a firm might legitimately use to its own advantage, and into the realm where it used them to maintain its market power.

The difficulty with Judge Hand's interpretation is that it is not clear what alternative conduct is open to a firm once it has attained a substantial market share through its own energy and efficiency. Does it then stay its hand and compete less actively than before and allow others to encroach on its market? In this case it might forestall any future antitrust action but at the cost of becoming internally slack. The losses to consumers from this development may then be greater than those which resulted from the firm's previous conduct, since internal slack will affect the whole of the firm's output and lead to higher prices.

In the event, Judge Hand was saved from having to follow through the full implications of his judgement of Alcoa's market conduct (which may have involved divestiture) by delaying any remedial measures until after the government had disposed of those aluminium plants built up during the Second World War. The programme resulted in the entry of two viable competitors to Alcoa (Kaiser and Reynolds) and the structure of the industry was then judged to be suitably competitive, although not without strong reservations from some economists (Adams, 1951). Subsequent judgements in dominant firm cases proceeded along more conventional lines and the core of the Alcoa decision never became the centrepiece of a new antitrust approach.

A much more recent US case before the Federal Trade Commission has focused directly and explicitly on strategic issues. It is of particular relevance in the present context because it assesses Du Pont's market conduct in the light of the recent theoretical discussion of predatory and strategic behaviour, citing a number of the papers mentioned in Section IV above. The case involved the expansion of the company's business in titanium dioxide pigments (used as a whitening agent in paints, plastics and paper).[14] The FTC was appealing against a decision by an administrative law judge who had found Du Pont not guilty of unfair methods of competition and practices by using its dominant position to monopolize the market. Most of the facts of the case were agreed by the parties, but their interpretation was disputed.

Just as in Alcoa, the crux of the case was whether Du Pont's strategy of building additional plant to meet forecast growth in demand should be interpreted as natural and efficient business practice or whether, given their position in the market, it amounted to an attempt to forestall entry and frustrate the growth of existing competitors. At the beginning of the period most relevant to the case (1972–7) Du Pont had a market share of about 30 per cent. By 1977, after the crucial expansion of its plant, its share stood at 42 per cent and at the time of the judgement (1980), it was forecasting a share of 55 per cent by 1985. Although its opening share of less than a third would not normally be regarded as 'dominant', nevertheless it was argued that Du Pont's conduct amounted to an attempt to monopolize the market. To sustain this argument, three points in the Du Pont strategy were emphasized. First, the expansion of capacity, while not in excess of anticipated demand, was such as to meet the company's growth objective only by pre-empting any expansion by competitors through the strategic announcement and start-up of the new plant. In addition it was claimed that, because the technology changed as the scale of operations increased, without the advantage of large-scale operations no competitor would be able to match the acknowledged Du Pont cost advantage of 'learning by doing'.

Secondly, it was argued that Du Pont had exploited its cost advantage by pricing its products high enough to finance the planned expansion but low enough to discourage rival firms from expanding their capacity. The strategy was underpinned by 'exaggerated announcements' of their expansion intentions from Du Pont. Thirdly, Du Pont refused to license the technology which it had previously developed and which now gave it a significant cost advantage over its rivals.

Thus the complaints in this case contained several elements emphasized in the analysis of strategic behaviour by dominant firms: building capacity ahead of demand and making known to rivals and potential rivals the implications for output, plus the exploitation of additional cost savings generated by moving rapidly down the learning curve. If the assessment of the case had followed the lead of Judge Hand in Alcoa, the decision would probably have gone against Du Pont. In that case, it would subsequently have had an important influence on the market conduct of dominant firms. Fortunately for both Du Pont and other large enterprises, the appeal was dismissed.

In the present context, the most important facet of the decision was the way in which each part of the Du Pont strategy was examined and found to have a legitimate business explanation. As far as the first two points outlined above were concerned, the Commission was convinced that there was no evidence 'that Du Pont planned to build excess capacity or that its plans to fulfil the foreseen demand with new and expanded plants were inconsistent with scale economies' (Salop, 1981, Appendix, p. 7). Having reviewed previous legal cases which raised somewhat similar issues, the Commission concluded that 'in the present case, Du Pont's conduct appears to be justified by [its] cost superiority over its rivals, demand forecasts and scale economies. There is no evidence that Du Pont's pricing or capacity strategies were unprofitable (regardless of the cost test employed) and ... the plant announcements do not appear to be misleading' (p. 38). On the last point the Commission was convinced that the reasons for announcing in advance plans for expanding capacity were mainly the long lead time required for obtaining environmental permits and completing construction. The firm had learned from an earlier experience when, for environmental reasons, it had had to abandon construction plans on its preferred site and settle for an inferior location where it also encountered strong resistance (p. 16). Furthermore, its customers were anxious for reassurance that Du Pont would be able to meet increasing demands and this also worked against exaggerated or distorted claims (p. 50). In the circumstances of the case, the Commission also saw no reason why Du Pont should have licensed its superior technology and thus allowed competitors to close the gap in costs more rapidly. It had acquired the know-how through its efforts and any imposition of a duty to license might serve to chill the very kind of innovative process that led to Du Pont's cost advantage (p. 49).

What comes through in this judgement, as in the Alcoa case, is the fine line that there is likely to be between strategic behaviour which is anticompetitive and exclusionary, and competitive behaviour which is legitimate and efficiency-enhancing. The Commission thus looked closely at whether Du Pont both built plant which took advantage of all scale economies and then used the plant at or near to its designed capacity. Satisfied on these points, it was then able to conclude that the company's efficiency rationale for its conduct, along with its announcements, was justified. However, nothing in the judgement precludes the possibility that, in other cases, where dominant enterprises have been less cautious in their approach to capacity plans and forecast demand, the judgement would go the other way.

The Commission's view is summed up as follows:

> Antitrust policy wisely disfavors monopoly, but it also seeks to promote vigorous competitive behavior. Indeed the essence of the competitive process is to induce firms to become more efficient and to pass the benefits of the efficiency along to consumers. That process would be ill-served by using antitrust to block hard, aggressive competition that is solidly based on efficiencies and growth opportunities, even if monopoly is a possible result. (p. 51)

A similar view has ultimately prevailed in other cases brought in the late 1970s and early 1980s which sought in one way or another to extend the reach of antitrust to cope with more complex forms of behaviour. One irony of this development was the great stimulus it gave to theoretical modelling of some of the problems involved, without as yet having a direct impact on antitrust outcomes in the USA, while in the UK and EU, apart from some attempts to deal with the problem of predatory pricing, which we discussed in Chapter 5, no cases have so far had to grapple with other complex questions of strategic behaviour.

Of the three other US examples to which we can refer briefly, two concerned innovation and the responsibilities of a dominant firm, while the third involved the brand proliferation strategies of a group of oligopolists. A number of cases in the 1970s were brought against IBM and had as a key characteristic the allegedly anticompetitive effects of innovation against a background of systems (as opposed to product) rivalry. Thus IBM produced whole systems involving a central processing unit linked to a number of peripheral devices such as memory units, tape drives and disks. Rival firms had grown up supplying these peripherals which were compatible with IBM central processing units. However, several manufacturers of peripherals brought actions for treble damages against IBM because of its methods of reacting to their competition.[15] In particular, if the main manufacturer introduces an entirely new system with units incompatible with those of its rivals, their continued ability to compete in the final system market could depend on the continued availability of compatible units. As Ordover and Willig (1981b, p. 348) point out, this situation can lead to a double disadvantage for the rival firms. First, if the new system is superior to the old, demand for the old system will tend to decline even if prices remain unchanged. Secondly, the innovator can raise the prices of the old system either by increasing the prices of the old components that are compatible with those of its rivals' equipment or by withdrawing the old components altogether.

Clearly in some cases the introduction of a new system will lead to net benefits to consumers and an improvement in social welfare. In others, however, the situation may be more ambiguous; the 'innovation' may serve mainly to weaken the competition. For antitrust policy purposes, it is important to be able to distinguish the two.[16] So far the courts in the USA have come down in favour of the innovator. For example in *Telex*, the initial verdict in favour of the plaintiff (and the award of $260 million damages) was overturned on appeal. In essence the Court held that IBM's response to competition was 'well within the boundaries of permitted competition'. A similar view was taken in *California Computer Products*.

The second example involving 'systems' rivalry and innovation had an equally well known defendant. In 1972, Kodak, the dominant firm in the markets for cameras and films, introduced a new pocket instamatic camera which required a new type of film. Berkey, a rival producer of cameras and processor of films, claimed that, because it had had no prior notice of Kodak's innovation and the film, it was unable for a long while to produce a suitable new camera of its own to take the special film. It therefore argued that, because of Kodak's dominant position in both camera and film markets, it had a duty to pre-notify competitors of any change in film format which might affect competition. The 'system' in this case was thus the complementary film and camera. The court ruled, however, that the antitrust laws imposed no duty on a firm, even a dominant firm, to disclose in advance information about their innovations which might allow rivals to continue to compete successfully in the future.

The courts have thus so far resisted that part of the argument in *Alcoa* which suggested that dominant firms embracing each new opportunity as it arose were effectively using their market power to exclude competitors. They apparently see a greater danger in the possibility that successful treble damages suits against firms with market power may force the latter into providing a cosy but inefficient environment for their competitors.

The last case we shall consider involved the leading manufacturers of breakfast cereals in the USA. The case had a number of interesting features, not least that in it the Federal Trade Commission sought to establish the charge of monopolization against a group of oligopolists rather than a single firm. Those originally involved in the case were Kellogg, with a market share of 45 per cent (in 1970), General Mills, with 21 per cent, General Foods, with 15 per cent, and Quaker, with 9 per cent.[17] The FTC sought the dramatic remedies of divestment into eight more evenly sized firms as well as compulsory licensing of cereal products and trademarks.

In the present context the most significant aspect of the case was the FTC's emphasis on the role of brand proliferation in deterring entry to a market where post-tax rates of return on capital had averaged more than twice the level for manufacturing industry over the period 1958–70 (Scherer and Ross, 1990, p. 465). Between 1950 and 1971, the number of nationally distributed brands marketed by the six leading firms rose from 27 to 74, and the FTC sought to establish that the effect, if not the purpose, of this increase was to deter the entry of new competitors.[18] The principal effects of brand proliferation, according to Scherer and Ross, were well known to marketing managers in consumers' products firms and from 1978 onwards Schmalensee's well-worked-out model of the process was also available. In the event, however, even before the controversial ending of the case, the judge had determined practically every substantive point in favour of the companies and it was eventually dismissed without the complete appeals procedure being fully employed as is usual in important cases.[19]

The US antitrust system, being the oldest and most highly developed, might be expected to be most sensitive to new analytical insights from economic theory. In one sense this is true, in that the economists helping to prepare cases on the government side are certainly familiar with these developments and in some cases have themselves made significant contributions.[20] As yet, however, the courts have not been convinced that pre-commitment of resources and the subsequent market conduct by a dominant firm have been sufficient to constitute monopolization of an industry. The central problem, as we anticipated in Section IV above, is that the conduct will appear to a third party as pro-competitive and probably welfare-enhancing rather than a buttress of market power.

VI Conclusion

The role of potential competition as opposed to actual competition in constraining the behaviour of dominant firms has long fascinated economic theorists and frustrated policy makers. Two recent developments in economic analysis underline this point: the theory of contestable markets and the strategic behaviour of dominant firms vis-à-vis potential entrants.

Despite misgivings about its robustness, contestability theory was rapidly applied to US policy making, particularly at a crucial stage in the development of the civil aviation industry post-deregulation. Several large mergers were allowed, mainly on the strength of contestability analysis, despite the presence of considerable barriers to entry in the relevant markets. In the UK, although the theory was much discussed in the period immediately prior to the privatization and (partial) deregulation of the large public utilities, in the event it has not featured prominently in any antitrust decisions. Indeed in the deregulated local bus industry, which has greatly exercised the antitrust authorities since 1986, its applicability has been implicitly rejected.

The second development, exploring strategic behaviour, has led to an explosion in the theoretical literature but has so far had very little positive impact on antitrust decisions, despite the arguments of bodies like the FTC and the impetus given to some theoretical contributions by US cases. Writing originally in 1983, Williamson expected that 'antitrust enforcement regarding strategic behaviour will be in much better shape at the end of the decade as a result of intervening scholarship' (Williamson, 1987, p. 343). With the possible exception of predatory pricing, which we discussed in Chapter 5, his optimism has so far proved unfounded. In particular, antitrust authorities are no closer to having ground rules about whether the focus of their attention should be on ex ante investments or on ex post contingent responses. Similarly, very little progress has been made on the question of what remedies should be sought if strategic behaviour is found to have impaired competition. Both of the developments discussed in this chapter, however, lead us to concur with Williamson's final conclusion of the continued need for a strong antitrust policy.

Notes
1. See Baumol *et al.* (1982).
2. The results for markets with one firm are slightly modified, but for most purposes can be regarded in the same way.
3. The significance of this decision can be judged by the price American and United were prepared to pay purely for these rights, $445 million and $290 million, respectively (*Financial Times*, 22 May, 1991).
4. The point is not quite as universal as is suggested in the text. Where demand over a small area is especially high (for example, the City of London), it may be feasible to establish a new network.
5. This assumes that all long-distance companies are competing for the same group of customers. If, however, some specialize in long-distance business calls, while others cater for the

'domestic' market, the local company may have scope for discriminatory pricing, as discussed in the previous chapter.

6. Mergers are discussed fully in Chapters 8 and 9. They are considered here as an example of the way contestable market analysis affected US policy.

7. Prior to the Airline Deregulation Act of 1978, the CAB had overall authority for the structure, conduct and performance of the US civil aviation industry. In particular it had responsibility for entry, exit, fares, services and mergers.

8. Booking agents have increasingly used a computerized system to display seat availabilities on particular flights. They will tend to make bookings from amongst the first half-dozen or so flights shown on the display. Airlines that can ensure that their flights are always shown amongst the first will retain or enlarge their market shares at the expense of new entrants. By the early 1980s, the systems provided by three airlines included more than 90 per cent of all computerized travel agents. In the opinion of one distinguished observer, attempts to regulate the use of computer systems to prevent such biases are almost inevitably doomed to failure (Fisher, 1987b).

9. Including British Telecom (1984), British Gas (1986), British Airports (1987), water companies (1989), electricity supply and distribution (1990), railways (1996–7), as well as British Airways (1987) and the National Bus Company (1988).

10. Examples from other industries, especially their mergers, will be discussed in later chapters.

11. The case is discussed in Section V below.

12. The analogy is with a group of firms at different locations competing within the same geographic area. Firms producing a number of brands may compete within the same product space.

13. *United States* v. *Aluminum Co. of America*, 148 F2d 416 (1945).

14. The transcript of the case is reproduced as an appendix in Salop (1981). Page references are to this source.

15. For example, *California Computer Products Inc.* v. *International Business Machines Corp*, 613 F2d 727 (9 Cir 1979); *Telex Corp.* v. *International Business Machines Corp*, 510 F2d 894 (10 Cir. 1975).

16. Ordover and Willig's paper is an attempt to establish a framework for making these distinctions.

17. Quaker was dropped from the case in 1978.

18. In this respect it was similar to an earlier UK antitrust investigation into the duopolistic detergent market where the very heavy levels of advertising and large number of brands were seen as a major deterrent to entry to even large petrochemical companies, despite being highly profitable to the participants (MMC, 1966b).

19. The outcome of the case had become politically sensitive in the run-up to the presidential election and Congress had been subject to intense lobbying. For details, see Scherer and Ross (1990).

20. At an important time for these developments, Steven Salop, for example, was Associate Director at the FTC.

7 Market dominance and collusion

I Introduction

It was clearly seen in Chapter 3 that overt collusion received the greatest degree of unanimity of treatment by the three antitrust jurisdictions. Agreements to restrict the terms of trading (covering price, output, rebates, discounts and so on) are per se illegal under Section I of the Sherman Act and Article 81 of the EU Treaty. In the UK the new Competition Act incorporates in its Chapter 1 a similar prohibition. Why is there this unanimity of approach to collusion while for single-firm dominance or merger policies are much more varied? A large part of the answer to this question is that the economic analysis of overt collusion gives much more unequivocal results than it does, say, for horizontal mergers where, as we shall see in the next chapter, complicated trade-offs may be involved.

As in much else, Adam Smith anticipated these conclusions more than 200 years ago in what has become the second most quoted passage from the *Wealth of Nations*:

> People of the same trade seldom meet together, even for merriment and diversion, but the conversation ends in a conspiracy against the public, or in some contrivance to raise prices. It is impossible to prevent such meetings, by any law which could be executed, or would be consistent with liberty and justice. But although the law cannot hinder people of the same trade from sometimes assembling together it ought to do nothing to facilitate such assemblies; much less to render them necessary. (Smith, 1776, as given in the Glasgow edition, 1979)

The contrivances they may use to raise prices above competitive levels are likely to generate several different types of inefficiency, if, that is, they are successful. Thus prices above costs will create allocative inefficiency and generate welfare losses and income transfers. To the extent that the collusive price guarantees higher-cost firms positive profits and slows the mechanism for reallocating resources towards lower-cost firms, technical efficiency suffers. Since successful collusion removes active competition, the longer it persists the greater the likelihood that members of the group will become internally slack or X-inefficient. Many would argue further that for the same reason collusion will tend to blunt incentives for innovation and hence impair technical progress. On this point, however, there is less agreement, since some economists have argued persuasively that in some industries collaboration among firms is a necessary condition for innovation.

In previous chapters of Part II we have been concerned with single-firm dominance and its likely effects. In this chapter we focus on the attempts of a group of firms to achieve essentially the same outcome. The centre of our attention is on the conditions that facilitate successful collusion and those that might cause it to break down. At first glance it may seem intuitively obvious that, if firms acting individually in a market cannot achieve a monopoly price and profit, they will rapidly choose the next best option, which may be a share in a monopoly profit earned by a group acting collectively. Indeed, at least one very illustrious economic theorist came to just such a conclusion. Chamberlin (1933), impressed by the implausibility of oligopoly analysis at the time (whereby individual firms were assumed to optimize their output or price in the belief that their decisions would have no affect on others), argued that they were much more likely to learn that their individual position could be improved by tacit collusion. He concluded that, under certain circumstances, especially where the number of competitors was small, a group of oligopolists would achieve a monopoly result.[1] Since then much effort has been expended in trying to pin down precisely when overt and tacit collusion will succeed and whether or not the weight of the law is required to minimize the impact.

The chapter proceeds as follows: Section II contains an analysis of the incentives to collude; Section III discusses the problems that collusion is likely to encounter, whether it is legal or illegal, secret or overt, with an emphasis on the need for agreement, compliance and monitoring if it is to persist. In Section IV, we consider some famous cases that have featured in the USA, the EU and the UK.

II   The incentive to collude

We begin with the simplest case and deal subsequently with more complex cases. Assume initially that there are a large number of firms with identical costs producing a homogeneous product. There are no barriers to entry. Under these circumstances we know from simple competitive analysis that the sum of all firms' short-run marginal cost curves forms the industry supply curve. Panel (b) of Figure 7.1 shows the market demand curve and this supply curve. The market would clear at the competitive price P_c with a total output sold of Q_c. Panel (a) shows the position of the typical profit-maximizing firm. In the short run it could produce q_c of the industry output which is sold at the market price, P_c. The firm thus makes a short-term positive profit of $P_c bed$. In these circumstances why should such a firm contemplate giving up some of its independence by participating in a collusive group? The answer is that, while no one firm acting independently could improve its profits (any single-handed attempt to raise price would fail as customers switched to other firms), if they act collectively they can participate in a monopoly profit.

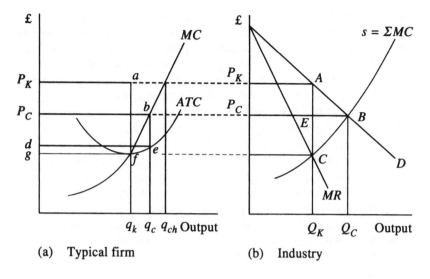

Figure 7.1 Collusion to raise price

Assume now that all existing firms agree to meet to fix the industry price and to persuade the government to introduce regulations preventing further entry to the industry.[2] Both conditions are met. At the meeting the firms agree to raise the product price to the monopoly level P_K which means that industry output has to be reduced to Q_K. The new price is determined by the intersection of the supply curve and the marginal revenue curve, *MR* (Figure 7.1, panel (b)). For the firm this implies that it has to reduce its output from q_c to q_k. If all firms reduce their output in the same fashion marginal costs will be the same across all firms and costs for producing the cartel output, Q_K, are minimized. The profit earned by the typical firm at the new monopoly price is P_K *afg* and must exceed the previous profit earned by the firm since (with unchanged cost curves) the monopoly profit for the whole industry exceeds the total profit of all firms when they priced competitively. Given our second assumption that the government is persuaded to block further entry to the market, there is in principle no reason why such profits should not persist into the long term. We can also observe from panel (b) of Figure 7.1 that the price increase causes a deadweight welfare loss of *ABC*. Part of this, *ABE*, was previously consumer's surplus and the other part, *BCE*, was producer's surplus. Thus the formation of the collusive agreement creates allocative inefficiency.

Even in this simple case, however, with rather stringent assumptions, the agreement may not persist (hence our caution when referring above to long-term monopoly gains). The heart of the problem can be illustrated by referring again to Figure 7.1, panel (a). Under the agreement the typical firm is expected to restrict its output to q_k, for which it receives a price of P_K per unit. Since the individual firm under current assumptions supplies only a fraction of the total output, it may reason as follows: 'Any additional output we produce over the range q_k–q_{ch} will increase our revenue more than our cost (that is, P_K > marginal cost) and hence increase our profits. As we are only one of many firms, the risk of our being identified as the culprit violating the agreement is very small. We will therefore sell more than q_k, even if it means shading our price below P_K. As long as price is greater than marginal cost it is worth our while.'

The flaw in this reasoning, of course, is that, if a number of firms think the same way, total industry output will exceed Q_K and the collusive price P_K will collapse. As more and more firms increase their output either initially, because they wish to cheat, or subsequently when they realize that they cannot sell their output at the agreed price because of cheating by others, the market price will decline towards the competitive level. Hence the claim made by a number of observers that collusive agreements are inherently unstable.

III   The problems of collusion

The argument is strengthened if more realistic cases are considered. Suppose, first, that firms in the market have differing rather than identical costs, but attempt to arrive at a price agreement similar to that described above. The problem can be illustrated in the duopoly (two-firm) case, but the principle extends to the more general case where the market is served by the two groups of firms, those with low costs and those with high costs.[3] In Figure 7.2 the marginal cost conditions for the high-cost firm and the low-cost firm are shown in panels (a) and (b), respectively.[4] In panel (c) industry demand and marginal revenue are shown as D and MR, respectively. The industry supply curve is formed by summing the two marginal cost curves horizontally. The profit-maximizing price for the colluding firms is P_K for a total output of Q_K. How should this output be allocated between the two firms? To ensure that the costs of producing Q_K are minimized, outputs should be allocated between the two firms so that marginal costs at that output are equal, that is, $MC_A = MC_B$. On this basis firm A would be expected to produce an output q_A and firm B an output q_B. At price P_K this would yield firm A a total profit of *abcd* (the difference between total revenue and total cost) while firm B could earn the much larger amount of *efgh*. The incentive to cheat identified above is increased. Both firms can observe that additional sales made at or near P_K would add more to their revenues than their costs and hence increase their profits, but in addition firm A is likely to feel disgruntled that its output quota and profit-making capacity are much smaller than those of firm B. This point is very much strengthened if we regard the industry as consisting of a large number of high-cost and low-cost firms, of which those shown in Figure 7.2 are typical examples. In this

case, as we observed above, individual firms will reckon that the risk of identification as a cheater will be relatively slight. Thus where costs differ substantially the incentive for firms to cheat is increased, unless additional
provisions are made for reconciling the aims of all members. We refer below
to some methods that have been used to try and counter this problem.

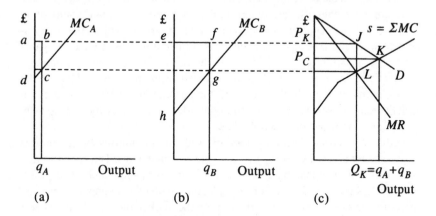

Figure 7.2   Duopoly with differing costs

A second factor concerns entry conditions to the market. Adam Smith was
acute enough to realize that governments ought to do nothing to facilitate
collusive agreement although for a variety of reasons they frequently ignore
this advice. However, in markets where firms cannot rely on government intervention to protect them from fresh competition and where their own efforts
(perhaps in the form of strategic behaviour, as discussed in the previous chapter)
prove unsuccessful, collusive agreements will suffer a further source of
instability. The whole point of the agreement is to raise price to the monopoly
level in order to enjoy the abnormal profits that result. In the absence of an
effective barrier to entry the abnormal profits may be short-lived. Other firms
both within the same country and beyond will be attracted by the profit prospects
and their additional supplies will tend to undermine the agreed price even if
the members themselves are strictly adhering to their output quotas. The recent
familiar example of OPEC illustrates the point. One of the strengths of OPEC
in the early 1970s was its extraterritoriality. Membership consisted of the
governments of the major oil-exporting nations which were obviously out of
reach on any national antitrust laws. For a considerable time, therefore, their
agreed price increases held. The same reason, however, created one of the major
weaknesses of OPEC. It had no control over new entry to the international
crude oil market. As a result its share of total production fell from about two-

thirds at the time of the first 'oil-price shock' in late 1973 to less than 40 per cent by the early 1990s.

The foregoing discussion allows us to identify those characteristics which will help participating firms to sustain an initial increase in prices. Freedom from 'outside' competition may, as we have just seen, play a crucial role and helps to explain the persistent petitions to government from groups of domestic firms hoping to gain official support for their objections to 'unfair' competition from abroad. A second important factor for participants will be the relationship between the probable punishment if collusion is detected and the gains from an effective price rise. If costs, in the form of fines and imprisonment, are relatively high, as in the USA, the rewards from collusion will have to be correspondingly high. In the UK, until the passage of the 1998 Competition Act, the range of punishments for an initial offence were very modest, so even slight gains may have been worthwhile.

Thirdly, the costs of actually administering and monitoring the agreement need to be relatively low compared with the potential gains. The level of these costs will in turn depend on a number of factors (Jacquemin and Slade, 1989; Salop, 1986b; Stigler, 1964). For example, the smaller the number of firms and therefore the more concentrated the sales in the market, the easier and faster it will be for the group to detect not only when 'cheating' is taking place, but who is the culprit. Five firms of roughly equal market share will almost immediately feel the impact of any decline in sales and from the reports of its sales staff identify the secret price cutter. On the other hand, in a market supplied by 50 similar firms, an individual firm may be more inclined not only to see the cartel price as outside its control but also to feel that any increase in output that it attempts to sell will not easily be detected by its rivals. Similarly, monitoring an agreement is likely to be simpler and therefore less costly the greater the homogeneity of the product. Where products with slightly different characteristics and customer appeal would sell for different prices in the absence of a formal agreement, the price differentials would have to be embodied in any formal arrangement and subsequent product modifications are likely to be the source of much haggling and dispute. Products that are easily specified and graded (raw materials and agricultural produce, for example) do not have this cause of friction.

Finally, the presence of a well established trade association which organizes regular meetings may make the coordination of price and output policies easier, even in the face of hostile antitrust laws. As Smith predicted, the ostensible purpose of such meetings may be innocuous but the unwritten agenda may be to ensure continued price discipline or, in the more euphemistic phrase of such associations, 'orderly marketing'.

The presence of all or some of these factors will assist in the formation of the cartel. Once formed, its continued success (from the point of view of its members) will very much depend both on the means of detection and punishment of cheating, and on the strength of the incentives to cheat in the first place. We have already indicated that fewness of firms aids cartel formation and eases the problem of detection. Another structural characteristic having the same effect is one where all participants are at the same stage of the production process. If some firms are vertically integrated while others are not, it will be more difficult for the cartel to monitor the 'price' at which transactions are taking place between different parts of the organization. The problem does not arise if all firms essentially buy inputs and sell output across the same markets. Similarly, if price is widely known amongst buyers and sellers and is relatively stable, cheating on an agreement will be relatively easy to detect. In contrast, where input prices and demand can fluctuate violently, causing frequent price changes, it will be difficult to establish whether individual firms are cheating or simply responding to factors outside their control.

In some cases the cost structures of participating firms may considerably reduce the incentive to cheat. Where, for example, marginal cost curves are relatively inelastic, firms will not wish to cut price in order to increase sales because these will meet with sharply increasing costs. For this reason, it is usually argued that cheating is less likely in times of high market demand.[5] Similarly, where fixed costs are a small proportion of total costs, firms are more likely to reduce output than price in times of slack demand and thus there is less pressure to cheat on the agreement. The corollary is in industries where fixed costs are a high proportion of the total. Firms will then face a strong temptation to cut prices in order to maintain output from their expensive plant.

The most successful devices for the prevention of cheating are those which antitrust lawyers and economists do not know about. The great variety of arrangements that have been used and detected in the past suggest, however, that there are still probably a great many which remain undiscovered and successful. We give below a number of methods which have been used. Especially where firms in the industry have different cost levels, much may hinge on the comprehensiveness of the arrangements for dividing the market. In other words, much more than simple price fixing will be involved. If the cartel price is to hold, output shares will have to be agreed and monitored. To ensure adherence to the scheme high-cost firms may be compensated by levies on the profits of low-cost firms. A mechanism for administering the arrangements including arbitration in the case of dispute will also be necessary. A complex apparatus of bureaucracy and committees may thus be required to cope with the apparently simple task of monitoring prices above competitive levels. Part of the bureaucracy may be assigned the task of administering the division of the market. If individual members are allocated particular geographic regions or specified customers, cheating will be relatively easy to detect.

Less obviously, the adoption by members of terms which on the surface appear to work in favour of lower prices may, by increasing the penalties borne by any firm caught cheating, actually help to preserve higher prices. One such device is an adoption of the 'most favoured nation clause'.[6] In the present context, a firm guarantees that it is not giving better terms to its existing customers than those currently offered. The implication is that if better terms are detected the firm will not only have to offer them to its existing customers but also probably to compensate them for not keeping to the original agreement. In the terms of Chapter 6, a firm offering a 'most favoured nation' clause is making a pre-commitment to its customers that it will not offer better terms to others and they are therefore likely to have more confidence in the contract. The incentive to keep to the terms of the cartel are thereby strengthened. Similarly, a firm which runs a campaign of being 'never knowingly undersold' undertakes to match the price-cut of any rival. Potential customers are thus encouraged to report any price variations, with the result that cartel members are more, rather than less, likely to adhere to the agreement.

Thus the main reason for relative uniformity of treatment of collusion has been the strong analytical framework that has underpinned the policy. At least this is the mainstream view. Some observers have been prepared to argue in favour of allowing various degrees of cooperation (if not complete collusion) in certain circumstances. In particular, Richardson (1965) has suggested that, in industries with high ratios of fixed to variable costs and with long lags between starting and completing capital investments, information exchanges amongst firms on their investment plans will allow a more efficient outcome and corresponding welfare benefits. Under certain conditions, mentioned above in Chapter 3, it is possible for firms to be given exemption from Article 81 in the EU. Dewey (1990), who has also made a case for collusion in some circumstances, nevertheless points out that entry conditions remain crucial: 'Conceivably the real world is now so riddled with entry barriers created by tax laws, franchise requirements, safety standards, import quotas, zoning regulations, etc. that a presumption in favour of collusion based on a premise of free entry is not strong enough to justify a major change in [US] present policy' (p. 119).

An important additional reason for maintaining a tough policy towards collusion has been the view that tolerance of cartels, even given their tendency, in many cases, to disintegrate, imposes considerable welfare losses on consumers. They benefit, of course, from the lower prices that cheating brings. In terms of Figure 7.2 (right-hand panel), the cartel price imposes a deadweight loss equal to *JKL*. A reduction in price (and consequent increase in sales) will reduce the size of the loss. If the cartel breaks down completely, price will fall to P_c and the loss will be completely eliminated.[7] The important question is then how great are the welfare losses from cartel activity likely to be? If they are trivial, as the original estimates made of market power losses implied,[8] they may not justify the resources allocated to the detection and elimination of cartels by the antitrust authorities.

The direct and indirect evidence that is available on the effects of cartels suggests that they can generate significant welfare losses. When we were discussing more generally the possible losses from market power in Chapter 1, we made the point that the loss of consumer surplus alone (represented geometrically by the Marshallian triangle) substantially underestimated the full social loss because of the attempts by firms to acquire and retain market power. In the limit, competition amongst firms or groups of firms to acquire such power will fully exhaust the monopoly rents available. On this view, therefore, the full social costs of market power are represented not only by the consumer surplus loss, but also by the monopoly profit of the industry. Using this analysis Posner (1976) makes some estimates of the likely social costs of a number of international cartels which have operated at different times. As is usual with such estimates, they should be treated with caution because of the assumptions on which they are based and because the data were not ideal. However, even if we allow for wide margins of error, the social costs, ranging from the equivalent of 36 per cent of total industry sales in the cases of sugar and copper to 75 per cent in the cases of aluminium and rubber, suggest that cartels can impose substantial burdens. A similar analysis applied, for example, to the effect of OPEC's pricing policy during most of the 1970s and early 1980s would doubtless show even greater losses.[9]

IV   Cartel policy in the USA, the EU and the UK
In the USA the language of Section 1 of the Sherman Act seems unequivocal. It prohibits 'every contract, combination ... or conspiracy in restraint of trade or commerce among the several states'. A major result of the case law that has built up since the Act is that agreements amongst firms to fix prices are per se illegal. The plaintiff (the US Justice Department) merely has to show that the restriction exists for it to be struck down by the courts.

The very baldness of the language of Section 1, however, has created some problems. As a very distinguished member of the Supreme Court, Justice Brandeis, wrote in one important decision:

> Every agreement concerning trade, every regulation of trade, restrains. To bind, to restrain is of the very essence. The true test of legality is whether the restraint imposed is such as merely regulates and perhaps thereby promotes competition or whether it is such as may suppress or even destroy competition. To determine that question the Court must ordinarily consider the facts peculiar to the business to which the restraint is applied.[10]

Every contract, in one sense, restricts and restrains, but clearly Section 1 was not meant to be applied in this way. Similarly, some restrictions require detailed examination and a rule of reason approach which may end in their favour. There was thus the possibility of some exceptions to the per se rule. In the event, however, such exceptions have been relatively few and far between.

It was clear from the earliest cases determined by the Supreme Court in the 1890s that agreements to restrict prices could be struck down whatever the attempted justification offered by the defendants. Thus in *Trans-Missouri Freight* (1897)[11] an agreement amongst a group of railway companies over what rates to charge was held to violate Section 1. The Court rejected the argument that the agreement merely allowed 'reasonable' rates to be charged. In the Court's view competition should determine what was or was not 'reasonable'. Similarly, an agreement to set prices and share out the market in certain cities between a group of cast iron water and gas pipe manufacturers who together accounted for about two-thirds of the Middle West and West market was declared illegal.[12] The industry was notoriously prone to excess capacity and sharp price reductions in the face of fluctuating demand. However, the defence that the agreement avoided ruinous competition and that the prices charged were reasonable was again dismissed.

The aftermath of this case is interesting. Within a few months of the Supreme Court decision all members of the agreement merged to form one company. At the time such a merger was legal. Hence what Section 1 of the Sherman Act prevented the firms from achieving independently, they sought through unification. Swann *et al.* (1974, pp. 172–8) also report a flurry of mergers in some UK industries which abandoned restrictive agreements in the wake of the early decisions of the Restrictive Practices Court. We shall see in the next chapter, however, that given current merger policy in both countries such a solution is no longer generally available.

From these early decisions there should have been little remaining doubt that an agreement clearly intended to fix prices was a per se violation of Section 1. Two subsequent cases further refined and clarified this position. The first, involving suppliers of about 82 per cent of the bathroom fixtures market, aimed to ensure adherence to an agreed price list circulated by their trade associations. The Court made it clear that, regardless of the success or otherwise of the agreement, or whether the association was able to enforce adherence to the stipulated prices, the presence of the agreement in itself constituted a violation. Reasonableness of prices was irrelevant: 'The power to fix prices, whether reasonably exercised or not, involves power to control the market and to fix arbitrary and unreasonable prices. The reasonable price fixed today may through economic and business changes become the unreasonable price of tomorrow'.[13]

Although there was some attempt in the early 1930s, in the depths of the Depression, to allow price fixing as a means of alleviating hardship suffered in many industries,[14] the change of course was short-lived. *Socony–Vacuum Oil* (1940) marked a decisive return to the per se rule against price fixing and the decision remains the established precedent. At a time when surplus or 'distressed' oil from independent refineries was having a depressing effect on the 'spot' market price for oil in the USA, the major oil companies agreed to establish a system whereby each one would purchase the surplus oil from an individual independent, known as its 'dancing partner', and so help to maintain the spot price of oil. The joint effort of the majors in buying a relatively small total amount of oil could thus have a significant effect on the price.[15] The Supreme Court had no trouble dealing with the defence of the restriction which was in the familiar terms of preventing ruinous competition and helping to preserve stability. It made no difference that the companies had not agreed to a uniform and inflexible price (as they had in the *Trenton Potteries* case). The restriction tampered with the price structure and was therefore unlawful. Wishing to leave no further shred of doubt about such cases, Justice Douglas wrote: 'Under the Sherman Act a combination formed for the purpose and with the effect of raising, depressing, fixing, pegging or stabilising the price of a commodity in interstate or foreign commerce is illegal per se.'

For agreements where it is clear to the Court that price fixing is a central purpose the uncompromising per se rule applies. However, where it is incidental or subsidiary to an agreement which seems to be conducive to a more competitive market, the court has been prepared to apply a modified 'rule of reason' approach. Thus, in an early case involving the Board of Trade of the City of Chicago, the court found in favour of an agreement amongst grain dealers. They competed against each other for buying and selling grain contracts and agreed not to make any sales after the market closed at other than the closing price. The Court accepted that the restriction had the effect, first, of ensuring that more grain contracts were exchanged while the market was open and as a result more information was processed. Secondly, it prevented others from 'free-riding' on the information embodied in the market's closing price, by concluding deals after hours at different prices if circumstances had changed, yet without paying any market fees. Having considered the facts 'peculiar to the business to which the restraint is applied', the Court concluded that it tended to enhance rather than stifle competition and was therefore not a violation of the Sherman Act.

The court has much more recently been prepared to accept that an efficiency-enhancing restriction was not automatically anticompetitive. Broadcast Music Inc. (BMI) and the American Association of Composers, Authors and Publishers (ASCAP) are two organizations which collect fees on behalf of copyright holders of musical compositions played, for example, in radio and television programmes. It would clearly be extremely costly and inefficient for individual composers to attempt to monitor all conceivable occasions when their compositions are played, and similarly for radio and television companies to seek and conclude separate contracts with individual composers or their heirs. Composers therefore contract with one or other of BMI or ASCAP to collect fees on their behalf. The organizations issue blanket licences to cover whole lists of compositions and collect fees on behalf of their composer clients. They fix the fees to be paid for licences and in this sense fix the price. Most countries have evolved a similar system of rewarding composers as a way of reducing the horrendous transaction costs that would otherwise be involved. The court recognized that the arrangements seemed to enhance efficiency and were if anything pro-competitive in encouraging the amount of use that could be made of musical compositions: 'The blanket licence, as we see it, is not a "naked restraint of trade" with no purpose except the stifling of competition, but rather accompanies the integration of sales, monitoring and enforcement against unauthorised copyright use.'[16]

We mentioned in Chapter 3 that at various times a number of organizations or classes of agreement have been exempted from the antitrust laws. In particular, trade unions, agricultural marketing boards and export agreements have been given exemption. For a long while it was also considered that certain professional associations (for example, in medicine, dentistry, architecture, law and engineering) were outside the scope of the laws. Indeed, some observers have suggested that in *Board of Trade*, the Supreme Court may have contributed indirectly to this view (see, for example, Scherer and Ross, 1990, p. 322). The position was undermined by a case judged by the court in 1978 involving the National Society of Professional Engineers. The Society argued that their rule against discussing the price of their services until after an engineer had been chosen by a customer was in the interest of maintaining high engineering standards and hence public safety and should therefore be exempt from Section 1. The court roundly rejected this argument, saying that it was not their task to determine whether competition was good or bad.

Thus, with the relatively few exceptions noted, horizontal agreements to fix prices and other terms of trading remain per se illegal in the USA, with the sanction of heavy penalties for those who violate the law.[17] In the cases considered so far, a formal agreement between the parties existed and formed the centrepiece of the dispute. What is the position, however, in markets with few sellers and no apparent agreement, but where the prices of individual firms move in concert, with remarkable consistency over time? After all, the essence of oligopoly is interdependence of decision making: no one firm can make important decisions about price changes without gauging the probable response of its major rivals. Firms with roughly equal market shares and cost levels may be expected to respond similarly to changes in market conditions. Indeed, it can be shown formally that under certain circumstances oligopolistic firms acting independently to secure the maximum advantage may earn abnormally high profits if all make the same assumptions about the others' behaviour.[18]

The problems for antitrust policy makers is to determine how far the laws can be applied across the wide spectrum of different forms of oligopolistic behaviour. Overt formal agreements are illegal but parallel pricing with no formal contact or information exchange between firms does not, in most circumstances, infringe the law. As Scherer and Ross summarize the current US position: 'The accumulated precedents seem to call for "parallelism plus". The key question remains, of what can the "plus" consist?' (Scherer and Ross, 1990, p. 345). In what was probably the high-water mark of the doctrine of conscious parallelism, the Supreme Court in 1946 appeared to take the view that very little, if any, direct contact was required: 'No formal agreement is necessary to constitute an unlawful conspiracy ... Where the circumstances are such as to warrant a jury in finding that the conspirators had a unity of purpose or a common design and understanding, or a meeting of minds in an unlawful arrangement, the conclusion that a conspiracy is established is justified.'[19] Taken literally, this passage seems to suggest that even independent action by leading firms in a concentrated oligopoly would infringe the law if it appeared to be taken in concert. This interpretation poses a severe problem for the firms concerned because such behaviour results naturally and rationally from the structure of the market.

More recent decisions have marked something of a retreat from this extreme position. In a 1954 case involving the boycott of nine film distributors of a new cinema, the Supreme Court, finding for the distributors, agreed that it has 'never held that proof of parallel business behavior conclusively established agreement or ... that such behavior itself constitutes a Sherman Act offense ... "Conscious parallelism" has not yet read conspiracy out of the Sherman Act entirely.'[20] Subsequent cases have tended to confirm the position that some form of direct communication between companies is required, in addition to their parallel action, if the courts are to find against them. However, even then there is scope for different interpretations, given the particular facts of a case. Thus anything as blatant as blacklists or circular letters would be sufficient, but advance warning of price changes to customers (as well as notification of the warning period) plus a 'most favoured customer' provision, all of which facilitated uniform pricing, was not an infringement.[21] No direct communication between competitors had taken place in this case, but in addition it was also shown that the warning and other provisions had all been in place prior to the emergence of competition and could not therefore be viewed as a means of suppressing it. It is an open question whether the decision would have gone the other way had these provisions been adopted once the several competitors were established in the market.

Thus, in the absence of a formal agreement, parallel action is a necessary but not sufficient condition for an infringement of the law. What precise additional practices are required to convert the 'necessary' into the 'sufficient' conditions is still subject to interpretation by the courts. In this respect some interesting comparisons can be made with the EU doctrine of concerted practices. As we saw in Chapter 3, Section 1 of Article 81 declares that agreements between enterprises which have the effect of preventing, restricting or distorting competition in the EU are prohibited. To this extent, the position is similar to that of the USA. Section 3, however, provides for exemptions where the agreement contributes to improving the production and distribution of goods or to promoting technical progress, as long as consumers share in the resulting benefits. This provision has no direct counterpart in US law.

Strictly speaking, the scope of Article 81 extends only as far as inter-state trade. Agreements which both directly and indirectly have a purely local effect within one member state (for example, an agreement to fix fares between bus companies providing services in one city) are not covered, but they are subject to the national antitrust laws. The 'reach' of the provision is, however, wider than may at first be thought. Since the wording of Article 81 refers to agreements between enterprises and concerted practices 'which *may* affect trade between Member States' (emphasis added), it is not necessary to show that inter-state trade has actually been harmed, but only that the potential for harm is there. The ramifications of this are considerable. For example, an agreement between all manufacturers in one country to grant aggregated rebates (based on total purchases from all the firms) to customers may have the effect of excluding imports from a firm in another member state which cannot match the rebate level, even though it may be as efficient as the individual domestic producers. Such an agreement thus has the effect of restricting and distorting competition and falls within Article 81, even though the agreement only involves firms in one member state. On the other hand, it is not necessary for all participants in a restriction to come from a member country for the law to apply. For example, a reciprocal exclusive dealing arrangement between a German and Japanese company which resulted in very high prices in the EU led to both being fined.[22]

More obviously, as we shall illustrate below, an agreement between a manufacturer in member country A and distributors in member country B that the latter will not re-export the product back to country A is also covered. This example also brings out the point that, since Article 81 is concerned with the effects rather than the substance of an agreement, it can be applied to both horizontal and vertical restrictions. A horizontal restraint refers to an arrangement between firms at the same stage of the production process (for example, manufacturers), whereas a vertical restraint refers to an arrangement between firms in a supplier–customer relationship (for example, manufacturers and distributors).

In fact one of the key early cases to be decided by the Court involved a vertical restriction and came close to establishing a per se rule. The essentially vertical nature of the restriction means that, strictly speaking, it should be considered in Chapter 10 below. However, because of its central importance in the development of EU competition law, it is more convenient to introduce the case here. The German manufacturer of electrical equipment, Grundig, gave exclusive distribution rights in France to Consten. In return, Consten agreed to place minimum orders, provide an effective back-up service, not to sell competing products, and not to resell the products in other territories, including Germany. These terms also applied to Grundig distributors in other countries. Under the terms of a related agreement, Consten was allowed to use the Grundig trademark, GINT, in France. When a competitor to Consten, UNEF, began importing Grundig products into France and selling them on more favourable terms, Consten took action in the French courts on grounds of unfair competition and infringement of the trademark. UNEF complained to the Commission, which carried out an enquiry. In its decision, the Commission ruled that the prevention of parallel imports imposed by the exclusive distribution and trademark arrangements infringed Article 81(*i*) and were therefore wholly void and unenforceable. On appeal, the European Court agreed with the Commission on the most fundamental point.[23] Agreements which tended to frustrate the development of trade between member states and to reinforce national divisions struck at the very heart of the founding Treaty and were void, even if this principle was upheld sometimes at the expense of efficiency in distribution systems:

> In this connection, what is particularly important is whether the agreement is capable of constituting a threat, either direct or indirect, actual or potential, to freedom of trade between Member States in a manner which might harm the attainment of the objectives of a single market between states. Thus the fact that an agreement encourages an increase, even a large one, in the volume of trade between States is not sufficient to exclude the possibility that the agreement may 'affect' such trade in the above mentioned manner.[24]

The completion of a single unified market was paramount and any agreement having the effect of allocating national markets to particular firms would almost invariably be found to affect inter-state trade and therefore be struck down. Subsequent decisions by the Commission and the Court have consistently maintained this position.[25]

The other most important cases under Article 81(i) have clarified the precise meaning of an 'agreement' and distinguished the concept of a 'concerted practice'. It is convenient to deal with the second point first. The Commission and the Court had US experience on which to draw and in the dyestuffs and sugar cases have arrived at a position close to that of the US Supreme Court. While recognizing the commercial realities of heavily concentrated markets and the need for firms to take account of their rivals' actions in formulating their own decisions, both Commission and Court have emphasized that no formal agreement is necessary for an infringement under Article 81 to take place. Thus, in the dyestuffs case,[26] ten manufacturers responsible for 80 per cent of EU production had engineered equal prices more or less simultaneously in 1964, 1965 and 1967. The market was effectively segmented into five national markets where there were differing costs and structures, making it highly unlikely that, with genuine competition, prices would be identical. The Commission had evidence that the companies had met and discussed prices, although no formal agreement was concluded. Such circumstantial evidence provided the kind of 'plus' factor regarded as necessary in similar US cases. In the event, when the case went on appeal to the Court, it did not rely on this additional evidence but was satisfied simply by the price behaviour of the firms that an infringement had occurred. It defined a 'concerted practice' as 'a form of co-ordination between undertakings which, without having reached the stage where an agreement properly so called has been concluded, knowingly substitutes practical co-operation between them for the risks of competition ... which becomes apparent from the behaviour of the undertakings'.

The requirement of both parallel behaviour and additional evidence to establish a concerted practice was made clearer in the subsequent sugar cartel case,[27] where the Court relied very heavily on the detailed evidence of apparent collusion. It argued that independent action did 'strictly preclude any direct or indirect contact between such operators the object or effect whereof is either to influence the conduct on the market of an actual or potential competitor or to disclose to such a competitor the course of conduct which they themselves have decided to adopt'.

On the basis of these cases, therefore, the position in the EU is very similar to that in the USA, with an infringement requiring clear evidence of parallel behaviour and additional evidence of some direct or indirect contact or communication between the parties on which they knowingly rely for framing their subsequent coordinated action.

The relationship between an 'agreement' and a 'concerted practice' was set out by the Commission in the *Polypropylene* cartel case.[28] The case involved 15 companies, including some of the most prestigious chemical companies in the world, and ended with the Commission imposing fines totalling ECU 57.9 million. Appeals by a number of the defendants to the Court were rejected early in 1992. Polypropylene is the material used in a multiplicity of plastic products and the companies involved were responsible for more than 90 per cent of EU supplies. The four largest suppliers, Montepolimeri (Montedison), Hoechst, ICI and Shell, accounted for more than 50 per cent. Documents recovered from a number of companies gave detailed accounts of regular meetings which discussed a whole range of issues to do with prices, including price fixing itself, the machinery for implementing price changes, restriction of sales, control of stocks and division of the market, reporting of contract volumes and target sales for each company, monitoring market shares, as well as possible approaches to new, non-participating producers and methods of dealing with pricing 'anomalies' (para. 21). The list reads like a practical guidebook for cartel practice, and yet the Commission noted that it was neither written down nor intended to be legally binding on participants. In rejecting the argument of some defendants that it did not therefore infringe Article 81, the Commission concluded:

> It is not necessary in order for a restriction to constitute an 'agreement' within the meaning of Article 81(i) for the agreement to be intended as legally binding upon the parties. An agreement exists if the parties reach a consensus on a plan which limits or is likely to limit their commercial freedom by determining the lines of their mutual, actual or abstention from action in the market. No contractual sanction or enforcement procedures are required. Nor is it necessary for such an agreement to be made in writing.
>
> In the present case, the producers, by subscribing to a common plan to negotiate prices and supply in the polypropylene market, participated in an overall framework agreement which was manifested in a series of more detailed sub-agreements worked out from time to time. (para. 81)

The Commission was thus convinced that the regular meetings and the panoply of issues discussed and acted upon amounted to an agreement. It also observed, however, that the behaviour of some participants at certain times 'may display the characteristics of a concerted practice'. In this connection it cited the expressed scepticism of Shell about quota schemes while indicating to ICI what allocation was acceptable to it (para. 87).

It concluded that 'the importance of the concept of a concerted practice does not thus result so much from the distinction between it as an "agreement" as from the distinction between forms of collusion falling under Article 85(i) and mere parallel behaviour with no element of concertation' (ibid.). The important point is therefore made that within a particular market the conduct of some firms may amount to an agreement and that of others to a 'concerted practice'. The two forms of collusive behaviour do not fall into different watertight compartments. One may spill into the other at different times.

However, the standard of proof required for establishing a 'concerted practice' was raised considerably by the outcome of the appeal in the *Wood Pulp* case.[29] The Commission had been satisfied that a 'concerted practice' existed between more than 50 companies from a number of different countries (at the time most outside the EU). The companies involved accounted for two thirds of the EU market. Fines ranging from ECU 50 000 to ECU 500 000 were imposed. On appeal the fines were revoked and costs were awarded against the Commission. In making its assessment the Court relied largely on a specially commissioned report from economists who were asked to determine whether, on the basis of the facts, collusion was the *only* explanation of the behaviour of prices. The economists argued that non-collusive oligopolistic behaviour could produce the same pattern of price behaviour. In particular they stressed the following points. First, the amount of price information available in the market was at the request of customers, not engineered deliberately by producers. Secondly, the slow price response by individual firms to changed market circumstances was characteristic of oligopolists to any of their competitors' reactions. Thirdly, a high proportion of total market supplies (upwards of 40 per cent) came from firms which were not part of the allegedly colluding group. To maintain effective collusion in such circumstances was extremely difficult. Finally, similar prices amongst firms with different costs were not unusual in oligopolistic markets. The different costs would be reflected in different profitability levels. The economists concluded, therefore, that a plausible, non-collusive explanation of the facts in the case was possible (Van Gerven and Varona, 1994). The Court accepted this argument and therefore allowed the appeal.

In future, proof of a 'concerted practice' is thus likely to need three elements: parallel behaviour on prices, information exchanges *plus* no convincing alternative explanation of observed price patterns. It is likely to be extremely difficult to prove that a 'concerted practice' has occurred.

In the case of the USA, as we have seen, although the Sherman Act makes no provision for exemptions to the Section 1 ban on agreements that restrict trade, the authorities have been prepared to apply a 'rule of reason' approach to some cases where a restriction clearly leads to greater efficiency and benefits to consumers. Within the European Union, Article 81(iii) allows for the Commission to exempt an individual restriction under certain circumstances. The exemption is granted for a specified time period (not normally exceeding ten years) and the Commission can ask for further information from time to time to assure itself that the circumstances in the market have not significantly changed. If they have, then the Commission may alter the renewal conditions.[30] Thus under Article 81(iii) an agreement or concerted practice may be granted an exemption if it

> contributes to improving the production or distribution of goods or to promoting technical or economic progress, while allowing consumers a fair share of the resulting benefit and which does not:
> (a) impose on the undertakings concerned restrictions which are not indispensable to the attainment of these objectives;
> (b) afford such undertakings the possibility of eliminating competition in respect of a substantial part of the products in question.

In effect the clause has four distinct components, two positive and two negative. On the positive side, to gain exemption a restriction must first contribute to the improvement of the production and distribution of goods or to the provision of technical or economic progress, and secondly, if it does, it must ensure that consumers gain a fair share of the resulting benefits. On the negative side, the agreement must not impose more restrictions than are strictly necessary for achieving the benefits and must not facilitate the elimination of competition. If any of the conditions are adverse, the restriction will not receive exemption. Thus it is possible that a restriction may improve production or distribution methods, but if it simultaneously helps to reduce competition it will not pass Article 81(iii). There is thus no possibility of a trade-off between the positive and negative components. Although some have regarded the clause as allowing the Commission to adopt a 'rule of reason' approach to restrictions, similar to the US practice, according to one legal authority this is far from being the case. Whereas the US courts can take into account all positive and negative features of a restriction without any restraint, by comparison, 'the Commission, must operate within a rigid conceptual framework which allows less freedom of manoeuvre and requires the restriction to pass, not a single balancing test, but a cumulative series of four separate tests ... There cannot be an "overall" balancing of debits and credits under the system laid down by [Article 81](iii)' (Goyder, 1998, p. 145).

A leading case which neatly illustrates the significance of each part of the procedure is *Transocean Marine Paint*.[31] A series of short-term exemptions were granted to a group of 20 medium-sized manufacturers of marine paint located in different countries of the Community. Their total market share was of the order of 5–10 per cent. The restriction involved standardization of quality and supply arrangements with the purpose of making the firms more competitive. Initially there were also some territorial restrictions whereby a firm selling in the territory of a fellow member had to pay a modest commission. Clearly, therefore, the restriction fell within Article 81(i). The Commission was satisfied, however, that there were significant benefits from the rationalized distribution system which increased members' competitiveness vis-à-vis other larger firms. Without the agreement, the individual firms lacked the resources to establish their own complete distribution network. The restriction therefore passed the first test. The Commission also considered that it passed the second, because consumers were provided with a wider range of stocks from port to port and also received more comprehensive technical advice. In the first period exemption the Commission accepted that all of the restrictions were necessary for the effective operation of the agreement. However, when the first renewal was applied for, the Commission, noting the increased sales of the member firms, insisted on the abandonment of the territorial restriction mentioned above. Without this added restriction it was satisfied that the remaining terms were necessary. Finally, given the modest aggregate market share of the members and the presence in the market of much more powerful competitors, the Commission also accepted that the restriction would not lead to the elimination of competition.

The requirement to pass all four tests is thus severe. In some cases a restriction may pass the two positive sections but fail on the negative sections. For example, in *Rennet*, involving an exclusive purchasing agreement imposed on all members of a Dutch agricultural cooperative, both the Commission and the Court agreed that there were efficiency gains and benefits to purchasers through lower prices, but refused exemption under the negative tests.[32] Members were required to buy all of their requirements from the cooperative and were fined if they did not. They also had to make a large payment if they withdrew from the agreement. Neither was held to be strictly necessary to obtain the efficiency benefits. Furthermore, those involved in the restriction were responsible jointly for market shares ranging from 80 to 100 per cent of the products, and would have a significant impact on competition. Agreements covering a large part of the market are highly unlikely to be granted exemption even if there are apparently significant improvements in manufacture and distribution.

Many of the arguments presented to the Commission by members of agreements seeking exemption under Article 81(iii) would be familiar to students of UK policy prior to the passage of the 1998 Competition Act. Restrictive agreements (including information agreements) were presumed to be illegal unless that presumption was successfully rebutted in the Restrictive Practices Court, a special section of the high court. Contrary to expectations the early decisions of the Court were hostile to restrictive agreements and as a consequence many were abandoned or modified. By 1986, when the DGFT last reported on this issue, 3706 agreements had either been given up or altered so as not to infringe the law. Only a handful of agreements had ultimately been accepted by the Court as being in the public interest, and some of these were abandoned or collapsed shortly after the decision. (For a full discussion, see Swann *et al.*, 1974).

With the benefit of hindsight, many observers would agree that it would have been better to have followed the recommendation of the majority in a key report by the Monopolies and Restrictive Practices Commission (as it was then called) and to have made restrictive agreements illegal, with perhaps a tightly drawn exemption clause (MMC, 1955). That, of course, is now the position following the passage of the 1998 Competition Act. As we saw in Chapter 3, restrictive agreements and concerted practices between firms that affect or may affect trade within the UK and have as their object or effect the prevention, restriction or distortion of competition are prohibited, under Chapter 1 of the Act. With the appropriate modification for the UK, this provision follows exactly Article 81 section (i) of the European Treaty. Agreements are thus to be judged on the basis of their *effects* on competition compared to the precise *form*, which was the position under the previous law. Similarly the UK Act contains a replica of the exemption clause (Article 81(iii)) which provides for agreements to be given exemption on precisely and narrowly drawn lines (p. 50 above).

Although the pure analysis discussed in Sections II and III above shows clearly that efficiency will very likely suffer under a cartel, in the three jurisdictions we are discussing, the resulting opposition ends at the national boundaries. Cartels concerned only with exports have been given special treatment in the USA. The Webb–Pomerene Act (1918) exempts from the antitrust laws cartel-like arrangements which deal exclusively with exports, although in recent years it has been invoked very infrequently (Scherer and Ross, 1990, p. 324). In the EU, Article 81 is concerned with restrictions which may impair intra-community trade. An agreement designed purely to foster exports from the EU is, therefore, in principle, not covered by Article 81. In practice, it may be very difficult for members to convince the Commission that there are no direct or indirect effects of their export agreement on trade within the Community. If firms meet to collude for the promotion of exports, it is highly improbable that domestic sales are not also discussed. The same point now applies to the UK under the Competition Act, even though under earlier legislation export cartels could be allowed to continue. The latter part of Adam Smith's conclusion quoted at the beginning of this chapter should be heeded in this respect: the law 'ought to do nothing to facilitate such assemblies [of businessmen]'.

V   Conclusion

The widespread support for policies designed to curb collusion is founded on fairly unequivocal results from economic analysis. A successful cartel will damage efficiency in a number of ways. Many of the arguments formerly used to justify such restrictions have been shown to be false or unsustainable. Some observers have argued that the conditions necessary for the long-term maintenance of a cartel are so lengthy and complex that they will only be met infrequently. The majority will collapse after a short time and therefore there is only a very limited need for legal remedies. The experience over a long period and from many countries suggests this view is exaggerated. Certainly many attempts at restriction are short-lived, but there is sufficient evidence of others living well on into middle age, to justify a tough legal stance.

The antitrust laws have led to the widespread abandonment of overt collusion and in the USA and the EU doctrines of 'conscious parallelism' or 'concerted practices' have been developed to cover situations where no formal agreement exists. A strict interpretation of Article 81(iii) in the EU has allowed the exemption of a narrow range of agreements which clearly enhance efficiency by reducing costs. Under the new Competition Act (1998) a similar procedure, allowing for limited exemptions, has been adopted for the UK.

Notes

1. His oligopoly analysis, although much less famous than his theory of monopolistic competition, was to have a very significant impact on subsequent empirical work in industrial organization. Bain, whose own work shaped several decades of this research, wrote: 'perhaps the most fruitful effort devoted to exploiting the potential of Chamberlinian theory has centred on the theory of oligopoly, and not improperly so if empirical relevance is introduced as a criterion' (Bain, 1967).

2. Those readers who believe this last assumption is too fanciful are referred to the experience of both the USA and the UK in the 1930s when, admittedly in the trough of the Depression, both governments effectively sanctioned cartelization of many industries and forbade price cutting. In the USA the experiment was short-lived because it was declared unconstitutional by the Supreme Court, but in the UK it lasted for more than a decade, with highly undesirable results. See, in particular, Allen (1968).

3. There is considerable evidence (much of it from antitrust cases) that at any one time existing firms in a market may have substantially different costs.

4. To keep the illustration as simple as possible, marginal costs are shown as linear and average total costs are not shown.

5. However, that view is not unanimous. Rotemberg and Saloner (1986) have argued that firms are more likely to cheat during a boom in order to take advantage of the favourable conditions. The evidence so far tends to support the more conventional view; see Suslow (1988).

6. The phrase was originally used in trade policy to describe the arrangement whereby a new trading partner was granted terms similar to those given to the 'most favoured' existing nation.

7. In the illustrative case given in Figure 7.2, a competitive price is unlikely to remain for long. With only two firms in the industry some new arrangement is likely to emerge fairly rapidly and cause prices to rise again. In the more realistic case with more firms, the factors discussed in the text will obviously apply.

8. Discussed in Chapter 1 above.

9. The point is taken up again in Chapter 12 below.

10. *Board of Trade of City of Chicago* v. *United States*, 246, US 231 (1918).

11. *United States* v. *Trans-Missouri Freight Association*, 166, US 290 (1897).

12. *United States* v. *Addyston Pipe and Steel Co.* 175, US 211 (6th Cir., 1899).

13. *United States* v. *Trenton Potteries et al.*, 273 US 392 (1927).

14. Notably *Appalachian Coals, Inc.* v. *United States*, 288 US 344 (1933).

15. *United States* v. *Socony–Vacuum Oil Co., Inc.*, 310 US 150 (1940).

16. *Broadcast Music Inc.* v. *Columbia Broadcasting System Inc.*, 441 US 1 (1979).

17. See Chapter 11 below.

18. For an accessible treatment of Cournot–Nash equilibrium see, for example, Carlton and Perloff (2000, ch. 6).

19. *American Tobacco Co. et al.* v. *US*, 328 US 781, 809–810 (1946).

20. *Theatre Enterprises, Inc* v. *Paramount Film Distributing Corp. et al.*, 346 US 537, (1954).

21. In the matter of *Ethyl Corp. et al.*, 101 FTC 425 (1983).

22. *Siemens-Fanuc*, OJ (1985) L.376/29.

23. In two respects it disagreed with the Commission. First, it did not agree that an exclusive distribution system alone was sufficient to create artificial barriers to trade between members. Secondly, it did not agree that all terms of a restrictive arrangement should be annulled. Only the restrictive terms should be affected.

24. *Consten and Grundig* v. *Commission* (1966), CMLR 418.

25. See, for example, Merkin and Williams (1984, p. 185).

26. *ICI* v. *Commission* (1972) CMLR 557.

27. *Suiker Unie and Others* v *Commission* (1975) CMLR 295.

28. *Re Polypropylene Cartel: The Community* v. *ICI plc and Others* (1988) 4 CMLR 347.

29. *Ahlstrom and Others* v. *Commission* (1993) 4 CMLR 407.

30. This is in addition to the power delegated to the Commission by the Council under Regulations 19/65 and 2821/71, allowing it to grant block exemptions for certain classes of agreements.

31. *Transocean Marine Paint Association* (1967) CMLR, D9; (1974) 1CMLR, D11

32. *Co-operative Stremsel en Kleurselfabriek* v. *Commission* (1982) 1CMLR 240.

8 Horizontal mergers and market dominance

I Introduction

According to Dr Johnson, patriotism is the last refuge of a scoundrel. According to some economists, merger is the last refuge of corporate conspirators. If the laws reviewed in the previous chapter prevent independent firms from colluding to raise prices, then, in the last resort, they may give up their separate identities and become a single enterprise to achieve the same purpose. The first point to note about mergers, therefore, is that those between sizeable firms operating in the same market, horizontal mergers, are likely to have the most direct impact on market power. Mergers between firms operating at different stages in the production process (as with a food manufacturer merging with a food supermarket chain) may have consequences for market power, but we postpone consideration of such vertical mergers until Chapter 9. The effects of mergers between firms operating in quite different markets (for example an electronics company merging with a clothing manufacturer) have been hotly disputed in the past but are now generally regarded as having little or no market power effects. Thus we confine ourselves in this chapter to horizontal mergers.

Secondly, in any one year, many mergers may occur for a wide variety of reasons. Some may simply arise because the founding owner of a company wishes to retire. Conversely, others may come about because two firms of modest size wish to pool their resources to increase their rate of growth. Again, one management group may bid for the assets of another company because they estimate that they can make better use of them, and hence enhance their value. Firms with complementary assets and expertise may merge in order to increase technical efficiency. Finally, firms may reckon that a merger would enable them to increase market power and hence increase prices. There are thus many possible motives for merger,[1] and at any one time only a comparatively small sub-set of cases is likely to concern antitrust agencies because of their possible effects on market power.

When discussing formal collusion, we mentioned that there was a good deal of agreement about the harmful effects on efficiency that could result. In all three of the jurisdictions considered, there was therefore effectively a per se rule. With horizontal mergers, the position is much more ambiguous. Some horizontal mergers, while increasing the market share of the new concern, may have a negligible effect on market power. Others may also hold out the promise of improved technical efficiency. In neither case would the antitrust authorities wish to intervene. A third category of merger may simultaneously enhance market power and increase technical efficiency. The question then is whether such mergers should be blocked. In practice it may be a major task for the authorities to distinguish those mergers falling into the different categories. It will seldom be clear how great the increase in market power may be or how far the prospective efficiency improvements will actually be realized.

Another source of ambiguity, at least in the UK and the EU, has been what may be termed the 'industrial policy' aspect of large mergers. At various times over the past 40 years or so several European governments have positively sought to reshape important industrial sectors by promoting mergers. The philosophy lying behind this largely discredited policy was to create firms large and efficient enough to compete in international markets with the best foreign enterprises.[2] The possible conflict with antitrust is clear. While governments retain lingering aspirations in this direction, however, they may not encourage any moves to block sizeable mergers on competition grounds. At the level of the EU, where individual members had experienced varying levels of merger activity in the recent past, with and without government support, those who felt they had some ground to make up tended to oppose moves to introduce a systematic community-wide merger policy.

In contrast with the laws on collusion, therefore, the approach to mergers is more circumspect and a rule of reason is applied. It is also worth noting that in all three jurisdictions merger policy was the last major branch of antitrust to be introduced: in the USA (effectively) in 1950, in the UK in 1965 and in the EU in 1990. Some of the reasons for this have been noted above, but another part of the explanation probably stems from priorities. Initially, the problem of market dominance is seen in terms of single-firm monopoly or joint action by a group of firms. Once policies to curb these abuses are in place, further measures to prevent their creation or re-emergence in a different form are required.

Section II of this chapter analyses the main issues raised by large horizontal mergers and the particular problems that the analysis reveals. Section III then discusses merger policy as it has evolved in the three jurisdictions. Of all the major areas of antitrust, merger policy is at once the most complex and the most interesting, largely because it must be concerned with projection rather than simply past events.

II   The analysis of horizontal mergers

Although mergers for market power may be the ultimate form of collusion, unless the merged firm is assured of market control it will suffer from the same problems as an imperfect cartel. As Stigler noted long ago, where there are relatively few firms in the market, the major difficulty for the merging firms is that it is more profitable to be outside than to be a participant: 'Hence the promoter of a merger is likely to receive much encouragement from each firm – almost every encouragement, in fact, except participation' (Stigler, 1968, p. 98). When the merged firm reduces output below the level previously produced by the participating firms and raises price, firms outside the merger can expand their own output in an attempt to take advantage of the higher price. As long as total output is less than that prior to the merger, some increase in price can occur, but far from all of the benefit accrues to participants in the merger. One source of instability suffered by a cartel, cheating by individual members, is clearly eliminated by merger. Another source, however, increased output by non-participating firms, remains. In addition, unless the market is protected by substantial barriers to entry, the higher price that the merged firm is attempting to introduce will attract further competition. Increased output from new entrants will thus place further strain on the post-merger price.

In short, two conditions are necessary if a merger is to create market power. The merged firm must have direct or indirect control of the market, which implies that it can manage not only its own output level but that of independent competitors. Secondly, entry conditions must be such that no significant entry can occur once post-merger price is raised above competitive levels. An antitrust body has therefore to assess (usually in a comparatively short space of time) the likely impact of a merger on these two highly complex issues: market and entry control.

For an antitrust policy aimed solely at preventing the creation and misuse of market power, these two criteria would be sufficient to block a merger, although, as we saw in Chapter 1, the extent to which prices can be raised persistently above competitive levels will depend on the degree of market power. According to US antitrust law, mergers which substantially lessen competition or tend to create a monopoly are illegal. It was in response to this position that Williamson (1987) argued that rational economic policy required consideration not only of market power effects but also of the efficiency effects of mergers. The strength of the opposition to this view at the time may be gauged by the opinion of the Supreme Court in 1967: 'Possible efficiencies cannot be used as a defense to illegality.'[3]

Part of Williamson's argument can be illustrated by Figure 8.1. The simplest case is shown in panel (a). The market is initially supplied by a large number of firms whose aggregate supply is shown as C_1 (horizontal for simplicity). Market demand is D and the pre-merger, competitive price and output are P_C and Q_C respectively. Price is equal to marginal cost and consumer surplus is maximized. A merger then occurs which creates some market power.[4] The model then assumes that three effects occur. First, by reorganization costs of supply are reduced to C_2. Secondly, the creation of market power raises price to P_M and reduces output to Q_M. Thirdly, entry to the market is blocked; otherwise, as we noted above, price at P_M would be short-lived. The creation and exercise of market power causes a loss of consumer surplus. Part (represented by $P_M BEP_C$) is transferred to the firm with market power. In welfare terms, this is merely a transfer rather than a loss. The area *EBK*, however, is the Marshallian deadweight loss and represents a reduction in consumer welfare.

In addition to the welfare loss, the reduction in costs for the reduced output (represented by the area P_cEFH) amounts to a saving in resources: the output Q_M is produced with fewer resources as a result of the amalgamation than without it. That remains true even though the gain accrues entirely to the firm with market power (rather than to any other group, such as consumers).

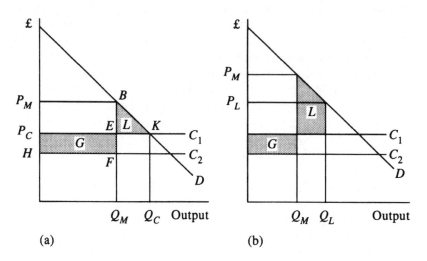

Figure 8.1   The welfare trade-offs in horizontal mergers

A merger policy concerned with market power effects alone would need only to establish that the loss *L* was likely to occur to block the merger. In contrast, Williamson argued that, in cases where efficiency gains resulted from mergers which simultaneously created market power, the gain, *G*, should be traded off against the loss *L*. If the gain exceeded the loss, *ceteris paribus*, then the merger should be allowed even though market power was created. Williamson showed that, since the scope of the gain extended over the entire output produced by the merged firms, whereas the loss was generated only by the contraction of output that occurred, quite modest cost savings would offset substantial increases in price for feasible values of the elasticity of demand. We should stress at this point that we have dealt only with the simplest case in order to highlight the central issue. There are many refinements that also need to be considered and some of these are mentioned below.

The case shown in Figure 8.1, panel (a), involves an extreme change from perfect competition to complete monopoly. The more likely case in practice is where a firm already in possession of some market power seeks to improve its position further by merger. The effects in this case are shown in panel (b) of the figure. Market demand is again shown as D. The costs of the company assumed to have some pre-merger market power are shown by C_1. Its pre-merger price is P_L and output Q_L. In other words, pre-merger price is already above cost. The merger is assumed to increase market power further, so that price rises to P_M and output is restricted to Q_M, but costs are reduced to C_2. In such cases the net benefits of the merger are less likely to be positive, that is, L is more likely to be greater than G. The reason for this is that, as market power increases, the benefits of further concentration diminish (because the scale of output is falling) while the costs of further exploitation rise (because the value of lost output is increasing) (Fairburn and Kay, 1989, p. 9). In fact, Williamson indicates that, where pre-merger market power exists, the cost savings necessary to offset further price increases following merger are significantly greater than in the first case considered above. Even at this stage of the analysis, therefore, he concludes that antitrust agencies should look very closely at mergers which threaten significant increases in market power.

The simple trade-offs illustrated in Figure 8.1 are merely a starting-point. A number of extensions have to be considered for a more comprehensive analysis. The first point concerns the treatment of the income redistribution that occurs as a result of the merger. Referring back to panel (a) of Figure 8.1, the income transfer from consumers to producers, represented by the area $P_C P_M BE$, is regarded as welfare neutral in the partial equilibrium framework used. The justification for this treatment in the present context is that antitrust is not concerned with income distribution, which is more the province of government taxation policy. On the other hand, because the size of the income redistribution in relation to both G and L is likely to be large, any modification of this view is likely to have a significant impact. Thus, if even part of the income redistribution were to be treated negatively rather than neutrally, the net effect of the merger might become negative. For example, if the merger occurred at a time of high general unemployment to which it would contribute through the reduction in output, the effect on labour unrest might be worsened if it became clear that the merger substantially increased monopoly rents but that these were accorded no part in the antitrust assessment. The efficiency implications might then be quite serious.

A related issue, also concerned with efficiency, has been taken up by Posner (1975) and was introduced in Chapter 1. He argues that in general any policy which permits the earning of economic rents is likely to generate 'rent-seeking' behaviour. Firms will expend resources in competing to achieve positions of market dominance and in the limit this would result in the dissipation of all potential economic rent. In the present context, referring again to Figure 8.1, panel (a), this implies that the full social costs of the merger are represented by the areas $P_M BFH$ and EBK. The first of these costs represents the alternatives forgone by attracting resources into an activity with no positive social (as opposed to private) value. On this analysis, therefore, there is no trade-off: mergers for market power are unambiguously welfare-reducing and should accordingly be blocked. This statement of Posner's argument takes the extreme view that there is perfect information about market power opportunities. In practice this is unlikely to be the case. Only some firms will have full information and rent-seeking expenditures may fall short of the total amount. However, two important points emerge from the analysis. First, it emphasizes again that, even if only part of the area $P_M BFH$ is treated negatively, the merger may create social losses rather than gains. Secondly, it draws attention to the point which is often overlooked: that, in a rent-seeking competition, most firms will fail even though they have expended resources in the attempt.

Central to the trade-off approach is that a merger creates the opportunity for reducing costs: product lines may be rationalized to produce longer production runs, distribution networks may similarly be more fully utilized, and so on. While cases of this sort undoubtedly arise and can be represented schematically in Figure 8.1 by the downward shift in the cost curve, many observers over a very long period have recognized that, if a firm moves from a highly competitive environment to one of substantial market power, costs may rise rather than fall. In other words, X-inefficiency may emerge as a result of a general slackening of internal control. Managers may award themselves and the workforce large pay rises as well as luxurious fringe benefits. As Williamson puts it, 'Economies which are available in theory but, by reason of market power, are not sustainable are inadmissible' (Williamson, 1987, p. 20). In effect, what is happening in this case is an income transfer from the owners of the firm (who would benefit from higher profits if technical efficiency was maintained) to the employees of the firm. A legitimate question is then, why should this transfer be treated differently from that in the 'naive' model discussed above? The answer is that, in the context of merger policy analysis, the whole rationale of a trade-off approach is undermined if costs rise as a result of merger, rather than fall. A merger which creates market power with no change in costs in unequivocally bad. A fortiori, a merger which creates market power but also leads to a rise in costs is worse, regardless of who within the firm happens to benefit.[5]

In dealing with extensions to the simple cases shown in Figure 8.1, we have so far used a static framework without considering the time sequence of possible costs and benefits arising from merger. Two issues are important: the effect on other firms in the market and the possibility that any cost savings forecast for the merger could be achieved by internal growth. Williamson was writing at a time of considerable concern in the USA over the increasing concentration of industry. He therefore makes the point that one significant merger in a market may induce others, perhaps for defensive reasons, to seek mergers of their own. Within a short space of time, therefore, a fundamental change may occur in the market structure, with possible further consequences for price. The simple welfare loss shown in Figure 8.1 clearly does not show these secondary effects and therefore understates the full effect. On the other hand, an initial merger undertaken for efficiency reasons may simply be an indication that technical conditions in the industry are changing and that firms are likely to respond by joining larger groups. In this case, for an antitrust authority to block a merger on grounds of what Williamson terms 'incipiency' may be to deny customers longer-term gains from lower costs. In practice, the authority may have to make a general assessment of probabilities: is the current merger likely to spark off a series of defensive acquisitions by competitors, the effect of which may be almost entirely negative, or is it merely a signal that changed market conditions allow mergers to generate important efficiency gains?

The second issue has a narrower focus and is concerned with the question of whether the market power effect may be avoided altogether. If the firm could achieve the same cost savings by internal reorganization and expansion without merger, then, for policy purposes, this course of action is preferable. Costs would be reduced and if anything the level of competition in the market would be increased rather than diminished. The question is likely to be a complex one because the timing of the efficiency gains may be different with a merger than with internal expansion. In principle, the problems can be resolved by comparing the present value of net benefits (that is, efficiency gains minus market power effects) with the present value of benefits (from internal expansion). Williamson suggested, on the basis of varying assumptions about the timing and magnitude of the savings and losses from merger, that the alternative of internal expansion would have to produce its benefits fairly rapidly, generally within 3–5 years, for the merger to be blocked on this ground alone. As Cowling *et al.* (1980) point out, however, this conclusion rests on the assumption that both the cost savings and the market power effects occur instantaneously whereas, if the increase in price (and therefore the market power effect) precedes the cost savings, the result may change substantially and mean that internal expansion becomes the preferred social option. Given the trauma that mergers frequently cause to firms and the highly ambiguous results regarding their effects on performance (see Hughes, 1989, for an excellent survey) the cost savings may come later than the price increases.

It should by now be more than clear that the policy issues raised in a trade-off analysis of mergers are extremely complex. For this reason, some authorities have claimed that the approach has little, if any, practical application. In particular Posner (1976) has argued that the difficulties involved in trying to make reliable forecasts of both cost savings and market power effects are too great to form the basis of an antitrust assessment. While Williamson himself did not anticipate that a full-blown cost–benefit analysis should be undertaken in merger cases, he was convinced that even an informal recognition of the overall framework and an admission that efficiencies could be important would improve merger policy:

> Merely to display efficiency consequences in qualitative or crude quantitative terms should help to create and sustain an enforcement atmosphere in which economies are socially valued. Allowing economies to be introduced informally into pre-trial discussions with the antitrust enforcement agencies and to be presented favorably to the courts should further contribute to this simple but basic and worthwhile purpose. (Williamson, 1977a, pp. 734–5)

As we shall see in Section III below, the central thrust of Williamson's argument has now been accepted by the US antitrust authorities, although rather surprisingly not by those of the EU. Whether or not the overall framework is used, it is still necessary for an assessment to be made, first, of the extent of the relevant market and the most appropriate measure of the effect of the proposed merger on the degree of concentration; and secondly, of the entry conditions to the market. We have already discussed the problems involved in correctly defining the market in Chapter 4, Section III above. There is no need to repeat that discussion here, except to remind the reader that questions of both demand and supply substitution need to be considered and that evidence of consumer substitution of alternative products signifies the presence rather than the absence of pre-merger market power.

There has been considerable discussion recently of the way in which the effect of a merger on the correctly identified market should be measured. The two most widely used indices are the concentration ratio and the Herfindahl index of concentration. Both can be directly derived from models of oligopoly, but the latter has received much closer attention since its formal incorporation into the Merger Guidelines used by the US Department of Justice since 1982 (see Section III below). The concentration ratio is simply the share of the largest firms in the market and data using this measure were given in Table 2.1. The number taken usually depends on the purpose for which the measure is to be used and the rules governing the collection of the data. Thus in a market where prior to merger six firms had shares of 40, 20, 15, 10, 10 and 5 per cent, respectively, a merger between, say, the first and fifth largest firms would raise the four-firm concentration ratio from 85 per cent to 95 per cent. In this illustration, the market is already dominated by the largest firm, whose share was already twice that of its closest rival and, unless entry to the market is very easy, an antitrust authority is likely to need a great deal of convincing that the merger should be allowed.

The main advantage of the concentration ratio in an antitrust case is that its meaning is immediately apparent to all concerned as it is based directly on market shares. In this context also the major drawback of the measure, namely that it only gives the cumulative share of the n largest firms, without any indication of the overall distribution, does not apply because the antitrust authority will have access to the market shares of all significant firms. (For a full discussion of the merits and drawbacks of this and other measures, see Scherer and Ross, 1990, ch. 3, or Singer, 1968, ch. 13.)

The second concentration measure widely used in discussion of antitrust cases is the Herfindahl index, which will be denoted by H. It is defined as follows:

$$H = \sum_{i=1}^{n} S_i^2,$$ (8.1)

where S_i denotes the market share of the ith firm. The index is thus the sum of the squared shares of all the firms in the market. An illustrative example of the calculation of the H index is given in Table 8.1. In keeping with current US antitrust practice, the market shares are expressed in percentage form (rather than proportions). The index can therefore vary from 10 000 for a complete monopoly to a value approaching zero for a market populated by a great number of very small firms.

Table 8.1   Calculation of the Herfindahl (H) index in a market with six firms

Firm ranking	Pre-merger market share (S_i) (per cent)	Squared pre-merger market share	Post-merger market share (S_i) (per cent)	Squared post merger market share
1	40	1 600	50	2 500
2	20	400	20	400
3	15	225	15	225
4	10	100	10	100
5	10	100	5	25
6	5	25	—	
		$H = 2\ 450$		$H = 3\ 250$

The pre-merger index is thus 2450 and a merger between the first and fifth-ranked firms raises it by 800 points to 3250. The index incorporates the shares of all firms in the market and, although this may appear to place a large burden on data requirements where there are a large number of small firms, their contribution to the index is relatively unimportant. For example, in the pre-merger case given in Table 8.1 if, instead of the smallest firm having 5 per cent of the market, there were four firms, one with a 2 per cent share and the remainder with 1 per cent each, the pre-merger H index would be 2432, that is 18 points (or less than 1 per cent) lower than the original. The corollary of this point is that, by squaring the shares, the index gives particular weight to the largest firms, which is important in an antitrust enquiry. In practical applications, however, the main disadvantage of the H index may be its unfamiliarity and counter-intuitive construction. Businessmen and lawyers are familiar with market shares and the possible implications of increases in shares. The sum of squared market shares does not have such a direct appeal.

To counterbalance this, it has the property of being related to market power, under certain assumed structural and behavioural conditions. Thus in an n-firm oligopoly where the firms have different but constant marginal costs and where they all assume that their own output decision will have no effect on the output of their rivals (that is, the basic Cournot assumption), the following relationship holds:

$$\frac{P - \overline{MC}}{P} = \frac{H}{e}, \tag{8.2}$$

where the left-hand expression is the weighted average price cost margin for firms in the market, H is the Herfindahl concentration index and e is the market price elasticity of demand. In this model, therefore, there is a direct relationship between concentration, measured by the H index, and the ability of firms to raise price above costs. (The derivation of the expression is given in the appendix to this chapter.)

Thus, in certain basic oligopoly models, market power and concentration are related, *ceteris paribus*.[6] This strengthens the supposition underlying Williamson's analysis, that sizeable horizontal mergers may well increase market power, even though simultaneously they may promise efficiency savings. Whichever model is used, however, the ability to maintain prices above competitive levels depends crucially on entry conditions. The third major element, therefore, in the analysis of horizontal mergers is an assessment of barriers to entry. The sequence of the analysis is, first, the correct delineation of the market; secondly, the effect of the merger on concentration within this market; and thirdly, the degree of difficulty involved in entering the market. If for a variety of reasons, mentioned briefly below, it is hard or impossible for capital to flow into the market, the ability of the merged firm persistently to maintain prices above the competitive level will be possible and the observed increase in concentration will be converted into market power. Monopoly profits are likely to follow.

An important corollary of this conclusion needs to be emphasized. Even if a horizontal merger increases dramatically the market share and thus the level of concentration in the market, if entry to the market is easy the firm will gain no market power. Its ability to raise price will be constrained by the threat of entry. In terms of the Williamson analysis, if some economies from the merger are likely, yet no increase in market power occurs, then the merger creates net benefits and can proceed without antitrust intervention. In the relevant market, an increase in concentration is a necessary but not sufficient condition to trigger a trade-off analysis.

Entry conditions were discussed in Chapters 1 and 2 and at this stage we need only underline the more important points. First, easy entry does not imply that firms do not have to expend resources to enter a market, merely that the size of those expenditures is no greater than those previously incurred by the incumbent firms. As we have seen, in some cases the existing firms may have made a strategic commitment of resources which makes credible their threat of a particular course of action (for example, an increase in output) if entry occurs or seems likely. Secondly, as Baumol and his colleagues (1982) have emphasized in their theory of 'contestable' markets, where an important part of the necessary investment to start producing in a market represents a sunk cost (that is, it is irretrievable should the firm wish subsequently to withdraw), this may deter entry. In other words, important barriers to exit in the form of sunk costs can act as a significant deterrent to entry. In the case of expenditures required to promote product differentiation (including advertising) entrants may thus not only have to incur a greater volume of expenditure than the incumbents who may have been the first in the field, but recognize that a large part of it may be irretrievable should their entry effort fail. For these reasons product differentiation advantages broadly interpreted may constitute some of the most formidable barriers to entry. Thirdly, many of the recent contributions to the theory of strategic behaviour have emphasized the interaction between market conduct and market structure. This has important implications for the analysis of horizontal mergers. When Bain (1956) published his pathbreaking work on barriers to new competition, he was working within the market–structure–conduct–performance framework which he did much to develop. Within this framework entry conditions were a highly significant element of market structure which was expected to have a direct influence on market conduct. If entry barriers and market concentration were high, for example, there would be scope for maintaining price above competitive levels, *ceteris paribus*. Conventional merger policy analysis has been concerned therefore with the impact on concentration and existing entry conditions. The significance of the more recent strategic contributions is that they demonstrate that many forms of market conduct may heighten barriers to entry. The examples given in Chapter 4 (covering excess capacity, brand proliferation and pre-emptive patenting sustained by high R & D) may all make it much more difficult for a potential entrant to gain a viable market share. Perceiving this, the firms will therefore stay out of the market. In the context of a merger enquiry, therefore, an important question is whether the change in market structure would also increase the probability of strategic behaviour. In other words, would the merger lead to a deterioration in future entry conditions? A full analysis of a sizeable merger therefore, requires some assessment of current entry conditions but also some consideration of the likely increase in entry barriers in the future, should the merger proceed. To the extent that more concentrated markets tend to generate greater commitment to strategic behaviour, this underlines the need for accurate measurement of the effect of a merger on concentration.[7]

Given the importance of entry conditions, how can they be assessed, especially when the time available is severely constrained, as it frequently is in merger enquiries? In a recent analysis written mainly for lawyers having a very practical interest in this question, Salop (1986a) focuses essentially on three factors:

1. If entry takes a long time or, what amounts to the same thing, if actual entrants only obtain small market shares, there are two reasons why incumbent firms will feel less constrained in their pricing behaviour. First, it may not be worthwhile in these circumstances for the established firms to reduce their prices before entry occurs. As a result, consumers suffer longer from the higher prices. Secondly, a strong likelihood that entrants will not achieve a viable market share rapidly raises their financial exposure and the risk of failure. The threat of entry will therefore be reduced and existing firms will feel less constrained in raising their prices above competitive levels.

2. If new entrants face cost or demand disadvantages relative to established firms, they will be unable to constrain price increases up to an amount approximately equivalent to the extent of the disadvantage. Thus, if entrants suffer a 10 per cent cost disadvantage, incumbents will be able to raise their prices by an amount marginally below this without any restraint. Whether this amounts to a permanent barrier, or is merely transitory, will depend on the circumstances and is linked to the next point.[8]

3. Where economies of scale or of scope (that is, the cost of producing a range of products is less than of producing them individually) are important, the entrant faces the choice of attempting to market on a small or large scale. Marketing on a small scale may not ensure an adequate market share and therefore poses no threat to established firms. Marketing on a large scale in order to gain available economies exposes the firm to two risks. First, as we have mentioned above, promotional expenditures may be largely sunk

costs and therefore constitute an important barrier to exit. Secondly, attempted entry on a large scale is more likely to promote a price response from established firms. Consumers benefit from the lower prices but, to the extent that the interaction of the two factors tends to keep effective entry out, established firms will be able to maintain prices above competitive levels.

Of the three main points that we have emphasized in this section (market definition, appropriate concentration index and entry conditions) the last is probably the most difficult and controversial. Not only is there still considerable debate over what should properly be treated as barriers to entry (Gilbert, 1989), but there is still no agreement on the relative weights that should be given to the effectiveness of actual as opposed to potential competition in restraining prices (compare, for example, Baumol, 1982, with Shepherd, 1984). A sizeable horizontal merger will have the immediate and obvious effect of removing the independent influence of an important competitor, with the added possibility that the merged firm may have the option of affecting future market structure by its strategic behaviour. In contrast, the threat of entry may be perceived by the antitrust agencies as a much more insubstantial restraining force, and one which may be weakened by the merger.

III   Merger policy

For any merger to infringe the amended Clayton Act in the USA, it must result in a substantial lessening of competition or in a tendency to create a monopoly in any line of commerce in any section of the country. The original Act, passed in 1914, contained a loophole. It referred to acquisition of the stock or other share capital of a company, rather than its assets. Firms were thus able to acquire directly the assets of another company without infringing the law. In practice, of course, there is no economic difference between acquiring a controlling interest in a company by a purchase of its shares and a purchase of its assets. This provision of the Act therefore remained largely ineffective until the amendment provided by the Celler–Kefauver Act of 1950.

Precisely the same market definition problems arise in a horizontal merger enquiry as in a dominant firm enquiry, discussed in Chapter 6. The market must be delineated in terms of both products and geographic area. It was clear from the first decisions on horizontal mergers that the Supreme Court was going to interpret the market narrowly and, equally important, was then prepared to infer significant increases in market power from relatively modest increments in market share by firms whose opening position seemed far from dominant. Four examples illustrate the point: a merger between an aluminium cable maker and one specializing in copper cable with small output of aluminium cable increased the acquiring firm's market share from 27.8 to 29.1 per cent when copper cable was excluded from the market definition; a merger of a metal container firm with a glass bottle manufacturer (but excluding containers of other materials) increased market share from 22 per cent to 25 per cent; a merger in the Los Angeles grocery retailing market increased the share from 4.7 per cent to 7.5 per cent; and finally, a merger between brewers in Wisconsin increased market share in the state from 13 per cent to 24 per cent.[9]

In each of these cases, the definition of the 'market' for antitrust purposes does not bear close scrutiny. There is little if any attention to the fundamental question of market power and whether the position of the merged firm in the market, even as defined, gives it leverage over price. Even if the market is correctly defined in these cases, the resulting market share makes it extremely doubtful whether the firm achieved a monopoly or caused a substantial decline in competition. Yet in each of these cases, and others during the 1960s and early 1970s, the Supreme Court found an infringement of the amended Clayton Act and blocked the mergers. Many decisions seemed to be at such variance with economic logic that one dissenting judge was moved to conclude that 'The sole consistency that I can find is that in litigation under section 7, the Government always wins.'[10] In retrospect, an explanation of this aspect of US antitrust policy during this period is that a relatively liberal Supreme Court was interpreting what it took to be the will of Congress at the time of the passage of the amendment to the Clayton Act in 1950. Alarmed by a post-war merger wave, which by later standards was more of a ripple, Congress wished to halt what it saw as a relentless increase in concentration. The amended Act was a means to halt this trend. This interpretation also helps to explain the particular emphasis on market shares to the practical exclusion of other factors. A merger which resulted in a 'significant' increase in concentration was seen by the court at this time as so inherently likely to lessen competition that it would be prevented unless there was overwhelming evidence to the contrary. Judging from the market shares created in the cases listed above, such a presumption would almost certainly be made in cases involving market shares in the 25–30 per cent range.

The focus on market shares was enshrined in the first set of Merger Guidelines published by the Justice Department in 1968. The Guidelines were to indicate to the business community those mergers which the Department would be likely to challenge. A distinction was made between markets where concentration was already high (for example, four-firm concentration ratio of 75 per cent or more) and where it was lower. In the first category, if the acquiring firm had a share of 15 per cent or more, any acquisition of a firm with a share of 1 per cent or more would be challenged. Even the case of a firm with a market share as low as 4 per cent acquiring another with a similar share would provoke a challenge. In the more moderate concentration category, the relevant market share thresholds were lower but even here the Antitrust Division would spring into action against mergers where, for example, the acquiring company had a 15 per cent share and the acquired company 3 per cent or more, or again if an acquiring company with 5 per cent of the market tried to acquire another with a similar share.[11] Two observations can be made about these Guidelines. First, they are firmly fixed in a market structure framework with an overriding emphasis on market share, even though no general guidance is given about the correct principles for defining the market. Secondly, the low level of the market shares potentially involved in a challenge is remarkable. It implies that a significant decrease in competition can occur following trivial increases in the market share of a quite modest participant.

The 1968 Guidelines probably marked the high point of the structuralist approach to merger policy. Thereafter the antitrust authorities had a much harder time convincing the Court that a merger infringed the Clayton Act. A significant case in this respect was *General Dynamics*, settled in 1974.[12] The Department of Justice challenged the merger on what appeared the familiar ground of market share. The combined share of the two coal companies involved amounted to just under 22 per cent in the Illinois area. The case is interesting not only because the Court found for the companies, but because of the much more rigorous view of what constituted the relevant market. The court recognized that, in this market, the ability to compete depended on the ability to win future long-term contracts from electricity companies. This in turn depended on the availability of coal reserves. There was clear evidence that the acquired company had already committed its reserves and could not easily gain access to others. In effect, therefore, the acquisition had no impact on competition and the merger could be allowed. The court looked behind the market share data and the apparent increase in concentration to the realities of actual competition in the market and decided that future competition would not decline despite the undoubted increase in concentration of current output.

The change in administration in the 1980s taking a more favourable view towards business, and the appointment of more conservative judges to the court, helped to reinforce the emphasis in US merger policy first noted in the *General Dynamics* case. In particular, the influence of economic principles rather than the presumed intention of Congress was apparent in the revised Merger Guidelines published in 1982.[13] Although there were undoubted problems with the application of the Guidelines, they have generally received favourable comment from economists as marking a considerable advance over the previous approach (see in particular the Symposium introduced by Salop, 1987, whose comments we draw on in what follows).

According to Salop, the Guidelines involve a five-point procedure. First, the relevant market is defined for the purpose of establishing the competitive effects of the merger. Secondly, pre- and post-merger concentration in the market is calculated, using the Herfindahl index (rather than the concentration ratio as in the 1968 Guidelines). Thirdly, the likelihood of entry is evaluated. Fourthly, any other competitive factors likely to affect post merger collusion possibilities are considered. Finally, many years after Williamson argued in favour of including efficiencies in the defence of merger, potential cost savings are estimated (Salop, 1987, pp. 6–7). The data assembled under this five-point procedure are then weighed in order to decide whether the particular merger will be challenged. In view of the novel approach used, the first of these five points deserves particular attention. In the Guidelines, a market is defined as follows:

> a product or group of products and a geographic area in which it is sold such that a hypothetical, profit maximising firm, not subject to price regulation, that was the only present and future producer or seller of those products in that area likely would impose at least a 'small but significant and non-transitory' increase in price, assuming the terms of sale of all other products are held constant. (US Dept of Justice and Federal Trade Commission, *Horizontal Guidelines*, Washington, 1992, p. 7)

The definition reveals quite clearly, therefore, that the purpose of an antitrust intervention in a horizontal merger is the evaluation of increases in market power. If applied consistently, it should cut through the often irrelevant discussion of whether the 'wider market' really consists of a number of 'market segments', 'sub-markets' or 'market niches'. All of these terms may have their legitimate uses in planning sales and marketing campaigns but in an antitrust enquiry they merely serve to obscure or fudge the main issue: would the ownership of a product or range of products by a hypothetical monopolist give the firm additional leverage over price? If it would, then the products should be included in the market. If it would not, then, as far as the antitrust enquiry is concerned, it belongs to another market. The Department could start with a narrowly defined product and ask whether a hypothetical monopolist of that product could impose a significant price increase. If the increase could be undermined by buyers shifting to other products, those chosen substitutes should be included in the market. The question should then be repeated until the narrowest group of products over which the price increase would hold has been determined. The principle is equally applicable to what the Guidelines term the 'product market' and the 'geographical market', although in practice it may be easier to delineate the latter than the former. In the geographic market, where firms have roughly similar production costs at different locations, transport costs will effectively determine which plants should be included in the market. In the 'product' market delineation will have to be determined by other, less direct factors.

In most cases the authorities have taken a 5 per cent price increase as 'small but significant' and one year as signifying a 'non-transitory' period of time. Thus, in trying to determine whether products A and B are close enough substitutes to be included in the same market, the authorities may ask customers of product A whether they would seriously consider switching to product B if the price of A was increased by 5 per cent. If there was clear evidence that important customers would switch, then both products should be included in the market. Similarly, technical data showing that equipment could be adjusted relatively easily to produce A rather than B in response to the price change would lead to the same conclusion. Statistical data showing close alignment through time of the product prices may under certain circumstances indicate that they belong to the same market. In fact the publication and use of the 1982 and 1984 Guidelines with the need for accurate market assessment has produced a large literature discussing the merits of alternative methods. For a review, see Sherwin and Stigler (1985) and Scheffman and Spiller (1987).

One possible pitfall in the approach concerns the so called 'cellophane fallacy', to which we have already referred. In the context of a merger case, the acquiring firm may already have market power and be charging a price above the competitive level. The firm may well be operating on an elastic portion of its demand curve, implying that at the prevailing price other products are regarded by customers as relatively close substitutes. The market definition exercise may therefore include such products in the relevant market, even though this is merely a reflection of the pre-merger use of market power. The proper test is whether a non-trivial price increase above the competitive level would produce a significant substitution between products. In other words, unless the antitrust authority is very careful in its assessment of pre-merger price levels, it may end up defining the market too widely, including products which have only become 'substitutes' because of the use of market power.

The Guidelines approach to market definition is thus not without its difficulties. Although data problems and time constraints may mean that the authorities cannot undertake a sophisticated statistical survey to define the market, the central focus on market power should ensure that they are asking the right questions and discarding irrelevant information.

Market definition, however, is only the first important stage of the procedure. Once it has been defined, the calculation of the Herfindahl concentration indices is merely a matter of arithmetic. For this stage, however, the Guidelines distinguish three categories. If the post-merger index remains below 1000 (approximately equivalent to a four-firm concentration ratio of 50 per cent (White, 1987), then, whatever the other circumstances in the market, such as entry conditions, the merger will not be challenged. Mergers in this category are in a 'safe harbor'. At the other extreme where the merger leads to an *H* index of 1800 or above (approximately equivalent to a four-firm concentration ratio of 70 per cent or more) the authorities would probably challenge the merger if the index was increased by at least 50 points and if entry was judged to be difficult. If the index was increased by at least 100 points the merger would almost certainly be challenged. In the middle category, where the merger would result in an index of between 1000 and 1800, the authorities could attempt to block it only if the index was increased by 100 points or more. Entry conditions and other factors would also be given most weight when considering mergers in this category.

Measuring the ease of entry is approached in the same way as for market definition. In response to a hypothetical price increase, would sufficient new capacity enter the market within two years to render the price increase ineffective? The focus is clearly on market power and the extent to which the threat of entry would constrain the merged firm from raising its prices. The factors discussed at the end of the previous section can be used to make the actual assessment. The interplay between post-merger concentration and entry conditions is likely to be most important in the middle category, where the presumption of collusive behaviour and effective exercise of market power is not so strong. However, even if entry is judged to be difficult and concentration high, other factors may allow the merger to be passed. Much attention at this stage of the analysis is likely to be given to those factors which facilitate tacit collusion, discussed in Chapter 7. The presence of powerful, skilled buyers and a degree of product heterogeneity may, for example, work against successful collusion even after the merger. On the other hand, if it is felt the merger will help to facilitate price coordination by making information exchanges easier, it is more likely to be challenged, *ceteris paribus*. Taken together, therefore, the approaches used to define the market and assess the ease of entry take account of both demand- and supply-side factors affecting market power, which we discussed in Chapter 4.

The final stage of the procedure is, in principle, highly significant and innovatory. It allows for a merger which will lead to a price increase due to a rise in market power to be saved if it can be shown convincingly that the merger is 'reasonably necessary' to gain significant cost savings or economies of scale. Cost reductions that could be achieved in some other way (for example, by internal growth) would not be counted in this part of the analysis. Surprisingly, in view of Williamson's results referred to in Section II above, no discussion of the size of any cost savings is given in the Guidelines. It is not clear, for example, whether the intention is that they should be sufficient simply to outweigh any possible deadweight loss from the price increase, in which case they need only be quite modest in most instances.

The overall approach embodied in the Guidelines has considerable appeal to economists and has received some very distinguished support (see, for example, the papers by Fisher, Schmalensee and White in the Symposium introduced by Salop, 1987). It should be remembered, however, that the Guidelines are essentially a screening procedure to sort out those mergers which merit challenge from the large majority that do not. Fisher in particular was concerned that what was merely the prologue should not be regarded as the main action: 'the Guidelines are not a substitute for serious analysis, and the

Department of Justice staff has tended to focus narrowly on issues of market definition and concentration measures as though such issues were dispositive. That is a mistake. In the present (and likely future) state of our knowledge, serious analysis of market power and oligopoly cannot be subsumed in a few spuriously precise measurements' (Fisher, 1987a, p. 39). The fact that the effect of the merger can be measured with such apparent precision on a numerical scale tends to give it an aura of scientific verisimilitude and weight disproportionate to its underlying significance. On the other hand, some observers have suggested that in practice the Guidelines have not been applied as written (Krattenmaker and Pitofsky, 1988) or that the efficiency defence has been used to swamp more traditional concerns (Lande, 1988). According to one of the few empirical studies of merger policy in the 1980s, however, no one part of the five-stage procedure appeared to dominate the others. On the whole the application of US policy since the early 1980s has followed the spirit if not the letter of the Guidelines and been consistent with economic principles (Coate and McChesney, 1992).

The current state of US merger policy is unusual in a number of ways. The precedents handed down by the Supreme Court in the 1960s, which reflected a very narrow structuralist approach and the perceived desire of Congress to halt increasing concentration, still stand. Yet the fundamental change in understanding and approach, in part reflected in a noticeable drop in the rate at which sizeable mergers were challenged in the 1980s (Scherer, 1989) and embodied in the new Guidelines, has not so far received the formal seal of approval from the Supreme Court, which has not had to adjudicate recently on a horizontal merger case. Given its current composition, however, and the recent analytical slant, any future judgement is likely to be very different from the leading cases of the 1960s.

Merger policy in the UK was introduced in 1965 in the wake of the first post-war merger or takeover wave. No changes to the policy were made in the 1998 Competition Act despite long-standing and serious criticisms. Two of the more serious complaints were as follows. First, many observers considered that the policy was weakened by the degree of political control exercised by the relevant minister. He or she was ultimately responsible for determining which mergers were examined by the MMC and, where action was necessary following an adverse finding, the minister could determine the outcome. Secondly, once a merger had been referred the MMC had to determine whether or not it would operate against the public interest. It did not have to be satisfied that the merger would operate positively *in* the public interest. This neutral stance that the MMC was instructed to take meant that the evidence submitted by the proponents of the merger was often superficial and sketchy. It was argued that a more robust approach would force the parties to provide more detailed and substantial information in those relatively few mergers that were challenged (George, 1989; Hay and Vickers, 1988).

Following the re-election of the Labour Government in June 2001, a White Paper was published setting out in detail proposals for a fundamental reform of merger policy.[14] The relevant measures were to be incorporated into the Enterprise Bill (2002). Both of the above criticisms are met under the new proposals. Responsibility for control of mergers would lie in the hands of the Office of Fair Trading, save for a very small minority of cases involving an 'exceptional public interest issue' (such as defence and public security). In these cases the minister retains authority as to whether or not the merger can proceed. Equally important is the change in the test for a merger applied by the Office of Fair Trading. The broad 'public interest' test is to be replaced by a competitive impact test. Thus only those mergers which result in a substantial lessening of competition will be prohibited. The new test brings UK law broadly into line with that applied both in the EU and the USA. However, in certain cases the test can be modified. The way this modification was phrased in the White Paper seems to recognize the central point behind Williamson's trade-off analysis which we discussed above (pp. 173–5). Thus 'the authorities will – exceptionally – be able to clear a merger or allow it to proceed with less stringent competition remedies than would otherwise be the case, where they believe that the merger will bring overall benefits to UK consumers affected by the merger. The authorities will be able to take account of consumer benefits which take the form of lower prices, or greater innovation, choice or quality of products or services' (Department of Trade and Industry, 2001, para.5.10). We have used the word 'seems' advisedly because the passage is ambiguous. Williamson argued that, where a merger would result in both cost reductions and increases in market power, it could be allowed if benefits outweighed costs, *ceteris paribus*. The White Paper takes the position that a merger which will lead to a substantial lessening of competition might be saved if it will also lead to consumer benefits, for example, in the form of lower prices. The difficulty is that a merger which substantially reduces competition would in most instances lead to *increased* prices for precisely that reason. Only in cases where the merger generated such enormous cost savings that the combined firm was able to lower its price would the condition in the Act be met. However, the overwhelming body of evidence on the efficiency effects of mergers indicates that such cases are very rare (Mueller, 1997; Ravenscraft and Scherer, 1987). There is a danger that promoters of mergers may see this clause as a means of acquiring market power in exchange for a promise of future cost and price reductions which fail to materialize.

Prior to the 2002 proposals there were two tests which could qualify a merger for investigation. The first involved market share: any merger creating or increasing a 25 per cent share of supply of a particular good or service in the

UK (or a substantial part of it) qualified for investigation. This test is to be retained. The second test involved the volume of assets to be acquired: any merger involving the acquisition of gross worldwide assets of £70 million or more could be investigated. This test has been dropped in favour of a turnover threshold. Any acquisition of a company with a UK turnover of £45 million or more is liable to investigation. Given the growing importance of service industries and intangible assets, it was thought a turnover test was now more appropriate than one based on assets.

Mergers above either of these thresholds may then be subject to a two stage enquiry, as under the previous rules. The first, preliminary stage by the OFT, taking a maximum of 30 working days, determines whether a more detailed investigation is required. If it is, then the merger is referred to the Competition Commission which must normally submit its report within 24 weeks, although exceptionally this can be extended to 32 weeks. Companies failing to supply information required by the Commission may be fined.

The range of possible remedies has been extended. As well as divestment of assets or outright prohibition, the OFT will now have the power to require companies to grant licences to competitors, and to publish information in a specified form. Since companies are still allowed to complete an acquisition which passes the thresholds and which may therefore be subject to Competition Commission enquiry, the OFT will have the power to prevent companies from integrating their activities before a final decision on an enquiry has been made. This ensures that the ultimate remedy of prohibition is not frustrated by merged companies claiming that their operations would be irreparably damaged because they had become fully integrated.

Once implemented, the proposals will thus remedy most of the previous shortcomings of UK merger policy. Of course none of the analytical difficulties inherent in merger analysis have gone away. It will still be necessary to determine the extent of the relevant market in terms of products and geography. Predicting the extent to which a merger may increase market power because of the decline in competition remains a highly imperfect art. However, the new procedures together with the guidelines on these issues published by the DGFT, mean that UK policy will be as well placed as any to make sound and consistent decisions.

Increasingly, of course, UK companies proposing large mergers will have to take EU policy into account. As we noted in Chapter 3, the European Treaty contained no provisions for dealing with mergers. Prior to September 1990, therefore, the Commission had to rely on Articles 81 and 82. In Chapter 3 we mentioned the two important cases which established a rather limited jurisdiction for the Commission over large horizontal mergers. In 1973, in the *Continental Can* case, the European Court determined that a merger could constitute abusive behaviour under Article 82 even though the acquiring firm had not used its dominant position to initiate the merger.[15] Although the decision was welcome to the Commission, the principle could only be applied to companies already in a dominant position. Mergers which themselves created dominance were not covered. Furthermore, the control could only be applied after the event and could not therefore be used to prevent undesirable mergers from taking place. In the wake of the decision the Commission tabled its first proposed merger regulation. Revised proposals were to follow with inexorable regularity throughout the 1980s. The decision in 1987 in the *Philip Morris* case probably played an important part in persuading member states that some proper machinery for merger control was urgently needed. In this case the Commission cleared the acquisition by Philip Morris of a 30 per cent holding in its major rival, Rothmans. Two other competitors, BAT and Reynolds, then challenged the purchase as inconsistent with the EU. The Court upheld the Commission's decision that in this particular case the share purchase did not restrict competition. However, it went on to make it clear that in other cases, where a share purchase was used for or could lead to joint control or cooperative action, Article 81 would apply. As a result of the case, there was a good deal of uncertainty about which shareholdings might be found to violate Article 81 and, if they did, how Section (ii) (restrictive agreements are void) was to be applied, and so on. The Commissioner for competition at the time had also made it plain that, if a suitable merger regulation could not be agreed, he would not hesitate to use Articles 81 and 82 for this purpose.

Not without a good deal of reluctance on the part of some member states, Regulation 4064 was finally agreed late in 1989 and the procedures came into operation in September 1990.[16] Mergers involving a worldwide turnover of the two (or more) firms in excess of EURO 5 billion qualify for examination by the Commission. The aggregate Community-wide turnover of at least two of the firms concerned must exceed EURO 250 million and each firm must do less than two-thirds of its business (measured by turnover) in one EU country. In other words, the merger must have a clear 'Community' dimension. Depending on the circumstances, a stake in another company as low as 20 per cent may be regarded as a 'merger' for this purpose.[17] A detailed notification procedure and timetable are laid down. Mergers of this size must be notified to the Commission within one week of the bid or acquisition of control and they cannot then be completed during the three weeks following notification. The Commission thus has one month for its preliminary enquiry. It must then decide either to give clearance to the merger or to undertake a full investigation. In the latter case it normally has a further four months to complete its full enquiry and reach a decision. Thus at most five months can elapse between an initial bid and the final outcome.

There are essentially three kinds of exception that can be made to the above rules, and it is a reflection of the difficulties that the Commission had in gaining acceptance for the regulation that these were normally referred to by the name of the country whose special interest or concerns they represented. Thus the so-called German clause refers to a procedure which allows a national merger authority to consider special cases. In particular, where any member state believes that a merger would create or strengthen a dominant position within its borders, it can apply to the Commission for authority to carry out its own investigations. If the Commission agrees with this assessment, it can refer the case to the authorities of the member state. If it feels that no distinct market can be identified in the member state, it can refuse to authorize this transfer of jurisdiction and the member then has the right of appeal to the Court. The clause is an expression of the concern felt by the Germans that the EU approach may tend to weaken their own tough merger policy.

In sharp contrast stands the so-called French clause which allows the Commission in making its appraisal of dominance to weigh up the need to preserve and encourage competition against 'the development of technical and economic progress, provided that it is to consumers' advantage and does not form an obstacle to competition'. This part of the Regulation has generated a good deal of suspicion or even hostility in Germany and Britain because of its apparent mixture of competition and industrial policy elements. The fear was that it might be used as a means of allowing industrial restructuring by merger rather than to control dominance. According to one authoritative source, it was 'the result of a political compromise between the big European countries (England [*sic*], France and Germany) and it was accepted by the German Federal Government for political reasons (to further European integration)' (Schmidt, 1991).

The other exceptions are less controversial. The so-called Dutch clause allows a member state to request that the Commission investigate a particular merger within its borders, even though it did not meet the turnover criteria. The clause was to protect the interests of the smaller members, some of which do not have established machinery of merger controls. Finally, the so-called English clause allows the national authority to take appropriate measures to protect its legitimate interests such as 'public security, plurality of the media and prudential rules'.

As far as remedies are concerned, the Commission has substantial powers under the Regulation. It can order divestiture, impose conditions on a merger and impose fines if the Regulation is infringed (for example, companies can be fined up to 10 per cent of their combined turnover for not following instructions made under the regulation and up to EURO 50 000 for a breach of the notification or information rules).

Mergers which create or strengthen a dominant position and which are likely to impede competition in the EU or a significant part of it will be prohibited. In making its assessment the Commission has to consider a whole list of factors set out in Article 2 of the Regulation. It has to take into account:

(a) the need to preserve and develop effective competition within the Common Market in view of, among other things, the structure of all the markets concerned and the actual or potential competition from undertakings located within or without the Community;

(b) the market position of the undertakings concerned and their economic and financial power, the opportunities available to suppliers and users, their access to suppliers or markets, any legal or other barrier to entry, supply or demand trends for the relevant goods or services, the interests of the intermediate and ultimate consumers, and the development of technical and economic progress provided that it is to the consumers' advantage and does not form an obstacle to competition. (Article 2.1)

In one form or another, therefore, the factors included in the US Guidelines also appear in Article 2.1. The effect on competition within the relevant market has to be assessed, including potential as well as actual competition; competitors within the EU as well as outside; and the height and character of any barriers to entry. Instead of dwelling on indices of concentration, the article refers to the 'market position of the undertakings concerned', but then adds rather vaguely 'and their economic and financial power', implying that in some cases the depth of a company's purse may be a relevant consideration. Although the same factors appear as in the US Guidelines, they are not so structured or tightly drawn in the Regulation.

Rather surprisingly, the Regulation makes no provision for an efficiency defence. The penultimate draft Regulation did contain such a provision but ran into strong opposition from some countries who feared that a rather loosely drawn 'efficiency' clause might be used by some members who viewed mergers as a means of promoting 'national champions'. If large mergers which threatened to cause a substantial reduction in competition could be success-fully defended on the grounds that they would reduce costs and (say) improve exports from the EU, the actual outcome was likely to be greater concentration and inflexible market structure (George and Jacquemin, 1990). Part of the original intention appears to have been retained in the French clause mentioned above. However, given that the main concern is to be the impact on competition, the other concerns are redundant. No merger can be saved under the Regulation if it will lead to a substantial reduction in competition and the strengthening of dominance, even if it promises large technical advances, all of which would accrue to consumers. Alternatively any merger which will bring these benefits without substantially reducing competition would in any case be allowed. Formally this must be the conclusion, given the wording of the Regulation. George and Jacquemin, however, considered that in practice there may be more scope for a persuasively argued efficiency case before the Commission than would appear: 'Doubts concerning the competitive impact together with a strongly argued case for technical and economic progress may result in several mergers being approved mainly on grounds of dynamic efficiency gains and the need to meet competition from large firms outside the Community – a situation little different to that which could have prevailed with an explicit efficiency defence' (ibid., p. 243).

There is little evidence that their expectation has been borne out. Commenting on the first year's operation of the policy, the Director of the 'Merger Task Force' explained that in none of the cases considered did the terms 'efficiency' or more generally 'benefit to the economy' appear (Overbury, 1991, p. 84). He was at pains to assure his readers that all decisions were taken purely on competition grounds, as the Regulation stipulates. At the same time, he met head-on the fear of many observers that the Regulation would be used as an instrument of industrial rather than strictly antitrust policy. In his judgement the wording does not allow such an interpretation:

> If the operation creates a dominant position which significantly impedes competition 'it *shall* be declared incompatible with the common market'. The existence of the word '*shall*' here seems very important. If the Regulation envisaged the possibility for the Commission to undertake a competition-based analysis and then commence an industrial/social policy balancing test to see whether the operation may nonetheless be approved, the wording would surely be different, and would, at least, have permitted some discretion on the part of the Commission. (Ibid., p. 83, italics in the original)

Prior to the introduction of the Regulation it was anticipated that between 50 and 60 merger proposals would be considered each year. In the event, during the first decade of the Regulation the annual average number of notifications of proposed mergers was 156. In all, more than 1500 proposals were notified to the Commission, more than 1400 were cleared after the first stage of the procedure and of those progressing to the more detailed second stage only 13 were prohibited, although another 120 were permitted subject to complying with specified commitments (Morgan, 2001).

The first merger to be blocked by the Commission was highly controversial. The case, which was the fifty-second notified to the Commission, involved a bid through a joint venture (ATR) by Aérospatiale and Alenia, the French and Italian state-owned aircraft manufacturers, for de Havilland, the Canadian subsidiary of Boeing.[18] The bidding companies were the leading producers of regional or commuter turboprop aircraft both in the Community and the world. De Havilland was the second largest producer. The market for such aircraft was divided into three, according to seat capacity, with the main focus of attention on aircraft with 40–59 seats where ATR's share of the world market would have increased from 45 per cent to 64 per cent (with its European share rising to 72 per cent) and on aircraft with 60–70 seats where ATR's share in both markets would have risen to about three-quarters. The merger would also have increased ATR's product range and left it as the only manufacturer producing a comprehensive range. The Commission decided that the merger would create a position of dominance and significantly curtail competition, especially because of the difficulties of new entry to a mature market. Rather worryingly, in view of the US experience in the 1960s, the suggestion that the merger would lead to cost reductions and marketing gains was regarded as detrimental to consumers because they would put existing producers at a disadvantage and make entry even more unlikely. In the view of the minority report on the case the Commission 'is not so much protecting competition but rather protecting the competitors of the parties to this proposed concentration'.[19]

There was a feeling in a minority of the Commission that the merger should have been allowed in order to strengthen the European aerospace industry, and in fact the French and Italian ministers rejected the majority view and demanded a re-examination of the case. The Commission replied that any appeal had to be made to the European Court. The European Parliament called for the amendment of the Regulation to take account of wider issues of industrial, social and regional policy, while the Commissioner for Industry questioned the authority of his fellow Commissioner with responsibility for competition policy, arguing that the final decision on crucial mergers should be taken jointly.

While the decision, taken purely on competition grounds, is generally thought to have strengthened the position of the fledgling merger policy, the sound and fury that it created over the question of whether 'industrial policy' issues should also have been considered tended to overshadow a proper consideration of its actual analysis. It is debatable whether the merger affected three separate markets for regional or commuter aircraft (as the Commission claimed) or whether the effective market was much wider, involving aircraft with seating for up to 110 passengers. In the former case, as we have seen, the merged group would have had a share of around three-quarters of the market, and this formed a major part of the Commission's objection. On the wider definition, the new grouping would have had only about 20 per cent and the merger would probably have been allowed. In reaching its judgement about the market, the Commission appears to have been much impressed by the views of customers and competitors as well as by the time necessary for manufacturers to switch from producing one size in the range to another. Although such evidence is suggestive it is less convincing than the Commission appears to have believed. The relevant question is not whether under existing prices it is profitable or not for companies to switch aircraft between uses, but whether, if relative prices were to change, it would become profitable to use, say, slightly larger aircraft (with seating for up to 110 passengers) where previously smaller models had been used. Under the current US Guidelines, this question would have been asked at the market definition phase of the enquiry. On the evidence in the published report, if the Commission had used this approach, it might well have decided differently about the size of the market.

Although highly controversial, at least in this case the controversy was confined to the EU. Potentially much more serious was the complete disagreement between the EU and US authorities over the proposed acquisition by Boeing of McDonnell Douglas (hereafter MDC) in 1996. For a number of uneasy months in the first half of 1997 the dispute seemed likely to provoke a serious breakdown in trading relations. It was eventually settled by means of a compromise and the acquisition proceeded.

Both of the companies were American and their plants were in the USA. It was agreed, however, that the market for the products in question, large civil aircraft, was worldwide. Consequently the EU authorities felt fully entitled to consider the merger under Regulation 4064 particularly because the airlines of most member states purchased aircraft from Boeing. They also, of course, purchased aircraft from the only other competitor in the world market, Airbus Industrie, owned (and heavily subsidized in its formative years) by a consortium of European governments.[20] In the 20-year period prior to the merger, Airbus had gradually replaced MDC as the second largest firm in the market. By 1995, the respective market shares were approximately Boeing 60 per cent, Airbus 30 per cent and MDC about 6 per cent. It was generally recognized that, while MDC retained a formidable presence in the market for military aircraft and equipment, it had failed to keep pace with technical advance in the market for civil aircraft.

The different interpretations placed by the EU and US competition authorities on the present and future position of MDC in the market were central to their conclusions and underline the continuing policy conflict. In the USA the case was investigated by the FTC, which concluded that US law would not be infringed and the merger could therefore proceed. Unusually where it was decided not to challenge a merger, the FTC gave the reasons for its decision. Its assessment was that MDC had lost the ability to have a significant impact on competition. Extensive interviews with executives from more than 40 domestic and foreign companies convinced the FTC that the MDC's situation in this market was irreversible and that Boeing was the only realistic purchaser. Citing the precedent of the *General Dynamics* case (1974), the FTC ruled that, since the future competitive impact of MDC in the market was effectively zero, there was no antitrust objection to the merger.

In sharp contrast, the EU authorities focused on what has become known as the 'entrenchment' doctrine. Boeing was already dominant in the market and for a number of reasons, argued the Commission, the acquisition of MDC would further strengthen its position. For example, Boeing's expertise would be able to revive the fortunes of MDC's civil aircraft and in the process Boeing would be able to solidify the relations with MDC's customers and induce them to buy from Boeing. Furthermore there would be two distinct 'portfolio' effects. Boeing would be able to offer a wider range of aircraft and therefore be in a stronger position to sign exclusive contracts with customers. Also MDC's continued strength in military aircraft would allow the civil aircraft divisions to be cross-subsidized, but also increase the scope for Boeing to use 'offsets' as an inducement to (mainly government) customers in emerging markets. In this context an 'offset' would provide for sub-contracts for military work to companies in the 'home' country if the state airline agreed to purchase Boeing's aircraft. All of these factors, according to the Commission, would further 'entrench' Boeing's dominant position to the disadvantage of Airbus. In the Commission's view the dangers inherent in these 'portfolio' effects were illustrated by the exclusive contracts recently concluded by Boeing with three leading US airlines, American, Continental and Delta. If the merger went ahead Boeing's ability to sign even more exclusive contracts would be enhanced. The merger should therefore be blocked.

Fortunately for future trading relations between the EU and the USA, a compromise was reached whereby the merger was allowed to proceed, subject to a number of conditions. Boeing agreed that for a period of 10 years MDC would be maintained as a separate legal entity and provide the EU authorities with regular reports on its commercial operations. In addition Boeing undertook to make available to other aircraft manufacturers for a reasonable fee its portfolio of government-funded patents and know-how. Perhaps most significantly, Boeing agreed to scrap the exclusivity provisions in the contracts with American, Continental and Delta.

It is this last condition which has received most comment. Some observers have suggested that the EU's real objective was to have the exclusive contracts removed. Attacking the merger was more likely to be successful in this respect than, for example, proceeding under Article 82, 'abuse of a dominant position' (Kovacic, 2001, pp. 834–5). Such a Machiavellian approach to antitrust matters seems unlikely given the way that merger control is organized within the EU Commission, through a specially instituted Merger Task Force. The Commissioner for Competition could argue persuasively that the reasoning behind the initial Boeing decision was completely consistent with the earlier de Havilland case. Furthermore, in a subsequent and equally contentious case, the same divergence of views occurred but with the EU again using its 'portfolio'-type analysis to block the merger, with the US authorities concluding there would be no competitive impact and therefore no impediment to the merger.

At the time, the proposed union between General Electric (GE) and Honeywell worth $43 billion was the largest industrial merger on record. The two US companies with substantial interests in Europe agreed terms in October 2000, and by May 2001 the Justice Department had said it would not challenge it. Soon afterwards, however, the EU submitted a lengthy statement of objections. The basic approach by the Commission was similar to the cases mentioned above but the terminology used was rather different. In this case at the centre of the Commission's objections was the additional leverage over contract terms the combined company would be able to wield. The term used was 'bundling', but the argument amounted to the same 'portfolio effect' stressed in the previous cases. For example, in aircraft leasing the Commission argued that the combined company might be able to persuade aircraft mainframe producers to use exclusively GE engines and avionics at the expense of more specialized engine makers. With some justice GE pointed out that, since the combined company would still only have about 8 per cent of the aircraft leasing market, it would be impossible for it to dominate in the way suggested. Rather ironically in view of the earlier case, both Boeing and Airbus as important customers were enthusiastically in favour of the proposed merger but their views appear to have been swamped by the objections of competitors.[21]

In this case no face-saving compromise was found and, despite considerable political pressure from the USA, the merger was blocked by the EU authorities. The aftermath rumbled on, however, for many months. The insensitivity of the then chief executive officer of GE, Jack Welch, was blamed by his counterpart at Honeywell for the opposition of the EU. More significantly, the Justice Department made it clear that it regarded the whole approach used by the EU authorities in this and the earlier case as 'neither soundly grounded in economic theory nor supported by empirical evidence, but rather as antithetical to the goals of sound antitrust enforcement'.[22]

Although many cases have been satisfactorily resolved in the first decade or so of the EU merger regulation, the gulf between US and EU thinking on these matters has been vividly exposed by the Boeing and GE cases. To avoid possible serious damage to trading relations some attempt at convergence is now urgently required. We take up this issue again in the final chapter.

IV   Conclusions

For a number of reasons, merger policy remains the most controversial area of antitrust. Market structures can be changed fundamentally and at great speed by a series of acquisitions. If the change is allowed to occur and market power is established, it may take a long while before market forces apply the necessary corrective, particularly if recent theoretical analysis is right that dominant firms have a formidable array of strategic weapons with which to protect themselves. On the other hand, practically no sizeable merger is announced without the promoters giving a rapturous account of the enormous public benefits that will result, once reorganization has taken place. Periodically, intoxication with possible efficiency gains that mergers can bring has gripped politicians, with the result that government itself becomes the promoter and market power considerations are all but forgotten. The UK is taking steps to remove political influence on merger policy as far as possible, but political pressures have been all too evident in recent transatlantic cases.

In all three jurisdictions, control over mergers was the last element to be included in antitrust policy. The USA, where policy became effective in 1950, has seen the greatest changes in emphasis. Initially, the Supreme Court was not only prepared to find monopolizing tendencies in mergers of quite modest size but was also hostile to the very notion that improved efficiency might 'save' a merger. The Guidelines adopted by the US Department of Justice since 1982 now permit potential cost savings to be taken into account by the antitrust authorities. Surprisingly, the merger Regulation finally agreed by the EU in 1989 does not. The emphasis in EU merger policy is supposed to be on competitive effects. Generally the approach seems to have worked reasonably well except in some especially sensitive international cases where the Commission has been accused of applying outdated theories of 'portfolio effects' and tending to protect competitors rather than competition. It would be ironic if EU policy in the current decade were to repeat the fallacies of US policy in the 1960s.

Notes

1. For a full discussion of the many possible motives for merger, see Steiner (1975).
2. The two UK institutions closely associated with this policy were the Industrial Reorganisation Corporation and the National Enterprise Board. For a detailed discussion, see Grant (1982). For further examples from 'high tech' industries, see Tyson (1992).
3. *Federal Trade Commission* v. *Proctor and Gamble Co. et al.*, 386 US 568, 580 (1967).
4. Attempts to monopolize in such a fashion are now ruled out precisely because of antitrust policy, but they were frequent at the turn of the 20th century in both the USA and the UK (see, for example, Stigler, 1968; Utton, 1972).
5. As is usual with partial equilibrium analysis, we are ignoring second best effects.
6. Stigler (1968) has also constructed a model of oligopoly in which the H index and the degree of collusion are related. For a review of other results, see Scherer and Ross (1990).
7. For a fuller discussion of this point, see Caves and Porter (1977).
8. If the cost or demand disadvantages are those incurred by *any* entrant to the market, including the established firms when they first appeared, then a number of authorities would not regard these as entry barriers (Stigler, 1968).
9. Cases all cited by Scherer and Ross (1990, p. 177): *United States* v. *Aluminum Co. of America et al.*, 377 US 271 (1964); *United States* v. *Continental Can et al.*, 378 US 441 (1964); *United States* v. *Von's Grocery Co. et al.*, 384 US 270 (1966); *United States* v. *Pabst Brewing Co. et al.*, 354 (1964).
10. *United States* v. *Von's Grocery Co. et al.*, 384 US 270 (1966).
11. US Department of Justice, *Merger Guidelines*, Washington, 30 May 1968.
12. *United States* v. *General Dynamics Corp.*, 415 US 486 (1974).
13. US Department of Justice, *Merger Guidelines*, Washington, 14 June 1982. The Guidelines were modified slightly in 1984 and again in 1992 and 1997. Most of our references will be to the 1992 version.
14. *Productivity and Enterprise: A World Class Competition Regime* Department of Trade and Industry, Cmnd 5233, Norwich: The Stationery Office, At the time of writing the reforms embodied in the Enterprise Bill are before Parliament.
15. *Europemballage and Continental Can* v. *Commission* (1973) CMLR 199.
16. A Regulation is legally binding on all member states.
17. In recognition of the increasing problem of multiple jurisdiction in many large mergers the Regulation was extended in March 1998. Mergers too small to qualify for EU investigation, but where three or more separate jurisdictions would be involved, can be investigated by the

EU as long as global turnover is more than EURO 2.5 billion and combined EU turnover is more than EURO 100 million. In each member state involved at least two merging companies have to have revenue of more than EURO 25 million before the EU can claim jurisdiction.

18. *Re the Concentration between Aérospatiale SNI and Alenia-Aeritalia e Selinia SpA and de Havilland* (1992) 4C.M.L.R.M2.
19. Ibid. p. M35.
20. For extensive discussions of the economic, political and legal implications of the case, see Kovacic (2001), Boeder and Dorman (2000) and Gifford and Sullivan (2000).
21. *Financial Times*, 6 July, 2001.
22. *Financial Times*, 18 October, 2001.

Appendix: the Herfindahl index and Cournot oligopoly

Consider an n firm oligopoly where each firm assumes that the others will hold their output fixed (the Cournot assumption). Entry to the market is blocked and the products of all firms are homogeneous in the eyes of consumers. Profits for the ith firm will be:

$$\Pi_i = Pq_i - TC_i,$$

where P is market price, q_i the ith firm's output and TC_i its total costs.

The firm maximizes profit by differentiating the expression with respect to q_i and setting the result equal to zero:

$$\frac{d\Pi_i}{dq_i} = q_i \frac{dP}{dQ}\frac{dQ}{dq_i} + P - \frac{dTC_i}{dq_i} = 0,$$

where Q is market output.

Rearranging terms and noting that $\dfrac{dTC_i}{dq_i}$ is marginal cost (MC_i), we can write

$$q_i \frac{dP}{dQ}\frac{dQ}{dq_i} = MC_i - P.$$

Under the Cournot assumption $\dfrac{dQ}{dq_i}$ equals 1 and multiplying through by $\dfrac{Q}{Q}$

gives:

$$\frac{q_i}{Q}\frac{dP}{dQ}Q = MC_i - P.$$

Multiplying through by $\dfrac{1}{P}$ and noting that $\dfrac{dP}{dQ}\dfrac{Q}{P}$ is the reciprocal of the elasticity of demand e, the expression can be rearranged to give:

$$\frac{q_i}{Q}\frac{1}{e} = \frac{P - MC_i}{P}.$$

The market share of the ith firm, S_i, is given by $\dfrac{q_i}{Q}$, so the expression becomes

$$\frac{S_i}{e} = \frac{P - MC_i}{P}.$$

Multiplying each side of the last expression by the market shares S_i and summing over all firms gives an expression relating the weighted average price cost margin to the Herfindahl index of concentration:

$$\frac{\sum S_i^2}{e} \equiv \frac{H}{e} = \frac{P - \overline{MC}}{P},$$

where $\overline{MC} = \sum S_i MC_i$.

PART III

MARKET DOMINANCE: VERTICAL ISSUES

9 Vertical integration and vertical mergers

I Introduction

Our major concern in part II (Chapters 4–8) was the antitrust issues raised by horizontal dominance, whether this came from a single firm or a group of firms acting overtly or covertly together. In this chapter and the next we discuss vertical dominance, that is, the possibility that a firm having market power at one stage of the production process may, by one means or another, increase its market power and hence its profits by operating in other, related production stages.

Most finished products in the modern economy go through a number of 'production' stages. What starts out as a collection of raw materials may have to go through a whole series of successive refining, manufacturing and distribution stages before it ends up in the retail showroom or store. The number of different stages and the degree to which a product is processed or refined at any one of them will vary from product to product. Some, such as fresh fruit and vegetables, may pass through few vertical stages, although in the case of those flown halfway across the world even this may need to be modified. Others, such as motor cars, drawing on a multiplicity of different materials often manufactured by independent firms, may involve many separate stages.

It will help in what follows if we abstract from this real-world complexity and think of a production process having just three vertical stages: raw material extraction, manufacturing and distribution. Vertical integration occurs when a producer at one stage, say a manufacturer, decides to carry out its own distribution. In this case it may build or buy warehousing and retail establishments for the distribution of its product. Partial vertical integration occurs when a firm at one stage starts to provide some of its requirements at an earlier or later stage in the production process. A manufacturer, for example, may buy ore deposits which are sufficient to supply, say, half of its total needs. The analysis of vertical integration and the antitrust issues that it raises are discussed in the present chapter.

However, it is important to keep clear the distinction between vertical integration and vertical restraints. As we have just seen, vertical integration involves a firm undertaking itself successive stages in the production process. If a manufacturer decides to undertake its own distribution by acquiring a chain of retail stores, it substitutes internal transactions between its manufacturing and distribution divisions for what had previously been market transactions between separate firms. In this sense, an increase in vertical integration in an industry reduces market transactions and increases internal or hierarchical transactions (Williamson, 1975). In contrast, vertical restraints do not change the mode of operation. The volume of market and internal transactions remain unchanged, but a firm at one level imposes restrictions on the terms and conditions of trading by firms at another level. Many, but not all, vertical restraints occur between manufacturers and distributors, and we will take examples from these stages. One of the most well known and controversial vertical restraints is resale price maintenance, whereby a manufacturer sets the price at which a distributor may sell the manufacturer's product. Another example is a geographical restriction in which a manufacturer designates a limited number of distributors of its products in a particular region. Some manufacturers may insist on a tying arrangement whereby distributors of product A from a particular manufacturer have to undertake to distribute products B, C and D from the same firm. The variety of such vertical restraints is considerable, but the essential point is that firms at the different stages retain their separate identities and the transactions on which the restraints are imposed are carried out across the market.[1] The analytical and antitrust issues raised by vertical restraints are discussed in Chapter 10.

There are almost as many motives for vertical integration as there are for merger, but in both cases only a relatively modest sub-set involves the acquisition or increase of market power. We examine a number of different cases in Section II of this chapter. It should be clear that vertical integration can occur either through internal expansion (a manufacturer builds up from scratch its own new distribution outlets) or through acquisition, that is, external expansion. As far as antitrust policy is concerned, although vertical integration by internal expansion may be considered in relation to horizontal market dominance, it is more likely to arise as a distinct issue when vertical merger is involved. Section III of this chapter is therefore mainly concerned with the treatment of vertical mergers by the antitrust authorities in the USA and Europe.

II   Motives for vertical integration and the effects on market power

Although vertical integration has long been discussed in the literature of industrial economics,[2] the focus has been greatly influenced in recent years by Oliver Williamson's analysis of transactions costs (Williamson, 1975). Drawing on the earlier classic paper by Coase (1938), he argues that the costs of actually using the market, broadly interpreted, may largely explain many decisions by firms to integrate their activities vertically, and these may have nothing to do with market power. Thus against a background of uncertainty and in cases where contracts of great complexity may be required, the limited ability of individual or group decision makers to take account of all possible future contingencies that may arise during the life of a contract may encourage them to seek vertical integration as a means of minimizing the difficulties. The unforeseen circumstances will still arise but, according to Williamson, the vertically integrated concern can handle such difficulties more easily and therefore at a smaller cost. First, transactions between different parts of the same enterprise should be more easily monitored than those between separate enterprises. The firm should have earlier warning of unforeseen problems and adjust more promptly. Secondly, there will be less scope within an enterprise for individuals or groups to try to use the difficulties to their advantage. Thirdly, where disputes do arise over liability, the integrated firm can use its own auditing and control mechanisms for settling the dispute, without having to resort to the law or arbitration. Clearly the greater the complexity and uncertainty attending the firm's operations, the greater the incentive it may have for vertical integration. Similarly, a firm may feel vulnerable to the opportunistic behaviour of suppliers where these are few in number. When there are many potential suppliers, any customer disapproving of the terms offered by one has many other alternatives. Where the numbers are few, the choice will obviously be limited and, once one supplier has satisfactorily completed an initial contract, it may be in a very powerful position to win future contracts because of the detailed knowledge it will have gained of its customer's precise requirements and mode of operation. Rather than laying itself open to the exploitation of this power gained by a supplier, a firm may decide to provide some or all of its own supplies.

A variation on this type of incentive for vertical integration occurs when production at a particular stage requires very specific equipment, effectively custom-built or located to meet the special needs of a particular customer. A high proportion of the costs embedded in such plant are likely to be sunk. Any firm committed to this stage of production alone is therefore effectively locked into the demands of one customer and highly vulnerable. Highly specialized assets at one stage may thus provide a strong incentive for a firm to integrate forwards to avoid dependency on individual customers. Transaction cost savings may therefore provide perfectly innocent incentives for vertical integration. To the extent that they lead to a reduction in costs compared with the non-integrated alternative, they are also likely to benefit consumers, in the form of lower prices.

A comparatively small proportion of all mergers challenged by antitrust authorities are vertical. Yet vertical integration is widespread throughout industry. These facts reflect the point that most vertical integration is not in the pursuit of market power, but is intended to reduce transactions costs. However, where market power is bound up with vertical integration, the different cases can be varied and complex. Market power depends on market structure. Vertical integration involves (at least) two market structures, such as manufacturing and distribution, and can therefore generate much greater complexity than market dominance at one stage in the production process. For example, what are the market power consequences of a monopoly manufacturer integrating forwards into a perfectly competitive distribution market or a monopoly distributor merging with his monopoly supplier of manufactured goods? The cases can be multiplied by changing one of the initial market structures involved. In order to keep the analysis that follows as clear as possible, we shall consider the implications of vertical integration between a manufacturing industry and a distribution industry.

One result we may note at the outset is that, if perfect competition prevails at each phase of the production and distribution process, no individual has a profit incentive to integrate either backwards (from distribution into manufacturing) or forwards (manufacturing into distribution). Whether or not integration takes place, competition will ensure that long-run profits remain at the normal level. In such markets, transactions costs will be either zero or minimal.[3] The cases which we are to consider involve monopoly at one or other of the production stages. Our task will be to analyse under what circumstances this market power at one stage can be transmitted via vertical integration to another stage and so enhance the profits of the monopolist. To focus precisely on that issue, we shall assume transactions costs are zero. In practice, of course, a firm may integrate out of a mixture of incentives and part of the job of an antitrust body is to assess their relative importance. We will also assume that the monopoly at one stage is legal, deriving perhaps from a patent. If the monopoly is questionable, then we would in effect be dealing again with the problems of horizontal dominance rather than vertical integration.

Integration to increase monopoly profit

Until comparatively recently, it was thought that a monopoly input supplier had no profit incentive to integrate forwards to take over a competitive industry. The monopolist could sell at a monopoly price, which would be incorporated in the product price of the competitive firms. Any increase in price by the monopolist would have to be accepted by the competitive firms. The monopolist could wring out all of the monopoly profit available by selling at the monopoly price.

This result, however, depends on the downstream competitive industry (hereafter called R) having a fixed proportions production function; that is, at any level of output there is a unique optimum combination of inputs, with no possibility of substitution. The case is illustrated in panel (a) of Figure 9.1. We will assume that competitive industry R requires two inputs for providing its final output. One input, N, is available from a competitively structured industry and the price, P_N, is a competitive price. The other input, M, is purchased at a monopoly price, P_M, from the monopoly supplier. The right-angled isoquant Q represents a particular level of output. The point E on the isoquant represents the optimum (and unique) combination of inputs for producing the output Q. Any other input combination for producing an amount Q indicates inefficiency: more of one input is being used than is required to produce Q. The isocost lines ab and cd are tangential to the isoquant at E. Their slopes represent different relative prices for the two inputs. Given the fixed proportions production

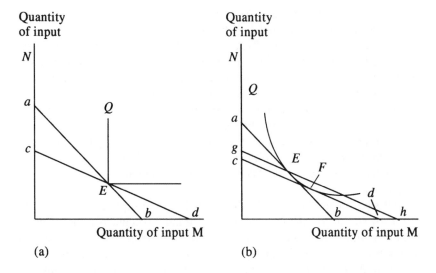

Figure 9.1 Incentives to integrate under different production conditions

function, therefore, whatever the relative prices of the inputs there is only one unique combination which minimizes production costs. The same point, of course, applies to any other specified production level. Any change in price by the monopoly input supplier will have no effect on the intensity of usage of the input, because there are no substitution possibilities. Any price increase will simply pass through to the final product selling price. Under these circumstances there is no profit incentive for the monopoly input supplier to integrate forwards. It receives the full monopoly profit simply from supplying the input.

We can contrast this result with the more realistic case where some input substitution is possible for producing the output in industry *R*. This case is represented in panel (b) of Figure 9.1. All other assumptions remain unchanged. Instead of the right-angled isoquant, *Q* is now a smooth downward-sloping curve indicating the substitution possibilities for producing the specified output. The isocost line *ab* reflects the relative prices of the two inputs used by the competitive industry *R*. Given the monopoly price of input *M* and the competitive price of input *N*, the competitive industry would optimize its production of *Q* by purchasing the input combination represented by *E* where the isocost line is tangential to the isoquant.

If the input *M* was supplied to the competitive industry not at a monopoly price but at a competitive price, the slope of the isocost line would change and there would be a new optimum input combination for producing *Q*. In Figure 9.1, panel (b), the isocost line would then be *cd* tangential to the isoquant at *F*.

In effect, the competitive industry would be able to substitute input M, now competitively priced, for input N. While it was priced at the monopoly level, it caused a distortion in usage by industry R. The key question is, how much saving is available to the competitive industry R if input M can be purchased at the competitive rather than the monopoly price? The extent of the saving can be represented in the figure in terms of units of input N. The line gh is drawn parallel to cd, therefore reflecting the same input prices, but also to pass through the point E, thus representing the same total costs as the line ab which also passes through E. Thus the savings to the competitive industry R if input M is available at a competitive price amount to cg, in units of input N. (The monetary saving can obviously be calculated by simply multiplying cg by the price per unit of N.)

This saving could be made by the monopoly input supplier by integrating vertically with the competitive industry R. The input M could then pass between the two stages of the integrated firm at an imputed competitive price. Vertical integration in this case eliminates the distortion in input use and increases the profits of the integrated concern. However, the integration has substituted a monopoly at the final product stage for the previous competitive industry. The integrated monopoly has lower costs, but do consumers also benefit, in the form of lower prices? Unfortunately for antitrust agencies, there is no clear-cut answer to this question. Prices can either rise or fall, depending on the size of the cost saving involved and the price elasticity of demand for the final product (Warren-Boulton, 1974). Just as in the case of third degree price discrimination, examined in Chapter 5, more detailed information about conditions in the market concerned are required before the question can be answered. For consumers, the final outcome of vertical mergers fitting approximately into this category is ambiguous.

Integration to avoid a double monopoly mark-up
Instead of a monopoly supplying a competitive industry, we shall now consider the case of a monopoly manufacturer, M, selling to a monopoly retailer, R, although at this stage we also assume that the retailer cannot exert any bargaining influence on the price set by the manufacturer. Again the question is, does the manufacturer have a profit incentive to integrate forwards and, if so, does the consumer also benefit from any integration that takes place?

The case is illustrated in Figure 9.2, where the left-hand panel shows the position prior to vertical integration and the right-hand panel the results if the two monopolies integrate. In both panels, the demand for the final product is shown as D_R and the related marginal revenue curve MR_R. The (constant) marginal costs of the manufacturing monopoly are MC. For simplicity of exposition, we assume that there are no separate retailing costs. The price at which the manufacturer is prepared to sell the product to the retailer will depend on its marginal costs and its marginal revenue. The manufacturer's demand curve is derived from the demand for the final product and is given by $MR_R = D_M$, the marginal revenue curve of the retailer. The manufacturer's marginal revenue curve is marginal to D_M and is marked as MR_M in Figure 9.2, panel (a). The manufacturer's profit-maximizing price is then P_M and the amount sold is Q_M. This price is then regarded as the marginal cost by the retailer. The monopoly retail price is then fixed at P_R according to the intersection of the retailer's marginal revenue, MR_R, and marginal cost, P_M.

As a result of this double mark-up, the profit on output Q_M is $P_M BFH$ for the manufacturer and $P_R ABP_M$ for the retailer. Both firms, however, have an incentive to integrate. The manufacturer, having established its monopoly price at P_M, would prefer to sell as much as possible at this price. The fact that the retailer then adds its own monopoly margin restricts sales. Similarly, seen from the viewpoint of the retailer, if it could receive the product at marginal production cost (without the mark-up) the final price would be lower and more would be sold. If vertical integration does take place,[4] the results can be illustrated by Figure 9.2, panel (b). Final product demand and marginal revenue remain unchanged, and are denoted D_R and MR_R, respectively. Marginal cost is MC. The integrated monopoly can now transmit the manufactured product to the retail stage at marginal cost. The monopoly final product price is P_M, determined by the intersection of MC and MR_R. As a result of the lower price, output increases. In fact, given the linear demand and cost functions used in the example, it doubles, from Q_M to $2Q_M$.[5] The total profit earned by the integrated firm rises to $P_M EGH$.

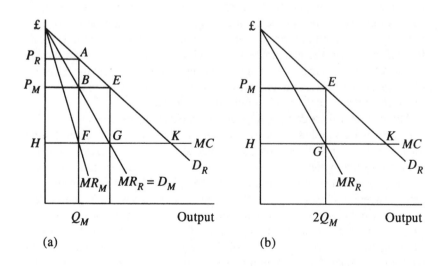

Figure 9.2   Double monopoly mark-ups and vertical integration

The integrated monopoly is thus better off than previously, but in this case so are consumers. The lower price and increased output that flow from the vertical integration also mean that consumer surplus is increased. The total deadweight loss imposed by the non-integrated market structure was $AEGF + EGK$. In addition, $P_R ABP_M$ was retained by the retailer. Once the integration has taken place and the price is reduced, consumer surplus is increased by an amount represented by the area $P_R AEP_M$. The area $BEGF$ represents part of the monopoly profit, while the triangle EGK is the remaining deadweight loss attributable to the restriction of output by the integrated monopoly below the level that would be produced by a competitively structured industry.

A somewhat similar result, although rather more complex to derive, follows from the case where we drop the assumption that the final monopoly seller has no bargaining power over the price at which it purchases the product. In this case, in addition to the successive monopoly mark-ups, the uncertainties of bargaining are injected into the negotiations between manufacturer and retailer. Both will know that, if the product can be exchanged between them at the appropriate imputed competitive price, the final price on the market will be lower and the joint profit higher than if the intermediate price approaches the monopoly level. In practice, lack of trust between independent firms and the scope there may be for opportunistic behaviour may mean that they depart considerably from the joint profit maximization solution. In order to avoid these bargaining problems, therefore, the firms may decide to integrate their operations.

Thus in the cases of successive monopolies we arrive at the rather surprising result that vertical integration which creates an even larger concern covering (in our example) two stages of the production process results in benefits not only to the enterprise, in the form of higher profits, but also to consumers, in the form of lower prices, and a greater output, yielding a larger consumer surplus and smaller welfare loss. The result is counter-intuitive because the cohesion of monopoly between separate stages might be thought to worsen the position of the consumer. Yet the result is quite unambiguous.

Although he had not derived the above result formally, the general conclusion was known to Marshall, who was much more circumspect in the policy inferences he drew than more recent commentators: 'the prima facie arguments in favour of the fusion of monopolistic cartels, or other associations, in complementary branches of industry, though often plausible and even strong, will generally be found on close examination to be treacherous. They point to the removal of prominent social and industrial discords; but at the probable expense of larger and more enduring discords in the future' (Marshall, 1919, p. 410). Those made uneasy by the prospect of allowing vertical mergers which would consolidate rather than weaken monopoly have turned their attention to the effect on the condition of entry and have argued that a merger which significantly increases entry barriers at either or both stages should be blocked. We examine this issue in more detail below.

Before leaving the question of integration to avoid a double monopoly mark-up, it is worth repeating one of our initial assumptions. In order to focus clearly on the vertical integration issue, we have assumed that existing market power is legal, otherwise the question resolves into one of horizontal dominance. In the present case, that assumption implies that both the manufacturing and retailing monopolies are acceptable. Although there may be circumstances where this is the case, they are probably rare. It seems unlikely, therefore, that an antitrust body would have to consider many cases where two legal monopolies seek to justify their integration in terms of the above analysis. The market power of at least one of them is likely to rest on dubious grounds and therefore be the main focus of antitrust.

Integration to avoid market power
In the cases considered so far, firms with market power sought vertical integration as a means of increasing their profits. The obverse case is where a firm may seek vertical integration as a means of avoiding the payment of monopoly prices for its inputs. Under what circumstances will such a move be cost-effective for the firm? A number of different circumstances can be considered.

For convenience, we shall continue to refer to the possible integration of manufacturing and retailing stages, but of course the analysis can be applied to any other stages in the production and distribution process. A retailer confronted by the monopoly price of a manufacturer may consider integrating backwards either by building its own plant or by acquisition. It needs to consider carefully, however, just how firmly based is the market power of the manufacturer. In particular, if the retailer can seriously contemplate entering the manufacturing stage, it is likely that others, possibly better placed, may be coming to the same conclusion. In that case entry will begin to erode the manufacturer's market power and the retailer may have no need to integrate. In practice, much may depend on the speed at which effective entry can occur.

If the monopoly manufacturer's market power is more firmly based, that is entry is blockaded, vertical integration by new investment will not be possible, but the retailer may consider acquisition. Whether or not such a move is worthwhile for the retailer depends on the price of purchasing the manufac-turer and the type of production available to the retailer (Carlton and Perloff, 2000). The monopoly power held by the manufacturer will be reflected in the purchase price: that is, the stock market price of the shares in the firm will represent the present value of the future monopoly profits. The retailer then has the choice of continuing to pay the monopoly price every time it takes supplies from the manufacturer or pay the monopoly price in one transaction by buying the firm. Unless there is scope for the retailer to make savings if the acquisition proceeds, there is no difference in the two alternatives: the retailer would pay the monopoly price. Whether or not there is scope for savings will depend on the retailer's production function.[6] The analysis of pp. 210–12 can now be applied in the present context. If the retailer has a fixed coefficient production function there will be no scope for input substitution and the merger option is unlikely to be considered. With the more likely flexible production function (illustrated in Figure 9.1, panel (b)), merger would allow the integrated firm to adjust its input combination. The product previously supplied at a monopoly price could be transferred between the two stages at a competitive price and could therefore be used more intensively. As long as the implied savings from this adjustment outweighed the costs of completing the merger, including a possible antitrust challenge, it would be in the retailer's interest to integrate. As we saw above, however, whether consumers benefit depends on the elasticity of the final product demand and the size of the cost saving.

Integration to facilitate price discrimination
We saw in Chapter 5 that price discrimination by a firm will maximize its profitability. In some contexts vertical integration may be used by a firm to ensure the success of its policy. For example, suppose that there is a monopoly supplier of an intermediate product which is used to make two quite distinct products. Numerous examples occur in metal fabrication, where the refined copper, aluminium, brass, tin and so on is fashioned into products serving quite distinct markets. The markets for these products have different demand elasticities and there is thus scope for price discrimination to increase profits. However, if the input supplier sells on the open market for use in the various industries, there will be nothing to prevent a low-cost purchaser reselling to a high-cost purchaser at a price slightly below that charged by the monopoly. In other words, arbitrage would undermine the attempted price discrimination. This behaviour provides an incentive for the monopolist to integrate forwards into the market where demand is more price-elastic and hence price lower. By internalizing supplies to the lower-priced market, it can then successfully charge the higher price to the other markets. Furthermore, to the extent that the prevailing antitrust laws circumscribe the use of price discrimination (as is the case in the USA and the EU – see above, Chapter 5) the vertical integration helps to disguise what is actually going on. Following integration there are market prices only for the less elastic market. Transactions for the other market are purely internal, between one division of the enterprise and another.

Vertical integration to sustain price discrimination may thus increase the profitability of the firm, but its effects on the different groups of consumers are ambiguous and follow from the conclusions already derived on this issue in Chapter 5. Compared with a unified price, discrimination will raise the price paid and reduce the amount purchased in the market with the less elastic demand, but reduce price and increase the amount purchased in the market with the more elastic demand. Without knowing more about the respective demand curves and in particular the demand elasticities, it is not possible a priori to determine whether or not there is a net welfare gain following the introduction of price discrimination.

Barriers to entry and the 'foreclosure' doctrine
We have so far discussed no motives for a firm to integrate vertically in order to create or enhance market power. We have established that under certain circumstances a firm already in possession of (legally held) market power may integrate so as to increase its profitability either through (transactions) cost savings or through a more efficient input combination. In neither case, however, was market power increased. Yet antitrust agencies, as we shall see in the next section, continue to be concerned with vertical integration in general and vertical mergers in particular. The main sources of their concern, especially in the USA, have been the effects on entry conditions and on 'foreclosure'.

The discussion of vertical integration and entry barriers has generally focused on capital requirements. Where the level of integration in the relevant markets is already high, further vertical integration, it is argued, may mean that entry can only be contemplated at both levels. For example, if most manufacturers have already integrated forwards into distribution, entrants may feel obliged to come in as an integrated manufacturing–distributing concern. Clearly the capital requirement for entry at two stages rather than one will be greater and the terms on which the entrant can raise the capital may be inferior. The last point has been the subject of much controversy. One view is that, given the degree of uncertainty and less than perfect information on the part of providers of capital to entrants, the costs are bound to be higher the larger the sum required. An alternative view is that there will be no difference in the terms on which entrants can raise larger rather than smaller amounts of capital. Hence there is no special barrier to entry arising from this source, as far as vertical integration is concerned. To the extent that the first view is correct, incumbent firms may have an incentive to integrate (either backwards or forwards, according to the circumstances) in order to raise their potential rivals' costs. In effect, they would be investing in entry barriers (Comanor, 1967). The short-run profits of the integrated firm might be lower (for example, because of the managerial diseconomies incurred) but longer-term profits would be higher than if entry and therefore competition increased. A successful policy of restraining entry by vertical integration will therefore lead to a gain for the incumbent firm or firms but a loss to consumers, who continue to pay higher prices.

The reverse case is that where vertically integrated firms have lower costs, perhaps because of a reduction in transactions costs. Firms wishing to enter at a single stage will therefore have higher costs. It is clearly incorrect in these circumstances to argue that vertical integration raises entry barriers. Consumers as well as the firms themselves are better off as a result of the integration.

It is thus possible that in some cases further vertical integration by the established firms may oblige entrants to come into the market at more than one stage and increase entry barriers by unduly raising the costs of capital. We should note, however, how restricted these cases are likely to be. Before the additional integration occurs, a large part of the production and distribution stages concerned must already be in the hands of integrated enterprises, otherwise entry at one stage will still be feasible: a new manufacturer, say, can still find sufficient independent retail outlets for its products. In addition, a potential entrant's costs can only be raised by the vertical integration activities of the incumbent firms if the conditions of entry at other stages are onerous. For example, raising the capital requirements (and hence entry barriers) for potential entrants by manufacturers integrating into retailing will only be effective if there are severe entry barriers into the retailing market. Otherwise there will be no problem for the entrant in finding distributors for its products. Vertical mergers where both of these conditions prevail (a high degree of existing integration and formidable entry barriers at the relevant stages) may therefore be a legitimate cause of antitrust concern. Otherwise they may be either welfare-neutral or positive.

Leading US cases, however, have turned largely on other considerations. The doctrine of 'foreclosure' has, until comparatively recently, played a central role in the treatment of vertical mergers. According to this doctrine, a firm which integrates either backwards or forwards reduces the volume of transactions that take place on the open market and therefore 'forecloses' part of the market to its rivals, with possibly adverse competitive consequences. For convenience in discussing this issue, we will retain the example of a manufacturer integrating forwards into retailing, although it can be applied to any other type of vertical relationship. Thus, if a manufacturer responsible for 20 per cent of the market merges with a retail chain which subsequently distributes only the new owners' products, the 'foreclosure' doctrine implies that 20 per cent of the retail capacity that was previously available for distributing the products of any manufacturer is now closed to them and, in the words of a famous US case, this can act as a 'clog on competition' depriving rivals 'of a fair opportunity to compete'.[7] The clear inference is thus that such vertical integration will give a competitive advantage to the integrating firm and put non-integrated firms at a disadvantage. Closer examination of the argument, however, suggests that it is much less clear-cut.

Consider first a case that we discussed above: a manufacturer has a legitimate monopoly over production and integrates forwards into retailing. In principle it could apply a discriminatory pricing policy between retailers, charging a lower price to its acquired retail outlets than to independent retailers who would

then tend to lose market share. The policy could be pursued until the manufacturer had a complete monopoly also over retailing. Assuming that the
production function allows some input substitution, then, as we saw on pp.
210–12, the integrated monopolist could increase its monopoly profit. Whether
or not price to consumers is reduced depends on the size of the cost saving and
the elasticity of demand. The integrated monopoly will only endure if entry at
either production stage is blocked or very difficult. We return to this point
below. In the case just examined, the real problem is the horizontal monopoly
at the manufacturing stage. For illustrative purposes, we assumed it was
'legitimate'. In many practical instances this may not be the case and the focus
of antitrust attention will be on any horizontal concentration.

In fact the more likely market structure involved in vertical mergers is
oligopoly. Consider, therefore, as a second case, a manufacturer with a 25 per
cent share of the market who acquires a retail chain. The retailer may or may
not have previously distributed the manufacturer's products. If the retailer did
previously sell the new owner's products and if, following the merger, there is
no change in policy, then no 'foreclosure' arises. Suppose, however, the
integrated concern insists that the retail outlets carry exclusively their own
products. Some of these may previously have been sold through other retailers.
If the newly integrated firm's total sales remain unchanged, all that will have
happened is that the distribution outlets handling those sales will have changed.
Some independent retailers will suffer reduced sales, while some other manufacturers will be seeking alternative retail outlets to replace those that are now
'foreclosed' by the exclusive policy of the integrated firm. There is no reason
to suppose that some realignment will not take place, with independent manufacturers making new contracts with independent retailers to distribute their
products. If the integrated firm not only insists on exclusive distribution of its
products through its newly acquired retailers, but also seeks to retain its sales
through independent retailers, total sales will increase but at a lower price.
Consumers would therefore benefit. In these circumstances, vertical merger is
unlikely to enhance market power.

So far we have said little about actual entry conditions. In the first case,
involving a manufacturing monopoly which integrates forwards into retailing,
if entry into retailing is difficult, the integrated concern will be able to maintain
its enhanced monopoly profit. In the oligopoly case, the realignment of sales
amongst existing retailers can take place regardless of entry conditions.
Proponents of the 'foreclosure' argument, however, suggest that, where entry
at the retail level is difficult (for example, because of licensing or zoning
regulations), the trend of vertical merger activity will be important. An initial
important vertical merger may spark off a whole series as manufacturers seek
to secure their own outlets for their products rather than have to deal with an
integrated competitor. Left unchecked, it is argued that the scramble to acquire

retail outlets will result in a much more highly integrated industrial structure than is strictly necessary for productive efficiency. Furthermore, no potential entrant could in future contemplate coming in at the manufacturing stage alone because all retail outlets will be 'foreclosed'. Entry will therefore have to be at both stages (assuming the retail restriction allows it) and, to the extent that the greater capital that this will require is on less favourable terms, the 'foreclosure' will have caused an even greater level of entry barriers.

Two observations can be made about this line of argument. First, the real source of any problem lies in the restriction on entry at the retail level, which is a horizontal rather than a vertical problem. Secondly, it is unclear whether consumers will suffer a further deterioration in their position as a result of the increased vertical integration. By assumption, the manufacturing stage is oligopolistic and entry is difficult at the retail stage. There is no reason to believe that forward integration by manufacturers will lead to higher prices and reduced output. Whatever coordination on prices the oligopolists might have achieved before integration is unlikely to increase after it has taken place. Initially, therefore, prices to the consumer are likely to remain unchanged following the vertical integration. The one caveat which we have already mentioned and which was recognized by Marshall is the possible long-term effects of a rigidified and unchanging industrial structure. This may facilitate not only collusion, but also the internal or X-inefficiency that can accompany it. The remedy would be the relaxation of the constraints on entry at the retail stage. If this is not thought feasible even in the long run, an antitrust agency charged with assessing the competitive effects of a vertical merger may decide to block it.

III   Policies towards vertical integration and vertical mergers
Vertical integration in itself is not generally covered in the antitrust provisions of the jurisdictions being discussed. It can become an issue, however, where a firm has horizontal market power and is extensively integrated, and it is explicitly included in antitrust law where mergers are concerned. Thus under the revised Clayton Act in the USA, any merger (whether horizontal, vertical or conglomerate) where the effect 'may be substantially to lessen competition, or to tend to create a monopoly' is illegal.

Despite the rather exceptional circumstances which have to prevail for a vertical merger to enhance marker power, the US authorities have taken a generally hostile stance. Moreover, a continuous thread in their judgements has been the notion of 'foreclosure'. Although the general line of argument can be traced back to earlier cases,[8] the leading authority (or for some the nadir) on vertical mergers is the *Brown Shoe* case.[9] The merger had horizontal and vertical features. Here we confine ourselves to the latter. The Brown Shoe company, mainly a manufacturer of shoes, acquired the Kinney Company, largely a shoe retailer. On a national level, Brown made about 4 per cent of output and Kinney about 0.5 per cent. Kinney was responsible for 1.2 per cent of shoe sales, and the two companies accounted together for about 2.3 per cent of shoe outlets. Altogether there were about 800 shoe manufacturers in the USA at the time of the merger, and it was widely accepted that barriers to entry, especially at the retail level, were negligible: on the face of it, hardly the industry where a merger between the two firms would pose a threat to the consumer. The Supreme Court, however, thought differently: 'the diminution of the vigor of competition which may stem from a vertical arrangement results primarily from a foreclosure of the share of the market otherwise open to competitors'. A central consideration is thus the extent of the market 'foreclosed'. On the facts before it, the Court concluded that this case did not involve monopoly, but neither did it involve a negligible share. Consequently, it was necessary to review the various historical and economic factors in the market to determine whether such an intermediate case was illegal. According to the Court, the two factors which damned this particular merger were the trend towards vertical integration which had occurred in the industry and the stated policy of Brown of insisting that Kinney carry Brown's shoes in its retail outlets.

Both factors were superficially true, but on closer analysis the danger to competition was negligible. Thus the 13 largest shoe manufacturers operated 21 per cent of the nation's specialized shoe stores, but on a straight extrapolation of these figures this would still allow 60 manufacturers of an equal size to integrate to the same extent. In fact, this calculation greatly understates the scope for actual competition, because it takes no account of department and clothing stores which also sell shoes. In short, it is difficult to see how the recent integration in the industry posed any real threat to competition. As far as the second point is concerned, it is true that before the merger Kinney carried none of Brown's shoes, whereas two years after the merger about 8 per cent of its sales were of Brown's shoes. It was Brown's declared intention to get Kinney to distribute its products, hardly a surprising policy in view of the merger. Again, however, the threat to competition via 'foreclosure' seems negligible. As Bork points out, before the merger, Kinney supplied 20 per cent of its own shoe requirements. It was responsible for 1.2 per cent of total retail sales. Even if Brown 'foreclosed' all of the remainder of Kinney's retail capacity, this would amount to about one-tenth of 1 per cent of the national market. It is this which the Supreme Court in this case appeared to believe acted as a clog on competition (Bork, 1978). In fact, of course, Brown would not as a matter of sound commercial judgement seek to displace Kinney's former sales with its own products. Prior to the merger, Kinney had determined that the characteristics of Brown's products, such as quality, styling and price, were not the best available for its existing stores. For Brown to replace Kinney's current product range with its own would cost Kinney as much as it benefited Brown.

Despite the minute market shares involved and the evident freedom of entry to the market, the Court in this case pushed the theory of 'foreclosure' to its extreme in finding against the merger. The subsequent criticisms, especially by economists, were substantial and yet a decade later the Court reached a similar conclusion on largely the same grounds in *Ford Motor*.[10] Ford's acquisition in 1961 of the sparkplug manufacturer Autolite was challenged by the Antitrust Division. Prior to the acquisition, Ford had obtained its sparkplugs from Champion. General Motors was supplied by its own subsidiary, Chrysler purchased from Autolite, as did American Motors which was also supplied by Champion. A number of realignments took place following the merger. Champion no longer supplied Ford and Autolite stopped selling to Chrylser. The market leader, Champion, now supplied Chrysler, whose own market share was less than that of Ford. As a result, Champion's market share fell from 50 per cent in 1960 to 33 per cent in 1966. Price discrimination between the two markets for sparkplugs was well established. At the time of the case, an average of five sets of plugs was used throughout the life of a car. To establish a strong position in the replacement market, manufacturers such as Champion and Autolite sold to car manufacturers at prices below cost, but more than made up these losses by sales in the replacement market, since mechanics tended to fit replacement plugs of the same brand.

The Supreme Court condemned the merger, essentially on two grounds. First, Ford was a potential entrant to the sparkplug industry and thus had a pro-competitive influence on its performance. Its removal as a potential entrant therefore tended to lessen competition. Secondly, and more important in view of the foregoing discussion, the acquisition caused the foreclosure of Ford as a purchaser of about 10 per cent of total industry output. Thus, whereas in *Brown Shoe* the court decided that the merger foreclosed some retail outlets to Brown's competitors, in *Ford Motor* the acquiring firm was said to have foreclosed itself as a market. As Bork points out, whereas it is conceivable that a firm may wish to lessen competition from its rivals, it is quite unreasonable to argue that a firm should wish to lessen competition amongst its suppliers. Ford could have no interest in reducing the efficiency with which suppliers produced their sparkplugs. The acquisition could therefore have had no adverse effects on the original equipment market. In general, firms will decide between making or buying on the basis of relative cost (Bork, 1978, p. 236). As far as the replacement market was concerned, there was evidence that, if anything, since the merger competition had increased rather than diminished. Former managers of Autolite started producing their own brand independently, and a number of large retail chains increased sales of their own brands.

The Court thus appears again to have upheld a decision hostile to a vertical merger on grounds which most economists would find difficult to justify. After analysing 43 antitrust cases involving vertical mergers, Areeda and Turner concluded that the foreclosure doctrine was repeatedly at the heart of the argument. If concentration in either market was high and the apparent market 'foreclosed' non-trivial, then there was a strong presumption of an adverse finding (Areeda and Turner, 1980, pp. 296–319).

We saw in Chapter 8 that in the case of horizontal mergers the Department of Justice issued Guidelines at different times setting out the criteria that would be used to determine whether or not a particular merger would be challenged in the Courts. Similarly, in the case of vertical mergers, two sets of Guidelines have been issued, in 1968 and 1982. Not surprisingly, the first set relied very heavily on the 'foreclosure' principle. Thus, recognizing that vertical mergers may raise entry barriers by 'foreclosing' access either to potential customers or to potential suppliers, the Department made clear that it would normally challenge cases where the supplying firm had 10 per cent or more of the sales and the purchasing firm accounted for approximately 6 per cent or more of total purchases. Exceptions might be made where it was quite clear that no other significant entry barriers existed. These messages derived from the *Brown Shoe* case were thus enshrined in the 1968 Guidelines and together they amounted almost to a per se rule against vertical mergers of any size throughout the 1960s and 1970s.

Some observers go further and suggest that, although the revised Guidelines of 1982 do not actually mention 'foreclosure', 'one can still discern an underlying concern regarding foreclosure possibilities' (Blair and Kaserman, 1985, p. 336). The 1982 Guidelines distinguish three possible grounds for objecting to vertical mergers. First, they may raise entry barriers in some circumstances. In particular, where there is already substantial vertical integration between what are termed the primary and secondary stages, further integration may make it effectively a requirement for an entrant to come in at both stages. The probability of entry at the primary stage is thus less likely and, as a result, the performance of the primary stage will deteriorate. In view of these considerations, the Department makes it clear that it would therefore normally challenge a merger where the Herfindahl concentration index exceeds 1800 (that is, approximately equivalent to a four-firm concentration ratio of 70 per cent), the probability growing stronger, the higher the index. It is here that the echoes of the 'foreclosure' doctrine are at their strongest.

Secondly, vertical mergers may facilitate collusion. Again, the probability of this arising depends on the level of vertical integration already in existence. Where it is high, however, it may make collusion easier because retail prices are more visible than upstream prices. Hence under the Guidelines, the Department would normally challenge vertical mergers where the *H* index is greater than 1800 in the upstream market and 'a large percentage' of the product would be sold through vertically integrated concerns after the merger.

Thirdly, vertical mergers may be a means of avoiding price regulation by public utilities. A natural monopoly supplier which has its prices regulated by a special agency may be able to manipulate internal transactions to its own advantage following vertical merger. For example, the acquisition of an input supplier could allow the utility to inflate the input prices and thus depress its apparent profitability, or pass on the inflated prices as 'costs' to the final consumer.

In line with those for horizontal mergers, the current Guidelines are more tightly drawn than their predecessors, reflecting, in part, the changed emphasis in antitrust in general and vertical integration in particular that took place in the late 1970s and 1980s. The new direction of policy was reflected in the *Fruehauf* decision[11] Fruehauf had a share of 25 per cent in the market for truck trailers where the largest four firms had a combined share of 49 per cent. The acquired firm, Kelsey, held 15 per cent of the market for heavy duty wheels. The largest four firms in this market accounted for 70 per cent of sales. A finding against the acquisition by the Federal Trade Commission on grounds of foreclosure in the heavy duty wheel market was overturned by the Court of Appeals. It held that there was no evidence that the acquisition would lead to significant decline in competition in the market for heavy duty wheels which would still be available at competitive prices. Future entry to the truck trailer market would not require firms simultaneously to enter the market for heavy duty wheels. Furthermore there was no evidence to indicate that Fruehauf was ever a serious potential entrant to the heavy duty wheel market. Current policy, therefore, makes a much wider assessment of the likely impact of a vertical merger on competition than simply focusing on any apparent 'foreclosure' effect.

We have deliberately concentrated so far on policy towards vertical mergers rather than vertical integration because it is the merger cases which have had greatest prominence and, as we said above, integration per se is not covered by the antitrust laws. However, it is useful to mention at this point one other leading US case where vertical integration was an important issue. Before its break-up under a consent decree agreed in 1982, American Telephone and Telegraph (AT and T) was not only the largest company in the USA but was also completely integrated vertically. In the telecommunications industry it produced and installed a whole range of equipment (from longlines and switching gear to handsets and other consumer apparatus); it provided local, national and international telecommunications services and it also had a world-renowned research laboratory. For a long period until the early 1970s it had almost a complete monopoly in the USA over telecommunications services and for this reason was subject to regulatory control by the Federal Communications Commission (FCC). From the late 1960s onwards, however, its position was increasingly challenged by firms wishing to enter the various markets in which it operated, especially the equipment and long-distance services markets. The changing economic environment in which formerly regulated industries were expected to operate culminated in an antitrust action under Section 2 of the Sherman Act, which resulted in the break-up of the company in 1984. The case was unusually complex, involving regulatory issues as well as questions of horizontal and vertical dominance. In the present context we focus on the vertical problems, which played an important role in the final outcome of the case.

While natural monopoly factors were still relatively strong in the market for local services (subscribers wish to link into as dense a network as possible and more than one local network is wasteful), changing technology had made them far weaker in the long-distance market. In principle, therefore, new entry into the long-distance market was technically and economically feasible. For delivery of an acceptable service, however, an entrant to the long-distance market had to be assured that it had appropriate interlinkage arrangements with the local supplier. Prior to 1984, a major problem for new entrants to the long-distance US market was that they were either refused interlinkage to AT and T's total networks, or only allowed the links on prohibitive terms. The reason, of course, was that AT and T correctly regarded the entrants as direct competitors and consequently did all that it could to resist. Given their hitherto protected and completely integrated operation, new entry for a long while remained impossible. Entry at one stage (local services) was precluded by natural monopoly factors, and artificially inhibited at the other stage (long-distance services) by the discriminatory behaviour of AT and T.

To help resolve this part of the problem, the 1982 consent decree insisted that the provision of long distance services should be separated from local services. AT and T was split up into essentially eight separate components. Seven of the new companies operated as local or regional suppliers. (By European standards, some of these 'regions' covered very large areas indeed.) The eighth, still called AT and T, produced equipment, retained the research laboratories and provided long-distance and international services. The division between local and long-distance suppliers thus ensured that the local monopolists had no reason to favour one long-distance supplier rather than any other. Entry and increased competition in the long-distance market were thus facilitated by severing the vertical link that had previously existed under the old AT and T company.

In this regard, the US authorities were bolder than their UK counterparts. When British Telecom (BT) was privatized and partially deregulated in 1984, the difficulties of the US industry were well known. Despite this, however, the integrated UK concern was privatized intact. As a result the newly licensed entrant, Mercury Communications, initially encountered precisely the same problem that had beset the US industry: on what terms could Mercury link its long-distance service to BT's established local network? The question was only resolved by the regulator after several years of acrimonious dispute.[12]

In other respects, however, UK treatment of vertical relationships, especially vertical mergers, has been more soundly based than in the USA. Vertical mergers were covered by the Fair Trading Act in the same way as horizontal mergers. A reference to the MMC could be made as long as the merger involved a market share of one-quarter or more and/or involved the acquisition of assets valued at £70 million or more. The MMC usually had to decide within six months whether or not the merger was in the public interest and make recommendations to the minister.

Vertical mergers have not featured prominently in those referred to the MMC, but the very first case that the MMC had to consider when its powers were broadened in 1965 involved a textbook case of vertical integration between a motor car manufacturer and a supplier of car bodies. At the time of the report, Pressed Steel supplied about one-quarter of BMC's total body requirements and about one-third of its requirements of car bodies. A competitor of BMC, the Rootes Group, was almost entirely dependent on Pressed Steel for their supplies of car bodies, as were the more specialized car producers, Rover and Jaguar. The other large-volume car makers in the UK, Ford, Vauxhall and Standard Triumph, produced their own car bodies. The question thus arose of whether BMC's acquisition of Pressed Steel would threaten the continuity of supply to those manufacturers who did not have their own car body plant. Although the term is not used in the report, the MMC in effect had to consider the 'foreclosure' argument: would the merger foreclose to other car manufacturers, especially Rootes, which was in direct competition with BMC, their supplies of car bodies? The MMC noted the increasing trend in the world motor industry towards vertical integration and the fact that Pressed Steel was probably the largest remaining independent car body maker in that industry. Given the structure of the industry, the MMC therefore took very seriously the possible vulnerability of the non-integrated firms. However, in his statement to shareholders setting out the terms and conditions of the agreement with BMC, the Chairman of Pressed Steel had made it clear that BMC 'has given assurances that it intends to maintain the existing goodwill and business relationships with Pressed Steel's other customers in the industry' (MMC, 1966a, para. 59). These undertakings appear to have been accepted by Pressed Steel's customers because none made representations to the MMC opposing the merger. The Commission also asked the merging companies to set out, quite specifically, their commitment to continued supply of the independent customers (para. 61). Despite the high concentration in the industry at both production stages and the formidable entry barriers, the MMC was therefore satisfied that the merger would not operate against the public interest.

In *S and W Berisford* (MMC, 1981b), a leading commodity and merchanting firm which also distributed sugar wanted to integrate backwards to acquire one of the two remaining large sugar refiners, the British Sugar Corporation (BSC).

Until the proposed merger, Berisford had distributed the sugar of both BSC and Tate and Lyle. At the time of the merger, BSC was responsible for about 49 per cent of sugar sales in the UK, and Tate and Lyle about 43 per cent. The remainder was imported. Although Tate and Lyle 'did not feel able to comment upon the ownership of its principal competitors in the United Kingdom sugar market' (para. 8.23) it did feel that it would not be right for its sugar to be merchanted through a newly integrated company. In this case, however, it was clear from evidence presented in the report that more than adequate independent sources of distribution remained, including direct purchase from Tate and Lyle itself. Thus, although the acquiring company, Berisford, also thought it inappropriate that it should continue to distribute Tate and Lyle's products following its merger with BSC, a move which the US authorities might still interpret as 'foreclosure', the fact that alternative means of distribution were readily available to Tate and Lyle convinced the MMC that there would be no significant effects on competition. Indeed, in this case, the MMC recommended that, to ensure that these effects were kept to a minimum, Berisford should give an undertaking that after the merger it would cease to distribute Tate and Lyle's products.

It is appropriate to mention one more British case involving vertical integration by merger, particularly because it provides a useful comparison with the USA. In *British Telecom/Mitel* (MMC, 1986), the MMC had to investigate the acquisition by the newly privatized British telecommunications monopoly of a leading Canadian producer of telecommunications equipment, especially various sizes of private automatic branch exchanges (PABXs). We noted above that, when AT and T was split up in 1984, not only were long-distance operations kept separate from local services but equipment manufacture was also separated from local service supply where natural monopoly elements were still strong. As a result, after the split local suppliers had no reason other than efficiency to prefer one equipment manufacturer to any other. The consent decree had thus involved a large element of vertical disintegration.

The position in the UK was almost exactly the opposite. Despite a number of proposals for splitting up British Telecom before privatization, in particular to separate long-distance from local services, the enterprise was privatized intact, but regulated by the newly created Office of Telecommunications (OFTel). While in the public sector, British Telecom had collaborated with UK equipment manufacturers in the development of new products but had practically no equipment capacity of its own. The central question raised, therefore, by its proposed acquisition of Mitel was the competitive effects in the equipment industry. The equipment manufacturers argued strongly that the merger would seriously distort competition in the UK market. BT was likely to remain for the foreseeable future the overwhelmingly dominant enterprise in the provision and maintenance of telecommunications services. It was by far the most important purchaser of equipment and, as a result of its previous position as a nationalized monopoly, had an unrivalled knowledge of end-users' current and future requirements. Not only would BT tend to favour purchases from its own subsidiary (Mitel) but, because of its role as the major network installer and operator, it would necessarily have advance knowledge of future technical requirements and developments. Sensitive information which independent suppliers would inevitably have to disclose to BT if they were to gain future orders would be made available to Mitel. Eventually, it was argued, the independent equipment producers would be squeezed out of the UK market.

Given the level of concentration in both long-distance and local network services in the UK and the absolute entry barriers that prevailed,[13] there is a good case for agreeing with the equipment manufacturers that the merger should be blocked. In the event, the MMC largely agreed with this verdict: 'BT has been allowed as a privately-owned company to retain much of the monopoly power its predecessors enjoyed as a public corporation. It now wants to enhance that market power by acquiring control of a manufacturer. This situation is unprecedented' (MMC, 1986, para. 10.76). It concluded that the merger was likely to operate against the public interest, but a majority (of four to one) considered that the adverse effects could be sufficiently reduced if a number of conditions were met. Amongst the many conditions were that BT should not purchase from Mitel equipment for the UK market for at least three years; that BT should not cross-subsidize Mitel; and that the operations of the two companies should be kept strictly separate (para. 10.77). Apart from the hope that these conditions might be monitored in the long term by OFTel, it is not at all clear how they could be guaranteed.

BT was therefore allowed to purchase 51 per cent of the equity in Mitel. The story, however, did not have a happy ending. BT had envisaged combining its own and Mitel's expertise to develop office automation equipment through which all sorts of data and telephone traffic could be channelled. The strategy was based on the expected convergence of the telecommunications and computer technologies. However, the industries did not develop in the way expected and Mitel's performance continued to be weak. At the beginning of 1990, BT announced that it was putting its share of Mitel up for sale, but it was not until June 1992 that it was able to dispose of its holding, for a reported loss of about £116 millions.[14]

In a highly controversial case investigated by the MMC, the existing high degree of vertical integration was a central issue. Its enquiry into the supply of beer involved a 'complex monopoly',[15] which essentially refers to a market structure where no one firm has a share of 25 per cent or more but where a group of two or more independent firms 'so conduct their respective affairs as in any way to prevent, restrict or distort competition' (MMC, 1989a, para. 11.5). In this case, the six largest integrated brewing companies accounted for 75 per cent of beer production in Britain and approximately the same proportion of public houses. Thus they acted as producers, wholesalers and retailers of beer (para. 1.9). Although individual brewers differed in detail, the restrictive arrangements that they made for the distribution of their beers were sufficiently similar for the MMC to find that a complex monopoly existed (para. 11.23).

The retail distribution of beer (and all alcohol), whether through public houses or shops and off-licences, is controlled through a licensing system. In the case of public houses, new licences are granted very sparingly and this creates a formidable entry barrier to this highly important part of the retail trade. A major factor in the forward vertical integration by brewers over a long period has therefore been the need, as they saw it, to secure adequate retail outlets. Even in the 25 per cent of public houses not owned by the big six, they had an important influence over the beers sold by means of the 'loan-tie' system. In exchange for the exclusive purchase of their beers or a minimum guaranteed amount, brewers offered loans at rates of interest below the market rate. The MMC estimated that about one-half of these public houses had a loan tied in this way (para. 1.10). Hence, through vertical integration and the tied loan system, the major brewers jointly controlled the major part of production and distribution of beers. In addition, entry barriers at the retail end were very high.

We noted above when discussing the 'foreclosure' doctrine that the combination of high levels of horizontal concentration and vertical integration with severe entry barriers was precisely that circumstance most likely to require antitrust action. Although our reference there was to vertical mergers, the point has equal force in the case of an existing integrated market structure. In the case of the supply of beer, the MMC agreed, listing at the end of a long and complex report no fewer than 11 characteristics of the market conduct of the major brewers that operated against the public interest. These included the rate of real increases in price, the higher relative price of lager beers and the regional differences in wholesale prices. Most of their conclusions, however, concerned the way in which the vertical integration in the market reduced consumer choice. They condemned, for example, the limited independence of tenants in brewer-owned public houses, the highly restricted choice of beers and other drinks, the exclusion of independent cider and soft drinks from public houses of brewers which jointly owned cider and soft drink companies, and the practice of offering loans in return for secured trade (see Chapter 12 of the MMC report).

Given the wide-ranging scope of their criticisms of the way vertical integration was used so that 'competition [was] structured by producers rather than driven by the demands of consumers' (para. 12.109), it is not surprising that the recommendations of the MMC were equally dramatic. Their main recommendation was that no brewer should be permitted to own or lease more than 2000 public houses in the UK. Those brewers which currently owned more than this number should be required to divest themselves of an amount to bring them within this threshold. At the time of the report, this would have required the six national brewers to sell off nearly two-thirds of their public houses (paras 12.129–12.130). There were other recommendations dealing with the introduction of other beers and drinks into brewer-owned public houses and the future relationships between brewers and tenants, but the divestiture proposal was by far the most radical and controversial.

Initially, the Secretary of State indicated that he was inclined to accept the proposals as they stood. There followed an intense lobbying campaign which, in the event, appears to have paid off. The remedies actually introduced were far less severe than the MMC recommended. The report was published in March 1989 and in July the Secretary of State announced his decision. The central recommendation on divestiture was dropped. Instead, all brewers owning more than 2000 public houses in future would have to keep at least 50 per cent above that number free of any restraint on the beers that they could sell. As the press notice announcing the decision made clear, 'this will create 11 000 more free houses but will allow the brewers to retain their properties'. Other parts of the decision required all public houses owned by the national brewers to sell at least one 'guest' beer as well as other drinks from any other firm and proposed to give greater security of tenure to public house tenants. These provisions have been monitored by the OFT.

The new merger regulation in the EU discussed in Chapter 8 uses the terminology of Articles 81 and 82 by referring to 'concentrations'. Thus 'A concentration which creates or strengthens a dominant position as a result of which effective competition would be significantly impeded in the Common Market or in a substantial part of it shall be declared incompatible with the Common Market' (Article 2). As long as the proposed vertical merger meets the turnover criteria, it can be considered by the 'Merger Task Force' in the same way as horizontal mergers. Clearly, given the wording of the above clause, the markets affected would have to be fairly heavily concentrated before an investigation was triggered. Vertical mergers have not, so far, featured prominently in the cases considered by the 'Task Force'. However, vertical elements in two cases were thought important enough to require 'de-integration' before they were allowed to proceed. Thus Telefonica, the sole buyer of telecommunications equipment in Spain, sold its 5 per cent holding in Telettra to Alcatel. The latter were the two most prominent equipment manufacturers in Spain and their merger resulted in a market share of more than 80 per cent. The sale of the share broke the vertical link between Telefonica and the equipment industry but, given the modest size of the holding, the impact of the move was unlikely to be very profound (Neven *et al.*, 1993). The second case involved a joint venture between a transport firm, TNT, and five national postal organizations (Canada Post, DBP Postdirect, La Poste, PTT Post and Sweden Post). The aspect of the original proposal which the 'Task Force' found most objectionable was the exclusive access to national postal outlets for five years to be granted to the joint venture. In the view of the 'Task Force', this would have led to an unacceptable degree of foreclosure to these outlets for competitors of TNT. Before the merger was cleared, therefore, the parties had to reduce the period of exclusive access from five to two years, as well as modifying the extent of the exclusive access, although precise details on the latter point were not made public (ibid., p. 120).

Given the extensive attention that has been paid recently in the economics literature to vertical relationships, future decisions are more likely to be in line with recent UK experience than with that of the USA, especially those judgements dating from the 1960s.

IV Conclusions
There are many motives for vertical integration and nearly all stem from attempts to improve efficiency by reducing costs. Recent analyses of the transactions costs of using the market rather than the internal capacity of the firm have tended to strengthen this view. Many mergers apparently undertaken for market power purposes have had, on close examination, a different outcome. Some vertical integration may increase the firm's profitability, but may simultaneously benefit consumers by lowering prices.

There remain, however, a small number of cases where vertical integration may increase entry barriers and market power. For this reason, although vertical integration by internal growth is not covered by the antitrust laws, vertical mergers are included. The development of case law on this issue in the USA has been marked, some would say marred, by some leading decisions in the 1960s and early 1970s which few economists would now wish to defend. Relying on a very restrictive interpretation of 'foreclosure' applied to markets where concentration was low and entry barriers modest, the Supreme Court blocked vertical mergers whose primary purpose was almost certainly to increase efficiency. It is unlikely that, with the revised Guidelines adopted in 1982, similar cases could now be challenged. In the UK, the relatively few vertical mergers considered by the MMC have raised the issue of 'foreclosure', but the Commission has normally been satisfied that alternative channels remain open for independent firms, or the merged firm has committed itself to continue to serve existing customers. The exception, where the MMC had considerable misgivings about the merger, involved the highly unusual case of a newly privatized and regulated natural monopoly. The indications are that any future cases investigated by the new EU regulation will place a heavy emphasis on existing concentration and entry conditions.

Notes
1. We recognize that in some cases the complexities of ownership may not make the distinctions as clear-cut as we suggest in the text. A manufacturer may own 30 per cent of the voting

capital of a distributor and also impose vertical restraints. If 30 per cent is enough to secure effective control, the firms are in practice vertically integrated.

2. There is an interesting discussion in Marshall (1919) for example.
3. In its most complete form, the model assumes full information about current and future prices on the part of all participants and no uncertainty. Transactions costs would therefore be eliminated. Those wishing to pursue these matters can consult Stigler (1965).
4. It may not always be possible. For example, the manufacturer may be a multinational enterprise distributing through a series of locally owned monopolies, hostile to integration. In such cases the manufacturer may seek to achieve the same result as vertical integration by some kind of vertical restraint. See below, Chapter 10.
5. This result depends on the well-known result from simple monopoly theory that a linear marginal revenue function cuts the horizontal axis halfway between the origin and the horizontal intercept of the demand curve.
6. In order to focus on the central issue we are assuming that, for example, managerial or organizational savings are not available.
7. *Brown Shoe* v. *United States*, 370 US 294 (1962), at 323–4.
8. See, for example, Blair and Kaserman (1985, pp. 326–7).
9. Two hostile reviews are Peterman (1975) and Bork (1978, chs 9 and 11).
10. *Ford Motor Company* v. *United States*, 405 US 562 (1972).
11. *Fruehauf Corporation* v. *Federal Trade Commission*, 603 F.2d 345, 1989.
12. See, for example, Vickers and Yarrow (1988, pp. 217–20).
13. When BT was privatized, the government introduced a strict system of licensing for new network operators. One other licence was granted, to Mercury Communications (a subsidiary of Cable and Wireless), but its market share remained around 5 per cent throughout the 1980s.
14. *Financial Times*, 16 June 1992.
15. See Chapter 3.

10 Market dominance and vertical restraints

I Introduction

We made clear at the beginning of Chapter 9 the distinction between vertical integration and vertical restraints. In this chapter our major concern is to analyse the effect that a variety of vertical restraints imposed by firms at one stage of the production process on their suppliers or distributors can have on market dominance, and then to consider the antitrust response to these practices.

The term 'vertical restraint' correctly captures the essence of the process: one firm in a vertical relationship with another imposes conditions over the terms on which it is prepared to trade. Thus a manufacturer may insist that any retailer handling his products charges a specific price, a practice variously termed 'resale price maintenance' or 'fair trade'. Some firms may allocate a particular geographic region to a distributor, whose sales must be confined to that region; others may insist that, if distributors are to handle one of its products, they must also handle another (a tying arrangement) or they must also take the full product line (full-line forcing). Again, firms may insist and give special inducements to sweeten their insistence that distributors handle *only* their product (exclusive dealing) and, if they feel that the distributor is not keeping to the bargain, refuse to deal with the firm.

In short, the variety of industry ensures a great diversity of vertical arrangements. The complexity and ingenuity that firms often bring to these relationships with other traders suggest that an important part of their profitability hangs on their success. Why go to the trouble of imposing complicated conditions on your distributors and then incur the costs of monitoring them, if they have no effect on your profitability? As we shall see in Section III, despite attempts by the law to curb restraints which are thought to enhance or create market power, firms are still prepared to run the risk of punishment in order to reap, at least for a time, the rewards that the restraints provide.

The economic analysis of vertical restraints, discussed in Section II, has received a great deal of attention in recent years and in some cases this has led to a substantial revision of the policy implications. The laws, especially in the USA, have not been revised so rapidly. In some cases, judgements and laws have reflected the changed emphasis on the 'new' thinking, while in others both remain unrevised. These contrasts in the law, both as between one jurisdiction and another, and between one type of vertical restraint and another, are the subject of Section III.

II   The analysis of vertical restraints

For clarity of exposition, we will deal with the main types of restraint separately but, of course, in practice firms may employ a complex package of restraints. Similarly, we will usually refer to a restraint imposed by a manufacturer on its distributors but in some contexts another stage in the production process may be more appropriate. We discuss in sequence the following restraints: resale price maintenance, selective distribution systems and tying arrangements. The list is not exhaustive, but it does cover the main types of restraint found in practice.

Resale price maintenance

Conceptually, it is useful to think of product distribution as an input into 'manufacture'. Just as a manufacturer for any given product will wish to ensure that inputs are as cheap as possible, so he will wish to minimize the cost of any distribution inputs. Having decided the price at which he wishes to sell to distributors, the manufacturer will want to ensure that his product is sold in as great a volume as possible and that distributors earn no more than a 'normal' return on his product. Any greater return for them implies that their price is above the competitive level and therefore they are restricting sales. At the given price received by the manufacturer, therefore, returns will be reduced.

Largely on the basis of this kind of reasoning, many observers until about 1960 believed that the prime movers in the introduction of resale price maintenance (RPM) were distributors who collectively imposed their will on reluctant manufacturers. Although this may have occurred for a range of products where no product-specific services were involved, in other cases, as Telser (1960) showed in a pathbreaking article, the initiators of resale price maintenance were probably the manufacturers. The question that Telser posed was this: if manufacturers wanted their products distributed as widely as possible, given the price at which they were selling to distributors, why, as the evidence suggested, did they frequently insist on minimum resale prices? If distributors were free to set their own prices rather than have to keep to the minimum price imposed by the manufacturer, the more efficient would reduce the price and sell more. Both distributor and manufacturer would gain. In fact this was at the heart of the debate which led to the effective abandonment of RPM in the UK following the 1964 Resale Prices Act discussed in the next section.

Telser answered the question in approximately the following terms. Frequently the manufacturer may have little concern about the detailed arrangements for the distribution of his products. Some retailers may provide a minimum of service, with poor or non-existent display and few, elusive sales-persons. Others may be effusive in all aspects of presentation, service and personnel. As a result a range of retail prices will emerge according to the types of distributors available. Those catering well for customers' tastes will prosper, while those who do not will have to change their policy or disappear. However, the manufacturer's attitude towards distributors is likely to be very different where product-specific services are required. Where, for example, products are complicated to install and operate, customers may rely heavily on the expertise of sales staff for advice and after-sales service. If this is not available, sales of the product may be badly affected. The manufacturers will want to ensure that all distributors of their products provide this amount of product-specific services which, of course, raise distribution costs but increase the manufacturers' profits. The crux of Telser's argument was that frequently the services could be consumed separately from the product. Consumers could go to a store providing a full-service (explanation of how to use an appliance, test drives for a new model of car, detailed description about new computer software and so on) and, having obtained the information and weighed the various available options, go to the nearest discount store which provides no service and buy the product of their choice. Consumers would 'free-ride' on the full service, higher-priced distributors who eventually would reduce the amount of service or go out of business. In either case, the manufacturers' objective would not be fulfilled. The 'free-rider' problem, therefore, appeared to provide a rational explanation for manufacturers pressing for the introduction of resale price maintenance. A minimum price of the product is set by the manufacturer. Any distributor attempting to sell below this price runs the risk of having supplies cut off (assuming for the moment that this is allowed by the law). Having introduced resale price maintenance, the manufacturer will have to monitor its operation. As long as the increased profits generated by the maintained price are greater than the costs of monitoring, it is clearly in the manufacturers' interest.

The manufacturer may gain, but what of distributors and consumers? Does the introduction of resale price maintenance lead unambiguously to gains for either or both of these groups? If all groups gain or even if there is a net welfare gain (say, the gain to the manufacturer and consumers outweighs any loss to distributors) then resale price maintenance may be considered desirable and should not be blocked by the law. Broadly speaking, this is the position of a group of commentators who may be described loosely as representing the Chicago School (for example, in particular, Bork, 1978, ch. 14; Posner, 1977). It turns out, however, that the results are far more ambiguous. In order to illustrate the possibilities, we refer to Figure 10.1.

In panel (a), consumer's demand is shown by D_0. The manufacturer's marginal cost is assumed constant at MC_M. We also assume that he has sufficient market power to maintain a wholesale price of P_0. Distributors have costs per unit of P_1-P_0 but, because distribution is assumed to be highly competitive, the retail price settles at P_1 and they earn a normal return with no economic profit. In the absence of resale price maintenance, therefore, the quantity sold is Q_1 for a price P_1. If the manufacturer believes that the quantity of retail services is inadequate, it may insist on introducing a higher maintained price of P_2, in which case an amount Q_0 would be sold. Given the structure of the retail market, the whole of the additional retail margin apparently created by this price rise and represented by the area P_1P_2GE will be taken up by the provision of extra services. The area P_0P_1EF represents the normal costs of distribution for the output Q_0.

This cannot be the end of the story, however, because, with increased prices and costs and a reduced output, the manufacturer's profit would have fallen. From the manufacturer's point of view, the extra services generated by resale price maintenance are to stimulate total demand for his product. One such demand shift is shown as D_1 in panel (a) of the diagram. At the maintained price P_2, the new larger quantity Q_2 is sold. We now need to know which groups have benefited from the change in this case. First, the manufacturer gains from an increase in profit. Prior to resale price maintenance, total profit was equal to MC_MP_0NM. On the larger output following the introduction of resale price maintenance, profit is increased by $MNKL$. Secondly, as long as retailing remains highly competitive, the position of individual retailers is unchanged. They earn a normal return. The total amount of 'distribution costs', including those induced by the maintained price, is equivalent to P_0P_2HK. Thirdly, we can show that consumers have benefited in this case. Consumers are getting more services from retailers, which is a benefit, but the price has risen, which is unfavourable. More precisely, we can compare consumer's surplus before and after the introduction of resale price maintenance. Before the introduction, price was P_1 and quantity Q_1 and consumer surplus was the equivalent of P_1RT in the figure. After resale price maintenance has shifted demand to D_1, consumer surplus on the increased output is P_2HS. The two triangles have the area P_2GT in common, so we have to decide whether the increase in consumer's surplus created by the shift in demand (represented by $GHST$) is greater than the loss in consumer's surplus resulting in the costs of additional services (represented by P_1RGP_2). It is clear from inspection of the figure that $GHST > P_1RGP_2$.[1] Consumers gain more from the increased services than they lose in having to pay a higher price. In this case, therefore, since both consumers and producer gain while the retailer's position is unchanged, we conclude that the introduction of resale price maintenance produces a net benefit. If this result were quite general, we could all join the ranks of the Chicago School and call for the abolition of all laws restricting the use of resale price maintenance.

Unfortunately, as a number of writers, notably Comanor (1985) and Scherer (1983), have shown, the world is more complex than is suggested by this result. In particular, if the demand shift is different from that shown in panel (a) of Figure 10. 1, it is quite possible for manufacturers' profits to increase following the introduction of resale price maintenance, but for consumers' surplus to fall by a greater amount, so that the net effect is a welfare loss. The case is shown in panel (b) of Figure 10.1, where we rely on the discussion in Scherer and

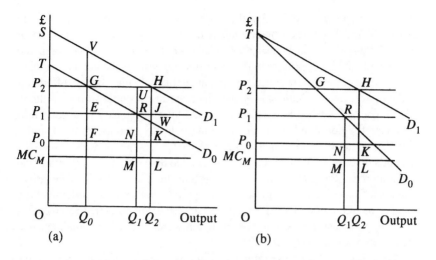

Figure 10.1   Welfare effects of resale price maintenance

Ross (1990, pp. 546–8). In the figure the introduction of resale price maintenance is assumed to cause the same increase in price and output as in the previous case. However, the demand shift which allows this is not parallel but as shown, where the higher demand D_1 increasingly diverges from the lower demand D_0 as the amount increases. The demand curve D_1 in the right-hand panel of Figure 10.1 is drawn so that the extra selling costs incurred following resale price maintenance lead to exactly the same price and output increases as in the previous case. Just as the parallel demand shift in panel (a) is a special case, so also is the case in panel (b). What it demonstrates, however, is that the introduction of resale price maintenance need not necessarily be welfare enhancing. In the case shown in panel (b) the increase in consumer surplus after the demand shift is GHT. This must be offset against the loss of consumer's surplus P_1P_2GR which is now taken up with the increased costs of distribution. In the case shown, $P_1P_2GR > GHT$, implying that consumers are worse off after the change. Even if the increased profit of manufacturers, represented by $MNKL$, is included as a gain, the additional costs are greater and there has been a net welfare loss as a result of the change to resale price maintenance. As Scherer and Ross explain, this need not necessarily be the result, but it is sufficient to show that the effects are not clear-cut (ibid., pp. 547–8). Indeed, the economic explanation of the demand shift shown in panel (b) is especially persuasive. The fact that the extra selling effort induced by resale price maintenance causes demand to increase by greater and greater amounts as we move down the demand curve means that consumers who previously were on the margin between buying and not buying the good (that is, those previously at R) are more affected than those who previously had very high reservation prices (for example, those previously near T). The latter group would have been prepared to pay a much higher price than P_2 rather than do without the good altogether. For them, additional distribution services are unlikely to make much difference, and therefore, as the figure shows, their increase in consumer surplus is slight. The impact is likely to be much greater for those previously just induced to purchase the good and for them consumer surplus increases significantly. Whether or not the case shown in panel (b) leads to a net increase in benefits depends on the size of the price increase and the demand shift. The greater the price increase the greater the likelihood that the net gain will be negative, whereas, for a given price increase, the greater the increase in demand the greater the likelihood of a net gain. Thus, since it is not possible to arrive at an unambiguous result, a permissive attitude towards resale price maintenance may lead to welfare losses.

The ambiguity is increased if we look more closely at the range of products to which resale price maintenance has been applied in the past. Frequently purchased, low-value items such as cigarettes, confectionery, package foods and household goods have been subject to resale price maintenance as well as complex, high-value items such as cameras, electrical appliances and consumer durables. While Telser's 'free-rider' argument may apply to the latter, it is difficult to apply to the former group of goods where consumers' experience and frequent purchase makes them a good judge of which brand suits them best. A contribution by Marvel and McCafferty (1985) goes some way to explain why resale price maintenance may be applied to a wider range of goods. They argue that retailers with a high reputation will stock products with maintained prices and wider margins and thus in effect certify to consumers that they are of good quality; otherwise they would not carry them. Manufacturers may thus wish to maintain prices as a means of ensuring that they are carried by outlets with the highest reputation for quality. This view is also connected to a much more traditional justification for resale price maintenance, namely that it will prevent the practice of 'loss leading'. A widely recognized, leading brand may be used by a distributor purely as a promotional tool. Its price may be cut drastically and the low price widely advertised as a means of encouraging consumers to use the distributor's stores, where they will probably purchase other items in addition to the 'loss leader'. Manufacturers may legitimately feel that, if consumers frequently judge quality by price, the widespread use of their products as 'loss leaders' will ultimately affect sales as consumers lose confidence in their quality and retailers providing a comprehensive service cease carrying the product. As we see in Section III below, even those jurisdictions which are generally hostile to resale price maintenance have been prepared to make special provisions against loss leading.

Two further explanations for the practice may be briefly mentioned. First, it is sometimes argued that manufacturers may favour resale price maintenance, at least in part, because it facilitates collusion. We saw in Chapter 7 that a perennial problem for manufacturers wishing jointly to maintain a monopoly price is the incentive this gives for cheating. Costly arrangements for monitoring the agreement will therefore have to be introduced. If resale price maintenance is employed by all members of the cartel, the incentive to cheat may be much reduced. An individual manufacturer seeking to boost sales by shading his price to the distributor will be largely disappointed because the retail price is maintained. Nevertheless, he may offer especially favourable terms to the distributor to push his products rather than those of his competitors. To counter this possibility, the cartel members may have to introduce a system of exclusive dealing; that is, a distributor handles the products of only one manufacturer. However, this in turn gives an incentive for manufacturers to offer secret deals in order to win over retailers to distribute their products. In short, resale price maintenance may be a very blunt instrument for trying to eliminate the inherent problems of collusion. Furthermore, according to a comprehensive US review, the average level of seller concentration in markets where resale price maintenance prevailed was too low to suggest that collusion would be successful (Overstreet, 1983).

Secondly, the villain's role has been assigned to distributors. They may use resale price maintenance as a means of preventing the erosion of margins and as a protection from competition. Instead of competing amongst themselves, retailers would like to establish a monopoly price from which they could jointly earn monopoly profit. Without special safeguards, as we saw in Chapter 7, such agreements are subject to cheating by individual members. If manufacturers can be persuaded to introduce and monitor resale price maintenance, this problem may be largely overcome: all retailers would have to sell at the maintained price, on pain of having supplies withdrawn if they attempted a price reduction. Resale price maintenance may, in this view, be a valuable buttress for a retailer's cartel.

There are two fairly obvious reasons, however, why any such reliance by retailers on resale price maintenance is likely to be misplaced. First, the collusive price desired by retailers would ideally be at the monopoly level, but this conflicts with the manufacturer's interest of making maximum sales, given the wholesale price. Any restriction caused by an elevation of the retail price to the monopoly level would reduce the manufacturer's own profits. Far from supporting and policing the retailer's collusive price, a manufacturer is likely to report the matter to the antitrust authority, or at the very least fail to enforce the resale price maintenance. In addition, given that entry is relatively easy in many retail markets, any abnormally high profits earned by colluding retailers are likely to attract new entrants or new stockists of the price-maintained products. With a regime of fixed prices, the abnormal returns would in the long run be eroded by increased selling costs, as a larger number of retailers competed for sales. Again, therefore, although there may be instances where pressure for resale price maintenance from retailers may have been partly influenced by collusive considerations, it seems unlikely to have played a major part.

The general point to emerge from our discussion of resale price maintenance is that, given the profit-maximizing wholesale price, manufacturers will wish to ensure that retail sales volume is as large as possible. In particular, they will want to avoid the 'successive monopoly mark-up problem' which would restrict their sales and profits. Maintaining resale prices does not conflict with their objective. If the 'free-rider' problem for some products is prevented or the reputation for high quality is underpinned in others, extra sales and manufacturers' profits may be generated. The welfare conclusions, however, are not unambiguously positive because in some cases consumers may be worse off with resale price maintenance than without it.

Selective distribution systems

In several types of vertical agreement the supplier selects the distributor of its products. For example, one type is the territorial agreement whereby the manufacturer selects one firm as the sole distributor for its products in a particular geographic area. In an exclusive dealing arrangement, a supplier insists that its distributors buy only from them. A variation on this arrangement is a franchise where the franchisee agrees not only to purchase materials and products exclusively from the franchisor but also to use his know-how, methods, logo and trademarks. For other products, suppliers may appoint as distributors only firms meeting certain levels of technical and other expertise. In each case distribution is constrained or restricted in some way and possible antitrust issues can arise.

The same tension between the interests of manufacturers and retailers can be observed in vertical restrictions which allocate a particular geographic area to a single distributor. Within that area the dealer has a monopoly over sales of the manufacturer's product. Why should the manufacturer be prepared to concede such a right when on the face of it the retailer will be free to charge a monopoly price which, as we have seen, will reduce the profit of the manufacturer? In addition we need to ask whether conferring a local monopoly on a distributor reduces consumer welfare by increasing the final price. Very broadly, therefore, do territorial restraints allow the exercise of market power or do they enhance efficiency?

From the manufacturer's point of view the advantage of an exclusive territory arrangement is that the offer of a wider margin to the distributors will encourage them to maintain a high quality of service, including an adequate stock of inventories. If the territorial restraint is coupled with exclusive dealing, the manufacturer can also expect the maximum effort on the part of the distributor to sell the product. For retailers, the territorial restriction should help to maintain higher margins than would prevail if there were an open policy by the manufacturer towards distribution outlets.

Just as in the resale price maintenance case, manufacturers may also have avoidance of 'free-riding' as a motive for an exclusive franchising agreement. The franchisee expects to benefit from the use of a known trademark or brand image. Its wide acceptance and reputation may command a high premium. Collectively all franchise holders as well as the manufacturer or supplier have a strong interest in ensuring that the reputation remains untarnished. Individually, however, some franchisees may seek to increase sales by reducing the quality of the product and so saving on costs. If only a small minority acted in this way not too much damage to the reputation of the product might occur. However, the same incentive to cut corners applies to all distributors and the supplier needs some method of eliminating the temptation. The exclusive franchise provides such an incentive structure. In return for an undertaking from the franchisee that the product will always be provided according to the meticulous conditions laid down in the contract, the franchisor guarantees that no one else will be granted a franchise in the area specified. In addition, the franchisee may be required to pay a lump sum for the franchise and this will be forfeited if standards fall below those stipulated.

Manufacturers and distributors may be happy with such an arrangement, but what of consumers? At first glance the grant of a local monopoly appears inimical to their interests. In practice exclusive franchise arrangements may be either marginally favourable for consumers or neutral. First, to the extent that the franchised products have gained wide acceptance and are highly regarded, a mechanism for maintaining those standards will be in the consumer's interest. The value of trademarking or branding to consumers is recognized and protected by the law. The franchise arrangements described are a relatively efficient means of underpinning this protection by minimizing the 'free-rider' problem. Secondly, although individual franchise holders may be granted exclusive rights in a particular area, the degree of market power that this confers is likely to be limited. Intra-brand competition is restricted by the exclusive franchise but inter-brand competition is unaffected. In any area, therefore, McDonald's will have to compete with other similar fastfood chains. Demand curves of franchise holders are likely to have negative but very gentle slopes. The ability of firms to hold prices consistently above costs will thus be relatively slight.

The franchising system is a particular form of exclusive dealing. The same general incentive structure holds, however, where distributors undertake to handle the products of only one firm (or, less rigidly, agree to take a specified percentage of their requirements for a particular product from one supplier). There may be substantial economies for both manufacturer and the distributors. For the manufacturer, supplying a relatively small number of specialized retailers should cut distribution costs while also ensuring a maximum sales effort. For distributors, handling the products of only one manufacturer can lead to reduced inventory costs.

Manufacturers may view exclusive dealing contracts as having many of the advantages and providing the same kinds of incentives as vertical integration. Just as some observers have emphasized the possible adverse consequences of foreclosure in some cases of vertical integration, similar objections may be made about exclusive dealing contracts. Clearly, if some distributors agree to handle the products of only one supplier, those outlets are 'foreclosed' to other manufacturers. Before we proceed to the conclusion that, as a result, barriers to entry are raised, we need to look much more closely at the market structures involved. If the manufacturer attempting to enforce exclusive dealing has a modest share of the market, the 'foreclosure' effect is minimal. Competitors can readily find other distributors for their products. Even where a manufacturer has a substantial market share, an exclusive dealing contract is likely to have little effect on competition if entry into distribution is easy. On the other hand, where zoning or licensing laws restrict retail outlets in a particular area, exclusive dealing by a leading manufacturer will put competitors at a disadvantage which may not reflect their relative inefficiency in production. Finally, to have a significant and negative impact on competition, the exclusive dealing arrangement must last longer than the normal contractual period, otherwise all competing manufacturers have an opportunity at contract renewal time to win the custom of the distributors of their choice (Blair and Kaserman, 1985, ch. 16).

In short, exclusive dealing *may* be a means of applying pre-existing market power, but does not in itself create it. Thus, if a dominant firm insists on long-term exclusive contracts with distributors where there is an exogenous constraint on entry into the retail market, then antitrust authorities should be concerned. However, if any parts of the condition are absent, the effectiveness of exclusive dealing as a vehicle for market power are correspondingly weakened.

Tying arrangements

Another variation on the vertical restraints theme which continues to receive theoretical and policy attention are tying arrangements or tie-in sales. A manufacturer of a major product X insists that customers also purchase related product or products Y and Z. At various times in the recent past, for example, manufacturers of photocopying machines have tied in with the lease of the machine sales of toner (ink) and paper. We also saw, in Chapter 5, that Microsoft's 'bundling' of its web browser into its operating system formed an important part of the antitrust case. As with the other restraints we have considered, there are often a variety of motives and effects of tying and only some of these are likely to be of concern to an antitrust authority. The practice is closely related to full-line forcing (insisting that customers purchase a whole line of products) and commodity bundling, whereby goods that could be sold separately are only made available as part of a package.

Two unexceptional motives for tying are the maintenance of product reputation and the improvement of technical efficiency. Sellers of technically advanced and sophisticated products which are used in conjunction with other materials (such as photocopiers and paper) may insist that a tied product is also purchased exclusively from them on the grounds that the use of an inferior product could damage the performance of the main (or tying) product or machine. If this occurred frequently, the reputation of the tying product would suffer, resulting in declining sales for the producer. Of course, it is a question of fact in individual cases whether or not the use of alternative materials or products can damage the performance of the tying product. An unsubstantiated claim suggests that the real purpose of the tie is different.

Distribution efficiency may be improved if tying and tied products can be delivered at the same time. In the photocopier case, supplies of toner and paper may be delivered while the machine receives its regular maintenance check. However, although there may be some instances where such cost savings are important, the majority of tying arrangements are probably inspired by other motives, and in any case the tie is not a necessary condition for the efficiency gain. For example, manufacturers could offer a lower price (reflecting the cost savings) to customers who take both (or all) products and a higher price to customers who wish to take only one product and buy the others elsewhere.

Three additional motives for tying are frequently mentioned: as a means of enforcing second degree price discrimination; more controversially, to raise the costs of entry; and to avoid regulation of profits or prices. On the face of it, all three involve market power and may therefore be of concern to antitrust policy. When discussing price discrimination in Chapter 5, it was clear that a firm with market power could substantially increase its profits if price discrimination were used. Specifically, with second degree price discrimination, output would be increased to the allocatively efficient level but a large income transfer from consumers to producers would take place, compared with a regime of simple monopoly pricing. We pointed out that the problem for a manufacturer wishing to introduce this kind of discriminatory pricing is to discover the intensity of demand by individual customers or groups. Tying may be a highly effective means of collecting such information. In the photocopying example, in the absence of a tie between machine and toner, the manufacturer would charge a single rental price, reflecting its market power. The same price would be paid by intensive users and occasional users alike. However, with a tie between the products, the toner could act as a metering device: the intensity of usage would be directly related to the quantity of toner required. The manufacturer can then generate higher profits from the more intensive users by loading the price of toner. The same result can, in principle, be achieved by fixing a meter to the machine. In this case, however, the manufacturer has to monitor usage to ensure that the meter is not tampered with. The tying arrangement is more discreet and avoids monitoring costs. The Internet provides many new opportunities for firms to gain detailed information about the intensity of consumer preferences and thus refine their price discrimination strategies (Shapiro and Varian, 1999).

Tying can thus be the vehicle for a manufacturer to earn higher abnormal returns through the transfer of consumer surplus. Output is likely to be higher in most instances than with simple monopoly pricing. However, as we saw in Chapter 5, the overall welfare effects of price discrimination are ambiguous. A similar ambiguity surrounds the net effects of tying. For this reason an antitrust agency may look particularly closely at a second, frequently mentioned motive for tying: as a means of raising the costs of entry. Without a tying agreement, the whole of the market for the tied product is potentially open to all firms. Once a tie is introduced, part of the market is 'foreclosed' to firms specializing in the production of the tied product. Where the effect is significant, potential entrants to the market for the tying product may be forced to consider entry at both production stages, involving both tying and tied products. To the extent that this requires a larger amount of capital which is only available to the potential entrant on less favourable terms, entry may be deterred. On this view, therefore, the tying arrangement has the effect of raising entry barriers to the tying product market where competition is impaired. The result, however, rests crucially on the share of the tied product market that is involved. If it is small, then clearly potential entrants to the tying product market can readily find alternative users of the tied product. In many cases the 'tied' product may have a number of uses, other than in conjunction with the tying product. The properly defined market for the tied product may thus be much broader than initially thought.

Finally, tying may be a means of evading government-imposed price or profit regulation. If products X and Y are used together, and where the price of X is regulated but the price of Y is not, then it is possible for the supplier to recoup whatever abnormal profit is being lost through the price regulation by raising the price of Y to the level allowed by the firm's market power and tying the sales of Y to those of X. The returns on the combined sales can then be equivalent to the level that would have been earned without the price regulation.

Refusal to sell

So far in this section we have discussed a number of ways in which suppliers may seek to regulate the number of their distributors and to control the terms on which they can trade. A refusal to sell occurs when a manufacturer or other supplier refuses to deal with a distributor at all, or only on terms less favourable than to other distributors. In the case of a complete refusal to deal, the practice is thus not strictly speaking a vertical restraint because no trading is taking place. However, because the practice may well be used in order to reinforce some other vertical restraint, it is appropriate to discuss it here.

Apart from cases where the supplier refused to deal with financially unsound distributors, the most common cases probably involve refusals to supply known price cutters. The practice may thus be used as a means to enforce resale price maintenance. We established earlier in our discussion of resale price maintenance that, given the price received by the manufacturer which will reflect any existing market power, he will wish to ensure as large a sale as possible. Since a lower retail price will generally increase sales, other things being equal, he would want to encourage rather than discourage retail price reductions. The 'free-rider' problem was one reason manufacturers might want to introduce resale price maintenance. The increased demand may more than outweigh the additional distribution costs and in some cases product reputation may be maintained. Even in the absence of formal resale price maintenance, some manufacturers see higher retail margins as a means of increasing market share and retaining their reputation for quality. They may therefore refuse to sell to distributors known for their policy of low margins and large sales volume.

The central question is, under what circumstances, if any, can a refusal to sell maintain or enhance market power? This question was examined in a general report by the MMC, although its discussion was cast in terms of the public interest (MMC, 1970b). It identified three necessary conditions for a refusal to sell to be against the public interest: (i) where the action was taken against a distributor with a reputation for price cutting; (ii) where the action was taken in response to a threatened boycott from other distributors; and (iii) where the supplier is not operating under reasonably competitive conditions (para. 37). The third condition clearly has to be present. Any firm operating under highly competitive conditions which refuses to sell to distributors will simply force them into the arms of competitors who may be more than happy to trade. If alternative sources of supply are available, there are thus unlikely to be any adverse consequences for consumers. Where a supplier with market power refuses to sell to distributors renowned for their price cutting, the outcome is more ambiguous, as we saw in the case of resale price maintenance. In some cases, maintaining wider margins at the retail level may benefit both producers and consumers, but in others consumers may be made worse off. Without more information on the type of products involved and the possible 'free-rider' effects, it is not possible a priori to decide what the outcome will be. A different issue arises where a supplier attempts to use its market power in conjunction with a refusal to sell as a means of suppressing competition. Thus a supplier may threaten to withhold supplies from customers who are dealing or planning to deal with other suppliers. This tactic may be used by a supplier against potential entrants and is clearly an attempt to maintain market power.

Where the balance of market power is reversed, the second condition mentioned by the MMC may apply. A group of retailers, which together account for a substantial portion of the sales by a supplier, may threaten a boycott unless the supplier refuses to deal, say, with a new entrant or a price-cutting competitor. The group taking this action must be important to the supplier, otherwise he is unlikely to respond. Similarly, the supplier must have a substantial share of the market, otherwise he will have little or no effective sanction over the entrant or price cutter because alternative sources of supply will be available. If these conditions are met, then refusal to supply will keep retail prices higher than they would otherwise be. The effective market power in such a case, however, is wielded by the large retail group rather than by the supplier. If he accedes to their demand he must consider that his interest is better served by retaining their custom than by turning to the entrant or price cutter.

What emerges from our discussion of some of the main forms of vertical restraints is the ambiguity of their effects. In some circumstances there may be an unequivocal net gain to consumers, as well as manufacturers or distributors. In others the most likely outcome may be the maintenance or enhancement of market power. Given these analytical results, we might expect the policy response to be equally flexible, adopting a rule of reason rather than a per se approach. In fact, as we shall observe in the next section, the policy response has often been characterized by inconsistency, not only as between one kind of restraint and another, but also between one time period and another.

III   Policy towards vertical restraints

United States

Considerable controversy has attended the interpretation of the antitrust laws in connection with vertical restraints. The discussion has focused on a number of interrelated issues. First, should the law apply per se rules or a rule of reason to such restraints? Secondly, as far as territorial restrictions are concerned, is the central issue the effect on intra-brand vis-à-vis inter-brand competition, or is this distinction irrelevant? Thirdly, is it correct to make a distinction between price and non-price restraints which should then receive different treatments, or are the effects similar and do they therefore deserve the same treatment by the law?

Resale price maintenance
Our discussion of these questions will follow the same sequence of restraints discussed in the previous section, beginning with resale price maintenance. Despite a somewhat chequered legal history and the economic analysis which suggests that in some circumstances a vertical price restraint can have beneficial

effects for consumers, a per se illegality rule has generally been applied. Since the key decision in 1911 in *Dr. Miles*,[2] the Supreme Court has held firmly to the view that resale price maintenance constitutes a violation of Section 1 of the Sherman Act.

For a time, however, the doctrine came under strong attack from what was known as the Fair Trade Movement which, at the height of the Depression in the 1930s, successfully promoted fair trade laws in all but four states of the Union. These laws enabled suppliers to fix minimum resale prices for their goods as long as inter-state trade was not involved. The Miller–Tydings Act (1937) exempted resale price maintenance contracts from prosecution under Section 1 of the Sherman Act where these were allowed under state laws. To ensure that recalcitrant distributors who did not want to be bound to a minimum price were brought into line, many states passed non-signer statutes whereby the restraint could be imposed on all distributors whether or not they agreed to the terms, as long as at least one had agreed. The Fair Trade Movement's finest hour was probably reached in 1952, when Congress passed the McGuire Act, effectively overturning a Supreme Court ruling of the previous year, which determined that non-signers of resale price maintenance contracts could not have the terms forced upon them. Together, the Miller–Tydings and McGuire Acts allowed for the enforcement of price maintenance in those states which had passed a fair trade law. Despite the hostility of the courts, therefore, the USA was in practice for several decades more tolerant of resale price maintenance than other jurisdictions with generally less developed antitrust laws (Scherer and Ross, 1990, p. 556).

The changed post-Second World War economic environment, the ingenuity of businessmen,[3] and undoubted cost reductions that could be made by large-scale, low-price retailing units, all tended to undermine the continued use of resale price maintenance. By the time the Miller–Tydings and McGuire Acts were eventually repealed in 1975, the range of products on which prices were still maintained had shrunk to a small minority (such as cosmetics, high-fidelity equipment, televisions, alcohol and prescription drugs) (ibid., p. 557).

In the absence of fair trading laws, the key question was whether the law reverted to the precedent established in *Dr. Miles*, namely that resale price maintenance was subject to Section 1 of the Sherman Act. Subsequent cases on this issue have been closely bound up with the practice of refusals to deal and it is therefore useful to consider them together. We have already mentioned that a firm may use the weapon of refusing to deal with price-cutting distributors as a means of enforcing resale price maintenance. However, if maintaining minimum prices is illegal (following the *Dr. Miles* decision), one might anticipate that the *means* of enforcing maintenance would also be illegal. In practice US law, as interpreted by the Supreme Court, is more complex, some might say mysterious. In the *Colgate* decision of 1919,[4] the manufacturer was allowed to refuse to supply a distributor who cut price below the minimum stipulated. The main reason for the decision appears to have been the lack of detailed contractual obligations on price between manufacturer and retailers who could sell at whatever price they wished as long as it was above the minimum. In thus upholding a trader's right to trade or not with whoever he wishes, the Supreme Court obscured the doctrine of *Dr. Miles*. It seemed that resale price maintenance (backed by refusal to sell) escaped prosecution under the Sherman Act if the contract of sale did not explicitly mention that prices would be maintained. The line between legality and illegality was very narrowly drawn. Subsequent cases suggested, for example, that illegality would be found where the manufacturer positively monitored retail prices, or reinstated retailers who gave an undertaking to abide by the minimum price in future, or assured retailers that those violating the price agreement would be punished.[5]

In the light of the ambiguous nature of the effects of resale price maintenance as revealed by economic analysis and following a consistent campaign by economist-lawyers of the Chicago School to have the *Dr. Miles* precedent overturned (see in particular Posner, 1981), it was increasingly felt that resale price maintenance as well as other vertical restraints should be treated under a rule of reason rather than under a per se rule. In a key case, the Justice Department made a submission to the Supreme Court effectively inviting them to give such a ruling. In the event, the Court ignored the proposal and gave a decision in line with previous precedent and the facts of the case. Thus in *Monsanto* a price-cutting distributor was refused further supplies by the manufacturer, allegedly following complaints by other distributors. The case turned on whether evidence of complaints was sufficient to prove a conspiracy between the manufacturer and distributors for price determination. Although the lower court and the Court of Appeals determined that it was, the Supreme Court disagreed and, citing the *Colgate* decision, argued that additional evidence indicating a lack of independent action on the part of supplier and distributors was required.[6] The Court was satisfied that there was additional evidence (in the form of the supplier pressuring distributors to maintain prices) and therefore found for the plaintiff. Evidently, the court is reluctant to give up the position in *Colgate*, establishing an independent trader's right to refuse to supply, and in addition has declined the opportunity to revise the per se rule against vertical price fixing.

Selective distribution systems

In addition to the question of a per se approach versus a rule of reason, the issue of intra-brand and inter-brand competition has featured prominently in discussion of the law on vertical territorial restrictions. Since some forms of territorial constraints can have benefits for the consumer while others benefit mainly the supplier, a rule of reason approach would again seem to be the most appropriate.

The issues were thrown into sharp relief in a case in 1963. In *White Motor*, the plaintiff defended its distribution system based on exclusive territories: dealers were given exclusive coverage of a particular geographic region but were allowed to sell only to customers in their region. The plaintiff argued in particular that, while intra-brand competition was constrained by the system, inter-brand competition was enhanced, to the benefit of consumers. In a surprising judgement, the Supreme Court admitted that, as this was the first case to come before them involving a territorial restriction, they were unable to reach a definite conclusion, and in particular they were not prepared to apply a per se illegality rule. Attention was drawn to the possible net benefits arising from the stimulus to inter-brand competition. The case was passed back to the lower court, but, before a decision was necessary, the company agreed to a consent decree involving the removal of the restraint.

Industry did not have long to wait, however, before a much more clear-cut decision was made by the Supreme Court. Unfortunately, in the view of many economists, it was a move in the wrong direction. In *Schwinn*, the defendant had a complex system for distributing its bicycles, including a number of vertical restraints. An important part of the system involved sales direct to franchised retailers who were only allowed to sell to final customers, not to discount stores. Retailers not keeping to the rules would have supplies cut off. The Court acknowledged that such a distribution system might sharpen inter-brand competition but emphasized that its concern had to be whether 'the effect upon competition in the market place is substantially adverse'.[7] In the event, however, the Court appears to have based its decision on other considerations. Legal title to the goods passed to the franchised retailers and the Court considered it wholly unreasonable for the manufacturer to place restrictions on the terms and conditions of trading for goods which they no longer owned. They concluded that such restrictions were a per se violation of Section 1 of the Sherman Act. Goods which the company supplied to retailers on a consignment basis (under which Schwinn retained the legal title until sale to the final customer) were not covered by the ruling. Thus, according to this decision, whether or not a non-price vertical restraint fell foul of the law depended on the form of the distribution contract (that is, consignment or sale), not on the actual competitive effects, which were likely to be identical. The decision satisfied neither those who wished to see all vertical restraints legalized nor those who wanted them to be judged on a rule of reason basis.

The latter had to wait a further decade before the Supreme Court made a substantial move towards their position. In *Sylvania*,[8] a distributor who had violated a territorial restraint imposed by the manufacturer had supplies cut off and sued, claiming a violation of the Sherman Act. On the face of it, the facts of this case are very similar to those in Schwinn: the manufacturer had sold goods to the distributor but was trying to impose a constraint on the retailer's actions. Indeed, the lower courts followed this interpretation and found against the manufacturer. The Court of Appeals attempted to distinguish the two cases and then, using a rule of reason, found for the manufacturer. The subsequent appeal to the Supreme Court provoked a landmark decision in the law on non-price vertical restraints. The Court refused to distinguish the cases but in effect reversed the decision in *Schwinn* and also applied a rule of reason in arriving at its decision. Of particular importance was its recognition of the efficiency-enhancing properties of some non-price vertical restraints. It accepted that, while territorial and similar restraints may suppress intra-brand competition, they tend also to sharpen distributors' incentives and hence inter-brand competition will probably be intensified. The effect should not therefore be viewed in the same way as those (essentially price) restraints whose impact on competition was irredeemably negative.

Following the *Sylvania* decision, therefore, territorial restrictions are judged according to a rule of reason with a particular focus on intra-brand and inter-brand competitive effects. However, the added attempt in the course of the court's judgement to sharpen the distinction between price and non-price restraints has led to continued controversy. The distinction is seen by some as without substance and if this is the case then, they argue, *all* vertical restraints (including resale price maintenance) should be judged according to a rule of reason.

Exclusive dealing Exclusive dealing as well as tying arrangements are proscribed under Section 3 of the Clayton Act, which deals with exclusionary practices, as long as there is a substantial adverse effect on competition. Although the courts have not systematically used either a per se or a rule of reason approach, they have been generally hostile to exclusive dealing. Much appears to turn on how the notion of a 'substantial effect' should be interpreted. Thus in an early case involving an exclusive arrangement for distributing patterns for women's and children's clothes, because the company controlled about 40 per cent of the pattern agencies in the country this was considered more than enough to have a significant effect on competition, and the agreement was struck down.[9]

The facts of any case are usually sufficient to establish the presence of an exclusive arrangement and the court may acknowledge the benefits derived by both the buyer and the seller. Yet, if the effect on competition is substantial, a Section 3 violation will be found. The question of how 'substantial' should be interpreted was central to a key decision in 1949. In the case usually known as *Standard Stations*,[10] Standard Oil had an exclusive dealing arrangement similar to that of its leading competitors with independent distributors of its petrol in the western states. The petrol stations involved accounted for about 16 per cent of the total in the area, although Standard's share of petrol sales was 13.5 per cent. The lower court interpreted 'substantial' in absolute rather than comparative terms: the company supplied a large number of outlets which were prevented from distributing the products of any other firm and this was sufficient to violate the Clayton Act. When the case reached the Supreme Court it had therefore to decide whether the presence of the restriction affecting a substantial amount of business amounted to an infringement. Deciding against the agreement, the Court argued that, given the restriction, it was not necessary to have proof that competition had *actually* diminished but merely that it might 'tend to' diminish. A majority of the Court determined that this condition was met and found against Standard Oil.

The implications that an exclusive dealing agreement covering a substantial volume of business but without close examination of the competitive effects was sufficient to establish an infringement of Section 3 was modified for a while by the *Tampa Electric* case. Nashville Coal agreed to supply the Tampa Electric Co. with its entire coal requirement. When the market price of coal subsequently increased, Nashville attempted to avoid the contract by claiming that it infringed the antitrust laws. Contrary to its previous practice in such cases, the Supreme Court examined the likely competitive effects on the basis of market share or relative rather than absolute importance of the volume of business affected. Since the estimated share involved was less than 1 per cent, the court found in favour of Tampa Electric.

This move towards a rule of reason approach in exclusive dealing contracts with an emphasis on the economic analysis of market structure was, however, short-lived. Five years later, in 1966, in the second *Brown Shoe* case, the Court reverted to its previous position. In striking down an agreement Brown had concluded with retailers representing about 1 per cent of shoe stores in the USA, the Court relied almost entirely on the notion that any exclusive deal foreclosed part of the market to other traders. As long as the amount of business was 'substantial', this was sufficient to establish the antitrust violation.

In retrospect, therefore, the more moderate and, to many economists, more tenable reasoning towards exclusive dealing in *Tampa Electric* was the exception rather than the rule. To a degree the Court in that case may have been responding to the unacceptable move by a company seeking to avoid a freely negotiated contract by claiming an antitrust violation. The traditional hostility of US law to exclusive dealing thus remains intact.

Tying arrangements   The law on tying arrangements for goods, which are also covered by Section 3 of the Clayton Act, has raised many issues similar to those of exclusive dealing. For tying restrictions, however, the original rulings which came very close to a per se interpretation have been softened in the last decade by a judgement which has applied a modified rule of reason. A key case early on was *International Salt*,[11] where the Supreme Court held that it was illegal per se to foreclose any substantial market from competitors in a tying arrangement. The decision did not depend on the degree of market power exercised by the tying firm. This view was reiterated just over a decade later in *Northern Pacific*. The Court was again unwilling to consider clearly the issue of market power, going so far as to say that 'tying agreements serve hardly any purpose beyond the suppression of competition'.[12] As long as the tying firm had the power to impose an appreciable restraint on free competition in the tied product, this was sufficient for an infringement to occur. By this stage the law had probably come closest to a per se illegality ruling for tying agreements.

Subsequently it has drawn back substantially from this position. In particular, in *Jefferson Parish*,[13] the Court laid down three criteria for establishing per se illegality. First, the products had to be genuinely distinct products in the sense that an independent market for the tied product must exist. Secondly, the seller had to have sufficient power to force a tie in the tied product market: a recognition that relative market position is central. Thirdly, the tying agreement must foreclose a substantial amount of trade. If the position of the plaintiff in the relevant market is insufficient for it to impose a tie on its customers, then the restriction is to be judged according to a rule of reason. Where the seller has a relatively small market share, there is unlikely to be an adverse judgement. The contrast with *International Salt* is substantial. The firm's ability to control the market is now recognized under the second criterion.

United Kingdom

With the exception of resale price maintenance, to which we refer below, there were no specific legal provisions dealing with vertical restraints under UK law prior to the 1998 Competition Act. The earlier law was specifically concerned with *horizontal* agreements and both implicitly and explicitly excluded vertical restraints. Thus it applied only where two or more parties accepted restrictions so that requirements contracts or tie-in sales could easily avoid the provisions of the law by careful drafting. Bilateral exclusive dealing agreements were explicitly exempted. Hence vertical agreements which may have restricted competition were not covered. They could, however, be examined as part of a dominant firm enquiry, or as a potential anticompetitive practice (Whish, 1989, p. 135).

This position has been largely retained under the 1998 Act. Vertical agreements are specifically exempted from *Chapter 1 Prohibition* (which we discussed in Chapter 7 above) with the exception of resale price maintenance. In his *Guidelines* for the application of the Act, the DGFT explains the rationale for the exemption: 'Vertical agreements do not generally give rise to competition concerns unless one or more of the undertakings [i.e. firms] involved possesses market power on the relevant market or the agreement forms part of a network of similar agreements' (Office of Fair Trading, 2000, p. 2).

He envisaged that exclusive distribution agreements, exclusive purchasing agreements, selective distribution agreements and franchise agreements would all benefit from the exclusion (ibid. p. 3).

Resale price maintenance

Before 1948, resale price maintenance was widespread in Britain. Indeed, until the passage of the Restrictive Trade Practices Act in 1956, it was underpinned by a system of collective enforcement. At its height in the mid-1950s it was estimated to apply to 44 per cent of consumers' expenditure on goods (Pickering, 1974). The position in many trades was for the manufacturer to sell to a wholesaler who sold on to a retailer. The manufacturer had no direct contract with the retailer and on an individual basis found enforcement of resale price maintenance difficult. However, the need for individual enforcement was avoided by means of collective action through a trade association. Any retailer attempting to cut prices below the maintained level of a single manufacturer's products faced the prospect of a collective boycott by all members of the manufacturers' association. Of course under US law such collective action would have been illegal under Section 1 of the Sherman Act and in the UK it was subsequently covered by the provisions of the 1956 Act. In the inter-war period, however, attempts to contest such collective action in the courts failed because they were regarded as legitimate business practices (Allen, 1968, ch. 8).

The legal position was changed in 1956. Section II of the Restrictive Trade Practices Act made *collective* enforcement of resale prices illegal but at the same time actually strengthened the hand of the individual manufacturer. Under the Act a manufacturer was given the right to take action against retailers who refused to maintain prices, even where no contract existed between them. According to one expert observer, there was no inconsistency between the treatment of collective and individual resale price maintenance. The provision strengthening the hand of the individual manufacturer was designed largely to help smaller firms. Larger firms operating in concentrated markets were powerful enough to protect their own interests once collective enforcement was abolished: 'But small firms were heavily dependent upon the collective enforcement machinery and could scarcely hope to preserve RPM without it. To increase the powers of legal enforcement was a means of redressing the balance between giant firms and others' (Allen, 1968, p. 110).

Significant developments in distribution, such as the growth of discount stores and supermarkets in the latter part of the 1950s, contributed to the breakdown of resale price maintenance in the grocery trade, but successful actions brought against price cutters in chemists and electrical goods suggested that the natural erosion of resale price maintenance was unlikely to occur at any speed in the absence of further revisions to the law. Eight years after the 1956 Act strengthened individual price maintenance, therefore, the Resale Prices

Act ensured that it would be subject to a procedure similar to that of horizontal restrictions. Individual resale price maintenance was presumed to be against the public interest, but that presumption could be rebutted on a number of grounds set out in the Act.[14] Thus a manufacturer could argue that the abolition of resale price maintenance was detrimental to consumers because (i) the quality or variety of goods would be substantially reduced, (ii) the number of shops would be substantially reduced, (iii) the long-run level of prices would increase, (iv) health would be endangered, and (v) the necessary pre- or post-sales services would be substantially reduced. In addition to being convinced on one or more of the above grounds, the Restrictive Practices Court also had to be satisfied that the detriment suffered by consumers would be greater than that resulting from the continuation of the resale price maintenance.

The Act also made it illegal for a manufacturer to withhold supplies from retailers who had sold below the recommended price or who were expected to do so. An exception was made in the case of 'loss leading'. A firm was allowed legitimately to withhold supplies where it had reasonable grounds for believing that its products would be used as 'loss leaders': that is, they would be sold at a very low price by a distributor as a promotional aid rather than as a means of making a profit. For reasons similar to those already discussed in connection with predatory prices (Chapter 5) it is particularly difficult to distinguish a 'competitive price' from a 'loss leading' price charged by an efficient distributor. Where price competition prevails, different distributors may be expected to charge different prices. It may be practically impossible to distinguish goods sold 'not for the purpose of making a profit ... but for the purpose of attracting to the establishment at which the goods are sold customers likely to purchase other goods or otherwise for the purpose of advertising the business of the dealer' (Resale Prices Act 1964, Section 3).

The failure of the confectioners in 1967 and the footwear manufacturers in 1968 to convince the Court of the net benefits of maintaining the prices of their products led to its widespread abandonment. According to Pickering (1974), by the time of the passage of the Resale Prices Act in 1964, resale price maintenance applied to about one-third of consumers' expenditure on goods. By 1974, the practice was confined to just two products, books and non-prescription medicines, accounting for 2 per cent of consumers' expenditure. The Net Book Agreement had been successfully defended as a horizontal restraint under the 1956 Act and was therefore not challenged again at this stage.[15] The only group of products successfully to pass through the procedure laid down in the 1964 Act was thus non-prescription medicines in 1970.[16]

We noted in Section II that much of the recent theoretical discussion of resale price maintenance has been concerned with the elimination of the 'free-rider' problem and net welfare effects. Neither of these points played very much part in the cases heard before the Restrictive Practices Court. With slight variations, the defence in all cases (including books) proceeded along similar lines. It was argued that abolition would allow supermarkets and multiple stores to reduce prices on a few popular lines. More specialized (smaller) stores would be unable to match these price cuts because of the extra service they offered, and their profits would suffer. As a result a number of changes would occur. Some specialists would go out of business. Those remaining would stock a narrower range of products and demand a higher margin from manufacturers. Prices would therefore rise.

In neither *Confectionery* nor *Footwear* was the Court convinced that prices would rise in the long run if resale price maintenance was abolished. It inclined to the view that increased competition would tend to reduce prices, although it did accept in *Confectionery* that the number of outlets might well be reduced. In contrast, the nature of the products concerned played a large part in persuading the court that the prices for medicaments should be maintained. The restriction in this case applied to wholesalers and ensured that they continued to stock a full range of prescription and proprietary drugs which could be made available at short notice to meet the needs of consumers. The role of the restriction in helping to preserve the number of retail outlets with their dispensary services was also recognized by the Court. To a degree, therefore, the Court's decision rested on the value judgement that the number of retail outlets sustained by the system of price maintenance was in itself desirable.

This line of reasoning was more comprehensible in the case of non pre-scription medicines than in the case of books. All of the arguments put in *Confectionery* and *Footwear* were given in *Books*, and the same outcome might have been expected. In the event, it was decided, in the words of the title of the volume published to celebrate the victory in the Court, 'books are different' (Barker and Davies, 1966). In this case, the Court thought it likely that the number of specialist stockholding booksellers, along with the range of titles carried, would be reduced if resale price maintenance were abolished, but also that as a consequence the price of books would rise in the long term, to the detriment of the public. As Pickering (1969) has argued, this conclusion appears to have been based on a faulty interpretation of the data on economies of scale in book production presented to the Court. The judgement was severely criticized at the time for its misapplication of economic analysis (see, for example, Stevens and Yamey, 1965; Sutherland, 1965). Ultimately, as Allen admits, the agreement was only defensible 'by reference to the (undemocratic) proposition that it is fitting that the reader of popular books should subsidize the student and the scholar' (Allen, 1968, p. 96).

By the late 1980s and early 1990s the agreement was coming under increasing pressure from newly established booksellers (in particular Pentos) and large retailers who regarded the relationship between publisher and bookseller as outmoded. Following the decision of the DGFT to seek to reopen the case several influential publishers withdrew from the agreement in 1995 and the Publishers' Association said it was no longer willing to defend it. As a result, resale price maintenance in books collapsed, and retailers were free to offer books at prices of their own choosing. However, in principle, the agreement could have been revived at any time and the DGFT, therefore, sought a ruling from the Court that the agreement was now against the public interest. The judge in the Restrictive Practices Court was persuaded that circumstances in the trade had substantially changed since 1962, not least because of the withdrawal of the support of the Publishers' Association. He concluded that the agreement which had lasted in one form or another for nearly 100 years was against the public interest and should be struck down (Utton, 2000b). A similar decision early in 2001 concerning non-prescription medicines meant that no products in the UK were any longer subject to resale price maintenance.

Selective distribution systems
We mentioned in the previous chapter a prominent industry (beer) which was the subject of lengthy investigation by the MMC, largely on account of its vertical integration. In petrol distribution as well, substantial vertical integration is coupled with vertical restraints on the market conduct of distributors. We refer to these restrictions below. but two other recent reports by the MMC deal specifically with the issue of territorial restriction. Thus, in *New Motor Cars* (MMC, 1992) and *New Cars* (Competition Commission, 2000) the central issue was whether the territorial restraints imposed by suppliers on their dealers through the selective and exclusive dealership system were against the public interest.

Under UK law, there were, as we have noted, no separate provisions dealing with territorial restraints of this kind, but they could be investigated as part of a monopoly enquiry. In the *New Motor Cars* case (as in beer), because no one supplier had 25 per cent or more of the market, the MMC had to be satisfied that a complex monopoly existed, that is, that two or more independent firms jointly holding more than one-quarter of the market so conducted their affairs as to prevent, restrict or distort competition. The MMC was satisfied that the form of the selective distribution system used by all major suppliers was sufficient to establish a complex monopoly.[17] Although the distribution agreements varied in detail, they frequently contained the following kinds of restrictions: (i) exclusive territories are allocated to dealers within which no other dealer will be supplied; (ii) dealers are not generally allowed to promote the sale of cars outside their territory; (iii) limits are placed on the number and location of dealerships and on the total number of new cars sold through them; (iv) limits are placed on the number and location of other suppliers' dealerships held by dealers; (v) restrictions are placed on the type of other car-related business dealers may undertake; (vi) dealers are prohibited from selling competing new cars from the same site; (vii) dealers may only sell new cars to final customers or to other franchised dealers. Finally, manufacturers refused to supply new cars for resale except through the franchised dealers (MMC, 1992, para. 13.31).

The common agreement between a supplier and his distributors is covered by an EU special block exemption (see below). The selective distribution system for cars is common throughout most of the world although not in the USA, and the exemption was granted on the grounds that consumers derived benefits in the form of a reliable servicing network for highly complex and potentially dangerous products which outweighed the resulting restriction on intra-brand competition. Under the exemption, there is provision for its withdrawal if price differences between national markets exceed certain limits (ibid., para. 13.10). However, the MMC in this case (as in beer) was quite clear that the block exemption from Article 81(i) in no way inhibited it in carrying out its own assessment of the effects of the distribution system: 'It is open to us, as a national competition authority, to examine the effects of the distribution system on the United Kingdom public interest, to make findings and, if we think fit, to make recommendations' (ibid., para. 13.37).

In common with the European Commission, the MMC in its first report concluded that in general the selective distribution system for new cars did not operate against the public interest. However, it did find certain features of the system objectionable and made recommendations for their correction. A central focus of the enquiry was on the level of prices of new cars in the UK compared with other members, following widespread claims that prices were substantially and persistently higher, despite moves towards the completion of the internal market. Although the MMC concluded that price differences were largely due to factors outside the distribution system, it also found that certain elements of the system contributed to higher prices, specifically 'restrictions by suppliers which limit advertising by a dealer outside his territory, limit the volume of cars he can sell, the extent to which he can hold competing franchises, or prevent him engaging in other car-related businesses' (ibid., para. 13.158). Essentially, the MMC saw these restraints as inhibiting the growth of the more efficient distributors. If they were removed, efficient distributors would be able to grow and achieve higher sales volumes, which should lead to lower prices, particularly if they were also able to widen their market by advertising. In turn, this could lead to an increase in their bargaining strength vis-à-vis suppliers, with further downward pressure on prices. The MMC also envisaged distributors being able to exploit inter-country price differences by offering to act as an intermediary for parallel imports according to individual customer requirements.

In its recommendations, the MMC therefore stopped short of any fundamental change in the selective distribution system, but proposed the removal in future of those restrictions on franchised dealers mentioned above. The report has been criticized for not examining in much more detail the central benefit claimed for the selective distribution system, namely that it is necessary to ensure proper servicing of a highly complex product. There was, for example, no attempt to compare servicing standards between franchised dealers and independent garages. Judging by its analysis of the inhibiting effects of the existing distribution system, the MMC clearly felt that there were disadvantages for consumers. For these to be outweighed by the superior servicing standards provided by franchised distributors, clear evidence should have been provided. No such evidence appears in a report which runs to more than 1000 pages.

Judging by the press comments when the MMC report was published, the motor industry was relieved that it had got off so lightly and there was criticism that an exercise which had apparently cost £15 million had so little impact on the industry (Groves, 1992; *Financial Times*, 6 February 1992).

Discontent amongst consumer groups and distributors intensified throughout the 1990s amid widespread reports that the restrictive distribution system was largely to blame for the continued high prices of new cars in the UK compared with other countries in the EU. In March 1999, therefore, the DGFT referred the industry again to the Commission, now renamed the Competition Commission, and a year later it produced another voluminous report. This time, however, the whole tone was different. The report amounts to a comprehensive condemnation of the selective distribution system for new cars. The requirement on dealers to supply all of a specified range of new cars, and deterring dealers from obtaining new cars from dealers in other EU member states, were both carried out 'for the purpose of exploiting or maintaining the monopoly situation' (Competition Commission, 2000, para 2.388). The Commission went on to list no fewer than 13 separate practices under the selective distribution system which operated against the public interest. Foremost amongst these were the allocation of exclusive territories to dealers; requiring dealers to offer servicing and repair services for the supplier's brand of cars; preventing dealers from selling other suppliers' new cars from the same premises as they sell the suppliers' cars; and refusing to supply new cars to resellers which are not dealers in the supplier's franchised network (para. 2.390). Taken together the Commission estimated that the operation of all of the restrictions in the selective distribution system caused the prices paid by UK private customers to be, on average, 10 per cent too high (para. 1.17).

Compared with the earlier report which concluded that substantial changes were unnecessary to produce improvements, the more recent report could see very little merit in the whole system as far as consumers were concerned, and the sooner it was swept away the better. Unfortunately, 'about half of the practices which we find to be against the public interest are explicitly allowed by the Block Exemption' (ibid, para 1.20). If these practices were to be prohibited or constrained the Commission concluded that one of three routes would have to be taken: (a) a unilateral withdrawal by the UK of the benefits offered by the block exemption; (b) a decision by the UK to prohibit specific provisions permitted by the block exemption; or (c) the block exemption itself would have to be changed or allowed to expire (para 1.20). Options (a) and (b) would have placed the UK authorities in direct conflict with their counterparts in Brussels and would probably have caused lengthy and expensive legal proceedings. In the event, as we discuss below, the EU is highly unlikely to extend the block exemption in anything like its current form beyond 2002.

Exclusive dealing Two years earlier in another weighty report, this time looking into exclusive distribution in petrol (the third for this industry in 25 years), the MMC was even more united in its recommendations. About two-thirds of all petrol stations in the UK are independent, but since, on average, they are smaller than those owned by the oil companies, they account for about one-half of total petrol sales. Most of the independent stations have an exclusive contract with one company to supply their petrol, the so-called 'solus tie' system. Previous reports by the MMC had found that such vertical arrangements did not generally operate against the public interest, and the Commission's views in the most recent report were similar. The MMC felt, however, that long-term agreements would tend to rigidify market structure, make entry more difficult and increase the influence of suppliers over retailers. Consequently, it recommended that exclusive agreements should continue to be restricted to five years, although it had no objection to associated loan agreements being spread over ten years as long as the retailer had the option of repaying in a shorter time (MMC, 1990b, paras 8.94–8.95). Under the block exemption granted by the European Commission in this industry, solus tie agreements can last up to ten years, but the MMC was not persuaded that such an extension should be permitted in the UK market. In general, it concluded that nothing in the current structure of the market, the behaviour of the wholesalers (the oil companies) or the resulting performance was against the public interest. However, it did consider that any further vertical integration by the oil companies thereby reducing the number of independent retailers could have adverse effects. It therefore recommended that the OFT should continue to monitor prices, profitability and the structure of the industry.

On a number of occasions, the MMC has been highly critical of attempts by dominant firms to impose exclusive terms on their customers. Thus, in the report on asbestos (MMC, 1972–3), the attempt by Turner and Newall, which at the time had approximately 43 per cent of the market, to restrict customers from buying asbestos textiles from its competitors was found to be against the public interest and was subsequently dropped by the company. Similarly, the Metal Box Company, which was even more dominant in the market for open-top cans, with a share of more than 75 per cent, was forced to modify a number of practices which, according to the MMC, seemed mainly designed to consolidate the position of the company and inhibit the growth of competitors (MMC, 1970a). The MMC took particular exception to discount arrangements based on total purchases from the company and unrelated to cost savings which gave a very strong incentive to customers to buy exclusively from Metal Box. It also objected to the contract terms which the company had used in the recent past whereby customers leasing their can-closing machines from Metal Box were prevented from closing the cans of any other company. Together with the very favourable rental and servicing terms, the contracts which in effect *tied* the use of Metal Box machines to the purchase of their cans made it very difficult for entrants or smaller competitors to make headway in the market.

Three examples can be cited where the DGFT has had to consider whether the exclusive provision of services rather than goods amounts to an anticompetitive practice. Two have involved British Rail and the exclusive use of their stations. Thus, in *British Railways Board and Brighton Taxis*, the DGFT concluded that the exclusive franchise allowed to one group of taxi firms whose members alone could ply for hire on the forecourt of Brighton station was anticompetitive. An undertaking which removed the restriction was given and the case was not therefore referred to the MMC. Similarly, in *British Railways Board and Godfrey Davis*, the DGFT took exception to the grant by British Rail of exclusive rights to the Godfrey Davis car hire firm on certain of its stations. Although considered anticompetitive, the effects of the restriction were thought to be too slight to merit a reference to the MMC for a public interest ruling. The British Airports Authority grant of an exclusive contract to one company for the supply of chauffeur-driven cars at Gatwick Airport was found to be anticompetitive. The DGFT's report made clear that exclusive contracts were not necessarily anticompetitive, but in this case the lack of competition in the market was crucial. Undertakings by the Authority were accepted and therefore a reference to the MMC was avoided.

Tying arrangements   Tying arrangements (and full-line forcing) have not attracted the same degree of hostility on the part of the antitrust authorities in the UK as in the USA. They have formed part of several single-firm investigations by the MMC. An early report by the MMC into a market dominated by a near monopolist was, however, highly critical of tying. Thus, in *Medical and Industrial Gases* (1956–7) contract terms which in effect forced gas users also to buy storage equipment (and vice versa) were condemned by the MMC. Two later cases subsequently had important ramifications. We have noted above that the Metal Box Company's policy of ensuring that customers took both open-top cans and closing machines from them was criticized by the MMC. Six years later, it opposed Rank Xerox's policy of insisting that lessees of their photocopying machines also use their toner (MMC, 1976–7). In all three cases, the firm concerned had a very large market share and the MMC saw the tying arrangement as a means of hindering competition. This conclusion appears to have impressed unduly the authors of the government's *Review of Restrictive Trade Practices Policy* (1979) who singled out tying and full-line forcing as deserving special treatment. In their judgement, the practices 'are likely almost invariably to operate against the public interest and to be capable of sufficiently precise definition' to merit a per se prohibition (para. 6.11). Fortunately, they recommended that, before such a drastic step were taken, a general reference should be made to the MMC. Its report was duly published in 1981 (MMC, 1981a) and, after a detailed analysis of a number of different forms of tying in a diverse range of industries, including cosmetics, shoe retailing, house insurance and farming supplies, it concluded that there was *no* general presumption that tying and full-line forcing was against the public interest. It therefore did not recommend the introduction of special provisions against the practice which it felt in a majority of instances was economically justifiable. In particular it concluded that ties that were simply the exercise of monopoly power were relatively rare.

Early on in the report the MMC made the important point that, apart from an expressly stated tying condition (the customer must purchase not only product A but product B from the supplier), a tie may be introduced implicitly as part of an exclusive dealing arrangement. Thus a supplier in such an agreement may make it clear that the purchaser's rights under the contract will be affected adversely if components or complementary products from another firm are used. In these circumstances, the purchaser may have little choice but to use components or complements provided by the supplier, even though it is not an explicit provision of the contract. Hence, as the MMC concluded, where there is already market power 'the anticompetitive effects of tie-in sales and line-forcing are likely to be much more significant if the practices are associated with an insistence on exclusive dealing' (ibid. para., 13.33). Some circumstances may arise where the intricacy of the product may require the use of components or complements controlled by the supplier in order to maintain the performance of the product and the reputation of the manufacturer. However, such cases are likely to be relatively infrequent and require detailed examination.

European Union

In contrast with the UK, where provisions dealing with horizontal restrictions explicitly excluded vertical restraints, the wording of Article 81 allows for the inclusion of both types of agreement. If the effect is to restrict, impair or distort competition, then Article 81(i) applies even though, as we shall see, exemptions may be granted. Indeed the Commission has taken a very positive view towards the efficiencies that certain vertical restrictions provide. For example, inter-country trade within the Community may be assisted if suppliers in one country can arrange for their products to be distributed in other member states by local companies with detailed knowledge of the language, regulations and customs. In addition, vertical agreements may help to keep entry barriers to a minimum by allowing firms to enter at one stage of the production and distribution process, rather than as vertically integrated concerns. Where, therefore, an exclusive distribution agreement stimulates inter-brand competition within the Community, without having any countervailing disadvantages, the Commission has generally taken a benign view.

On the other hand, it is well aware that vertical agreements may be used in a way to stifle or inhibit inter-country trade. Companies might, for example, attempt to maintain discriminatory pricing between countries by prohibiting parallel imports. Insulation of individual countries is wholly contrary to the basic objectives of the Community and has been fiercely opposed by the Commission.

Resale price maintenance
Given the basic objectives of the EU, it is not surprising that the Commission has been particularly anxious to eradicate collectively enforced resale price maintenance. An early case involved an association of Belgian perfume and toiletry manufacturers and distributors[18] whose original rules had contained detailed and rigid provisions for the collective enforcement of resale prices for both domestically produced and imported goods, backed, as necessary, by collective boycotts of any dealer who tried to cut prices. The association's application for negative clearance (under Article 81(iii)) was only granted once all traces of such collective enforcement had been removed from the agreement. Similarly, the detailed arrangements amongst Belgian wallpaper manufacturers and wholesalers for collectively maintaining prices and many other aspects of trading were condemned by the Commission (Goyder, 1998, p. 249).[19] Both of these cases had horizontal and vertical features. From the discussion in Chapter 7, it is clear that horizontal agreements covering collective resale price maintenance are illegal under Article 81(i).

In several key cases in the 1970s the Commission, backed up by the court, established that individual resale price maintenance infringed Article 81(i). Thus, in *Deutsche Grammophon* v. *Metro* (1971), the plaintiff sought an injunction to prevent Metro from reimporting its records into Germany and selling them below the maintained price. The Court ruled that a company could not prohibit imports in an attempt to enforce a restriction (resale price maintenance) which infringed Article 81. This effectively meant that Deutsche Grammophon had to abandon maintained prices in Germany because under the prevailing law it had to be applied universally. Two years later the Commission had little difficulty in finding that the Deutsche Philips policy of maintaining the prices of its electric razors throughout the Community also infringed Article

81. Taken together, the two cases are thought to have hastened the abolition of resale price maintenance in Germany (Goyder, 1998, p. 249). In fact, by the early 1980s, individual resale price maintenance had been prohibited (in Germany, France and Luxembourg) or very heavily circumscribed (UK, Ireland and Denmark) in a large part of the EU. Only in Belgium, the Netherlands and Italy was it still treated as lawful.

One exception, which we also noted when discussing the British position, concerned the treatment of books. Two cases involved agreements to maintain the price of books, and have also touched on the complex question of the relationship between national laws and Community law. The first case involved an agreement between two book-publishing trade associations in Holland and Belgium. They had an agreement covering the publication of Dutch books in Holland and Belgium which provided for each to enforce collective resale price maintenance directly on its own members and indirectly on members of the other association.[20] The agreement also laid down that members should deal exclusively with each other. In both countries the national law allowed collective resale price maintenance, but the European Court held that at issue was the effect of the agreement on inter-member trade. The national law on resale price maintenance was not at stake but, when an attempt was made to extend these national provisions into the realm of inter-country transactions, they came into direct conflict with Community competition law and no exemption under Article 81(iii) could be granted.

The second, more complex, case occurred not long afterwards. Under the French Book Prices Act of 1981, every publisher or importer of books is required to set a public selling price, and all retailers then have to charge a price between 95 and 100 per cent of this set price. Any book originally published in France sold abroad but then reimported has to be sold at the price set by the original publisher. When a bookseller well known for cutting prices was prevented by legal action by other booksellers from selling below the set prices, the question of whether the French law was enforceable, given the provisions of Article 81, was referred to the European Court. The special characteristics of the book trade were recognized. The Court accepted that individual member states retained the right to enact rules under which publishers or importers could fix prices binding on all retailers, as long as no other restrictions were imposed which were incompatible with the EU. National governments may thus continue to allow individual or even collective resale price maintenance. The Court even went so far as to allow national courts to enforce resale price maintenance on imported books where it was judged that they had first been exported and then reimported merely to circumvent the law. Where books had initially been exported in the normal course of trade but then reimported, price maintenance could not be enforced. Although this last point is clearly intended to maintain the basic principle of parallel importing even for the special case of books, it is not clear how the distinction can in practice be upheld. It appears to place particular importance on the identity of the importer (ibid., p. 254). The recent decision by the Court in the case of the British Net Book Agreement suggests that it will not be long before the distinction is tested.

Selective distribution systems

To encourage the use of efficiency-enhancing distribution agreements which may stimulate inter-country trade but which may formally infringe Article 81, the Commission has used the block exemption procedure, allowing a multitude of agreements which would otherwise require individual scrutiny to be dealt with en masse.

Prior to 2000 two important block exemptions covered distribution agreements (number 1983) and purchasing agreements (number 1984). Distribution agreements involve a *territorial* restriction whereby a supplier or manufacturer grants exclusive rights in a specified territory to a distributor. Purchasing agreements usually involve an undertaking by a distributor to purchase *exclusively* from a supplier. The territorial restriction is thus usually absent. However, the distinction is not always clear-cut, because some distribution agreements may also contain restrictive supply conditions, so that the distributor may agree to buy exclusively from one manufacturer.

The exemption for distribution agreements was broadly drawn and could apply to restrictions covering the whole of the EU. However, there were a number of circumstances where it could be withdrawn. For example, where competition for the affected goods was ineffective in the territory specified or where access by other suppliers to different stages in the distribution system was made particularly difficult, the block exemption would not apply. Similarly where it was not possible for users to obtain supplies from dealers outside the territory on normal terms or where exclusive distributors charged excessive prices or refused to sell to purchasers who could not obtain the goods elsewhere on customary terms, exemption would not be allowed.

The intention was to ensure, as far as possible, that the gains from allowing the development of an efficient distribution system for a particular supplier's goods were not outweighed by undue restrictions on competition. Intra-brand competition was reduced in the expectation that more effective inter-brand competition would be stimulated.

Similar reasoning lay behind the block exemption dealing with purchasing agreements. According to Goyder (1998, p. 201), Regulation 1984 applied to agreements which had the following five elements. First, the purchaser agreed to buy solely from the supplier for a period not exceeding five years. Secondly, the supplier agreed not to compete in the purchaser's principal sales area. Although the territory was not normally specified in a purchasing agreement, the purchaser's usual trading area would be obvious from the location. Thirdly, the purchaser agreed not to manufacture or distribute competing goods during the period of the agreement. Fourthly, the seller imposed on the purchaser only those restrictions necessary for efficient distribution. This could involve the purchaser taking a minimum quantity or a complete product range as well as selling under the trademark and packaging required by the supplier. Finally, reciprocal or non-reciprocal arrangements between *manufacturers* were not exempt (unless one of the parties in a non-reciprocal deal had an annual turnover of less than EURO 100 million). Exemption could be withdrawn, however, if the Commission concluded that one or other of the conditions mentioned above prevail.

The standard form of purchasing agreement involving exclusive dealing has long characterized the distribution arrangements for two sets of products, beer and petrol. Both require special storage and point of sale dispensing equipment, frequent deliveries in specialized vehicles to a large number of retail outlets, and both sets of products are heavily promoted through advertising. According to Goyder, there were upwards of 250 000 such agreements covering beer and 150 000 covering petrol in the EU at the time when Regulation 1984 was being considered. In addition to the main products, the exclusive dealing agreements often covered other products (such as soft drinks and spirits in the case of beer, and lubricants and tyres in the case of petrol) and complex tenancy arrangements where retail outlets were on lease from the supplier. Despite the difficulties thus raised for potential new entrants to these markets, arrangements covering both products were included under the Regulation as long as they complied with certain specified terms. In general these concerned the duration of the agreement: for exclusive purchase of beer only, the agreement could be for ten years, but for beer and other drinks the maximum period was five years; for exclusive purchase of petrol the maximum length was ten years.[21]

At the end of 1999 the Commission adopted Regulation 2790 on the application of Article 81(3) to categories of vertical agreements as well as conerted practices (Rivas and Stroud, 2000). The Regulation came into affect in June 2000. The new block exemption replaces the previous ones covering distribution and purchasing agreements, but also applies to *all* forms of vertical restrictions, as long as certain conditions are met. Agreements containing vertical restraints are covered by the block exemption as long as the market share of the supplier does not exceed 30 per cent of the relevant market and provided that the agreement does not contain so called 'hard core' restrictions. Probably the most prominent of these are resale price maintenance and territorial or customer resale restrictions. (A complete list is given in Rivas and Stroud, 2000, p. 238fn.) Where the market share threshold is exceeded an agreement may still benefit from *individual* exemption, assuming that it contains no 'hard core' restriction. However, it does mean that many firms which previously benefited from a block exemption, and whose share of a particular market exceeds 30 per cent, will not be eligible for block exemption under the new regulation (Whish, 2000, p. 909).

Apart from the market share threshold, an important characteristic of the block exemption is that it is much wider in scope than previous cases. It covers services as well as goods and extends to goods for incorporation or use compared with previous exemptions which applied only to goods for resale. The economic rationale underlying the new block exemption remains unchanged: many vertical restraints improve economic efficiency and, even though intra-brand competition is reduced, inter-brand competition is, if anything, increased. Only where a supplier has a substantial market share is the overall effect of a restraint likely to be negative.

Although the distribution arrangements, almost universal in the motor vehicle industry, have many similarities with those covered by Regulation 1983, they were thought both important and distinctive enough to merit separate exemption. When it came into force in July 1985, Regulation 123 was thus the first block exemption to deal specifically with one industry. Agreements covered by the Regulation allowed the supplier to insist that designated distributors do not sell the products or components of other manufacturers; do not actively seek customers outside the territory specified; do not subcontract distribution, servicing or repairs without the supplier's permission; and do not sell products or parts to dealers outside the authorized network. In return, the supplier agreed to appoint no other dealers within the specified territory.

Consumers were expected to benefit from the more reliable pre- and after-sales service for complex and potentially dangerous products which the exclusive dealership system was supposed to provide. These benefits were reckoned to outweigh the restrictions on intra-brand competition that the system involved. A unique feature of Regulation 123 was that it allowed the Commission to withdraw exemption if the distribution system was judged to have allowed wide differences in vehicle prices between member states. As we saw when discussing the reports of the MMC, the issue has remained highly complex and sensitive.

The original ten-year exemption granted to the car industry's distribution system expired in 1995 and after intense lobbying from the industry a seven-year extension was granted (Regulation 1475/95). Although the new regulation increased, to some extent, the independence of dealers (by allowing them, for example, to repair vehicles of different makes in the same workshop, and to sell cars outside their allotted territory) it was recognized that it did not include any effective mechanism to ensure reasonable uniformity of prices across the EU. As we have seen, the second report into the car industry concluded that car prices in the UK remained unacceptably high compared with those in other member states and as a result a government order enforced a widespread reduction in prices. The widely held view that car manufacturers continued to put pressure on their distributors to maintain price differentials was illustrated in spectacular fashion by the fine of EURO 102 million imposed by the Commission on Volkswagen early in 1998. The company was accused of preventing German and Austrian customers from buying cars from Volkswagen distributors in Italy over a ten-year period, and threatening to cut off supplies unless the distributors complied. In October 2001, Daimler/Chrysler, was fined EURO 72 million for similar retail practices.

As the expiry date for the block exemption (September 2002) drew closer it became clear that the European Commission was going to insist on a major overhaul, if not the outright withdrawal, of the exclusive distribution in cars which was increasingly seen as hampering cross-border sales, inflating prices and inhibiting inter-brand competition. The new system, after a suitable transition period, was likely to be much more tilted towards consumers with the abolition of exclusive trading areas and a severing of the link between sales and servicing. These changes would allow for the entry both of new car retailers (including supermarkets) and of specialist service firms.

Those block exemptions mentioned so far apply to systems of exclusive dealing: distributors have exclusive rights in a particular territory or agree to purchase solely from one supplier. Other restrictive distribution arrangements do not have this exclusive characteristic and therefore do not fall within the block exemptions. Suppliers of complex and expensive equipment, for example, may select distributors who meet certain technical and qualitative criteria to handle their products. There may be no territorial restriction and no exclusive purchase clause. Where such selective distribution systems involve criteria concerning the technical qualifications of distributors and the suitability of their premises, the Court has found in a series of cases that Article 81(i) does not apply as long as the restrictions are applied uniformly. The products involved have been of high value and technically complex (watches and clocks, cameras and film, electrical or electronic equipment and so on) or, somewhat surprisingly, highly priced and heavily promoted products (like jewellery and cosmetics).[22] Instead of emphasizing the benefits consumers may obtain from competent after-sales service (an argument difficult to apply in the case of cosmetics) the Court has concentrated on the stimulus to non-price competition:

> Systems of selective distribution, insofar as they aim at the attainment of a legitimate goal capable of improving competition in relation to factors other than price, therefore constitute an element of competition which is in conformity with Article [81](i). The limitations inherent in a selective distribution system are, however, acceptable only on condition that their aim is in fact an improvement in competition in the sense above mentioned. Otherwise they would have no justification inasmuch as their sole effect would be to reduce price competition. (AEG/Telefunken 1984, 3CMLR 325)

The benefit to consumers from intensified non-price competition may be more clearly apparent in hi-fi equipment and computers than in cosmetics. In the former, consumers may obtain a better understanding of how to use the products because distributors have been able to invest in the necessary equipment and expertise, protected from 'free-riders'. In the latter, what they obtain is altogether more esoteric, in keeping with the nature of the products. Ultimately the benefit seems to rest on the claim by the manufacturers that the sales of their products can only be maintained if they are sold in shops with the appropriate air of luxury, unsullied by lower-priced products. The claim has been accepted by the MMC, citing the exemption granted by the Commission (MMC, 1993a).

Since February 1989, a block exemption on franchising agreements has applied throughout the EU. Regulation 4087/88 covers distribution and service franchises of the kind discussed in Section II above. In return for the use of the franchisor's know-how, trademarks and methods, the franchisee agrees to certain restrictions on methods of trading (for example, to exploit the franchise only from agreed premises, not to seek actively customers from outside the stipulated territory or not to manufacture or sell competing products). In short, conditions which promote the use of the franchise while protecting the intellectual property which it embodies are covered by the Regulation. Attempts by franchisors artificially to segment the market or fix resale prices, however, will mean that the block exemption will not apply.

Tying arrangements   Both Articles 81 and 82 can be applied to tying arrangements. Thus, under Article 81(i)(*e*), an example of an unlawful agreement is one which makes 'the conclusion of contracts subject to acceptance by other parties of supplementary obligations which, by their nature or according to commercial usage, have no connection with the subject of such agreements'. Very similar wording appeared under Article 82(*d*). However, the general block exemptions covering distribution agreements both allowed a supplier to insist that the distributor purchase complete ranges of goods.[23]

The most significant moves against tying arrangements have been under Article 82. The Commission used Article 82 to ensure that IBM ended its system of so-called 'memory bundling' and 'software bundling' under which customers were unable to purchase the system 370 central processing units without also taking the main memory. The company gave an undertaking that in future the central processing units would be available without the main memory (or with merely sufficient memory for testing purposes).[24] Several recent cases have made it very clear that the Commission will readily challenge any attempt by a dominant firm to extend its position into a related or complementary product. Thus, for example, in *Eurofix-Banco* v. *Hilti*,[25] the Commission decided that the insistence by Hilti that purchasers of its patented nail cartridges also had to purchase its nails was an abuse of a dominant position and the company was heavily fined. The company's argument that this was a reasonable precautionary measure to protect operators from injury when using nail guns was rejected by the Commission on the evidence before it. Similar cases have involved a monopoly radio and television station insisting that advertisers use the company's own advertising manager or an agency appointed by it, and a sugar company refusing to supply customers at an ex-works price, so that they themselves could carry out the distribution.[26] Both were found to infringe Article 82. Thus tying by a dominant firm which serves no purpose other than to enhance the incumbent firm's position and impair competition from other suppliers of the tied product will be found incompatible with the EU.

IV   Conclusion

Much of the economic analysis of vertical restraints is ambiguous, in the sense that changed circumstances can alter the net welfare effects. Thus, for individual resale price maintenance, whether or not there is a net gain depends on the nature of the shift in demand resulting from its introduction. Exclusive dealing in many markets may bring gains from enhanced inter-brand competition which outweigh the loss created by the reduction in intra-brand competition. This result may not follow, however, if the manufacturing stage is dominated by one or two firms and entry into distribution is constrained.

Such ambiguity and complexity of different cases suggest that a rule of reason rather than a per se approach to policy will produce more efficient results. With very few exceptions this, broadly speaking, has been the approach adopted in the UK and the EU. Individual resale price maintenance has effectively been eliminated, while the collectively enforced variety, having the form of a horizontal agreement, is illegal under both jurisdictions. In contrast, the EU Commission allows exclusive distribution systems where these are reckoned to yield net benefits to the consumer. In the UK, the MMC has taken a similar view in industries such as cars and petrol.

In the USA, the position is not so clear. While resale price maintenance remains effectively per se illegal (despite attempts by the Chicago School and the Justice Department to encourage the use of a rule of reason approach) other restraints are more circumscribed than in Europe. Thus territorial restrictions are now likely to be judged according to a rule of reason, whereas exclusive dealing is generally treated much more harshly, even though logic points in the direction of greater tolerance. The attitude of antitrust authorities to tying arrangements is now rather similar, with an emphasis on market power by the firm imposing the tie and the extent to which the market of the tied product is foreclosed to competitors or potential entrants. Recent cases have tended to recognize the argument that firms may have a legitimate interest in ensuring that their products are used with the correct quality and specification of complementary or ancillary products. However, this will only justify a tie, *ceteris paribus*, if it is clearly shown to be necessary on the facts of the case.

In the EU the use of block exemptions, subject to safeguards, has proved to be a particularly flexible and time-saving system for dealing with a multiplicity of vertical agreements almost universally adopted in certain trades.

Notes

1. For those unconvinced by a simple visual comparison, a geometric proof of the statement in the text is as follows: consider the two parallelograms $STGV$ and P_2P_1EG. They lie between the same parallel lines OS and Q_0V but they have different widths, that is, $GV > GE$ (since $GV = HW$ and $HW > HJ$, because $HJ = GE$, then $GV > GE$). Hence, $STGV > P_2P_1EG$. Comparing triangle GER and GHV: triangle GER is equal to triangle GUR which in both base and height is less than triangle GHV.
2. *Dr. Miles Medical Co.* v. *John D. Park & Sons*, 220 US 373 (1911).
3. It was possible, for example, for mail order companies to set up in the states without fair trade laws and ship low-priced goods to states where prices were still maintained.
4. *United States* v. *Colgate and Co.*, 250 US 300 (1919).
5. For further examples, see Blair and Kaserman (1985, ch. 13).
6. *Monsanto Co.* v. *Spray-Rite Service Corp.*, 465 US 752 (1984).
7. *United States* v. *Arnold, Schwinn & Co.*, 388 US 365 (1967).
8. *Continental TV* v. *GTE Sylvania*, 433 US 36 (1977).
9. *Standard Fashion Co.* v. *Magrane Houston Co.*, 258 US 346 (1922).
10. *Standard Oil of California* v. *United States*, 337 US 293 (1949).
11. *International Salt Co.* v. *United States*, 332 US 392 (1947).
12. *Northern Pacific Railway Co.* v. *United States*, 356 US 1 (1958).
13. *Jefferson Parish Hospital District No. 2* v. *Hyde*, 466 US 2 (1984).
14. The previous law was consolidated under the Resale Prices Act 1976.
15. *Re Net Books Agreement* (1962) LR3 RP 246.
16. *Re Medicaments Reference* (1970) LR7 RP 267.
17. By the time of the second report the MMC had been transformed into the Competition Commission. See Chapter 3 above.
18. *Association Syndicale Belge de la Parfumerie* (1970) CMLR D 25.
19. *Groupement des Fabricants de papiers peints de Belgique* v. *EC Commission* (1976) 1 CMLR 589. On appeal, the fine imposed by the Commission was overruled for reasons unconnected with the collective enforcement terms.
20. Usually referred to as the 'Dutch Book' case, VBVB-VBBB (1985) 1 CMLR 27.
21. We noted above that for the UK the MMC has concluded that petrol agreements should not exceed five years.
22. The cases are discussed in Goyder (1998), pp. 216–28. They include the Omega watch case (1970), CMLR D 49; Kodak case (1970), CMLR D 19; the perfume cases (1981) 2CMLR 91, 143, 164; the electrical equipment cases Metro-Saba (1978) 2CMLR I and AEG/Telefunken (1984) 3CMLR 325.
23. Regulations 1983/83; 1984/83, Article 2(3)a.
24. Fourteenth Report on Competition Policy, points 94 and 95.
25. *Hilti* v. *Commission* (1994), 4 CMLR 614.
26. The cases are discussed in Whish (1989, pp. 638–40).

PART IV

PRIORITIES AND PROSPECTS FOR ANTITRUST

11 Priorities in antitrust policy

I Introduction

The centenary of the father of modern antitrust laws (the Sherman Act) in 1990 was seen by many in the USA as an appropriate occasion for appraisal and reflection on the purpose and achievement of antitrust policy (see, for example, Bittlingmayer, 1992). In the USA, there has been much discussion about what should be the fundamental objectives of antitrust policy and whether or not these are in accordance with the original intent of Congress or current interpretation by the courts (Bork, 1978; Brodley, 1987; Lande, 1982). The debate was sharpened by what was perceived by many observers to be a fundamental shift in policy in the 1980s during the Reagan and Bush administrations. With the Chicago School in the ascendant some prominent cases against large enterprises were dropped, and for many it seemed that little government action was being taken against exclusionary behaviour or mergers. For some even relative inactivity was insufficient. Nothing less than the complete revision of the antitrust laws would suffice (Armentano, 1982) or at least drastic curtailment to control only predatory pricing and cartels (Thurow, 1981).

Amongst those observers who took a less extreme position there was nevertheless a recognition that, given the pace of development in many national and international markets, antitrust policy should be responsive to the needs of such changes. Some of these questions, such as the possible overlaps or conflicts between antitrust and trade policies, are dealt with in the next chapter. In the present chapter we focus on three issues which have been prominent in the recent debate. First, the special characteristics of innovation and its overriding importance for economic efficiency have led to special provisions in the USA and the EU. In both jurisdictions the need for collaborative research and development (R&D) and joint ventures to achieve an efficient rate of innovation has to an extent been acknowledged and allowed to supersede the general ban on collusion (Section II). Secondly, and in direct contrast, there is the recognition that antitrust may be subverted by individuals or firms who seek to use it to gain an advantage or reward irrespective of their own or their competitors' market performance. Actions of this kind are part of a much wider class of rent-seeking behaviour (see, for example, Buchanan *et al.*, 1980) and are considered in Section III. The incentive and scope for rent seeking, in this context, may depend very much on the structure of antitrust penalties. The present position in the USA may lend itself more readily to this form of behaviour than is the case in either the UK or the EU. Antitrust penalties are discussed in Section IV.

II Innovative efficiency and collaborative R&D

In the first part of the book, when we were setting out the disadvantages for resource allocation of market dominance, there was considerable emphasis on allocative efficiency. Indeed market power was defined as the ability of a firm or group of firms persistently to hold price above marginal cost. Where market power is present, there is thus a misallocation of resources. Removal of the market power (by antitrust policy, for example) may improve resource allocation, *ceteris paribus*.[1] Allocative efficiency is concerned with the allocation of a given set of scarce resources.

Productive or technical efficiency, in contrast, occurs when a firm produces the maximum output for a given resource cost or, what amounts to the same thing, minimizes resource cost for a given output. It implies, for example, that firms take advantage of any available scale economies for their chosen output and do not waste resources by becoming slack or X-inefficient. Where economies of scale are substantial in relation to the prevailing market size there may be scope for only a few, technically efficient, firms. In the limit, of course, scale economies may be so great that the market is a natural monopoly. However, even in less extreme cases the possibility that markets dominated by a few technically efficient firms can exploit market power has been a major theme of the book. The trade-off between technical efficiency and market power has appeared in a number of different contexts, for example single-firm dominance, tacit collusion amongst a small group of dominant enterprises and mergers promising cost savings but also an increase in market power.

There is a third aspect of efficiency to which we have occasionally alluded but which we now need to deal with more explicitly. Innovative efficiency refers to the ability of firms to develop and introduce new products and production methods. While many interrelated factors may contribute to economic growth, technical change is recognized as having a key role. Thus, whereas allocative and technical efficiency are concerned with the static allocation of a given volume of resources, innovative efficiency is intimately related to economic growth and dynamic performance. We saw in Chapter 1 that markets dominated by single firms can cause static welfare losses as the result of allocative inefficiency. Suppose, however, that the rate of innovation and thence economic growth generated by such markets exceeds that of more fragmented markets where the static welfare losses are consequently smaller. The power of compound interest readily indicates that the incomes enjoyed by consumers in the economy which tolerates market dominance would rapidly exceed those in the economy with fragmented markets, even though the latter has a superior static performance. Much, therefore, turns on the empirical question of whether market dominance generates a faster rate of technical progress. Unfortunately, the data do not give a clear-cut answer to this question.

What is especially significant in the present context, however, is the *relative* importance of innovative compared with allocative and technical efficiency. Estimates suggest that the most important contributory factor to the productivity growth experienced by industrialized countries for the greater part of the 20th century was the application of new production methods and equipment. The growth of capital and the improved educational standard of the workforce also played a part, but were quantitatively far less important than technological change (Denison, 1967). These results can be considered alongside those estimates of the welfare losses resulting from the misuse of market power discussed in Chapter 1. At the lower end these suggested that the loss of output (attributable to allocative inefficiency) amounted to substantially less than 1 per cent of gross national product. Even if the subsequent revised estimates are used, the figures are still not substantial, although much depends on which assumptions we are prepared to accept. For present purposes, however, the important point is that innovative efficiency should be given at least as much weight in policy matters as allocative and technical efficiency. Some observers have gone further and argued strongly that innovative efficiency should be given priority, followed by technical efficiency, with allocative questions being ranked third (see, in particular, Brodley, 1987; Jorde and Teece, 1990, 1992). In any case the unusual circumstances surrounding the creation and introduction of new knowledge is now widely appreciated, along with the need for special antitrust treatment.

The law already recognizes the need to protect incentives for innovation by granting patents, even though this restricts the use of new information. The gain from granting a patent monopoly is thought to outweigh the loss suffered by consumers who pay a monopoly price. Patent protection, however, may solve only a small part of the problem of externalities or spillovers involved in the discovery of new scientific knowledge. Not all information occurs in a patentable form, secrecy may not be complete, new techniques may be discoverable by competitors' reverse engineering. As a result, individual firms undertaking R&D may not realize all of the value created by their discoveries. Consequently too little R&D will take place. Furthermore, in the absence of special provisions, collaboration on R&D could be prosecuted under the various anti-cartel laws in the USA and EU.

The advantages and disadvantages of research joint ventures (RJVs) have been set out by Grossman and Shapiro (1986) and we draw on their discussion in what follows. The first advantage refers to the point just made: an RJV largely overcomes the 'free-rider' problem which is inherent in the process of new knowledge creation. Participants agree ex ante to share the costs and can then all equally exploit the results. Some degree of spillover may still remain, however, if significant competitors remain outside the venture.

Secondly, RJVs are likely to generate substantial synergies and economies of scale in R&D. Given the highly specialized expertise required for successful R&D, participants in the venture can benefit from the complementary skills brought together under one organization. Economies of scale in R&D are related to the public good characteristics of new knowledge. Repeated and simultaneous use of the knowledge in many different applications at little or no extra cost does not impair its value. Some very large research projects may only be worthwhile as long as the results can be widely employed by a number of different producers. Where the minimum efficient scale of R&D is large in comparison with that of production, it would be wasteful to duplicate the facilities. This follows as long as the single R&D input produces the same total R&D output as a number of competing laboratories. RJVs may also allow individual firms to diversify the risks inherent in the innovatory process by allowing them to create a research portfolio. As Grossman and Shapiro explain, however, this aspect of RJVs should only be regarded as a secondary advantage. The need for the diversification of risks by firms in this way implies some imperfection in the capital market which prevents an efficient allocation of risk bearing amongst investors with diversified shareholdings. A further advantage of RJVs is that they may allow an economy to enjoy the benefits of R&D scale economies without having to endure the dangers of increased concentration in production. This solution may be preferable to the alternative of having a single firm undertake the R&D and then license the results to other production companies which become dependent on a sole source for the most recent technology.

Thirdly, RJVs can increase the dissemination of new knowledge and help to maintain competition at the production stage. Given the public good characteristics of new knowledge, it is socially efficient for it to be used as widely and intensively as possible. A joint research venture is in the nature of an ex ante licensing agreement with zero licensing fees. All participants can use the results of the venture without having to contribute anything above their original agreed cost of joining. It is thus likely to be a more successful dissemination mechanism for new knowledge, especially amongst rivals, than a conventional patent licensing system. To the extent also that firms which otherwise would not have undertaken R&D are drawn into the venture, competition at the production stage may be increased.

On the other hand, the disadvantages of RJVs are usually considered to be the threat they pose to competitors at both the research and production levels, or what Grossman and Shapiro term the 'research' and the 'product' markets, respectively. They envisage two possible dangers in the research market. First, static inefficiencies in the R&D market will occur if participants in the RJV deliberately pursue a restrictive licensing policy towards non-participating rivals. This outcome is analogous to the pricing problem of a monopolist. In the

R&D context, the fewer the number of firms competing to sell new knowledge, the higher the price is likely to be. Any limit on the use of the knowledge in the product market will raise costs in the case of a process innovation or inhibit competition in the case of a product improvement. Secondly, and potentially more serious, there is the dynamic counterpart to the previous point. Dynamic inefficiencies in the R&D market will occur if firms participating in an RJV collude in order to retard the pace of technical innovation. Collectively firms may benefit from a reduction in their R&D expenditures. The likelihood of such collusion is minimized if participating firms retain their own independent research facilities and personnel. They then have both the means and the incentive to cheat on any attempted collusive action.

The danger may be equally acute in the product market. Collaboration in R&D may breed collusion in the product market. A firm's perception of the way its rivals would behave following a particular competitive move may be subtly changed after participation in an RJV. The risk of collusion is clearly greater where the members collectively have significant market power and if the research agreement is supplemented by other restraints. One example would be participants agreeing to employ any new patents flowing from the venture in a way which segmented the market either geographically or by end use. Although such additional restrictions are not sufficient to condemn the venture, because they may be needed to provide an adequate incentive for firms to join, they do 'shift the burden of proof somewhat onto the firms, who must establish that they are necessary and that there exist compensating social welfare benefits from the venture' (Grossman and Shapiro, 1986, p. 325).

Despite the doubts raised by these disadvantages, the unusual characteristics of the innovation process have persuaded many observers that it therefore requires special antitrust treatment. Indeed the recent debate in the USA has focused primarily on possible impediments to R&D collaboration posed by the antitrust laws which have placed US industry at a technological disadvantage and thus played their part in the worsening performance of the economy, particularly its trade imbalance. This is certainly the view of Jorde and Teece, who quote an influential MIT report to support their case: 'Underdeveloped co-operative relationships between individuals and between organisations stand out in our industry studies as obstacles to technological innovation and the improvement of industrial performance'; and again, 'interfirm co-operation in the US has often, though not always, been inhibited by government antitrust regulation' (Dertouzos *et al.*, 1989, pp. 7, 105, quoted in Jorde and Teece, 1992, p. 47). A similar view is taken by Grossman and Shapiro (1986) who argue that 'Substantial evidence exists to suggest that antitrust uncertainties have discouraged US firms from entering with co-operative R&D projects' (p. 315). The position is made even worse, according to this view, because the major US international competitors in Western Europe and Japan suffer no such constraints and often receive direct government inducements to stimulate technical change (ibid., 1986, p. 319; Jorde and Teece, 1992, p. 47).

Not surprisingly, there is more unanimity about the underlying issue of the need to stimulate innovation than about the role of the antitrust laws. Thus Audretsch (1991) in his discussion of the Jorde and Teece (1990) position argues that the underlying reasons for the relatively poor US performance recently are to be found elsewhere (particularly in enormous budget deficits and high interest rates). In a similar vein, Brodley (1990) argues that, even before the National Cooperative Research Act (NCRA) was passed in 1984, research joint ventures were treated very permissively by the courts. The Act was thus 'not to redress an overly stringent enforcement policy, but to correct overdrawn perceptions of antitrust risk, particularly by smaller firms' (p. 100). It provides for a registration system of RJVs which then protects participants from triple damages if they are subsequently found to have violated the antitrust laws. Registered ventures are thus not immune from the laws, but the Act specifically provides for them to be judged under a rule of reason rather than a per se rule. According to Brodley, the Act has been highly successful in encouraging RJVs. Prior to the Act only about seven ventures a year were formed, whereas an average of 29 a year were formed in the five years after the Act. In fact in some respects the provision may have provided the wrong sort of stimulus, with collaboration occurring 'not in industries where research appropriability was likely to be low, but instead in industries where concentration was high, productivity growth strong, and where firms were already engaged in diversified R&D so as to be able to exploit R&D spillovers across industries' (Brodley, 1990, p. 101).

Since the passage of the NCRA, a number of other proposals have been made to extend the degree of antitrust exemption in various ways. These have included, for example, specifying in detail the criteria for applying the rule of reason; allowing cooperation to extend into the production and marketing of the results of collaboration; and setting up an administrative system with powers to clear ventures which might risk an antitrust challenge (Geroski, 1993; Brodley, 1990; Jorde and Teece, 1992). It has been these proposed additions, particularly those which would allow collaboration to extend from R&D into production and marketing, which have been at the heart of the current discussion in the US. For some, like Jorde and Teece, such a provision is a natural and necessary extension of the current position, which would place US industry on a par with its European competitors. For others, like Brodley and Audretsch, the risks of collaboration turning into full-blown collusion are too great, and any extension should therefore be resisted.

It is instructive at this point to compare the current position in the European Union with that in the USA. In the absence of special provisions, collaborative R&D agreements would be illegal under Article 81(i). As early as 1968, a

Notice dealing with collaboration between firms stated that such agreements relating only to R&D would not normally infringe Article 81(i). In 1985, this policy was significantly extended. Under block exemption 418/85, which lasted for 13 years, the original provision was left intact but agreements covering the exploitation of the results of R&D could also be given favourable treatment. Thus, under certain circumstances, agreements covering both R&D and production (but not marketing) could be given exemption from Article 81(i). The exemption applied if the work was carried out within a well defined programme; all parties had access to the results; each party was free to exploit the results independently where joint exploitation was not undertaken; and the fruits of the collaborative research made a substantial contribution to economic progress and were indispensable for the manufacture of the resulting product (Jacquemin, 1988). The original provisions were modified when, as part of a more comprehensive review, a new block exemption came into force in January 2001 lasting until 2010. Where participants have a combined market share of 25 per cent or less exemption is granted for seven years or possibly longer. If an agreement extends to joint distribution of jointly developed projects, the combined market share threshold is increased to 25 per cent (compared with 10 per cent previously) (Rivas and Stroud, 2001). The market share conditions try to ensure that the threat to competition in the product market is minimized. However, by extending the exemption into the realm of distribution and not merely R&D, the Commission has gone considerably further than current US provisions allow. It thus gives greater recognition to the need for stability in R&D agreements and appropriability of the results.

Thus, although both jurisdictions have now recognized the innovation process as a special case which requires modification of the antitrust rules, neither attempts to restrict acceptable collaboration to those sectors of industry where the spillovers are likely to be greatest, although the practical difficulties of identifying them in advance are great. The most important difference in treatment between the USA and EU is that the latter gives certain collaborative joint ventures complete exemption from the antitrust laws for a specified period, even when these extend into distribution, whereas the former merely allows for a softening of the penalties if the venture (which has to be confined to R&D) is subsequently found to have infringed the law. In practice, however, the difference may be much less important (at least as far as pure RJVs are concerned) because the US antitrust authorities have taken a very accommodating view and this has greatly increased the number of ventures registered. In contrast, in the EU, very few have been notified,[2] possibly because participants in unnotified agreements do not want to draw attention to possible anti-competitive clauses, although the risk of subsequent harsh antitrust treatment would remain acute (Geroski, 1993).

A final interesting point raised by Geroski is that neither the NCRA nor the block exemption deal explicitly with the possible alternatives to an RJV. At one extreme would be cases where no R&D would take place in the absence of collaboration. Assuming that some R&D is better than none at all, RJVs will have a positive effect. At the other extreme, firms denied R&D collaboration may seriously contemplate full merger. Since any market power effect is likely to be much more enduring from a merger than from restricted collaboration, the latter would again be preferable.

Measures in both the USA and the EU have modified the application of the antitrust laws towards R&D activities in the hope that they will contribute to improved innovative performance. The potential externalities and spillovers involved in the discovery and application of new scientific knowledge provide the theoretical underpinning for such moves. The measures have been introduced despite the rather unpersuasive evidence, extensively discussed in the recent US debate, that antitrust policy has actually stood in the way of innovation. The case for further policy modifications, therefore, especially in Europe where they are already more generous than in the USA, would be difficult to justify.

III   The misuse of antitrust

Antitrust policy, as we saw in Chapter 1, can be viewed as a response to market failure. The modification of antitrust discussed in the previous section was itself a response to another type of market failure (created by externalities). We now address a problem of a different kind. Firms or individuals may attempt to use antitrust policy for their own advantage and thereby defeat or at least weaken the very mechanisms that it is designed to correct. Thus, for example, firms feeling themselves vulnerable because of the superior competitive efforts of rivals may accuse them of predatory pricing or, in a different context, oppose a merger on the ground that it will create market power when what they really fear is its enhanced efficiency. In effect the firms are attempting to gain protection from the full rigours of competition, just as they may similarly seek protection from foreign competition by urging a government to impose tariffs or quotas. The use of the antitrust laws in this way is another example of the more general problem of rent seeking analysed by Buchanan *et al.* (1980) and specifically in the context of antitrust by Posner (1975). The central idea was discussed in Chapter 1 and in the present context may be interpreted as follows. Firms already in the fortunate position of earning economic rents clearly wish to maintain them. If the effort of competing with efficient rivals is perceived to be greater than that required to achieve the same objective by using the antitrust laws, and if the likely return from the latter is greater, then firms will use the laws in this way.

At least four potential sources of waste can be identified if such policies are pursued (Baumol and Ordover, 1985). First, to the extent that firms succeed in protecting their rents, a welfare loss results from the continued resource misallocation. Secondly, the resources expended (for example, on lawyers, consultants and lobbying fees) amount to a deadweight loss to society, given that they are being used to subvert the antitrust laws. In general, if the market for rent seeking is open, then competing firms will dissipate the whole of the potential rent in purchasing such services (Posner, 1975). Thirdly, firms successfully manipulating antitrust policy will have their incentives to retain their own internal efficiency weakened. In Chapter 1 this was termed 'X-inefficiency' and referred to a multitude of ways in which firms released from the immediate pressures of remaining competitive may allow their managerial and supervisory standards to slip, thus raising their costs. Unlike the first source of inefficiency just noted, X-inefficiency applies to the whole of current output. Fourthly, and more subtly, firms actively rent seeking in this way have their attention distracted from objectives which we normally associate with profit-maximizing firms. Instead of attempting to improve their productivity or products, time and money are expended planning the best strategy for weakening a rival by misusing the antitrust laws.

As Baumol and Ordover (1985) explain, the reason why the antitrust laws lend themselves to such misuse is the difficulty of drawing clear distinctions between legitimate and destructive forms of competition. The former maintain or improve efficiency and the consumer's interest, the latter are instruments of monopolization. Discussion in the previous chapters provides a number of examples of this difficulty. The most widely quoted is predatory pricing. Since active competition is supposed to promote lower prices and since at a particular time firms operating in a market may have very different levels of technical efficiency, distinguishing competitive from predatory pricing may be very difficult. Incumbent firms, however, may have a wide variety of variables at their disposal, including brand proliferation, intensified advertising, capacity creation and pre-emptive patenting, all of which may appear to be benign but which may be used strategically to prolong market dominance. In each case, making the correct analysis is difficult and hence the scope for attempting to manipulate the antitrust laws is multiplied. Generally, recent developments in the theory of industrial organization suggest that the task of antitrust authorities is much more difficult than was previously thought (Comanor and Frech, 1984; Schmalensee, 1982b).

Writing against the background of the US antitrust laws, Baumol and Ordover argue that a number of factors make the system especially prone to rent-seeking or 'protectionist' behaviour. These factors are considered in reverse order of importance. First, there is the vagueness of some antitrust criteria. Economic analysis can rarely give an unequivocal answer to a particular antitrust question.

Probably the only two circumstances where there is almost universal agreement is explicit price fixing by a group of firms, and a merger between large firms where entry barriers are high. For the rest, whether a particular action is anti- or pro-competitive depends on the detailed circumstances. A good case can therefore be made that most antitrust decisions should be based on a rule of reason. Compared to a per se rule, however, the outcome of a rule of reason is necessarily more uncertain. Hence there is a greater incentive for firms to use the antitrust laws for their own advantage where a rule of reason is applied: they may win and consolidate their position.

Secondly, the more severe the tests of anticompetitiveness applied by the antitrust authorities, the greater the likelihood of misuse. One example given by Baumol and Ordover in this connection is particularly instructive. In antitrust cases dealing with predatory pricing, a rule which used fully allocated costs rather than incremental or marginal cost to establish an infringement would give more scope for challenge by firms seeking protection. Efficient firms would be likely to feel far more constrained in their pricing policy under such a rule than under one which used marginal cost as a benchmark.

Thirdly, and most important, the provision in the Sherman Act (and later included in the Clayton Act) for successful plaintiffs to recover triple damages gives a very strong incentive for individuals or firms to misuse the antitrust laws. Together with the additional provision that unsuccessful plaintiffs in antitrust actions do not have to pay the costs of bringing the case, current US antitrust practice offers an enticing recipe for those seeking a profitable respite from the full rigours of competition. In the next section of this chapter we consider in more detail the whole issue of remedies and penalties in antitrust policy. For the moment we simply note that the US triple damages system has the large disadvantage of increasing the potential pay-off for protectionism or rent seeking. A successful action will not only hobble an efficient competitor and allow the less efficient to continue to use its market power but will also reward the latter into the bargain. In addition, trebled damages also increase the amounts it pays both defendant and plaintiff to expend in combating the case, for such damages increase the pool of rents to be disputed (Baumol and Ordover, 1985, p. 253). Expenditures will therefore tend to increase in proportion to the size of the rents available, but to a large extent the outlays by the plaintiff will be cancelled out by those of the defendant. As in the case of competitive advertising in a concentrated oligopoly, costs increase but both parties stay in the same place while imposing an equivalent burden of loss on society.

The triple damages system may thus stimulate an undue amount of protective behaviour in the USA. For a number of reasons, Baumol and Ordover suggest that the incentives for such abuse in the EU are much weaker. Plaintiffs are not entitled to triple damages and the notion of contingent fee agreements, whereby the size of the lawyer's fees depends on the amount awarded in a successful action, are unknown in the Union. Discovery procedures (of possibly incriminating documents) are also less well developed, although they are improving with experience. At the purely national level they are almost entirely lacking. In the USA, defendants have the right to trial by jury in cases involving money damages, whereas in the EU there is no such right. Finally, the usual European practice is that an unsuccessful plaintiff has to bear the defendant's costs, whereas in the USA this is not the case. Plaintiffs therefore have very little to lose in opening legal proceedings, in the expectation in many instances that the defendant will be intimidated into settling out of court to avoid the possibility of a harsher penalty at the eventual end of the trial.

The pattern of penalties available and imposed in the USA diverges considerably from that of the EU, and particularly from some individual members. There has been an extensive discussion in the USA about both the structure and level of antitrust penalties (see, for example, Salop and White, 1988; Landes, 1983). Widespread criticism of the lack of effective antitrust sanctions in the UK eventually led, as we saw in Chapter 3, to the much tougher provisions in the 1998 Competition Act. It remains true, however, that revising the system of remedies is near the top of the list of priorities in antitrust.

IV Antitrust remedies

Many of the issues discussed in previous chapters have been concerned with abusive market conduct either by a single dominant firm (such as predatory pricing or refusal to sell) or by a group of firms, jointly dominant, acting together (for example, price fixing or collective boycott). In the first case, none of the antitrust laws condemn dominance per se. Some additional abusive behaviour has to occur which is incompatible with the EU, or which tends to create a monopoly in the USA, for an infringement to take place. In the second case, the jurisdictions vary in their treatment, but a large class of joint behaviour is illegal. The differences relate to the degree to which exemptions or exceptions are tolerated. The one important area of antitrust policy which does not fall easily into either category concerns mergers. Some mergers may change market structure dramatically but do not in themselves constitute an abuse of a dominant position (although, as we saw in Chapter 8, the European Commission came close to this position in the *Continental Can* case, thereby highlighting the gap in EU antitrust provisions). Similarly, although it is recognized that merger may be a substitute for collusion, it is not normally thought of as an aspect of market conduct.

This difference between abusive conduct by a single firm or group of firms, on the one hand, and mergers creating or enhancing dominance, on the other, is reflected in the existing antitrust remedies in the three jurisdictions. The remedy against mergers found to infringe the law is broadly similar. Mergers that are planned but as yet unconsummated (usually the case in the UK and

EU) are simply blocked and that (once the appeal procedure in the EU has been exhausted) is the end of the matter; those that have been completed (frequently the case in the past in the USA) have to be unscrambled.

The position is much more complex and varied in the case of abusive market conduct. The different treatments and remedies are the subject of considerable controversy. To help with the subsequent discussion we give a (necessarily) brief review of the position in the three jurisdictions in turn, starting with the USA. Although details have changed, the structure of remedies set out in the Sherman Act remain substantially intact. Violations of the Act were originally classed as misdemeanors punishable by maximum fine and/or imprisonment. The maximum fine and punishment term have changed over the years and currently stand at $350 000 for an individual and $10 million for a company and three years' imprisonment. 'However the fines can be increased up to twice the violator's gain or twice the victim's loss' (Carlton and Perloff, 2000, p. 609). In 1974, violations of the price-fixing provisions were reclassified as felonies. Further remedies can take the form of injunctions granted on the application of either the Justice Department or an individual. Of particular importance more recently has been the provision allowing an individual or firm to sue the defendant for damages. Success in such a suit, as we mentioned above, automatically brings triple assessed damages plus a reasonable lawyer's fee. Infringement of the Clayton Act carries no criminal penalties but in other respects remedies are enforced in the same way as the Sherman Act. The separate and parallel proceedings under the Federal Trade Commission are enforced exclusively by the Commission itself and the only remedy has the force of an injunction, termed 'a cease and desist' order (Posner, 1976, ch. 3).

In practice the courts have been more lenient than the maximum provisions of the Acts allow. Prison sentences for executives found guilty of collectively fixing prices have been comparatively rare and the terms shorter than for other petty criminals, such as burglars and embezzlers. There is some sign, however, that since the change in maximum penalties in 1974 attitudes may have been hardening. Up to 1974, the longest sentence for participation in a price-fixing conspiracy was 90 days, whereas, in 20 cases started between 1975 and 1979, prison terms ranging from ten days to three years were handed down, with the average sentence lasting 130 days over the whole period. From 1955 to 1993 the average prison sentence was about three months. From the mid-1990s fines imposed on individual firms increased dramatically. Between 1990 and 1995 total criminal fines averaged less than $50 million per year. From 1996 to 1999 total fines rose from $205 million to more than $900 million per year (Carlton and Perloff, 2000, p. 609).

For the European observer, however, the most interesting recent development in US antitrust enforcement is probably the role of the private action: an individual or firm suing another firm or group of firms for damages. The right has been available since the passage of the Sherman Act, but it only took on practical significance after the Second World War, when a number of Supreme Court decisions led to simplified procedures and increased the prospect of plaintiffs receiving triple damages. The number of such private claims rose from an average of 221 per annum in the 1940s, to 696 in the 1960s. The rate reached its peak at 1313 per annum in the 1970s, before falling back somewhat in the 1980s to 1002 per annum (Salop and White, 1988; Viscusi *et al.*, 1992). For most of the 1970s and 1980s, private actions accounted for well over 90 per cent of the total. The government cases (brought by the Antitrust Division of the Justice Department or the Federal Trade Commission) are generally of more significance, involving monopolization (the lengthiest and most costly) and price fixing, followed by merger cases. Most private actions involve price fixing and vertical restraints, such as tying and exclusive dealing. The distinct possibility of a triple damages award has meant that a majority of private actions are settled out of court and, although the mean amount paid may be relatively modest ($50 000 in one published sample of cases – Salop and White, 1988), in a few cases spectacularly large amounts are passed to plaintiffs and their lawyers. For example, following the electrical equipment price-fixing case in the early 1960s, approximately $500 million were paid to settle the numerous follow-up suits and, more recently, a reported $300 million were paid by Cardboard Carton Manufacturers (Scherer and Ross, 1990). In the USA, therefore, the financial sanctions against abusive market conduct are considerable. We reserve our consideration of whether or not they now serve to enhance or weaken competition until after we have outlined the system in the other jurisdictions.

The EU system of remedies differs in important ways from that in the USA. An infringement of Articles 81 or 82 can lead to fines imposed on the companies involved. The level of fine is determined by the Commission and then, if necessary, by the Court, but it is levied against the company only and not individual executives. There is no provision for prison sentences. As we saw in Chapter 7, however, companies party to an agreement notified to the Commission are not subject to a fine if the agreement is subsequently found to infringe Article 81. Neither the Commission nor the Court has hesitated to use the power of fine where they consider it justified, especially in cases involving concerted practices. For example, firms in the polyethelene cartel were fined a total of EURO 37 million, and the polyvinyl chloride manufacturers, EURO 23.5 million. In the recent, most blatant case of formal collusion to fix the price of vitamins over a period of eight years the leading firms Roche and BASF were fined EURO 462 million and EURO 296 million, respectively. Total fines amounted to EURO 855 million. Similarly, abuse of a dominant position under Article 82 in the form, for example, of price discrimination (United Brands) or predatory pricing (AKZO) results in fines. Action under both articles is greatly assisted by the Commission's powers of entry, search and seizure of documents relevant to the case. Although formally it is open to an individual or firm to bring an action for damages, so far they have not played a significant part in the development of EU competition policy.

The lack of effective remedies under UK law prior to 1998 was largely corrected by the Competition Act whose provisions mirrored those of Articles 81 and 82. Colluding firms or an individual firm abusing a dominant position can be fined up to 10 per cent of their UK turnover. The first case, involving a pharmaceutical firm which had abused a dominant position, resulted in a fine of £3.2 million in March 2001 (*Financial Times*, 31 March 2001). In the White Paper published in mid-2001, however, the government proposed to go even further in the direction of having tough remedies for antitrust offences (Department of Trade and Industry, 2001). In the case of what the OECD had classed as 'hard-core' cartels, the government intended to introduce criminal penalties, for the first time. A 'hard-core' cartel was defined as 'an anti-competitive agreement, anti-competitive concerted practice or anti-competitive arrangement by competitors to fix prices, make rigged bids (collusive tenders), establish output restrictions or quotas, or share or divide markets by allocating customers, suppliers, territories, or lines of commerce' (ibid., p. 37). If implemented, the proposal would mean that individuals participating in this class of cartel would be guilty of a criminal offence and subject to a prison sentence. The White Paper invited views on what should be an appropriate level of sentence for what it regarded as 'serious conspiracies which defraud business customers and consumers and have wide economic impacts' (ibid., p. 43).

In the course of the widespread discussion of reform of antitrust remedies (especially in the USA) two issues have been prominent. First, the appropriate role of private actions by individuals or firms to recover damages suffered as a result of an antitrust infringement, and, secondly, the form and extent of other penalties. The two are interrelated and also depend on the central objective of antitrust policy. We saw in Chapter 3 that policy frequently has to tread a delicate path between the competing claims of different interest groups. For present purposes, however, we will assume that the prime purpose of antitrust policy is 'to promote and maintain a process of effective competition so as to achieve a more efficient allocation of resources' (Hay and Vickers, 1987, p. 2).

In the light of this we then have to consider whether this purpose is best served by penalties which deter the wrongdoer or compensate the victim of wrongdoing, or some combination of both. In their stimulating discussions of antitrust penalties, Elzinga and Breit (1976) and Breit and Elzinga (1985) suggest that the main emphasis should rest on deterrence administered by public agencies (such as the Justice Department in the USA or the Commission in the EU) on the grounds that antitrust policy is a 'public good'. Hence, if the matter is left in the hands of individuals seeking recompense for alleged infringements of the law, a non-optimal amount of antitrust will result. Certainly in the EU and UK, the penalties (for price fixing and abuse of a dominant position) have been publicly administered with deterrence rather than compensation in mind (although the UK government is actively seeking ways of enabling groups harmed by illegal behaviour to pursue actions for damages). The enormous growth of private actions in the USA and the size of some of the damages awarded have played a major role in the widespread calls for reform. At the risk of oversimplification, the consensus now seems to be that antitrust objectives are best secured by policy which is largely administered by a public body with appropriate sanctions (see below) while retaining (in the US case) or encouraging (in the EU and the UK) some scope for private suits.

Individual actions for damages can mobilize far more information about business practices than is available or discoverable with the limited resources of a central agency. An unknown number of abuses go undetected simply because the antitrust authorities have no knowledge of them. Furthermore, it may seem equitable for individuals to be able to recover at least what they have lost as a result of an antitrust abuse. The US experience, however, suggests that any move towards the encouragement of private actions for damages should be thought through very carefully.

For example, it is generally desirable for consumers who might suffer as a result of market power to attempt to minimize their injury by seeking out alternative products. If they know they will be able to recover at least the amount of any overcharging, then the incentive for taking evasive action is blunted (the more so if they might recover triple damages). Furthermore, individuals might be induced to make false claims for injury. Under the current US system, as we have seen, the only costs that a plaintiff incurs if the action fails are the fees of his lawyer. In a successful action these will be borne by the defendant as well as his own legal costs plus triple damages. The imbalance in potential costs, therefore, tends to encourage the spurious or flimsy claim. This tendency would be reduced, at least in part, if unsuccessful plaintiffs were usually required to pay the defendants' costs (as in the UK). The incentives to bring a private suit offered by the US system also tempt defendants to settle out of court even when they are convinced of their own innocence (as indicated by the figures quoted above). The uncertainty of proving their case to a Court, and the prospect of heavy damages if they should lose, may make this seem the most attractive solution. A system which therefore allowed a plaintiff to recover the amount of any loss suffered as a result of a clear-cut antitrust infringement plus legal costs would avoid the worst aspects of the US system, especially if any unsuccessful claimant had to pay the defendants' costs.

With major responsibility for antitrust policy retained in the hands of public authorities whose main objective is deterrence, what penalties should be available to ensure, as far as possible, optimal compliance with the law? It can be argued that the maximum fines levied or proposed in both the USA and

288 Market dominance and antitrust policy

Europe fall a long way short of what is necessary to achieve this objective. The reason for this assertion is as follows. Consider a case where a group of firms could earn a monopoly profit of £6 million if they colluded to fix prices. If they are certain to be detected, any fine less than £6 million would not deter them because they stand to gain from the infringement of the law. (To focus on the central issue we ignore, for the moment, costs of detection and prosecution.) Suppose, more realistically, that the probability of detection is less than one, say 0.5. The optimal size of the fine now depends on the expected value or size of the firms' punishment and their attitude towards risk. If the firms are risk-neutral (that is, they are indifferent in this context between the expected value of any fine and its certain equivalent[3]) then the fine must be large enough to ensure that their expected gain is at most zero. This implies that the size of the fine should be set at twice the value of the monopoly profit. The expected value of the fine would then be (0.5 × £12 million) or £6 million: collusion would not, on average, be profitable. If the chances of detection were smaller, the maximum fine would have to be increased to compensate. (This gives some theoretical underpinning for the idea of multiple damages, although there is no reason to believe that tripling is the correct factor to apply.) The numerical example, however, considered only the monopoly profit element of the collusion. It is clear from the discussion in Chapter 7 that the social cost of collusion also involves a deadweight welfare loss, as a result of the output restriction. If the antitrust policy is to promote allocative efficiency, this social cost of collusion should also be included in the calculation of the fine.[4]

Hence a good case can be made for substantial increases in the maximum fines that can be levied on companies which collude or abuse a dominant position. To avoid the distortion of incentives that can occur if individuals sue for triple damages (including the strategic misuse of antitrust policy) Baumol and Ordover (1985) suggest that for abuses which are hard to detect (such as collusive price fixing) the penalty should be three times the estimated damages caused, but the plaintiff would only receive single damages. The remaining two-thirds would go to the government. Successful plaintiffs would also receive costs but unsuccessful plaintiffs would not. Such a scheme of punishment may achieve a substantial amount of deterrence, but at the cost of limiting the number of private actions, including some where there is a good case. An alternative proposal by Posner (1976) would continue to allow private actions for triple damages but only to customers or suppliers, not to competitors. The incentive for competitors to use the antitrust laws to inhibit competition would thus be severely weakened. The same author is opposed to imprisonment as a sanction against executives who knowingly infringe the antitrust laws. His opposition is largely on grounds of efficiency. It is extremely difficult to convert the value of the loss imposed by the infringement into an equivalent non-pecuniary cost in the form of days of imprisonment. Hence, in Posner's view, an overlenient sentence will tend to be imposed. More to the point, a prison sentence is much more costly to administer than a fine. In addition to the obvious cost of locking up guilty executives, there is the real loss of their effort and output while serving their term. In the case of a fine, apart from the negligible cost of collection, the entire amount of the loss incurred by the infringement is offset by a transfer to the Treasury. In comparison, a prison sentence imposes a deadweight welfare loss (Posner, 1976, pp. 225–6).

There is sufficient apprehension about the desirability of the US system of punishments for antitrust violation, especially the award of triple damages in private suits, to make it highly unlikely that it will be emulated in Europe. Nevertheless, there is a feeling that individuals or firms harmed by an infringement should be able to gain compensation. Hence the proposals in both the UK and the EU to make it easier for individuals to bring a successful action for damages and costs. Given the public good nature of antitrust, there is general agreement that major responsibility for enforcement should remain with public bodies able and willing to impose substantially larger fines than hitherto.

V Conclusion

One way of interpreting the modifications to the antitrust measures in the USA and the EU in favour of collaborative R&D ventures is in terms of innovative efficiency. Proponents of such changes have argued strongly that an overemphasis on static objectives such as allocative and technical efficiency may be made at the cost of innovative efficiency, which appears to have a very large impact on the long-term growth of incomes. We saw in Section II that the EU, with its block exemption for R&D joint ventures, has been prepared to go much further than the USA, where the NCRA gives no exemption from the law but protects participants from triple damages should their registered agreement be found subsequently to have infringed the law. Calls for further relaxation of the law have so far been resisted. The special nature of R&D and its results are recognized, but so is the danger that collaboration at one level may spread to collusion at the marketing level. Thus, although the EU exemption is more generous than its US counterpart, it too stops short of allowing collaborative marketing. The issue illustrates clearly the possible clash of policy objectives that we have encountered at a number of points throughout the book and which we take up again in the next chapter.

If one priority in antitrust is to try and ensure that it prevents conspiracy without stifling useful collaboration, another is to block its use to subvert competition. Dominant firms may use strategic behaviour to prevent or inhibit entrants. Under certain circumstances smaller firms, or the inefficient, may use the antitrust laws to hamper their rivals rather than to correct a genuine infringement. In Sections III and IV we suggested that, unless the system of penalties was properly adjusted, the incentive structure of firms might be distorted in a number of ways. In particular the current US system of awarding triple damages to successful private plaintiffs (who do not have to pay defendants' costs if the action fails) seems especially open to abuse.

The recent debate on 'optimal' antitrust penalties has highlighted several interrelated points. First, antitrust has certain characteristics of a public good and therefore private enforcement would tend to be non-optimal. Secondly, mainly public enforcement through a system of fines can help to overcome the problem, especially if a prime purpose is deterrence rather than punishment. This emphasis, however, does not rule out a role for private actions for damages by individuals who have suffered from an infringement. Thirdly, the analysis of penalties in this context suggests that they should be set high enough to ensure that, on average, firms do not expect to gain from an infringement. Since this implies that the size of the fine should be some multiple of the private and social damage caused (dependent on the probability of detection) the current levels of fines imposed in the USA and the EU are probably too low.

Notes

1. This of course is a considerable oversimplification in the interests of brevity at this stage. The costs of removing the market power, including any loss of scale economies, should not outweigh the resource allocation gains.
2. Fewer than 15 notifications of RJVs were recorded by the EU antitrust authorities between 1986 and 1990. In contrast, nearly 160 registrations had been made in the USA by the end of 1989 (Geroski, 1993).
3. Thus, for example, an individual is risk-neutral if he or she is indifferent between a 1 per cent chance of paying a fine of £100 and the certainty of paying a £1 fine. A risk-averse individual prefers the certainty of paying the £1, whereas a risk-lover would prefer the alternative option.
4. If individuals retain the right to sue for damages caused by the restriction a case can be made for also allowing such a right to consumers who have been denied a product because of its monopoly price. The principle has, however, been resisted in the USA. Similarly, customers who purchased from firms outside a cartel, but were charged the cartel price, cannot sue (see, for example, Landes and Posner, 1979).

12 Antitrust policy in an international perspective

I Introduction

At a number of points in previous chapters, the importance for antitrust policy of international trading relations has been apparent. When discussing single firm dominance, for example, the definition of the 'market' was crucial and, in many instances, the correct definition may extend way beyond the national boundaries of a particular country. Indeed, as we saw, there is distinguished but controversial support for the view that, where imports into a country already occur, the whole foreign productive capacity should be included in the relevant market. Similar points can be made when trying to assess the potential market power effects of a proposed merger. In contrast, when discussing cartels, we noted that agreements formed solely to promote exports frequently escape prosecution altogether. The danger that collusion in one phase of companies' operations would spill over into other phases is thus thought to be outweighed by the benefits of promoting sales in other countries.

Thus the fact that most companies operate in an international rather than a purely domestic market environment impinges directly on antitrust policy in a number of ways. The list is readily extended. For example, if country A promotes its exports by allowing collusive behaviour, is it in the economic interest of recipient country B to restrain the resulting imports through its own antitrust policy? Do special factors apply to a merger between a leading domestic producer and a company registered and operating mainly abroad? A country may, as we saw in Chapter 5, attempt to eliminate predatory behaviour by dominant concerns in the domestic market. Can exactly the same analysis and solution be applied to a company located abroad and apparently using predatory behaviour in the domestic market?

Questions such as these are considered from a purely theoretical perspective in Section II. The antitrust response in the three jurisdictions is considered in Section III, including the controversial and still unresolved issue of jurisdiction. How far can the antitrust policy of, say, the USA reach? If the UK allows firms to collude and they export to the USA, can the firms be prosecuted under the US antitrust laws? If a UK firm is accused of predatory behaviour in the provision of an international service (such as civil aviation) can the victim sue in the USA or must any action be confined to the UK?

As technology, tariff reductions and financial deregulation widen the scope of many markets, so the tensions between different countries and the different interest groups within them also grow. While many recognize the benefits of freer trade, many others also see an advantage in special treatment for their particular group. There may thus be increased tension or even contradiction between antitrust and trade policies. The focus of this chapter is to explain the delicate but important role that antitrust policy may play in helping to maintain international trade.

II   Antitrust economics and international trade

An issue which highlights the complexity of the questions involved, and one which continues to cause great controversy, is dumping. In our discussion of price discrimination in Chapter 5 we emphasized that with third degree price discrimination firms find it profitable to charge different prices in different markets. Specifically in the present context, a firm with market power in its domestic market, but where competition in an overseas market is more intense, would find it profitable to sell at a high price at home and at a lower price abroad (assuming that re-export back to the domestic market was not possible). The profit-maximizing position would be where the marginal revenue generated in each market was equal, otherwise the firm would switch sales between the markets. The economic welfare consequences of third degree price discrimination are ambiguous but in a number of cases would be positive. Price in each market catered for remains at or above marginal cost. Although a necessary condition for price discrimination by a firm is market power, there is no suggestion of predatory behaviour. The presence of a foreign competitor in the overseas market may well improve the performance of the overseas industry. Consumers can buy the product at a lower price than would otherwise have occurred. Hence Ordover *et al.* (1983) conclude, 'It is undesirable to prohibit such sales since they benefit consumers and neither reflect anticompetitive objectives nor have anticompetitive consequences. Instead, they are the rational, generally pro-competitive response of a producer facing an overseas market with greater demand elasticity than his home market' (p. 328).

Although we have used the example of a single firm discriminating between markets, the same conclusion follows in the case of a government-tolerated cartel amongst domestic producers, which then has an incentive to export. The level of home prices guarantees a satisfactory overall rate of return even if foreign prices are significantly lower.

Predatory pricing bears some resemblance to an extreme form of price discrimination, but is different in a number of very important ways. The intention of predatory pricing is to eliminate or coerce rivals. Indeed, one definition of predatory behaviour refers to actions which are profitable if they cause the exit of rivals from the market but which are otherwise unprofitable. A practice may cause a rival's exit, but it is predatory only if it becomes profitable as a result of that exit (Ordover and Willig, 1981b). Predatory behaviour, or specifically predatory pricing, requires a number of conditions to hold for its success. The firm in question must already have substantial market power so that its actions can be properly directed. It is implausible and unrealistic that a firm with a modest market share could drive out sufficient of its rivals through predatory behaviour for an initially fragmented market to become concentrated. Secondly, considerable entry barriers must exist so that costs for an entrant are higher than for the incumbent. These may be particularly significant where an important part of total costs is irretrievable or sunk. In the absence of entry barriers, a predatory campaign will fail because of the constraint imposed on the incumbent firm by potential entrants. A related, third point concerns re-entry barriers. If re-entry costs for a firm previously in the market are negligible then again a predatory strategy will fail because any attempt by the incumbent to raise price so as to recoup previous losses will be met by re-entry.

Thus, in the case of price discrimination, the firm is maximizing its return, given the different elasticities of demand in the various markets. No price is below marginal cost and some consumers benefit from prices lower than if a single price were charged. We should also reiterate the point made in Chapter 5 that antitrust treatment of price discrimination remains highly controversial, particularly in the USA but also in the EU. As far as predatory pricing is concerned, it is certainly destructive of competition, but can only be effective if a number of important structural features are present in the market. We concluded in Chapter 5 that, although these features may occur in some markets, the occasions when predatory pricing might successfully be used are likely to be comparatively rare.

The reason for recapitulating these conclusions is their direct relevance to the emotive question of dumping. The standard definition of dumping is charging a price in a foreign market below that charged in the domestic market. In other words, 'dumping' is simply third degree price discrimination applied to markets located in different countries. It is easy to show that dumping can lead to a higher domestic price but a total output substantially larger than that sold by a domestic monopolist. In Figure 12.1, D and MR are the demand and marginal revenue curves, respectively, of a domestic monopolist. MC denotes marginal cost. If the monopolist serves only the domestic market and does not use price discrimination, an output of Q_M is sold at a price of P_M. Suppose, however, that the line P_W represents world demand for the product. For simplicity it is assumed to be perfectly elastic. If the domestic market is effectively isolated from the world market (because of tariffs, for example) the firm can maximize its returns by ensuring that marginal revenues are equivalent in the two markets and that, overall, marginal cost is equal to marginal revenue. Domestic and world marginal revenues are equal at the point A in Figure 12.1 and this indicates that sales on the domestic market will be OQ_N for a price of P_N. Marginal cost and world marginal revenue are equal at the point E. The firm's sales on the

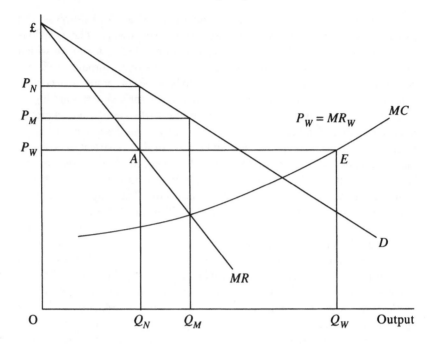

Figure 12.1   Dumping and price

world market would then amount to $Q_N Q_W$. The discrimination thus induces the firm to charge a higher price in the home market than would otherwise have been the case ($P_N > P_M$) but the total output sold is substantially larger ($OQ_W > OQ_M$). From the point of view of the importing country, the welfare effects are clear: consumers benefit from the lower price of the imported good than would have been the case without the discrimination. 'A welfare maximizing importing country would encourage dumping' (Caves *et al.*, 1993).

In practice, the near-universal response to dumping is hostility and action taken to curb what is seen as unfair and abusive market conduct. Action against dumping is part of trade policy which is generally in different hands from antitrust policy, as we shall see in the next section. While antitrust agencies may apply rigorous criteria to determine whether or not a competitor has used predatory pricing, when confronted with a claim of dumping, trade policy agencies have usually applied quite different criteria, even though the essence of the claim may be in terms of unfair or predatory conduct. For most purposes it may be sufficient to establish that the good is sold at a lower price in the foreign market than at home (with due provision for transport costs). No reference to the structural conditions in either the home or export markets, or to the relationship between price and cost may be necessary. Thus market conduct which an antitrust body may find unexceptional or even pro-competitive and certainly pro-consumer is likely to be found abusive by a trade policy agency.

A potentially more serious conflict has been emphasized by Messerlin (1989, 1990). A frequent penalty for dumping is the imposition of a levy or duty on the dumped goods to raise the price, normally at least to the level at which they are sold at home. Apart from the obvious points that consumers are denied the good at the lower price and producers are relieved of the burden of a powerful source of competition, the anti-dumping measure may become the vehicle for collusion. Following the imposition of the anti-dumping levy, the new higher-priced imports may provide a useful focal point for pricing by firms serving the market involved. Although the list of conditions necessary for successful collusion is a comparatively long one (Chapter 7), the removal of one potentially important source of disruption in the form of low-priced imports, especially since it is administered with government approval, may be crucial. There is some evidence (reviewed below) that it may have played precisely this role in EU cases. What one arm of government policy may thus be striving hard to prevent (under Article 81 and Directorate General IV) may be promoted indirectly by another arm (trade policy, administered by Directorate General I).

Once a tough anti-dumping policy is in place, many potential exporters may prefer a solution which for them is more profitable. A 'voluntary' export restraint (VER) is a form of quantity restriction. An exporter agrees to limit the total volume of sales in a foreign market to a specific level or share of the market. Since the firm knows that it can only sell a certain number of units, it will tend to supply those at the upper end of its price range in order to maximize its return; that is, it will set a price for the restricted volume of its product that will clear the market. The purpose of such restraints is to protect domestic producers from the full rigour of import competition, but one of the effects may be again to facilitate collusion. Furthermore, instead of the proceeds of the restriction accruing to the government, as they do in the case of an anti-dumping levy, the additional revenue from the higher price goes to the exporting firm. The extensive use of VERs throughout the 1980s as substitutes for tariff protection, and some damning evidence on their net effects on the countries promoting them, led to a reaction (Kostecki, 1987; Ordover and Goldberg, 1993). The final report of the Uruguay Round contained provisions for the phasing out of VERs.

In the cases considered so far, action against imports may indirectly facilitate collusion amongst domestic firms, even if the country concerned nominally has an active antitrust policy. The response to an alleged attempt to monopolize the domestic market by foreign companies (even though by normal definitions no predatory action may have occurred) is thus a cause of the resulting collusion.

Suppose we now change the perspective but still focus our attention on cartels or collusive behaviour. All three jurisdictions we have considered exempt export cartels from their antitrust laws. Given that the purpose of a cartel is to raise price (and assuming that collusion on exports does not lead to price fixing at home), a key question concerns the antitrust response in the overseas country to such arrangements. There may be some cases when real economies can be made by this type of collaboration (joint marketing operations, for example) and the cartel may be justified on efficiency grounds. In other cases the rationale may be quite simply to extract profits from abroad at the expense of foreign consumers. In effect, a successful export cartel transfers consumer surplus from abroad and converts it into higher profits and wages in the exporting country (Ordover, 1987).

For a variety of reasons, Ordover proposes that the overseas country should respond more vigorously in the face of collusion than when confronted by complaints about monopolization against a single foreign firm. Leaving aside the possibility that harsh anti-dumping measures may themselves generate collusion, he argues that successful predatory behaviour is comparatively rare, even for a domestic company. The probability of success for a foreign company is likely to be even more remote. Furthermore, the problems of correctly applying a test for predatory behaviour to a domestic firm are considerable. They are compounded when applied to a foreign firm. In contrast, price fixing is easier to determine than whether price has or has not been above marginal cost. A cartel is more pernicious than attempted predatory behaviour because at no time does it confer a benefit on consumers since prices are higher than they would otherwise be, whereas a predatory price strategy involves, at least in the short term, very low prices. Collusion is the exact opposite of competition and cannot be mistaken for it, unlike predatory behaviour which may often resemble normal strategic interaction. In short, the danger of a mistaken policy response is much greater in the case of single-firm 'monopolization' than in the case of collusion.

Despite the government support that an export cartel may receive, there are thus good reasons for an antitrust response by the foreign country, although the risk of retaliation may caution restraint. Other cases where the policy of one country spills over to affect foreign countries are more complex. In industries where there are significant learning effects coupled with scale economies, one sizeable country may gain an international competitive advantage by denying foreign firms access to its market. Domestic firms gain the advantages while the volume of foreign firms' sales are restricted, raising their unit costs. As a result, their ability to compete even in their own home market is reduced. In the extreme case they may be driven out of their own market. No predatory conduct has occurred but the effect is ultimately the same and results from the first country's policy of fostering its domestic producers. The original motive of the home government in giving special treatment to the industry may not have been to increase exports or to undermine foreign competition, but nevertheless this is the outcome.

A more blatant example may arise where one government provides subsidies to some industries, part of whose output is then exported. From the perspective of the country receiving the subsidized output, the welfare effects may be positive. Where, for example, there was previously no domestic production and where entry barriers to the market are minimal, the price charged can never for long remain above the competitive level. Hence consumers will derive a benefit from the imports. In perhaps a more realistic case, where the imports displace domestic production and where re-entry to the market is difficult, consumers may face the detriment of monopoly prices in the long term.

As far as producers are concerned, the situation may be quite complex. The costs imposed on domestic producers will be minimal if productive factors are mobile and easily accommodated in an alternative employment with comparable remuneration. If any of these conditions are removed, however, the result may be very different. Where productive factors have been earning substantial rents prior to imports and if these rents are not adjusted downwards to meet the new competitive challenge, the factors will have to move to an employment where they earn substantially less than before, or remain unemployed, perhaps for some considerable time. In such cases, imports impose large costs on rent-earning factors: in effect the rents are exported abroad. In terms of overall welfare, however, the elimination or reduction in rents caused by subsidized imports may not necessarily be negative. The reduction of monopoly prices for final products or of monopoly wages paid to certain groups of workers may generate a welfare gain to consumers which more than outweighs the loss suffered by resource owners.

Thus the net effects of subsidized imports are ambiguous. They are more likely to result in a net gain (i) the less they impair the productive capacity of domestic producers, (ii) the easier it is for displaced factors to move to alternative employment with comparable earnings, and (iii) the greater the possibility of downward adjustment of rents previously earned, in order to retain employment (Ordover *et al.*, 1983). Although the problem of subsidized imports may usually be dealt with by trade policy, it is clear that it may also arise in antitrust cases involving monopolization or collective action.

In all of the cases considered there is a danger that individual countries may seek a unilateral solution to what they perceive as unfair trading practices. The danger is that, once one important trading country adopts such a course, others will retaliate with similar measures, leading to a cumulative contraction of world trade: individual countries apparently pursuing their own best interests in a rational fashion produce an outcome where all participants are actually worse off. One solution would be to ensure the application of universal rules to trading secured by international agreement. Although some progress has been made in this connection in the last 50 years or so, the present arrangements still fall a long way short of the ideal.

III   Antitrust policy and international markets

The last point is well illustrated by two problems that continue to hamper international trading relations: the approach by different countries to dumping and conflicting views as to the territorial 'reach' of antitrust policy. A third issue which raises strong emotions and often calls for stringent policy restraints involves transnational mergers. Each of these is dealt with in turn.

Dumping

Formally, the anti-dumping measures used by the USA and the EU are within the code of practice adopted by members of the General Agreement on Tariffs and Trade (GATT, now administered through the World Trade Organisation (WTO)). In Article VI of the Agreement, the 'contracting parties recognise that dumping ... is to be condemned if it causes or threatens material injury to an established industry in the territory of a contracting party or materially retards the establishment of a domestic industry' (quoted in Stegemann, 1991, p. 376). The original intention was to establish the right of individual members to impose anti-dumping duties in certain narrowly specified circumstances but against a background of a general commitment to liberalization of world trade. There is now considerable agreement, at least amongst economists, that the way anti-dumping measures are actually used is protectionist and anticompetitive. Since the code was put in place (during the Kennedy round of trade negotiations), refinements to the way that anti-dumping regulations may be enforced have been adopted, with the result that 'the "legal" instruments of regulatory protection are thus harmonised on a higher plateau' (ibid., p. 378).

Anti-dumping measures are different from traditional restraints on trade, such as tariffs and quotas, in that they are imposed in a highly selective fashion on a case-by-case basis. There is considerable administrative discretion on such questions as the size of any injury, the extent of the dumping margins to be imposed and their duration. However, their effect is very similar to other non-traditional trade restrictions such as VERs, 'orderly marketing' arrangements and 'industry to industry' understandings. As Stegemann makes plain, they directly aim at a fairly narrow range of industries where import competition is at its most aggressive and where the result is often protection levels considerably higher than those allowed by WTO/GATT tariff arrangements.

Originally the distinction between 'fair' and 'unfair' trade practices may have been legitimate and may have been a necessary accompaniment to the trade liberalization movement which, without the provisions against 'unfair' trade, may have faltered in its first stages. Increasingly, however, the 'unfair' part of the procedures has been captured by protectionist forces to realize their objectives. They know that these are more readily achieved using trade rather than antitrust policy. North American commentators have underlined the gulf that now divides anti-dumping standards from those applied in antitrust actions. Anti-dumping actions are driven almost entirely by the interests of domestic producers against those of newcomers or outsiders in the form of importers. The established domestic producers are the complainants and the entrant or outsider firms are the defendants: an exact reversal of roles compared with many antitrust cases. Although the Clayton Act, as amended by the Robinson–Patman Act, contains provisions for dealing with geographic price discrimination (of which 'dumping' is simply a variant), we pointed out in Chapter 5 that the severe and sustained attack on what are regarded as misguided measures has had an effect on the application of antitrust.

In fact, the Justice Department recommended the repeal of the Robinson–Patman Act in 1979 and, although this has not occurred, there has been little pressure for it to be used more actively. In contrast to the effective abandonment by US antitrust authorities of the prosecution of price discrimination, the number of anti-dumping cases has continued to increase dramatically. For example, at the end of 1980, the number of orders outstanding was 84. By the end of 1990, the number stood at 197 (Anderson, 1993). Over the decade 1987–97 a total of 269 investigations into alleged dumping led to the imposition of remedial measures (Miranda *et al*, 1998).What is more, the procedures used under the trade laws are wedded to a standard that has practically no support among economists. The approved standard under the WTO/GATT is that dumping occurs when imports injure the interest of domestic producers of similar goods. This requires an examination of the volume of dumped goods and their effect on the domestic market for like goods, together with their impact on domestic producers. Although the code indicates that the examination should include an evaluation of all relevant factors in the market, in practice a finding of substantive injury on any single factor can be sufficient to involve an anti-dumping remedy (Stegemann, 1991). There need be no analysis of the likelihood that the importers will be able to monopolize the domestic market. In fact a domestic complainant with, say, a market share of 20 per cent may be afforded protection on a showing that an importer has increased its share from, say, 2 to 3 per cent at the expense of domestic producers. There is no analysis of the entry and re-entry conditions to the market and no assessment of the probability that the dumping firm will capture a large enough share of the market eventually to exploit a position of market power. Whereas US antitrust policy now frequently applies a modified Areeda–Turner rule to test for predatory conduct, essentially based on marginal cost, an anti-dumping case applies a 'full-cost plus profit' standard to determine whether import prices are 'less than fair value'. The scope that this standard gives for administrative discretion is very wide indeed.

If the incidence of predatory pricing is comparatively rare, the likelihood of genuine predatory dumping is even smaller. Indeed Stegemann concludes, having observed the anti-dumping policies of three jurisdictions for more than a decade, 'I am not aware of a single case for which it could be argued convincingly that exporters who were dumping could have hoped to attain lasting monopoly power to exploit buyers in the importing country' (Stegemann, 1991, pp. 384–5). In fact, if an antitrust rather than a trade policy standard were applied to dumping cases, the whole policy might cease to exist, or at least no new orders would be applied. It is possible that eventually the kind of intellectual pressure brought to bear against an over-harsh treatment of price discrimination under antitrust law may have a similar effect on the application of anti-dumping rules – possible but unlikely, given the much greater sensitivity of trade rules than of domestic antitrust.

The same tension between trade and antitrust policies exists within the EU, where they are administered by different Directorates General (I and IV, respectively). The EU also applies a version of the GATT anti-dumping code but, given that it periodically admits new members, the anomalies are thrown into sharper relief. Thus a non-member may have had an anti-dumping duty imposed on some of its products according to the usual standard. When it becomes a member, the code no longer applies because there are no anti-dumping provisions within the EU for intra-member trade. The new member is subject to Article 82 but, from what we have said above, it is practically certain that it would be inapplicable to the products and firms covered by the previous anti-dumping orders.

A most important aspect of this tension between the two policies is the recent claim that enforcement of the anti-dumping provisions actually helps to sustain collusive behaviour. The case has been strongly argued by Messerlin, especially after his detailed examination of two chemical cases (Messerlin, 1990; see also Messerlin, 1989). He first makes the point that in 30 of the anti-cartel cases initiated by the EU in the 1980s, parallel action had also been taken under the anti-dumping regulations. In contrast, the number of actions under Article 82 (dealing with price discrimination and predatory behaviour), which also involved products subject to anti-dumping, was very small, suggesting that 'the link between anti-dumping action and predatory intent is quite loose, contrary to the alleged goal of the anti-dumping regulations' (Messerlin, 1990, p. 466).

The two cases which he discussed in detail involved low-density polyethylene (LdPE) and polyvinylchloride (PVC). The cases had many characteristics in common. The anti-dumping complaints were both made by a trade association whose members were responsible for the vast majority of EU production and who were subsequently all found to be members of the two cartels. In both cases the initial anti-dumping complaints were made against East European producers then operating in non-market economies. Messerlin argues convincingly that the anti-dumping actions were decisive for the maintenance of the cartels which were comprehensive enough to control most of the EU market but, for the same reasons, size and number of members, were potentially unstable. Anti-dumping proceedings rapidly led to 'undertakings' given for both products by the countries concerned. Messerlin suggests that these probably took the form of increased prices to an extent which effectively doubled the duty on imports to the EU (ibid., p. 469). At the initiation of the anti-dumping action, prices stabilized within the EU and rose thereafter. Prior to the action, prices were declining slowly.

The way the anti-dumping procedure was carried out suggests strongly that it had been 'captured' by the complaining companies. For example, Sweden was used as the country of reference for computing the dumping margin, that is, the difference between the domestic and export price of an exporter. Under GATT (and EU) rules, where the exporting countries are 'non-market economies' it is permissible to ignore the actual overseas prices in determining dumping margins and to use instead the prices in a suitable 'country of reference' which should reflect conditions similar to those in the exporting countries were their markets uncontrolled. The choice of Sweden for this exercise seems odd, for two reasons. First, factor prices, especially wages, are much higher in Sweden than in eastern Europe, but, as wage costs are a small fraction of the total, this factor may not have been very important. Secondly, and much more significant according to Messerlin, was the claim by the EU anti-dumping unit that Sweden was suitable because a significant proportion of domestic demand for the products was imported and therefore market prices were likely to be competitive and form the basis of a fair comparison. What the anti-dumping authorities failed to recognize, however, was that the two cartels controlled all domestic Swedish production and 90 per cent or more of Swedish imports. Far from being competitive, therefore, the Swedish prices were set by the cartels. Hence the East European prices were compared with a cartel price in order to set the dumping margin. Although the cartel investigations under Article 81 succeeded the anti-dumping actions, Messerlin implied that a full analysis would have made it clear that Sweden was not an appropriate proxy for a free market competitive price. In his view, the error was compounded when the anti-dumping authorities sought to estimate the damage done to EU producers by dumping from eastern Europe. An important part of the case was that increased imports had adversely affected both prices and profits of domestic producers. The acceptance of this interpretation by the anti-dumping unit is, in Messerlin's view, a good example of 'indirect' capture: 'To treat an increase in import shares as an injury when markets are cartelised represents a major extension of the definition of injury. It implies that domestic cartels are *entitled* to restrict sales and to raise prices, and that, should foreign competition erode their market power, anti-dumping action should be taken to protect the rents of the domestic oligopolies' (Messerlin, 1990, p. 481, italics in the original).

The tension or even conflict between antitrust and trade policies is, perhaps, thrown into sharpest relief by Messerlin's comparison between the likely benefits accruing to cartel members as a result of the protection afforded them in the anti-dumping action (under the authority of DG.I) and the subsequent fines imposed for infringing Article 81 (under the authority of DG.IV). We noted in the last chapter that, although triple damages in antitrust suits had a number of shortcomings, the penalties actually imposed by the authorities frequently seem derisory in comparison with the potential gains to the lawbreaker and the welfare losses imposed on the economy. The point is reinforced by the two cases under review. Messerlin offers a range of estimates of the additional costs to consumers resulting from the anti-dumping action, based on various assumptions. As is usual with such exercises, the results should be treated with some caution. However, even his maximum estimate is based on the rather conservative assumption that the anti-dumping action would have allowed the cartels to survive for only two years. In the case of LdPE, he estimates that consumers had to pay an additional amount ranging from DM204 million to DM737 million and for PVC an additional DM127 million to DM660 million as a result of the action, depending on the assumption used. In contrast, the fines imposed for infringing Article 81 were DM37 million and DM49 million, respectively, which at the time were considered severe. Messerlin considers that for a number of reasons the higher estimates of the additional costs are closer to the mark but, whichever is taken, it is clear that the net benefits of collusion buttressed by anti-dumping action were substantial. They appear to give a clear signal to other producers that such action pays.

In principle there appears to be a strong case for unifying the treatment of price discrimination in all its forms under one authority. If jurisdiction in alleged dumping cases passed to DG.IV and if antitrust rather than trade policy criteria were applied, more efficient outcomes would be likely to result, not only in the sense that competition rather than competitors would be protected but also administrative resources would be saved by having cases dealt with by a single authority. In practice, given the hallowed tradition of anti-dumping actions, sanctified by the full authority of the WTO/GATT, plus the bureaucratic resistance from DG.I, such reform seems highly unlikely.

Extraterritoriality
In the chemical cases just considered, several of the firms involved in the two cartels were located outside the EU but were nevertheless fined for having infringed the antitrust measures of the Union. Although the cases raised no new

issues of principle in this respect, they do help to introduce the controversial issues raised by extraterritoriality, which in the present context refers to economic arrangements made by companies registered in country A which have important economic effects in country B. How comprehensive is country B's jurisdiction in dealing with these issues? We have already observed the favourable treatment usually granted to cartels expressly formed for the purpose of exporting. Do such cartels which are legal in the home country nevertheless infringe the law of, say, the EU and the USA, respectively? If companies agree in Geneva to share the world market between them by allocating territories, do the US and EU antitrust laws apply when the agreement is carried out? If domestic companies form a special agreement to bargain collectively with a dominant foreign seller, what, if any, is the role of the antitrust laws? These and many other examples raise complex issues concerning the 'reach' of antitrust. Although the principles involved are largely legal, they are specifically concerned with economic effects, particularly the various manifestations of market dominance. The increasing globalization of markets and multinational operations of many companies, even those of fairly modest size, suggest that the issues are likely to grow in importance.

There are two well established bases in international law for determining the scope of jurisdiction in such cases (Whish, 1989, ch. 11). The bases are defined in terms of 'territory' or 'nationality'. The first gives jurisdiction over any action committed within the country concerned, whatever the nationality or registration of the individuals or companies involved. The second allows a country to apply its laws to its citizens wherever they may have committed an offence. Much more controversial is the so-called 'effects' doctrine. In this case, regardless of the nationality of the companies concerned or where the action at issue was initiated, a country claims jurisdiction because the economic *effects* of the action are felt within its territory. Taken literally, the effects doctrine has very wide application indeed and, although embraced vigorously by the USA, it has been just as vigorously resisted by the UK. Clearly, under such a doctrine members of a cartel in, say, Sweden who trade with the USA would be subject to the US antitrust laws even though none of them had subsidiaries there. In fact, in the course of the judgement in the famous Alcoa case, to which we have frequently referred, it was said that 'it is settled law ... that any State may impose liabilities, even upon persons not within its allegiance, for conduct outside its borders which has consequences within its borders which the State reprehends'.[1] Since this case, the USA has drawn back somewhat from the all-embracing jurisdiction which it implies. An attempt has been made to develop a 'rule of reason' approach to the question. The 'effects' of the action should not only have been intended but also be direct, substantial and foreseeable. Furthermore, application of the principle should also have regard to the likely reaction of the other states involved and this should be weighed against the interests of the USA (Whish, 1989, p. 381, discussing the Timberlane case[2] and the Department of Justice's Guidelines[3]).

The modified US approach, however, has had little effect on the UK, which remains firmly against the whole 'effects' doctrine. According to Frazer (1992), its harshest criticism has been reserved for what has been interpreted as an attempt by the USA to export its economic policies to unwilling foreign countries. Many years of diplomatic efforts to resolve the question failed and, although it was not made explicit, it was clear at the time of the parliamentary discussions that the 1980 Protection of Trade Interests Act was heavily influenced by the US attitude to its jurisdiction (ibid., p. 239). Under the Act, the Secretary of State for Trade and Industry is given wide powers to forbid UK companies complying with the requirements of foreign courts where jurisdiction is being applied extraterritorially in a way which would be damaging to British trading interests. Where a British company has been found liable for triple damages, the Act also prevents any such judgement being enforced in the UK. Furthermore, where a company has had to pay triple damages, the Act provides for the 'multiple' portion to be reclaimed through the British courts. So far only one case under the Act has involved antitrust policy issues. Laker Airways was suing British Airways (and several others) in the USA, allegedly for using predatory tactics to eliminate Laker from the North Atlantic routes. British Airways sought a ruling from the British courts to prevent Laker pursuing his case. Eventually, the House of Lords determined that Laker should be allowed to proceed in the USA on the ground that otherwise there would be no other means open to pursue the claim, since the course of action was not recognized under UK law.

The provisions in the 1980 Act for reclaiming multiple damages paid out in another country illustrate vividly the hostility of the UK to the whole 'effects' principle. However, the UK stance had been made quite clear much earlier, before the UK had joined the EU. In the *Dyestuffs* case,[4] the European Commission relied on an effects doctrine to determine the involvement of a UK company (ICI) in price fixing. In an *aide-mémoire* following the Commission's decision, the UK government expressed in no uncertain terms its view that an effects doctrine had no basis in international law and should therefore be rejected. When the Court delivered its judgement on the case, instead of addressing the issue directly, it effectively side-stepped the central question by arguing that, where a wholly-owned subsidiary of a foreign parent company operated within the EU, the two should be treated as a single economic entity. If the subsidiary were a member of an illegal restriction so, on this basis, was the parent. In other words, by treating a foreign parent and its subsidiaries as one, the Court was able to use the well-established 'territorial' principle in arriving at its decision. At this stage, therefore, the Commission had embraced an 'effects' doctrine whereas the Court had managed to avoid it.

The question of how it would react to a cartel selling to the EU, but whose members were located abroad and which had no subsidiaries in the EU, had to be addressed in the subsequent *Wood Pulp* case.[5] The Commission had no problem in finding against the cartel in line with its previous decision. In a rather tortuously worded judgement, the Court as good as adopted an 'effects' doctrine without actually admitting it. It relied on the notion that, since the restriction had been *implemented* within the EU, it was therefore possible to employ the accepted territorial principle. Thus, whether or not the Court acknowledges explicitly the relevance of the doctrine, the use of the 'single economic entity' to cover a parent and its subsidiaries, together with the idea of 'implementation' as expressed in the *Wood Pulp* case, should allow it to deal with most cases.[6]

As far as cartels are concerned, therefore, the response of the USA and the EU to the growth of international operations has been to adopt what economic analysis suggests is a logical approach. Price-fixing agreements restrict output and cause welfare losses to consumers. Those losses will be felt wherever the cartel price is imposed, irrespective of the nationality or location of the companies involved and antitrust action will therefore be taken.

Transnational mergers

Mergers involving large companies frequently raise more passion amongst politicians and in the media than any of the other issues discussed in this book. If the mergers involve a foreign firm, the passion can reach fever pitch. There are a number of reasons for this concern. First, the takeover of a significant domestic firm by a foreign enterprise raises the question of where its true interest will in future lie. Not only may profits be channelled back to the parent, but future investment and employment in the domestic market may be curtailed and directed to another country. Where the domestic company is a significant local employer, such loss of ultimate control to a foreign company may have important political implications. The point is reinforced during recessions, when governments are under strong pressure to do all they can to maintain and increase employment. Secondly, to the extent that governments follow an 'industrial' policy which involves positive restructuring (to create 'national champions' to compete with foreign competitors), a foreign takeover may put key companies out of reach. Thirdly, it may be the case that a foreign company bidding to take over a domestic firm may not be vulnerable to a similar bid on its home ground because of legal differences in share ownership and company control. This question is most frequently raised when the foreign bid is regarded as hostile by the domestic management. Calls are made for reciprocity of treatment and an automatic ban on such bids where reciprocity does not apply.

A final point concerns the nature of the foreign enterprise involved. A foreign state-owned firm attempting to acquire a private sector domestic firm may face a hostile policy response quite unrelated to questions of market power. A UK example was when French state-owned water companies bid for newly privatized domestic water companies. In the event, the government's opposition to what it saw as an indirect reversal of its privatization programme was frustrated by the MMC's repeated conclusion (based on straight competitive criteria) that the mergers were not likely to operate against the public interest.

The central question in transnational merger cases is whether the accepted antitrust criteria should be overridden by other special factors, such as those outlined above. Despite considerable pressures, it is broadly speaking the case that, especially in recent years, a more or less strict antitrust analysis has been allowed to prevail. In particular, the US courts have made it quite clear that the provisions of the Clayton Act apply alike to foreign and domestic firms. Thus, for example, in a case involving the attempted takeover of a US firm by a foreign enterprise, the judge concluded:

> There are those in the public sector who would have the Court enjoin defendant merely because the thought of foreign control of American business is revolting. The argument eventually extends, considering the weakness of the dollar and our present struggle with the OPEC nations, to one of national security. There are others who point to the principle of economic reciprocity and adamantly maintain that infusion of foreign capital is just what our economy needs. The arguments are offsetting and, in any event, the Court shall treat foreign investment exactly like domestic investment in the absence of Congressional guidance.[7]

This remains the position under the antitrust laws, but we should also note that, following the passage of the Omnibus Trade and Competitiveness Act, which became law in August 1988, the US President has had in principle very wide-ranging powers to block any foreign investment in the USA which threatens to impair national security, broadly interpreted. The Act allows very wide discretion in the interpretation of those cases which might pose a threat to security. Although some observers at the time viewed it as a means of curbing the foreign control of US business, in practice it is seen very much as a power of last resort which is highly unlikely to be used in a way which runs counter to the traditional US policy of openness to foreign investment (Davidow and Stevens, 1990).

Experience so far with the EU merger Regulation also suggests that the same rules will be applied to foreign as to 'domestic' acquisitions of Community firms. The general criteria which can trigger an investigation, discussed in Chapter 8, are broad enough to deal with large acquisitions between companies located outside the EU but which have an effect on its internal trading. Two examples which were cleared were the joint venture between Mitsubishi of

Japan and Union Carbide of the USA and the acquisition of the US company MCA by the Japanese Matsushita (Jacquemin, 1993). Aérospatiale's attempt to acquire the Canadian subsidiary of Boeing illustrates the reverse point. Companies located within the EU acquiring a company outside it are also caught by the terms of the merger Regulation and if, as in the controversial Aérospatiale case, it is decided that the acquisition would have an adverse effect on competition within the EU, then it can be prohibited. As we saw, however, in Chapter 8, despite the enormous political pressure exerted on the Commission to apply other than a strict competitive analysis in reaching its decision, it was resisted. The *Boeing–McDonnell Douglas* case caused even greater problems and almost resulted in a breakdown of commercial relations between the USA and the EU. Although the USA has provided for its antitrust laws to apply to foreign companies, many in the Congress were incensed that a foreign authority (the EU Commission) should apply their antitrust laws to two strictly US companies (Kovacic, 2001). We noted in Chapter 8 that, although in this case a compromise solution was reached, despite the different antitrust analyses applied by the two authorities, the problem of dealing with large mergers where the impact was clearly international remains unresolved.

IV   The future of antitrust

At various points in the previous chapters we have indicated areas of antitrust where important changes in emphasis have taken place, underpinned usually by developments in economic analysis. This is perhaps most clearly seen in the case of vertical restraints, where a much more benign approach has been adopted, but it also applies to mergers, with the overriding emphasis on horizontal dominance, and to cooperative agreements covering R&D. We also pointed to areas where reforms were needed. One example was in making penalties large enough (in relation to the harm caused) to deter future infringements. Another need was to ensure that firms could not manipulate the antitrust laws to their own advantage. A particularly important example was discussed earlier in this chapter and concerns the apparent conflict between trade and antitrust policies. There is clearly a need for a unified approach both as to the concepts used ('dumping' v. 'predatory' pricing, for example) and to the policy bodies involved. Ideally, one agency should be used for dealing with all of the issues to maintain a consistent approach, although there is little sign of this occurring at present.

One important recent development which, given the growing significance of multinational operations and international trade, is likely to be of increasing importance in the future, is the completion of the European Commission–United States Government Competition Agreement in September 1991.[8] The issues discussed in the previous section made it clear that both the USA and the EU would benefit from a formal cooperative agreement. Preliminary discussions had been taking place for some years and the USA already had bilateral agreements with Germany (1976), Australia (1983) and Canada (1984). France and Germany had also concluded an agreement (1984) (see, in particular, Ham, 1993; Riley, 1992). The stated aim of the Agreement is to promote cooperation and coordination between the two parties in the application of their antitrust laws, especially so as to minimize the possibility that the application of the two sets of laws may overlap or conflict. There is specific provision for notification (Article II); exchange of information (Article III); cooperation and coordination of enforcement activity (Article IV); cooperation regarding anticompetitive activities in the territory of one party that adversely affect the interest of the other party (Article V); avoidance of conflicts over enforcement activities (Article VI); and consultation (Article VII).

The level of cooperation envisaged by the Agreement is thus substantial and goes way beyond a simple exchange of information. The parties undertake to keep each other informed of any antitrust action which may affect the other, but early enough in the proceedings to ensure that their views can be considered. Nevertheless, the Boeing–McDonnell Douglas and GEC–Honeywell cases illustrate the extent of the difficulties that remain. The continued growth of international trade and the widening of markets is likely to produce many more such cases, notably involving mergers but also other examples of individual firms or groups of firms attempting to exploit their market dominance internationally. For this reason the EU has proposed that some coordinated effort of antitrust control should be promoted through the WTO/GATT. In contrast, the USA remains firmly opposed to any movement towards a multilateral adoption of an antitrust code, fearing that this would lead to a severe dilution of its own policy. Its own preferred path, as we indicated above, is to sign bilaterial cooperative agreements. However, if sufficient cases of international market dominance continue to arise, the impetus for multilateral action is likely to grow.[9]

Notes

1. *United States* v. *Aluminum Co. of America et al.*, 148 F 2d 416 (1945).
2. *Timberlane Lumber Co.* v. *Bank of America*, 549 F 2d 597 (1977).
3. *Antitrust Guide for International Operations*, Justice Department, Washington (1977).
4. *ICI Ltd* v. *EC Commission*, case 48/69 (1972) CMLR 557.
5. *A Ahlstrom* v. *Commission*, case 114/85 (1988) 4 CMLR 901.
6. It is also worth noting that several members of the price agreement in the *Wood Pulp* case were also in a cartel authorized under the US Webb–Pomerene Act. Nevertheless, the European Court held that this was no defence since the Act merely exempted cartels, it did not compel them to be concluded (Whish, 1989, p. 390).
7. *Copperfield Corp* v. Imetal, 403 F supp. 579, 608; W.D.Pa, (1975) as quoted in Davidow and Stevens (1990).
8. Competition Laws, Co-operation Agreement 1991, 4 (1992) 4 CMLR. Following a legal challenge by France, Spain and Holland who questioned the authority of the Commission to conclude such an Agreement, its terms were fully reproduced in a 1995 Agreement between the Council and the USA.
9. For a detailed discussion of these issues, see Fox (1997) and Hoekman (1997).

References

Adams, W.J. (1951), 'The Aluminum Case: Legal Victory – Economic Defeat', *American Economic Review*, **41**, December, pp. 915–22.

Allen, G.C. (1968), *Monopoly and Restrictive Practices*, Allen and Unwin, London.

Anderson, K.B. (1993), 'Anti-dumping Laws in the United States', *Journal of World Trade*, **27**, April, pp. 99–117.

Areeda, P. and Turner, D. (1975), 'Predatory Pricing and Related Practices under Section 2 of the Sherman Act', *Harvard Law Review*, **88**, February, pp. 697–733.

Areeda, P. and Turner, D. (1978), *Antitrust Law III*, Little, Brown, Boston.

Areeda, P. and Turner, D. (1980), *Antitrust Law IV*, Little, Brown, Boston.

Armentano, D. (1982), *Antitrust and Monopoly: Anatomy of a Policy Failure*, Wiley, New York.

Arrow, K.J. (1962), 'Economic Welfare and the Allocation of Resources for Invention', in R. Nelson (ed.), *The Rate and Direction of Inventive Activity*, Princeton University Press, Princeton.

Audretsch, D.B. (1991), 'Antitrust Policy and Innovation: Taking Account of Performance Competition and Competitor Cooperation', *Journal of Institutional and Theoretical Economics*, **147** (1), pp. 145–51.

Bailey, E. (1981), 'Contestability and the Design of Regulatory and Antitrust Policy', *American Economic Review*, **71**, May, pp. 178–83.

Bailey, E. and Baumol, W.J. (1984), 'Deregulation and the Theory of Contestable Markets', *Yale Journal on Regulation*, **1** (2), pp. 111–37.

Bailey, E., Graham, D. and Kaplan, D. (1985), *Deregulating the Airlines: an Economic Analysis*, MIT Press, Boston.

Bain, J.S. (1956), *Barriers to New Competition*, Harvard University Press, Boston.

Bain, J.S. (1967), 'Chamberlin's Impact on Microeconomic Theory', in R.E. Kuenne (ed.), *Monopolistic Competition Theory*, Wiley, New York.

Bain, J.S. (1968), *Industrial Organisation*, 2nd edn, Wiley, New York.

Barker, R.E. and Davies, G.R. (1966), *Books are Different*, Macmillan, Basingstoke.

Baumol, W.J. (1979), 'Quasi-Permanence of Price Reduction: a Policy for Prevention of Predatory Pricing', *Yale Law Journal*, **89**, November, pp. 213–70.

Baumol, W.J. (1982), 'Contestable Markets: an Uprising in the Theory of Industry Structure', *American Economic Review*, **72**, March, pp. 1–15.

Baumol, W.J. and Ordover, J.A. (1985), 'Use of Antitrust to Subvert Competition', *Journal of Law and Economics*, **28** (2), May, pp. 247–65.

Baumol, W.J., Panzar, J. and Willig, R. (1982), *Contestable Markets and the Theory of Industry Structure*, Harcourt Brace Jovanovich, New York.

Beesley, M.E. (1990), 'Collusion, Predation and Mergers in the UK Bus Industry', *Journal of Transport Economics and Policy*, **24**, September, pp. 295–310.

Bergson, A. (1973), 'On Monopoly Welfare Losses', *American Economic Review*, **63**, December, pp. 853–70.

Bishop, W. (1981), 'Price Discrimination under Article 86: Political Economy in the European Court', *Modern Law Review*, **44**, May, pp. 282–95.

Bittlingmayer, G., (1992), 'Economics and 100 years of Antitrust: Introduction to a Symposium', *Economic Inquiry*, **30**, April, pp. 203–6.

Blair, R.D. and Kaserman, D.L. (1985), *Antitrust Economics*, Irwin, Homewood.

Boeder, T.L. and Dorman, G.J. (2000), 'The Boeing–McDonnell Douglas merger: the economics, antitrust law and politics of the aerospace industry', *The Antitrust Bulletin*, **XLV** (1), Spring, pp. 119–152.

Bork, R.H. (1978), *The Antitrust Paradox*, Basic Books, New York.

Borrie, G. (1991), *Financial Times*, 9 May.

Borrie, G. (1992), *Financial Times*, 4 June.

Breit, W. and Elzinga, K.G. (1985), 'Private Antitrust Enforcement: the New Learning', *Journal of Law and Economics*, **28**, May, pp. 405–43.

Brennan, T.J. (1982), 'Mistaken Elasticities and Misleading Rules', *Harvard Law Review*, **95**, June, pp. 1849–56.

Brodley, J.F. (1987), 'The Economic Goals of Antitrust: Efficiency, Consumer Welfare, and Technological Progress', *New York University Law Review*, **62**, November, pp. 1020–53.

Brodley, J.F. (1990), 'Antitrust Law and Innovation Cooperation', *Journal of Economic Perspectives*, **4**, Summer, pp. 97–112.

Buchanan, J.M., Tollison, R.D. and Tullock, G. (1980), *Toward a Theory of the Rent Seeking Society*, Texas A and M University Press, College Station.

Carlton, D.W. and Perloff, J.M. (2000), *Modern Industrial Organisation*, 3rd edn, Addison-Wesley, Reading, MA.

Caves, R.E. and Porter, M.E. (1977), 'From Entry Barriers to Mobility Barriers: Conjectural Decisions and Continued Deterrence to New Competition', *Quarterly Journal of Economics*, **91**, May, pp. 241–61.

Caves, R.E., Frankel, J.A. and Jones, R.W. (1993), *World Trade and Payments*, 6th edn, Harper Collins, New York.

Chamberlin, E.H. (1933), *Theory of Monopolistic Competition*, Harvard University Press, Cambridge, MA.

Clarke, R. (1985), *Industrial Economics*, Basil Blackwell, Oxford.

Clarke, R. (1993), 'Trends in Concentration in UK Manufacturing Industry: 1980–89', in M.C. Casson and J. Creedy (eds), *Industrial Concentration and Economic Inequality*, Edward Elgar, Aldershot.

Coase, R.H. (1938), 'The Nature of the Firm', *Economica*, **4**, November, pp. 386–405.

Coate, M.B. and McChesney, F.S. (1992), 'Empirical Evidence on FTC Enforcement of the Merger Guidelines', *Economic Inquiry*, **30**, April, pp. 277–93.

Comanor, W.S. (1967), 'Vertical Mergers, Market Power and the Antitrust Laws', *American Economic Review*, **57**, May, pp. 254–65.

Comanor, W.S. (1985), 'Vertical Price Fixing, Vertical Market Restrictions, and the New Antitrust Policy', *Harvard Law Review*, **98**, March, pp. 983–1003.

Comanor, W.S. (2001), 'The Problem of Remedy in Monopolisation Cases: The *Microsoft* case as an example', *The Antitrust Bulletin*, **XLVI** (1), Spring, pp. 115–33.

Comanor, W.S. and Frech, H.E. (1984), 'Strategic Behavior and Antitrust Analysis', *American Economic Review*, **74**, May, pp. 372–6.

Competition Commission (2000), *New Cars*, Cmnd.4660, HMSO, London.

Cowling, K. and Mueller, D.C. (1978), 'The Social Costs of Monopoly Power', *Economic Journal*, **88**, December, pp. 727–48.

Cowling, K., Stoneman, P., Cubbin, J., Cable, J., Hall, G., Domberger, S. and Dutton, S. (1980), *Mergers and Economic Performance*, Cambridge University Press, Cambridge.

Davenport, M. (1989), *The Charybdis of Anti-Dumping: a New Form of Industrial Policy*, Royal Institute of International Affairs, London.

Davidow, J. (1992), 'The Relationship Between Antitrust Laws and Trade Laws in the United States', *World Trade*, **14**, March, pp. 37–52.

Davidow, J. and Stevens, P.S. (1990), 'Antitrust Merger Control and National Security Review of Foreign Acquisitions in the United States', *Journal of World Trade*, **24**, February, pp. 39–56.

Davis, E. and Bannock, G. (1991), *The Nestlé Takeover of Rowntree*, David Hume Institute, Edinburgh.

Denison, E.F. (1967), *Why Growth Rates Differ*, Brookings, Washington.

Department of Prices and Consumer Protection (1979), *A Review of Restrictive Trade Practices Policy*, Cmnd 7512, HMSO, London.

Department of Trade and Industry (2001), *Productivity and Enterprise: A World Class Competition Regime*, Cmnd.5233, The Stationery Office, Norwich.

Department of Transport (1984), *Buses*, Cmnd 9300, HMSO, London.

Dertouzos, M.L., Lester, R.K. and Solow, R.M. (1989), *Made in America: Regaining the Productive Edge*, MIT Press, Cambridge, MA.

Dewey, D. (1990), *The Antitrust Experiment in America*, Columbia University Press, New York.

Easterbrook, F.H. (1981), 'Predatory Strategies and Counter Strategies', *University of Chicago Law Review*, **48**, Spring, pp. 263–337.

Easterbrook, F.H. (1984), 'The Limits of Antitrust', *Texas Law Review*, **63**, August, pp. 1–40.

Elzinga, G. and Hogarty, T.F. (1978), 'Utah Pie and the Consequences of the Robinson–Patman Act', *Journal of Law and Economics*, **21**, October, pp. 427–34.

Elzinga, K.A. and Breit, W. (1976), *The Antitrust Penalties*, Yale University Press, New Haven.

Evans, D.S., Nichols, A.L. and Schmalensee, R. (2000), 'An Analysis of the Government's Economic Case in US v. Microsoft', *The Antitrust Bulletin*, **XLVI** (2), Summer, pp. 163–251.

Fairburn, J.A. and Kay, J.A. (eds) (1989), *Mergers and Merger Policy*, Oxford University Press, Oxford.

Fairburn, J.A., Kay, J.A. and Sharpe, T.A.E. (1986), 'The Economics of Article 86', in G. Hall (ed.), *European Industrial Policy*, Croom Helm, London.

Fisher, F.M. (1987a), 'Horizontal Mergers: Triage and Treatment', *Journal of Economic Perspectives*, **1**, Fall, pp. 23–40.

Fisher, F.M. (1987b), 'Pan American to United: the Pacific Division Transfer Case', *Rand Journal of Economics*, **18**, Winter, pp. 492–508.

Fisher, F.M. and McGowan, J. (1983), 'On the Misuse of Accounting Rates of Return to Infer Monopoly Profits', *American Economic Review*, **73**, March, pp. 82–97.

Fisher, F.M. and Rubinfeld, D.L. (2001), 'US v Microsoft – An Economic Analysis', *The Antitrust Bulletin*, **XLVI** (1), Spring, pp. 1–69.

Fox, E.M. (1984), 'Abuse of a Dominant Position under the Treaty of Rome – a Comparison with US Law', *Annual Proceedings of the Fordham Corporate Law Institute*, Matthew Bender, Albany.

Fox, E.M. (1997), 'Towards world antitrust and market access', *American Journal of International Law*, **91**, pp. 1–25.

Frantz, R.S. (1988), *X-Efficiency: Theory, Evidence and Applications*, Kluwer, Boston.

Frazer, T. (1992), *Monopoly, Competition and Law*, 2nd edn, Wheatsheaf Books, Hemel Hempstead.

Galbraith, J.K. (1963), *American Capitalism*, Penguin Books, Harmondsworth.

Gallo, J.C., Craycroft, J.L. and Bush, S.C. (1985), 'Guess Who Came to Dinner: an Empirical Study of Federal Antitrust Enforcement for the Period 1963–1984', *Review of Industrial Organisation*, **2**, pp. 106–30.

Gates, B. (1995), *The Internet Tidal Wave*, Memorandum, 26 May.

George, K.D. (1989), 'Do We Need a Merger Policy?', in J. Fairburn and J.A. Kay (eds), *Mergers and Merger Policy*, Oxford University Press, Oxford.

George, K.D. and Jacquemin, A. (1990), 'Competition Policy in the European Community', in W.S. Comanor (ed.), *Competition Policy in Europe and*

North America: Economic Issues and Institutions, Harwood Academic Press, London.

Geroski, P.A. (1987), 'Do Dominant Firms Decline?', in D. Hay and J. Vickers (eds), *The Economics of Market Dominance*, Basil Blackwell, Oxford.

Geroski, P.A. (1993), 'Antitrust Policy Towards Cooperative R&D Ventures', *Oxford Review of Economic Policy*, **9**, Summer, pp. 58–71.

Gifford, D.J. and Sullivan, E.T. (2000), 'Can international antitrust be saved for the post-Boeing merger world?', *The Antitrust Bulletin*, **XLVI** (1), Spring, pp. 55–118.

Gilbert, R.J. (1981), 'Patents, Sleeping Patents and Entry Deterrence', in S. Salop (ed.), *Strategy, Predation and Antitrust*, Federal Trade Commission, Washington.

Gilbert, R.J. (1989), 'Mobility Barriers and the Value of Incumbency', in R. Schmalensee and R. Willig (eds), *Handbook of Industrial Organisation, I*, North Holland, Amsterdam.

Gilbert, R.J. and Katz, M.L. (2001), 'An Economist's Guide to *US* v. *Microsoft*', *Journal of Economic Perspectives*, 15 (2), Spring, pp. 25–44.

Gilbert, R.J. and Newbery, D.N.G. (1982), 'Pre-emptive Patenting and the Persistence of Monopoly', *American Economic Review*, **72**, June, pp. 514–26.

Goyder, D.G. (1998), *EC Competition Law*, third edition, Clarendon Press, Oxford.

Grant, W. (1982), *The Political Economy of Industry Policy*, Butterworths, London.

Gribbin, J.D. and Utton, M.A. (1986), 'The Treatment of Dominant Firms in UK Competition Legislation', in H.W. de Jong and W.G. Shepherd (eds), *Mainstreams in Industrial Organisation, II*, Kluwer, Dordrecht.

Grossman, G.M. and Shapiro, C. (1986), 'Research Joint Ventures: an Antitrust Analysis', *Journal of Law, Economics and Organisation*, **2**, Fall, pp. 315–37.

Groves, P. (1992), 'The Car Market: MMC's Report', *European Competition Law Review*, **13**, (3), pp. 97–100.

Ham, A.D. (1993), 'International Co-operation in the Antitrust Field and in Particular the Agreement Between the United States of America and the Commission of the European Communities', *Common Market Law Review*, **30**, (3), pp. 571–97.

Harberger, A.C. (1954), 'Monopoly and Resource Allocation', *American Economic Review*, **44**, May, pp. 77–87.

Hay, D.A. (1987), 'Competition and Industrial Policies', *Oxford Review of Economic Policy*, **3**, Autumn, pp. 27–40.

Hay, D.A. and Vickers, J. (eds) (1987), *The Economics of Market Dominance*, Basil Blackwell, Oxford.

Hay, D.A. and Vickers, J. (1988), 'The Reform of UK Competition Policy', *National Institute Economic Review*, **125**, August, pp. 56–68.

Hilke, J.C. and Nelson, P.B. (1984), 'Noisy Advertising and the Predation Rule in Antitrust', *American Economic Review*, **74**, May, pp. 367–71.

Hoekman, B. (1997), 'Competition Policy and the Global Trading System', *World Economy*, **20**, pp. 383–406.

Hughes, A. (1989), 'The Impact of Merger: a Survey of Empirical Evidence for the UK', in J. Fairburn and J.A. Kay (eds), *Mergers and Merger Policy*, Oxford University Press, Oxford.

Hurwitz, J.D., Kovacic, W.E., Sheehan, T.A. and Lande, R.H. (1981), 'Current Legal Standards of Predation', in S. Salop (ed.), *Strategy, Predation and Antitrust Analysis*, Federal Trade Commission, Washington.

Hymer, S. and Pashigian, P. (1962), 'Firm Size and Rate of Growth', *The Journal of Political Economy*, **120**, December, pp. 556–69.

Jacquemin, A. (1988), 'Cooperative Agreements in R&D and European Antitrust Policy', *European Economic Review*, **70**, December, pp. 556–69.

Jacquemin, A. (1993), 'The International Dimension of European Competition Policy', *Journal of Common Market Studies*, **31**, March, pp. 91–101.

Jacquemin, A. and Slade, M. (1989), 'Cartels, Collusion and Horizontal Merger', in R. Schmalensee and R. Willig (eds), *Handbook of Industrial Organisation, I*, North-Holland, Amsterdam.

Jewkes, J., Sawers, D. and Stillerman, R. (1969), *The Sources of Invention*, 2nd edn, Macmillan, Basingstoke.

Johnston, J.J. (1960), *Statistical Cost Analysis*, McGraw-Hill, New York.

Johnston, J. (1963), 'The Productivity of Management Consultants', *Journal of the Royal Statistical Society*, series A, part 2, pp. 237–49.

Jorde, T.M. and Teece, D.J. (1990), 'Innovation and Cooperation: Implications for Competition and Antitrust', *Journal of Economic Perspectives*, **4**, Summer, pp. 75–96.

Jorde, T.M. and Teece, D.J. (1992), *Antitrust, Innovation and Competitiveness*, Oxford University Press, Oxford.

Justice Department (1984), 'Merger Guidelines', *Antitrust and Trade Regulation Report*, 14 June, Washington.

Kamerschen, D.R. (1966), 'An Estimation of the Welfare Losses from Monopoly in the American Economy', *Western Economic Journal*, **4**, Summer, pp. 221–36.

Kay, J.A. (1987), 'Assessing Market Dominance Using Accounting Rates of Profit', in D. Hay and J. Vickers (eds), *The Economics of Market Dominance*, Basil Blackwell, Oxford.

Kay, J.A. and Bishop, M. (1988), *Does Privatisation Work?*, London Business School, London.

Klein, B. (2001a), 'The Microsoft Case: What Can a Dominant Firm Do to Defend Its Market Position?', *Journal of Economic Perspectives*, **15** (2), Spring, pp. 45–62.

Klein, B. (2001b), 'Did Microsoft Engage in Anticompetitive Exclusionary Behaviour?', *The Antitrust Bulletin*, **XLVI** (1), Spring, pp. 73–113.

Kostecki, M. (1987), 'Export Restraint Arrangements and Trade Liberalisation', *World Economy*, 10, pp. 425–53.

Kovacic, W.E. (2001), 'Transatlantic turbulence: the Boeing–McDonnell Douglas Merger and International Competition Policy', *Antitrust Law Journal*, **68**, pp. 805–73.

Krattenmaker, T.S. and Pitofsky, R. (1988), 'Antitrust Merger Policy and the Reagan Administration', *The Antitrust Bulletin*, **XXXIII**, Summer, pp. 211–32.

Lande, R.H. (1982), 'Wealth Transfers as the Original and Primary Concern of Antitrust: the Efficiency Interpretation Challenged', *Hastings Law Journal*, **34**, September, pp. 65–151.

Lande, R.H. (1988), 'The Rise and (Coming) Fall of Efficiency on the Rules of Antitrust', *The Antitrust Bulletin*, **XXXIII**, Fall, pp. 429–65.

Landes, W.M. (1983), 'Optimal Sanctions for Antitrust Violations', *University of Chicago Law Review*, **50**, Spring, pp. 652–78.

Landes, W.M. and Posner, R.A. (1979), 'Should Indirect Purchasers have Standing to Sue under the Antitrust Laws? An Economic Analysis of the Rule of Illinois Brick', *University of Chicago Law Review*, **46**, Spring, pp. 602–35.

Landes, W.M. and Posner, R.A. (1981), 'Market Power in Antitrust Cases', *Harvard Law Review*, **94**, March, pp. 937–96.

Lang, J.T. (1981), 'Community Antitrust Law – Compliance and Enforcement', *Common Market Law Review*, **18** (2), pp. 335–62.

Leibenstein, H. (1978), 'X-Inefficiency Xists – Reply to an Xorcist', *American Economic Review*, **78**, March, pp. 203–11.

Lerner, A. (1934), 'The Concept of Monopoly and the Measurement of Monopoly Power', *Review of Economic Studies*, **1**, June, pp. 157–75.

Levinson, R.J., Romaine, R.C. and Salop, S.C. (2001), 'The Flawed Fragmentation Critique of Structural Remedies in the Microsoft Case', *The Antitrust Bulletin*, **XLVI** (1), Spring, pp. 135–62.

Littlechild, S.C. (1981), 'Misleading Calculations of the Social Costs of Monopoly Power', *Economic Journal*, **91**, June, pp. 348–63.

Machlup, F. (1955), 'Characteristics and Types of Price Discrimination in National Bureau of Economic Research', *Business Concentration and Price Policy*, Princeton University Press, Princeton.

Marshall, A. (1919), *Industry and Trade*, Macmillan, London.

Marshall, A. (1920), *Principles of Economics*, 8th edn, Macmillan, London.

Martin, S. (1993), *Industrial Economics*, 2nd edn, Prentice Hall, New Jersey.

Marvel, H.P. and McCafferty, S. (1985), 'Resale Price Maintenance and Quality Certification', *Rand Journal of Economics*, **15**, Autumn, pp. 346–59.

McGee, J. (1980), 'Predatory Pricing Revisited', *Journal of Law and Economics*, **23**, October, pp. 289–330.

McGowan, F. and Trengove, C. (1986), 'European Aviation: a Common Market?', Institute of Fiscal Studies, London.

McKenzie, R.B. and Lee, D.R. (2001), 'How Digital Economics Revises Antitrust Thinking', *The Antitrust Bulletin*, **XLVI** (2), Summer, pp. 253–98.

Merkin, R. and Williams, K. (1984), *Competition Law: Antitrust Policy in the UK and the EEC*, Sweet and Maxwell, London.

Messerlin, P.A. (1989), 'The EC Anti-Dumping Regulations: a First Economic Appraisal 1980–85', *Weltwirtschaftliches Archiv*, **125** (4), pp. 563–86.

Messerlin, P.A. (1990), 'Anti-Dumping Regulations or Pro-Cartel Law? The EC Chemical Cases', *The World Economy*, **13**, December, pp. 465–92.

Miller, J.P. (1955), 'Measures of Monopoly Power and Concentration: their Economic Significance', *Business Concentration and Price Policy*, National Bureau of Economic Research, Princeton University Press, Princeton.

Miranda, J., Raúl, A. and Ruiz, M. (1998), 'The International Use of Antidumping: 1987–97', *Journal of World Trade*, **32** (5), pp. 5–71.

*Monopolies and Mergers Commission (1955), *Collective Discrimination*, Cmnd 9504, HMSO, London.

Monopolies and Mergers Commission (1956–7), *Supply of Medical and Industrial Gases*, HC 13, HMSO, London.

Monopolies and Mergers Commission (1959), *Chemical Fertilisers*, HC 267, HMSO, London.

Monopolies and Mergers Commission (1964), *Electrical Equipment for Mechanically Propelled Land Vehicles*, HC21, HMSO, London.

Monopolies and Mergers Commission (1966a), *British Motor Corporation and Pressed Steel*, HC 46, HMSO, London.

Monopolies and Mergers Commission (1966b), *Household Detergents*, HC 105, HMSO, London.

Monopolies and Mergers Commission (1968a), *Electric Lamps*, HC 4, HMSO, London.

Monopolies and Mergers Commission (1968b), *Flat Glass*, HC 83, HMSO, London.

Monopolies and Mergers Commission (1968c), *Manmade Cellulosic Fibre*, HC 130, HMSO, London.

Monopolies and Mergers Commission (1970a), *Metal Containers*, HC 6, HMSO, London.

Monopolies and Mergers Commission (1970b), *Refusal to Sell*, Cmnd 4372, HMSO, London.

---

* For convenience this title is used throughout, even though the title of the Commission was changed over the years.

Monopolies and Mergers Commission (1972–3), *Supply of Asbestos and Certain Asbestos Products*, HC 3, HMSO, London.

Monopolies and Mergers Commission (1976–7), *Indirect Electrostatic Reprographic Equipment*, HC 47, HMSO, London.

Monopolies and Mergers Commission (1981a), *Full-Line Forcing and Tie-In Sales*, HC 212, HMSO, London.

Monopolies and Mergers Commission (1981b), *S and W Berisford and British Sugar Corporation*, HC 241, HMSO, London.

Monopolies and Mergers Commission (1986), *British Telecommunications PLC and Mitel*, Cmnd 9715, HMSO, London.

Monopolies and Mergers Commission (1989a), *Beer*, Cmnd 651, HMSO, London.

Monopolies and Mergers Commission (1989b), *Labour Practices in TV and Film Making*, Cmnd 666, HMSO, London.

Monopolies and Mergers Commission (1989c), *Labour Practices in TV and Film Making*, Cmnd 666, HMSO, London.

Monopolies and Mergers Commission (1990a), *Highland Scottish Omnibuses Ltd*, Cmnd 1129, HMSO, London.

Monopolies and Mergers Commission (1990b), *The Supply of Petrol*, Cmnd 972, HMSO, London.

Monopolies and Mergers Commission (1992), *New Motor Cars*, Cmnd 1808, HMSO, London.

Monopolies and Mergers Commission (1993a), *Fine Fragrances*, Cmnd 2380, HMSO, London.

Monopolies and Mergers Commission (1993b), *Gas*, Cmnd 2314, HMSO, London.

Morgan, E.J. (2001), 'A Decade of EC Merger Control', *International Journal of the Economics of Business*, **8**, pp. 451–73.

Mueller, D.C. (1986), 'Antitrust at the Crossroads', in H.W. de Jong and W.G. Shepherd (eds), *Mainstreams in Industrial Organisation*, *II*, Kluwer, Dordrecht.

Mueller, D.C. (1997), 'Merger Policy in the United States: a Reconsideration', *Review of Industrial Organisation*, **12**, pp. 655–85.

National Bureau of Economic Research (1955), *Business Concentration and Price Policy*, Princeton University Press, Princeton.

Neale, A.D. and Goyder, D.G. (1980), *The Antitrust Laws of the United States of America*, 3rd edn, Cambridge University Press, Cambridge.

Neven, D., Nuttall, R. and Seabright, P. (1993), *Merger in Daylight*, Centre for Economic Policy Research, London.

Office of Fair Trading (1986), *Annual Report of the Director General of Fair Trading, 1985*, HMSO, London.

Office of Fair Trading (1988), *Becton-Dickinson UK Limited: the Supply of Hypodermic Syringes and Hypodermic Needles*, OFT, London.

Office of Fair Trading (1989), *Highland Scottish Omnibuses Limited: Local Run Services in Inverness*, OFT, London.

Office of Fair Trading (1999), *The Chapter II Prohibition*, OFT, London.

Office of Fair Trading (2000) *Vertical Agreements and Restraints*, OFT, London.

Ordover, J. (1987), 'Conflicts of Jurisdiction: Antitrust and Industrial Policy', *Law and Contemporary Problems*, **50**, Autumn, pp. 165–77.

Ordover, J. and Goldberg, L. (1993), *Obstacles to Trade and Competition*, OECD, Paris.

Ordover, J.A. and Willig, R.D. (1981a), 'An Economic Definition of Predation: Pricing and Product Innovation', *Yale Law Journal*, **91**, November, pp. 8–53.

Ordover, J.A. and Willig, R.D. (1981b), 'An Economic Definition of Predatory Product Innovation', in S. Salop (ed.), *Strategy, Predation and Antitrust Analysis*, Federal Trade Commission, Washington.

Ordover, J.A., Sykes, A.O. and Willig, R.D. (1983), 'Unfair International Trade Practices', *New York University Journal of International Law and Politics*, **15**, Winter, pp. 323–37.

Overbury, C. (1991), 'First Experiences of European Merger Control', *European Law Review, Competition Law Checklist, 1990*, **16**, pp. 79–88.

Overstreet, T.R. (1983), *Resale Price Maintenance: Economic Theories and Empirical Evidence*, Federal Trade Commission, Washington.

Pass, C. and Sparkes, J. (1980), 'Dominant Firms and the Public Interest: a Survey of the Reports of the British Monopolies and Mergers Commission', *The Antitrust Bulletin*, **XXV**, Summer, pp. 437–84.

Peterman, J.L. (1975), 'The Brown Shoe Case', *Journal of Law and Economics*, **18**, April, pp. 81–146.

Phlips, L. (1983), *The Economics of Price Discrimination*, Cambridge University Press, Cambridge.

Phlips, L. and Moras, I.M. (1993), 'The AKZO Decision: a Case of Predatory Pricing?', *Journal of Industrial Economics*, **41**, September, pp. 315–21.

Pickering, J.F. (1969), 'Would Prices Rise Without RPM?', *Oxford Economic Papers*, **21**, July, pp. 248–67.

Pickering, J.F. (1974), 'The Abolition of Resale Price Maintenance in Great Britain', *Oxford Economic Papers*, **26**, March, pp. 120–46.

Porter, M.E. (1980), *Competitive Strategy: Techniques for Analysing Industries and Competitors*, Free Press, New York.

Porter, M.E. (1985), *Competitive Advantage*, Free Press, New York.

Posner, R.A. (1975), 'The Social Costs of Monopoly and Regulation', *Journal of Political Economy*, **83**, August, pp. 807–27.

Posner, R.A. (1976), *Antitrust Law*, University of Chicago Press, Chicago.

Posner, R.A. (1977), 'The Rule of Reason and the Economic Approach: Reflections on the *Sylvania* Decision', *University of Chicago Law Review*, **45**, Fall, pp. 1–20.

Posner, R.A. (1981), 'The Next Step in the Antitrust Treatment of Restricted Distribution: per se Legality', *University of Chicago Law Review*, **48**, Winter, pp. 6–26.

Prais, S.J. (1981), *The Evolution of Giant Firms in Britain*, Cambridge University Press, Cambridge.

Pryke, R. (1971), *Public Enterprise in Practice*, MacGibbon and Kee, London.

Pryke, R. (1981), *Nationalised Industry: Policies and Performance since 1968*, Martin Robertson, Oxford.

Ravenscraft, D.J. and Scherer, F.M. (1987), *Mergers, Sell-Offs and Economic Efficiency*, Brookings, Washington.

Richardson, G.B. (1965), 'The Theory of Restrictive Trade Practices', *Oxford Economic Papers*, **17**, November, pp. 432–49.

Riley, A.J. (1992), 'Nailing the Jellyfish: the Illegality of the EC/US Government Competition Agreement', *European Competition Law Review*, **13**, (3), pp. 101–9.

Rivas, J. and Stroud, F. (2001), 'Developments in EC Competition Law in 1999/2000: an Overview', *Common Market Law Review*, August, pp. 235–90.

Robinson, J. (1969), *The Economics of Imperfect Competition*, 2nd edn, Macmillan, London.

Rotemberg, J.J. and Saloner, G. (1986), 'A Super-game Theoretic Model of Price Wars During Booms', *American Economic Review*, **76**, June, pp. 390–407.

Rowley, C.K. (1969), 'The Monopolies Commission and the Rate of Return on Capital', *Economic Journal*, **79**, March, pp. 42–65.

Salop, S. (ed.) (1981), *Strategy, Predation and Antitrust Analysis*, Federal Trade Commission, Washington.

Salop, S.C. (1986a), 'Measuring Ease of Entry', *The Antitrust Bulletin*, **XXXI**, Summer, pp. 551–70.

Salop, S.C. (1986b), 'Practices that Credibly Facilitate Oligopoly Co-ordination', in J. Stiglitz and F. Mathewson (eds), *New Developments in the Analysis of Market Structure*, Macmillan, Basingstoke.

Salop, S.C. (1987), 'Symposium on Mergers and Antitrust', *Journal of Economic Perspectives*, **1**, Fall, pp. 3–12.

Salop, S.C. and White, L.J. (1988), 'Private Antitrust Litigation: an Introduction and Framework', in L.J.White (ed.), *Private Antitrust Litigation*, MIT Press, Boston.

Scheffman, D. and Spiller, P. (1987), 'Geographic Market Definition under the US Department of Justice Merger Guidelines', *Journal of Law and Economics*, **30**, pp. 123–48.

Scherer, F.M. (1976), 'Predatory Pricing under Section 2 of the Sherman Act', *Harvard Law Review*, **89**, March, pp. 869–90.

Scherer, F.M. (1983), 'The Economics of Vertical Restraints', *Antitrust Law Journal*, **52** (3), pp. 687–707.

Scherer, F.M. (1987), 'Antitrust, Efficiency and Progress', *New York University Law Review*, **62**, November, pp. 1004–26.

Scherer, F.M. (1989), 'Merger Policy in the 1970s and 1980s', in R.J. Larner and J.W. Meehan (eds), *Economics and Antitrust Policy,* Quorum Books, Westport, CT.

Scherer, F.M. and Ross, D. (1990), *Industrial Market Structure and Economic Performance*, 3rd edn, Houghton Mifflin, Boston.

Schmalensee, R. (1978), 'Entry Deterrence in the Ready-to-eat Breakfast Cereal Industry', *Bell Journal of Economics*, **9**, Autumn, pp. 305–27.

Schmalensee, R. (1981), 'Output and Welfare Implications of Monopolistic Third-Degree Price Discrimination', *American Economic Review*, **71**, March, pp. 242–7.

Schmalensee, R. (1982a), 'Another Look at Market Power', *Harvard Law Review*, **95**, June, pp. 1788–816.

Schmalensee, R. (1982b), 'Antitrust and the New Industrial Economics', *American Economic Review*, **72**, May, pp. 24–8.

Schmalensee, R. (1987), 'Horizontal Merger Policy: Problems and Changes', *Journal of Economic Perspectives*, **1**, Fall, pp. 41–54.

Schmidt, I.L. (1991), 'The New EEC Merger Control System', *Review of Industrial Organisation*, **6**, (2), pp. 147–59.

Schumpeter, J.A. (1965), *Capitalism, Socialism and Democracy*, Allen and Unwin, London.

Schwartzman, D. (1960), 'The Burden of Monopoly', *Journal of Political Economy*, **58**, December, pp. 627–30.

Shapiro, C. and Varian, H.R. (1999). *Information Rules*, Harvard Business School Press, Boston, MA.

Shepherd, W.G. (1984), '"Contestability" vs Competition', *American Economic Review*, **74**, pp. 572–87.

Shepherd, W.G. (1988), 'Competition, Contestability and Transport Merger', *International Journal of Transport Economics*, **15**, June, pp. 113–28.

Sherwin, R.A. and Stigler, G.J. (1985), 'The Geographic Extent of the Market', *Journal of Law and Economics*, **28**, October, pp. 555–85.

Silcox, C.R. and MacIntyre, A.E. (1986), 'The Robinson–Patman Act and Competitive Fairness: Balancing the Economic and Social Dimensions of Antitrust', *The Antitrust Bulletin*, **XXXI**, Fall, pp. 647–61.

Singer, E.M. (1968), *Antitrust Economics*, Prentice-Hall, Englewood Cliffs.

Singh, A. and Whittington, G. (1975), 'The Size and Growth of Firms', *Review of Economic Studies*, **42**, January, pp. 15–26.

Smith, A. (1979), *The Wealth of Nations*, University of Glasgow, Glasgow.

Spence, A.M. (1981), 'Competition, Entry and Antitrust Policy', in S. Salop (ed.), *Strategy, Predation and Antitrust Analysis*, Federal Trade Commission, Washington.

Spence, A.M (1983), 'Contestable Markets and the Theory of Industry Structure: a Review', *Journal of Economic Literature*, **21**, September, pp. 981–90.

Stegemann, K. (1991), 'The International Regulation of Dumping: Protection Made Too Easy', *World Trade*, **14**, December, pp. 375–405.

Steiner, P.O. (1975), *Mergers*, University of Michigan Press, Ann Arbor.

Stevens, R.B. and Yamey, B.S. (1965), *The Restrictive Practices Court*, Weidenfeld and Nicolson, London.

Stigler, G.J. (1964), 'A Theory of Oligopoly', *Journal of Political Economy*, **72**, February, pp. 44–61

Stigler, G.J. (1965), 'Perfect Competition, Historically Contemplated', reprinted in *Essays in the History of Economics*, University of Chicago Press, Chicago.

Stigler, G.J. (1968),*The Organisation of Industry*, University of Chicago Press, Chicago.

Stigler, G.J. (1976), 'The Xistence of X-efficiency', *American Economic Review*, **66**, March, pp. 213–16.

Suslow, V.Y. (1988), 'Stability in International Cartels: an Empirical Survey', *Hoover Institution Working Paper*.

Sutherland, A. (1965), 'Economics in the Restrictive Practices Court', *Oxford Economic Papers*, **17**, November, pp. 385–431.

Sutherland, A. (1971), 'A Critique of Dr. Rowley', *Economic Journal*, **81**, June, pp. 264–72.

Swann, D., O'Brien, D.P., Maunder, W.P.J. and Howe, W.S.(1974), *Competition in British Industry*, Allen and Unwin, London.

Telser, L.G. (1960), 'Why Should Manufacturers Want Fair Trade?', *Journal of Law and Economics*, **3**, October, pp. 86–105.

Thurow, L. (1981), *The Zero Sum Society*, Penguin Books, Harmondsworth.

Tyson, L.D'A. (1992), *Who's Bashing Whom? Trade Conflict in High Technology Industries*, Institute for International Economics, Washington, DC.

Utton, M.A. (1972), 'Some Features of the Early Merger Movement in British Manufacturing Industry', *Business History*, **14** (1), pp. 51–60.

Utton, M.A. (1986a), *The Profits and Stability of Monopoly*, Cambridge University Press, Cambridge.

Utton, M.A. (1986b), *Economics of Regulating Industry*, Basil Blackwell, Oxford.

Utton, M.A. (2000a), 'Going European: Britain's New Competition Law', *The Antitrust Bulletin*, **XLV** (2), Summer, pp. 531–51.

Utton, M.A. (2000b), 'Books are not different after all: observations on the formal ending of the Net Book Agreement in the UK', *International Journal of the Economics of Business*, 7, pp. 115–26.

Utton, M.A., and Morgan, A.D. (1983), *Concentration and Foreign Trade*, Cambridge University Press, Cambridge.

Van Gerven, S. and Varona, E.N. (1994), 'The *Wood Pulp Case* and the future of concerted practices', *Common Market Law Review*, 31, pp. 575–608.

Vickers, J. and Yarrow, G. (1988), *Privatisation*, MIT Press, Cambridge, MA.

Viscusi, W.K., Vernon, J.M. and Harrington, J.E. (1992), *Economics of Regulation and Antitrust*, D.C. Heath, Lexington.

Warren-Boulton, F.R. (1974), 'Vertical Control with Variable Proportions', *Journal of Political Economy*, 82, July–August, pp. 783–802.

Waterson, M.J. (1988), *Regulation of the Firm and Natural Monopoly*, Basil Blackwell, Oxford.

Whinston, M.D. (2001), 'Exclusivity and Tying in *US v. Microsoft*, What We Know and Don't Know', *Journal of Economic Perspectives*, 15 (2), Spring, pp. 63–80.

Whish, R. (1989), *Competition Law*, 2nd edn, Butterworths, London.

Whish, R. (2000), 'Regulation 2790/99: The Commission's "New Style" Block Exemption for Vertical Agreements', *Common Market Law Review*, 37, pp. 887–924.

White, L.J. (1987), 'Antitrust and Merger Policy: a Review and Critique', *Journal of Economic Perspectives*, 1, Fall, pp. 13–22.

Wiles, P. (1961), *Price, Cost and Output*, 2nd edn, Basil Blackwell, Oxford.

Williams, M. (1993), 'The Effectiveness of Competition Policy in the United Kingdom', *Oxford Review of Economic Policy*, 9, Summer, pp. 94–112.

Williamson, O.E. (1972), 'Dominant Firms and the Monopoly Problem', *Harvard Law Review*, 85, June, pp. 1512–31.

Williamson, O.E. (1975), *Markets and Hierarchies*, Free Press, New York.

Williamson, O.E. (1977a), 'Economies As An Antitrust Defense Revisited', *University of Pennsylvania Law Review*, 125, April, pp. 699–736.

Williamson, O.E. (1977b), 'Predatory Pricing: a Strategic and Welfare Analysis', *Yale Law Journal*, 87, November, pp. 284–340.

Williamson, O.E. (1987), *Antitrust Economics*, Basil Blackwell, Oxford.

Worswick, G.D.N. (1961), 'On the Benefits of Being Denied the Opportunity to "Go Shopping"', *Bulletin of the Oxford University Institute of Statistics*, 23, August, pp. 271–9.

Yamey, B.S. (1972), 'Predatory Price Cutting: Notes and Comments', *Journal of Law and Economics*, 15, April, pp. 129–42.

Index